John Pizzamiglio
Oct. 1983.

D1352731

E. J. Hobsbawm was born in Alexandria and educated in Vienna, Berlin, London and Cambridge. He is now Professor of History at Birkbeck College in the University of London and Hon. Fellow of King's College, Cambridge. His publications include: *Primitive Rebels*; *Labouring Men: studies in the history of labour*; *Industry and Empire: an economic history of Britain since 1750*; and (also available in Abacus) *The Age of Capital: 1848–1875*.

E. J. Hobsbawm

THE AGE OF REVOLUTION
EUROPE 1789–1848

First published in Great Britain
by Weidenfeld & Nicolson Ltd 1962
Copyright © E. J. Hobsbawm 1962
First published by Sphere Books under the CARDINAL imprint 1973

This ABACUS edition published in 1977
by Sphere Books Ltd
30/32 Gray's Inn Road, London WC1X 8JL
Reprinted 1978, 1979, 1980

This book is sold subject to the condition that it shall not, by way of
trade or otherwise, be lent, re-sold, hired out or otherwise circulated
without the publisher's prior consent in any form of binding or cover
other than that in which it is published and without a similar condition
including this condition being imposed on the subsequent purchaser

Set in Baskerville Intertype
*Printed in Great Britain by Hazell Watson & Viney Ltd
Aylesbury, Bucks*

CONTENTS

LIST OF ILLUSTRATIONS

ACKNOWLEDGEMENTS

The author and publishers would like to thank the following for supplying photographs for use in this volume : Bildarchiv der Österreichischen Nationalbibliotek : Plates 4, 20; A. Castellanon : Plate 2; Crown Copyright : Plate 28; Galerie Marie Antoinette, Versailles : Plate 1; Gemälde Galerie, Dessau : Plate 3; Giraudon : Plates 1, 14; Historisches Museum der Stadt, Wien : Plates 4, 20; Louvre : Plate 17; Mansell Collection : Plates 8, 15, 16, 17, 19, 23, 25, 27, 29; Photo Marburg : Plates 3, 7, 11, 18, 22; Museum of Fine Arts, Budapest : Plate 24; Museo Nazionale di San Martino : Plate 26; National Gallery, Berlin : Plates 18, 22; Parker Gallery : Plate 10; Prado : Plate 2; Radio Times Hulton Picture Library : Plates 5, 12; Science Museum : Plate 13; Tony Scott : Plate 21; Soprintendenza Gallerie, Napoli : Plate 26.

LIST OF MAPS

PREFACE

This book traces the transformation of the world between 1789 and 1848 insofar as it was due to what is here called the 'dual revolution' – the French Revolution of 1789 and the contemporaneous (British) Industrial Revolution. It is therefore strictly neither a history of Europe nor of the world. Insofar as a country felt the repercussions of the dual revolution in this period, I have attempted to refer to it, though often cursorily. Insofar as the impact of the revolution on it in this period was negligible, I have omitted it. Hence the reader will find something about Egypt here, but not about Japan; more about Ireland than about Bulgaria, about Latin America than about Africa. Naturally this does not mean that the histories of the countries and peoples neglected in this volume are less interesting or important than those which are included. If its perspective is primarily European, or more precisely, Franco-British, it is because in this period the world – or at least a large part of it – was transformed from a European, or rather a Franco-British, base. However, certain topics which might well have deserved more detailed treatment have also been left aside, not only for reasons of space, but because (like the history of the USA) they are treated at length in other volumes in this series.

The object of this book is not detailed narrative, but interpretation and what the French call *haute vulgarisation*. Its ideal reader is that theoretical construct, the intelligent and educated citizen, who is not merely curious about the past, but wishes to understand how and why the world has come to be what it is today and whither it is going. Hence it would be pedantic and uncalled-for to load the text with as heavy an apparatus of scholarship as it ought to carry for a more learned public. My notes therefore refer almost entirely to the sources of actual quotations and figures, or in some cases to the authority for statements which are particularly controversial or surprising.

Nevertheless, it is only fair to say something about the material on which a very wide-ranging book such as this is based. All historians are more expert (or to put it another way, more ignorant) in some fields than in others. Outside a fairly narrow zone they must rely largely on the work of other historians. For the period 1789 to 1848 this secondary literature alone forms a mass of print so vast as to be beyond the knowledge of any individual, even one who can read all the languages in which it is written. (In fact, of course, all historians are confined to a handful of languages at most.) Much of this book is therefore second- or even third-hand, and it will inevitably contain errors, as well as the inevitable foreshortenings which the expert will regret, as the author does. A bibliography is provided as a guide to further study.

Though the web of history cannot be unravelled into separate threads without destroying it, a certain amount of subdivision of the subject is, for practical purposes, essential. I have attempted, very roughly, to divide the book into two parts. The first deals broadly with the main developments of the period, while the second sketches the kind of society produced by the dual revolution. There are, however, deliberate overlaps, and the distinction is a matter not of theory but of pure convenience.

My thanks are due to various people with whom I have discussed aspects of this book or who have read chapters in draft or proof, but who are not responsible for my errors; notably J. D. Bernal, Douglas Dakin, Ernst Fischer, Francis Haskell, H. G. Koenigsberger and R. F. Leslie. Chapter 14 in particular owes much to the ideas of Ernst Fischer. Miss P. Ralph helped considerably as secretary and research assistant. Miss E. Mason compiled the index.

E. J. H.

London, December 1961

INTRODUCTION

Words are witnesses which often speak louder than documents. Let us consider a few English words which were invented, or gained their modern meanings, substantially in the period of sixty years with which this volume deals. They are such words as 'industry', 'industrialist', 'factory', 'middle class', 'working class', 'capitalism' and 'socialism'. They include 'aristocracy' as well as 'railway', 'liberal' and 'conservative' as political terms, 'nationality', 'scientist' and 'engineer', 'proletariat' and (economic) 'crisis'. 'Utilitarian' and 'statistics', 'sociology' and several other names of modern sciences, 'journalism' and 'ideology', are all coinages or adaptations of this period.[1] So is 'strike' and 'pauperism'.

To imagine the modern world without these words (i.e. without the things and concepts for which they provide names) is to measure the profundity of the revolution which broke out between 1789 and 1848, and forms the greatest transformation in human history since the remote times when men invented agriculture and metallurgy, writing, the city and the state. This revolution has transformed, and continues to transform, the entire world. But in considering it we must distinguish carefully between its long-range results, which cannot be confined to any social framework, political organization, or distribution of international power and resources, and its early and decisive phase, which was closely tied to a specific social and international situation. The great revolution of 1789–1848 was the triumph not of 'industry' as such, but of *capitalist* industry; not of liberty and equality in general but of *middle class* or '*bourgeois*' *liberal* society; not of 'the modern economy' or 'the modern state', but of the economies and states in a particular geographical region of the world (part of Europe and a few patches of North America), whose centre was the neighbouring and rival states of Great Britain and France. The transformation of 1789–1848 is essentially the twin upheaval which took place in those two countries, and was propagated thence across the entire world.

But it is not unreasonable to regard this dual revolution – the rather more political French and the industrial (British) revolution – not so much as something which belongs to the history of the two countries which were its chief carriers and symbols, but as the twin crater of a rather larger regional volcano. That the simultaneous eruptions should occur in France and Britain, and have slightly differing characters, is neither accidental nor uninteresting. But from the point of view of the historian of, let us say, AD 3000, as from the point of view of the Chinese or African observer, it is more relevant to note that they occurred somewhere or other in North-western Europe and its overseas prolongations, and that they could not with any probability have been expected to occur at this time in any other part of the world. It is equally relevant to note that they are at this period almost inconceivable in any form other than the triumph of a bourgeois-liberal capitalism.

It is evident that so profound a transformation cannot be understood without going back very much further in history than 1789, or even than the decades which immediately preceded it and clearly reflect (at least in retrospect), the crisis of the *ancien régimes* of the North-western world, which the dual revolution was to sweep away. Whether or not we regard the American Revolution of 1776 as an eruption of equal significance to the Anglo-French ones, or merely as their most important immediate precursor and stimulator; whether or not we attach fundamental importance to the constitutional crises and economic reshuffles and stirrings of 1760–89, they can clearly explain at most the occasion and timing of the great breakthrough and not its fundamental causes. How far back into history the analyst should go – whether to the mid-seventeenth-century English Revolution, to the Reformation and the beginning of European military world conquest and colonial exploitation in the early sixteenth century, or even earlier, is for our purposes irrelevant, for such analysis in depth would take us far beyond the chronological boundaries of this volume.

Here we need merely observe that the social and economic forces, the political and intellectual tools of this transformation were already prepared, at all events in a part of Europe sufficiently large to revolutionize the rest. Our problem is not to trace the emergence of a

14

world market, of a sufficiently active class of private entrepreneurs, or even in England of a state dedicated to the proposition that the maximization of private profit was the foundation of government policy. Nor is it to trace the evolution of the technology, the scientific knowledge, or the ideology of an individualist, secularist, rationalist belief in progress. By the 1780s we can take the existence of all these for granted, though we cannot yet assume that they were sufficiently powerful or widespread. On the contrary, we must, if anything, safeguard against the temptation to overlook the novelty of the dual revolution because of the familiarity of its outward costume, the undeniable fact that Robespierre's and Saint-Just's clothes, manners and prose would not have been out of place in a drawing-room of the *ancien régime*, that the Jeremy Bentham whose reforming ideas expressed the bourgeois Britain of the 1830s was the very man who had proposed the same ideas to Catherine the Great of Russia, and that the most extreme statements of middle class political economy came from members of the eighteenth-century British House of Lords.

Our problem is thus to explain not the existence of these elements of a new economy and society, but their triumph; to trace not the progress of their gradual sapping and mining in previous centuries, but their decisive conquest of the fortress. And it is also to trace the profound changes which this sudden triumph brought within the countries most immediately affected by it, and within the rest of the world which was now thrown open to the full explosive impact of the new forces, the 'conquering bourgeois', to quote the title of a recent world history of this period.

Inevitably, since the dual revolution occurred in one part of Europe, and its most obvious and immediate effects were most evident there, the history with which this volume deals is mainly regional. Inevitably also, since the world revolution spread outwards from the double crater of England and France it initially took the form of a European expansion in and conquest of the rest of the world. Indeed its most striking consequence for world history was to establish a domination of the globe by a few western régimes (and especially by the British) which has no parallel in history. Before the merchants, the steam-engines, the ships and the guns of the west – and before its ideas – the age-old civilizations and empires of the world capitulated and collapsed. India became a province administered by British pro-consuls, the Islamic states were convulsed by crisis, Africa lay open to direct conquest. Even the great Chinese Empire was forced in 1839–42 to open its frontiers to western exploitation. By 1848 nothing stood in the way of western conquest of any territory that western governments or businessmen might find it to their advantage to occupy, just as nothing but time stood in the way of the progress of western capitalist enterprise.

And yet the history of the dual revolution is not merely one of the triumph of the new bourgeois society. It is also the history of the emergence of the forces which were, within a century of 1848, to have turned expansion into contraction. What is more, by 1848 this extraordinary future reversal of fortunes was already to some extent visible. Admittedly, the world-wide revolt against the west, which dominates the middle of the twentieth century, was as yet barely discernible. Only in the Islamic world can we observe the first stages of that process by which those conquered by the west have adopted its ideas and techniques to turn the tables on it : in the beginnings of internal westernizing reform within the Turkish empire in the 1830s, and above all the neglected and significant career of Mohammed Ali of Egypt. But within Europe the forces and ideas which envisaged the supersession of the triumphant new society, were already emerging. The 'spectre of communism' already haunted Europe by 1848. It was exorcized in 1848. For a long time thereafter it was to remain as powerless as spectres in fact are, especially in the western world most immediately transformed by the dual revolution. But if we look round the world of the 1970s we shall not be tempted to underestimate the historic force of the revolutionary socialist and communist ideology born out of reaction against the dual revolution, and which had by 1848 found its first classic formulation. The historic period which begins with the construction of the first factory system of the modern world in Lancashire and the French Revolution of 1789 ends with the construction of its first railway network and the publication of the Communist Manifesto.

NOTES

1 Most of these either have international currency, or were fairly literally translated into various languages. Thus 'socialism' or 'journalism' are fairly international, while the combination 'iron road' is the basis of the name of the railway everywhere except in its country of origin.

PART I

Developments

I

The World in the 1780s

Le dix-huitième siècle doit être mis au Panthéon. – Saint-Just[1]

I

The first thing to observe about the world of the 1780s is that it was at once much smaller and much larger than ours. It was smaller geographically, because even the best-educated and best-informed men then living – let us say a man like the scientist and traveller Alexander von Humboldt (1769–1859) – knew only patches of the inhabited globe. (The 'known worlds' of less scientifically advanced and expansionist communities than those of Western Europe were clearly even smaller, diminishing to the tiny segments of the earth within which the illiterate Sicilian peasant or the cultivator in the Burmese hills lived out his life, and beyond which all was and always would forever be unknown.) Much of the surface of the oceans, though by no means all, had already been explored and mapped thanks to the remarkable competence of eighteenth-century navigators like James Cook, though human knowledge of the sea-bed was to remain negligible until the mid-twentieth century. The main outlines of the continents and most islands were known, though by modern standards not too accurately. The size and height of the mountain ranges in Europe were known with some approach to precision, those in parts of Latin America very roughly, those in Asia hardly at all, those in Africa (with the exception of the Atlas) for practical purposes not at all. Except for those of China and India, the course of the great rivers of the world was mysterious to all but a handful of trappers, traders or *coureurs-de-bois*, who had, or may have had, knowledge of those in their regions. Outside of a few areas – in several continents they did not reach more than a few miles inland from the coast – the map of the world consisted of white spaces crossed by the marked trails of traders or explorers. But for the rough-and-ready second- or third-hand information collected by travellers or officials in remote outposts, these white spaces would have been even vaster than in fact they were.

Not only the 'known world' was smaller, but the real world, at any rate in human terms. Since for practical purposes no censuses are available, all demographic estimates are sheer guesses, but it is evident that the earth supported only a fraction of today's population; probably not much more than one-third. If the most usually quoted guesses are not too wide of the mark Asia and Africa supported a somewhat larger proportion of the world's people than today, Europe, with about 187 million in 1800 (as against about 600 million today), a somewhat smaller one, the Americas obviously a much smaller one. Roughly, two out of every three humans would be Asians in 1800, one out of every five Europeans, one out of ten African, one out of thirty-three American or Oceanian. It is obvious that this much smaller population was much more sparsely distributed across the face of the globe, except perhaps for certain small regions of intensive agriculture or high urban concentration, such as parts of China, India and Western or Central Europe, where densities comparable to those of modern times may have existed. If population was smaller, so also was the area of effective human settlement. Climatic conditions (probably somewhat colder and wetter than today, though no longer quite so cold or wet as during the worst period of the 'little ice age' of *c.* 1300–1700) held back the limits of settlement in the Arctic. Endemic disease, such as malaria, still restricted it in many areas, such as Southern Italy, where the coastal plains, long virtually unoccupied, were only gradually peopled during the nineteenth century. Primitive forms of the economy, notably hunting and (in Europe) the territorially wasteful seasonal transhumance of livestock, kept large settlements out of entire regions – such as the plains of Apulia : the early nineteenth-century tourist's prints of the Roman campagna, an empty malarial space with a few ruins, a few cattle, and the odd picturesque bandit, are familiar illustrations of such landscapes. And of course much land which has since come under the plough was still, even in Europe, barren heath, waterlogged fen, rough grazing or forest.

Humanity was smaller in yet a third respect. Europeans were, on the whole, distinctly shorter and lighter than they are today. To take one illustration from the abundance of statistics about the physique of conscripts on which this generalization is based : in one canton on the Ligurian coast 72 per cent of the recruits in 1792–9 were less than 1·50 metres (5 ft. 2 in.) tall.[2] That did not mean that the men of the later eighteenth century were more fragile than we are. The scrawny, stunted, undrilled soldiers of the French Revolution were capable of a physical endurance equalled today only by the under-sized guerillas in colonial mountains. A week's unbroken marching, with full equipment, at the rate of thirty miles a day, was common. However, the fact remains that human physique was then, by our standards, very poor, as is indicated by the exceptional value kings and generals attached to the 'tall fellows', who were formed into the *élite* regiments of guards, cuirassiers and the like.

Yet if the world was in many respects smaller, the sheer difficulty or uncertainty of communications made it in practice much vaster than it is today. I do not wish to exaggerate these difficulties. The later eighteenth century was, by medieval or sixteenth century standards, an age of abundant and speedy communications, and even before the revolution of the railways, improvements in roads, horse-drawn vehicles and postal services are quite remarkable. Between the 1760s and the end of the century the journey from London to Glasgow was shortened from ten or twelve days to sixty-two hours. The system of mail-coaches or *diligences*, instituted in the second half of the eighteenth century, vastly extended between the end of the Napoleonic wars and the coming of the railway, provided not only relative speed – the postal service from Paris to Strasbourg took thirty-six hours in 1833 – but also regularity. But the provision for overland passenger-transport was small, that for overland goods transport both slow and prohibitively expensive. Those who con-ducted government business or commerce were by no means cut off from one another : it is estimated that twenty million letters passed through the British mails at the beginning of the wars with Bona-parte (at the end of our period there were ten times as many); but for the great majority of the inhabitants of the world letters were useless, as they could not read, and travel – except perhaps to and from markets – altogether out of the ordinary. If they or their goods moved overland, it was overwhelmingly on foot or by the slow speeds of carts, which even in the early nineteenth century carried five-sixths of French goods traffic at somewhat less than twenty miles a day. Couriers flew across long distances with dispatches; postilions drove mail-coaches with a dozen or so passengers each, shaking their bones or, if equipped with the new leather suspension, making them violently seasick. Noblemen raced along in private carriages. But for the greater part of the world the speed of the carter walking beside his horse or mule governed land transport.

Under the circumstances transport by water was therefore not only easier and cheaper, but often also (except for the uncertainties of wind and weather) faster. It took Goethe four and three days respectively to sail from Naples to Sicily and back during his Italian tour. The mind boggles at the time it would have taken him to travel overland in anything like comfort. To be within reach of a port was to be within reach of the world : in a real sense London was closer to Plymouth or Leith than to villages in the Breckland of Norfolk; Seville was more accessible from Veracruz than from Valladolid, Hamburg from Bahia than from the Pomeranian hinterland. The chief drawback of water transport was its intermittency. Even in 1820 the London mails for Hamburg and Holland were made up only twice a week, those for Sweden and Portugal once weekly, those for North America once a month. Yet there can be no doubt that Boston and New York were in much closer contact with Paris than, let us say, the Carpathian county of Maramaros was with Budapest. And just as it was easier to transport goods and men in quantity over the vast distances of the oceans – easier, for instance, for 44,000 to set sail for America from Northern Irish ports in five years (1769–74) than to get five thousand to Dundee in three generations – so it was easier to link distant capitals than country and city. The news of the fall of the Bastille reached the populace of Madrid within thirteen days; but in Péronne, a bare 133 kilometres from the capital, 'the news from Paris' was not received until the 28th.

The world of 1789 was therefore, for most of its inhabitants, incalculably vast. Most of them, unless snatched away by some awful hazard, such as military recruitment, lived and died in the county, and often in the parish, of their birth : as late as 1861 more than nine out of ten in seventy of the ninety French departments lived in the department of their birth. The rest of the globe was a matter of government agents and rumour. There were no newspapers, except for a tiny handful of the middle and upper classes – 5,000 was the usual circulation of a French journal even in 1814 – and few could read in any case. News came to most through travellers and the mobile section of the population : merchants and hawkers, travelling

22

journeymen, migratory craftsmen and seasonal labourers, the large and mixed population of the vagrant and footloose ranging from itinerant friars or pilgrims to smugglers, robbers and fairground folk; and, of course, through the soldiers who fell upon the population in war or garrisoned them in peace. Naturally news also came through official channels – through state or church. But even the bulk of the local agents of such state-wide or ecumenical organizations were local men, or men settled for a lifetime's service among those of their kind. Outside the colonies the official nominated by his central government and sent to a succession of provincial posts was only just coming into existence. Of all the subaltern agents of the state perhaps only the regimental officer habitually expected to live an unlocalized life, consoled only by the variety of wine, women and horses of his country.

II

Such as it was, the world of 1789 was overwhelmingly rural, and nobody can understand it who has not absorbed this fundamental fact. In countries like Russia, Scandinavia or the Balkans, where the city had never flourished excessively, between 90 and 97 per cent of the population were rural. Even in areas with a strong though decayed urban tradition, the rural or agricultural percentage was extraordinarily high : 85 per cent in Lombardy, 72–80 per cent in Venetia, more than 90 per cent in Calabria and Lucania, according to available estimates.[3] In fact, outside of a few very flourishing industrial or commercial areas we should be hard put to it to find a sizeable European state in which at least four out of every five inhabitants were not countrymen. And even in England itself, the urban population only just outnumbered the rural population for the first time in 1851.

The word 'urban' is, of course, ambiguous. It includes the two European cities which by 1789 can be called genuinely large by our standards, London, with about a million, and Paris, with about half a million, and the score or so with a population of 100,000 or more : two in France, two in Germany, perhaps four in Spain, perhaps five in Italy (the Mediterranean was traditionally the home of cities), two in Russia, and one each in Portugal, Poland, Holland, Austria, Ireland, Scotland, and European Turkey. But it also includes the multitude of small provincial towns in which the majority of city-dwellers actually lived; the ones where a man could stroll in a few minutes from the cathedral square surrounded by the public buildings and the houses of the notables, to the fields. Of the 19 per cent of Austrians who, even at the end of our period (1834), lived in towns, well over three-quarters lived in towns of less than 20,000 inhabitants; about half in towns of between two and five thousand. These were the towns through which the French journeymen wandered on their Tour de France; whose sixteenth-century profiles, preserved like flies in amber by the stagnation of subsequent centuries, the German romantic poets evoked in the background of their tranquil landscapes; above which the cliffs of Spanish cathedrals towered; among whose mud the Chassidic Jews venerated their miracle-working rabbis and the orthodox ones disputed the divine subtleties of the law; into which Gogol's inspector-general drove to terrify the rich, and Chichikov to ponder on the purchase of dead souls. But these also were the towns out of which the ardent and ambitious young men came to make revolutions or their first million; or both. Robespierre came out of Arras, Gracchus Babeuf out of Saint-Quentin, Napoleon out of Ajaccio.

These provincial towns were none the less urban for being small. The genuine townsmen looked down upon the surrounding countryside with the contempt of the quick-witted and knowledgeable for the strong, slow, ignorant and stupid. (Not that by the standards of the real man of the world the sleepy back-country township had anything to boast about: the German popular comedies mocked 'Kraehwinkel' – the petty municipality – as cruelly as the more obvious rural hayseeds.) The line between town and country, or rather between town occupations and farm occupations, was sharp. In many countries the excise barrier, or sometimes even the old line of the wall, divided the two. In extreme cases, as in Prussia, the government, anxious to keep its taxable citizens under proper supervision, secured a virtually total separation of urban and rural activities. Even where there was no such rigid administrative division, townsmen were often physically distinct from peasants. In a vast area of Eastern Europe they were German, Jewish or Italian islands in a Slav, Magyar or Rumanian lake. Even townsmen of the same religion and nationality as the surrounding peasantry *looked* different: they wore different dress, and indeed were in most cases (except for the exploited indoor labouring and manufacturing population) taller, though perhaps also slenderer.[4] They were probably, and certainly prided themselves on being, quicker in mind and more literate. Yet in their mode of life they were almost as ignorant of what went on outside their immediate district, almost as closed-in, as the village.

The provincial town still belonged essentially to the economy and society of the countryside. It lived by battening on the surrounding peasantry and (with relatively few exceptions) by very little else except taking in its own washing. Its professional and middle classes were the dealers in corn and cattle, the processers of farm-products, the lawyers and notaries who handled the affairs of noble estates or the interminable litigations which are part of land-owning or land-holding communities; the merchant-entrepreneurs who put out and collected for and from the rural spinners and weavers; the more respectable of the representatives of government, lord or church. Its craftsmen and shopkeepers supplied the surrounding peasantry or the townsmen, who lived off the peasantry. The provincial city had declined sadly since its heyday in the later middle ages. It was only rarely a 'free city' or city state; only rarely any longer a centre of manufactures for a wider market or a staging-post in international trade. As it had declined, it clung with increasing stubbornness to that local monopoly of its market which it defended against all comers : much of the provincialism which the young radicals and big city slickers mocked, derived from this movement of economic self-defence. In Southern Europe the gentlemen and even sometimes the nobles lived in it on the rents of their estates. In Germany the bureaucracies of the innumerable small principalities, themselves barely more than large estates, administered the wishes of Serenissimus there with the revenues collected from a dutiful and silent peasantry. The provincial town of the late eighteenth century might be a prosperous and expanding community, as its townscape, dominated by stone buildings in a modest classical or rococo style still bears witness in parts of Western Europe. But that prosperity came from the countryside.

III

The agrarian problem was therefore the fundamental one in the world of 1789, and it is easy to see why the first systematic school of continental economists, the French Physiocrats, assumed as a matter of course that the land, and the land rent, was the sole source of net income. And the crux of the agrarian problem was the relation between those who cultivated the land and those who owned it, those who produced its wealth and those who accumulated it.

From the point of view of agrarian property relations, we may divide Europe – or rather the economic complex whose centre lay in Western Europe – into three large segments. To the west of Europe there lay the overseas colonies. In these, with the notable exception of the Northern United States of America and a few less significant patches of independent farming, the typical cultivator was an Indian working as a forced labourer or virtual serf, or a Negro working as a slave; somewhat more rarely, a peasant tenant, share-cropper or the like. (In the colonies of the Eastern Indies, where direct cultivation by European planters was rarer, the typical form of compulsion by the controllers of the land was the forced delivery of quotas of crops, e.g. spice or coffee in the Dutch islands.) In other words the typical cultivator was unfree or under political constraint. The typical landlord was the owner of the large quasi-feudal estate (hacienda, finca, estancia) or of a slave plantation. The characteristic economy of the quasi-feudal estate was primitive and self-contained, or at any rate geared to purely regional demands : Spanish America exported mining products, also produced by what were virtually Indian serfs, but nothing much in the way of farm-products. The characteristic economy of the slave-plantation zone, whose centre lay in the Caribbean islands, along the northern coasts of South America (especially in Northern Brazil) and the southern ones of the USA, was the production of a few vitally important export crops, sugar, to a lesser extent tobacco and coffee, dye-stuffs and, from the Industrial Revolution onwards, above all cotton. It therefore formed an integral part of the European economy and, through the slave-trade, of the African. Fundamentally the history of this zone in our period can be written in terms of the decline of sugar and the rise of cotton.

To the east of Western Europe, more specifically to the east of a line running roughly along the river Elbe, the western frontiers of what is today Czechoslovakia, and then south to Trieste, cutting off Eastern from Western Austria, lay the region of agrarian serfdom. Socially, Italy south of Tuscany and Umbria, and Southern Spain belonged to this region, though Scandinavia (with the partial exception of Denmark and Southern Sweden) did not. This vast zone contained its patches of technically free peasants : German peasant colonists scattered all over it from Slovenia to the Volga, virtually independent clans in the savage rocks of the Illyrian hinterland, almost equally savage peasant-warriors like the Pandurs and Cossacks on what had until lately been the military frontier between Christian and Turk or Tartar, free pioneer squatters beyond the reach of lord and state, or those who lived in the vast forests, where large-scale farming was out of the question. On the whole, however, the typical cultivator was unfree, and indeed almost drenched by the flood of serfdom which had risen almost without a break since the later fifteenth or early sixteenth centuries. It was least obvious in the Balkan areas which had been, or still were, under the direct administration of the Turks. Though the original agrarian system of the Turkish pre-feudalism, a rough division of the land in which each unit supported a non-hereditary Turkish warrior, had long degenerated into a system of hereditary landed estates under Mohammedan lords, these lords seldom engaged in farming. They merely sucked what they could from their peasantry. This is why the Balkans, south of the Danube and Save, emerged from Turkish domination in the nineteenth and twentieth centuries substantially as peasant countries, though extremely poor ones, and not as countries of concentrated agricultural property. Still, the Balkan peasant was legally unfree as a Christian, and *de facto* unfree as a peasant, at least so long as he was within reach of the lords.

Over the rest of the area, however, the typical peasant was a serf, devoting a large part of the week to forced labour on the lord's land, or its equivalent in other obligations. His unfreedom might be so great as to be barely distinguishable from chattel slavery, as in Russia and those parts of Poland where he could be sold separately from the land : a notice in the *Gazette de Moscou* in 1801 advertised 'For sale, three coachmen, well-trained and very presentable, also two girls, aged 18 and 15, both of good appearance and skilled in different kinds of manual work. The same house has for sale two hairdressers, one, aged 21, can read, write, play a musical instrument and do duty as postilion, the other suitable for dressing ladies' and gentlemen's hair; also pianos and organs.' (A large proportion of serfs served as domestics; in Russia almost 5 per cent of *all* serfs in 1851.)[6] In the hinterland of the Baltic Sea – the main trade-route with Western Europe – servile agriculture produced largely export crops for the importing countries of the west : corn, flax, hemp and forest products mostly used for shipping. Elsewhere it relied more on the regional market, which contained at least one accessible region of fairly advanced manufacturing and urban development, Saxony and Bohemia and the great capital of Vienna. Much of it, however, remained backward. The opening of the Black Sea route and the increasing urbanization of Western Europe, and notably of England, had only just begun to stimulate the corn-exports of the Russian black earth belt, which were to remain the staple of Russian foreign trade until the industrialization of the USSR. The eastern servile area may therefore also be regarded as a food and raw-material producing 'dependent economy' of Western Europe, analogous to the overseas colonies.

The servile areas of Italy and Spain had similar economic characteristics, though the legal technicalities of the peasants' status were somewhat different. Broadly, they were areas of large noble estates. It is not impossible that in Sicily and Andalusia several of these were the lineal descendants of Roman latifundia, whose slaves and *coloni* had turned into the characteristic landless day-labourers of these regions. Cattle-ranching, corn-production (Sicily is an ancient export-granary) and the extortion of whatever was to be extorted from the miserable peasantry, provided the income of the dukes and barons who owned them.

The characteristic landlord of the servile area was thus a noble owner and cultivator or exploiter of large estates. Their vastness staggers the imagination : Catherine the Great gave between forty and fifty thousand serfs to individual favourites; the Radziwills of Poland had estates as large as half of Ireland; Potocki owned three million acres in the Ukraine; the Hungarian Esterhazy's (Haydn's patrons) at one time owned nearly seven million acres. Estates of several hundreds of thousands of acres were common.[7] Neglected, primitive and inefficient though these often were, they yielded princely incomes. The Spanish grandee might, as a French visitor observed of the desolate Medina Sidonia estates, 'reign like a lion in the forests whose roar frightens away whatever might approach him',[9] but he was not short of cash, even by the ample standards of the British milord.

Below the magnates, a class of country gentlemen of varying size and economic resources exploited the peasantry. In some countries it was inordinately large, and consequently poor and discontented; distinguished from the non-noble chiefly by its political and social privileges and its disinclination to engage in ungentlemanly pursuits such as work. In Hungary and Poland it amounted to something like one in ten of the total population, in Spain at the end of the eighteenth century to almost half a million – or, in 1827, to 10 per cent of the total European nobility;[10] elsewhere it was much smaller.

IV

In the rest of Europe the agrarian structure was socially not dissimilar. That is to say that for the peasant or labourer anybody who owned an estate was a 'gentleman' and a member of the ruling class, and conversely noble or gentle status (which gave social and political privileges and was still nominally the only road to the highest offices of state) was inconceivable without an estate. In most countries of Western Europe the feudal order implied by such ways of thinking was still politically very alive, though economically increasingly obsolete. Indeed, its very economic obsolescence, which made noble and gentle incomes limp increasingly far behind the rise in prices and expenditure, made the aristocracy exploit its one inalienable economic asset, the privileges of birth and status, with ever-increasing intensity. All over continental Europe the nobleman elbowed his low-born rivals out of offices of profit under the crown : from Sweden, where the proportion of commoner officers fell from 66 per cent in 1719 (42 per cent in 1700) to 23 per cent in 1780,[11] to France, where this 'feudal reaction' precipitated the French Revolution (see below Chapter 3). But even where it was in some ways distinctly shaky, as in France where entry into the landed nobility was relatively easy, or even more in Britain where landed and noble status was the reward for any kind of wealth, provided it was large enough, the link between estate-ownership and ruling-class status remained, and had indeed lately become somewhat closer.

Economically, however, western rural society was very different. The characteristic peasant had lost much of his servile status in the late middle ages, though still often retaining a great many galling marks of legal dependence. The characteristic estate had long ceased to be a unit of economic enterprise and had become a system of collecting rents and other money incomes. The more or less free peasant, large, medium or small, was the characteristic cultivator of the soil. If a tenant of some sort, he paid rent (or, in a few areas, a share of the crop) to a landlord. If technically a freeholder, he probably still owed the local lord a variety of obligations which might or might not be turned into money (such as the obligation to send his corn to the lord's mill), as well as taxes to the prince, tithes to the church, and some duties of forced labour, all of which contrasted with the relative exemption of the higher social strata. But if these political bonds were stripped away, a large part of Europe would emerge as an area of peasant agriculture; generally one in which a minority of wealthy peasants tended to become commercial farmers selling a permanent crop surplus to the urban market, and a majority of small and medium peasants lived in something like self-sufficiency off their holdings unless these were so small as to oblige them to take part-time work in agriculture or manufacture for wages.

Only a few areas had pushed agrarian development one stage further towards a purely capitalist agriculture. England was the chief of these. There landownership was extremely concentrated, but the characteristic cultivator was a medium-sized commercial tenant-farmer operating with hired labour. A large undergrowth of small-holders, cottagers and the like still obscured this. But when this was stripped away (roughly between 1760 and 1830) what emerged was not peasant agriculture but a class of agricultural entrepreneurs, the farmers, and a large agrarian proletariat. A few European areas where commercial investment traditionally went into farming, as in parts of Northern Italy and the Netherlands, or where specialized commercial crops were produced, also showed strong capitalist tendencies, but this was exceptional. A further exception was Ireland, an unhappy island which combined the disadvantages of the backward areas of Europe with those of proximity to the most advanced economy. Here a handful of absentee latifundists similar to the Andalusian or Sicilian ones exploited a vast mass of tenants by means of extortionate money-rents.

Technically European agriculture was still, with the exception of a few advanced regions, both traditional and astonishingly inefficient. Its products were still mainly the traditional ones : rye, wheat, barley, oats and in Eastern Europe buckwheat, the basic food of the people, beef cattle, sheep, goats and their dairy products, pigs and fowl, a certain amount of fruit and vegetables, wine, and a certain number of industrial raw materials such as wool, flax, hemp for cordage, barley for beer, etc. The food of Europe was still regional. The products of other climates were still rarities, verging on luxury, except perhaps for sugar, the most important foodstuff imported from the tropics and the one whose sweetness has created more human bitterness than any other. In England (admittedly the most advanced country) the average annual consumption per head in the 1790s was 14 lb. But even in England the average *per capita* consumption of tea in the year of the French Revolution was hardly 2 ounces per month.

The new crops imported from the Americas or other parts of the tropics had made some headway. In Southern Europe and the Balkans maize (Indian corn) was already quite widespread – it had helped fix mobile peasants to their plots in the Balkans – and in Northern Italy rice had made some progress. Tobacco was cultivated in various principalities, mostly as a government monopoly for revenue purposes, though its use by modern standards was negligible: the average Englishman in 1790 smoked, snuffed or chewed about one and a third ounces a month. Silkworm culture was common in parts of Southern Europe. The chief of the new crops, the potato, was only just making its way, except perhaps in Ireland where its ability to feed more people per acre at subsistence level than any other food had already made it a staple of cultivation. Outside England and the Low Countries the systematic cultivation of root and fodder crops (other than hay) was still rather exceptional; and only the Napoleonic wars brought about the massive production of beet for sugar.

The eighteenth century was not, of course, one of agricultural stagnation. On the contrary, a long era of demographic expansion, of growing urbanization, trade and manufacture, encouraged agricultural improvement and indeed required it. The second half of the century saw the beginning of that startling and henceforward unbroken rise in population which is so characteristic of the modern world : between 1755 and 1784, for instance, the rural population of Brabant (Belgium) rose by 44 per cent.[12] But what impressed the numerous campaigners for agricultural improvement, who multiplied their societies, government reports and propagandist publica-

31

tions from Spain to Russia, was the size of the obstacles to agrarian advance rather than its progress.

V

The world of agriculture was sluggish, except perhaps for its capitalist sector. That of commerce, manufactures, and the technological and intellectual activities which went with both, was confident, brisk and expansive, and the classes which benefited from them, active, determined and optimistic. The contemporary observer would be most immediately struck by the vast deployment of trade, which was closely tied to colonial exploitation. A system of maritime trade currents, growing rapidly in volume and capacity, circled the earth, bringing its profits to the mercantile communities of North Atlantic Europe. They used colonial power to rob the inhabitants of the East Indies [13] of the commodities exported thence to Europe and Africa, where these and European goods were used to buy slaves for the rapidly growing plantation systems of the Americas. The American plantations in turn exported their sugar, cotton, etc. in ever vaster and cheaper quantities to the Atlantic and North Sea ports whence they were redistributed eastwards, together with the traditional manufactures and commodities of European East-West trade: textiles, salt, wine and the rest. From 'the Baltic' in turn came the grain, timber, flax. From Eastern Europe came the grain, timber, flax and linen (a profitable export to the tropics), hemp and iron of this second colonial zone. And between the relatively developed economies of Europe – which included, economically speaking, the increasingly active communities of white settlers in the northern British colonies of America (after 1783, the Northern USA) – the web of trade became ever more dense.

The *nabob* or planter returned from the colonies with wealth beyond the dreams of provincial avarice, the merchant and shipper whose splendid ports – Bordeaux, Bristol, Liverpool – had been built or rebuilt in the century, appeared to be the true economic victors of the age, comparable only with the great officials and financiers who drew their wealth from the profitable service of states, for this was still the age when the term 'office of profit under the crown' had its literal meaning. Beside him the middle class of lawyers, estate managers, local brewers, traders and the like, who accumulated a modest wealth from the agricultural world, lived low and quiet lives, and even the manufacturer appeared little better than a very poor relation. For though mining and manufactures were expanding rapidly, and in all parts of Europe, the merchant (and in Eastern Europe also often the feudal lord) remained their chief controllers.

This was because the chief form of expanding industrial production was the so-called domestic or putting-out system, in which the merchant bought the products of the handicraftsmen or of the part-time non-agricultural labour of the peasantry for sale in a wider market. The mere growth of such trade inevitably created rudimentary conditions for an early industrial capitalism. The craftsman selling his wares might turn into little more than a worker paid on piece-rates (especially when the merchant supplied him with his raw material, and perhaps leased out productive equipment). The peasant who also wove might become the weaver who also had a small plot. Specialization of processes and functions might divide the old craft or create a complex of semi-skilled workers from among peasants. The old master-craftsmen, or some special groups of crafts, or some group of local intermediaries might turn into something like sub-contractors or employers. But the key controller of these decentralized forms of production, the one who linked the labour of lost villages or back streets with the world market, was some kind of merchant. And the 'industrialists' who were emerging or about to emerge from the ranks of the producers themselves were petty operators beside him, even when they were not directly dependent upon him. There were a few exceptions, especially in industrial England. Ironmasters, men like the great potter Josiah Wedgwood, were proud and respected, their establishments visited by the curious from all over Europe. But the typical industrialist (the word had not yet been invented) was as yet a petty-officer rather than a captain of industry.

Nevertheless, whatever their status, the activities of commerce and manufacture flourished brilliantly. The most brilliantly successful of eighteenth-century European states, Britain, plainly owed its power to its economic progress, and by the 1780s all continental governments with any pretence to a rational policy were consequently fostering economic growth, and especially industrial development, though with very varying success. The sciences, not yet split by nineteenth-century academicism into a superior 'pure' and an in-

33

ferior 'applied' branch, devoted themselves to the solution of productive problems : the most striking advances of the 1780s were those of chemistry, which was by tradition most closely linked to workshop practice and the needs of industry. The Great Encyclopaedia of Diderot and d'Alembert was not merely a compendium of progressive social and political thought, but of technological and scientific progress. For indeed the conviction of the progress of human knowledge, rationality, wealth, civilization and control over nature with which the eighteenth century was deeply imbued, the 'Enlightenment', drew its strength primarily from the evident progress of production, trade, and the economic and scientific rationality believed to be associated inevitably with both. And its greatest champions were the economically most progressive classes, those most directly involved in the tangible advances of the time : the mercantile circles and economically enlightened landlords, financiers, scientifically-minded economic and social administrators, the educated middle class, manufacturers and entrepreneurs. Such men hailed a Benjamin Franklin, working printer and journalist, inventor, entrepreneur, statesman and shrewd businessman, as the symbol of the active, self-made, reasoning citizen of the future. Such men in England, where the new men had no need of transatlantic revolutionary incarnations, formed the provincial societies out of which both scientific, industrial and political advance sprang. The *Lunar Society* of Birmingham included the potter Josiah Wedgwood, the inventor of the modern steam engine James Watt and his business partner Matthew Boulton, the chemist Priestley, the gentleman-biologist and pioneer of evolutionary theories Erasmus Darwin (grandfather of a greater Darwin), the great printer Baskerville. Such men everywhere flocked into the lodges of Freemasonry, where class distinctions did not count and the ideology of the Enlightenment was propagated with a disinterested zeal.

It is significant that the two chief centres of the ideology were also those of the dual revolution, France and England; though in fact its ideas gained widest international currency in their French formulations (even when these were merely gallicized versions of British ones). A secular, rationalist and progressive individualism dominated 'enlightened' thought. To set the individual free from the shackles which fettered him was its chief object : from the ignorant traditionalism of the Middle Ages, which still threw their shadow across the world, from the superstition of the churches (as distinct from 'natural' or 'rational' religion), from the irrationality which divided men into a hierarchy of higher and lower ranks according to birth or some other irrelevant criterion. Liberty, equality and (it followed) the fraternity of all men were its slogans. In due course they became those of the French Revolution. The reign of individual liberty could not but have the most beneficent consequences. The most extraordinary results could be looked for – could indeed already be observed to follow from – the unfettered exercise of individual talent in a world of reason. The passionate belief in progress of the typical 'enlightened' thinker reflected the visible increases in knowledge and technique, in wealth, welfare and civilization which he could see all around him, and which he ascribed with some justice to the growing advance of his ideas. At the beginning of his century witches were still widely burned; at its end enlightened governments like the Austrian had already abolished not only judicial torture but also slavery. What might not be expected if the remaining obstacles to progress such as the vested interests of feudality and church, were swept away?

It is not strictly accurate to call the 'enlightenment' a middle class ideology, though there were many enlighteners – and politically they were the decisive ones – who assumed as a matter of course that the free society would be a capitalist society.[14] In theory its object was to set all human beings free. All progressive, rationalist and humanist ideologies are implicit in it, and indeed came out of it. Yet in practice the leaders of the emancipation for which the enlightenment called were likely to be the middle ranks of society, the new, rational men of ability and merit rather than birth, and the social order which would emerge from their activities would be a 'bourgeois' and capitalist one.

It is more accurate to call the 'enlightenment' a revolutionary ideology, in spite of the political caution and moderation of many of its continental champions, most of whom – until the 1780s – put their faith in enlightened absolute monarchy. For illuminism implied the abolition of the prevailing society and political order in most of Europe. It was too much to expect the *anciens régimes* to abolish themselves voluntarily. On the contrary, as we have seen, in some respects they were reinforcing themselves against the advance of the new social and economic forces. And their strongholds (outside

Britain, the United Provinces and a few other places where they had already been defeated) were the very monarchies to which moderate enlighteners pinned their faith.

VI

With the exception of Britain, which had made its revolution in the seventeenth century, and a few lesser states, absolute monarchies ruled in all functioning states of the European continent; those in which they did not rule fell apart into anarchy and were swallowed by their neighbours, like Poland. Hereditary monarchs by the grace of God headed hierarchies of landed nobles, buttressed by the traditional organization and orthodoxy of churches and surrounded by an increasing clutter of institutions which had nothing but a long past to recommend them. It is true that the sheer needs of state cohesion and efficiency in an age of acute international rivalry had long obliged monarchs to curb the anarchic tendencies of their nobles and other vested interests, and to staff their state apparatus so far as possible with non-aristocratic civil servants. Moreover, in the latter part of the eighteenth century these needs, and the obvious international success of capitalist British power, led most such monarchs (or rather their advisers) to attempt programmes of economic, social, administrative and intellectual modernization. In those days princes adopted the slogan of 'enlightenment' as governments in our time, and for analogous reasons, adopt those of 'planning'; and as in our day some who adopted them in theory did very little about them in practice, and most who did so were less interested in the general ideals which lay behind the 'enlightened' (or the 'planned') society, than in the practical advantage of adopting the most up-to-date methods of multiplying their revenue, wealth and power.

Conversely, the middle and educated classes and those committed to progress often looked to the powerful central apparatus of an 'enlightened' monarchy to realize their hopes. A prince needed a middle class and its ideas to modernize his state; a weak middle class needed a prince to batter down the resistance of entrenched aristocratic and clerical interests to progress.

Yet in fact absolute monarchy, however modernist and innovatory, found it impossible – and indeed showed few signs of wanting – to break loose from the hierarchy of landed nobles to which, after all, it belonged, whose values it symbolized and incorporated, and on whose support it largely depended. Absolute monarchy, however theoretically free to do whatever it liked, in practice belonged to the world which the enlightenment had baptized *féodalité* or feudalism, a term later popularized by the French Revolution. Such a monarchy was ready to use all available resources to strengthen its authority and taxable revenue within and its power outside its frontiers, and this might well lead it to foster what were in effect the forces of the rising society. It was prepared to strengthen its political hand by playing off one estate, class or province against another. Yet its horizons were those of its history, its function and its class. It hardly ever wanted, and was never able to achieve, the root-and-branch social and economic transformation which the progress of the economy required and the rising social groups called for.

To take an obvious example. Few rational thinkers, even among the advisers of princes, seriously doubted the need to abolish serfdom and the surviving bonds of feudal peasant dependence. Such a reform was recognized as one of the primary points of any 'enlightened' programme, and there was virtually no prince from Madrid to St Petersburg and from Naples to Stockholm who did not, at one time or another in the quarter-century preceding the French Revolution, subscribe to such a programme. Yet in fact the only peasant liberations which took place from above before 1789 were in small and untypical states like Denmark and Savoy, and on the personal estates of some other princes. One major such liberation was attempted, by Joseph II of Austria, in 1781; but it failed, in the face of the political resistance of vested interests and of peasant rebellion in excess of what had been anticipated, and had to remain uncompleted. What *did* abolish agrarian feudal relations all over Western and Central Europe was the French Revolution, by direct action, reaction or example, and the revolution of 1848.

There was thus a latent, and would soon be an overt, conflict between the forces of the old and the new 'bourgeois' society, which could not be settled within the framework of the existing political régimes, except of course where these already embodied bourgeois triumph, as in Britain. What made these régimes even more vulnerable, was that they were subject to pressure from three directions: from the new forces, from the entrenched, and increasingly stiff resistance of the older vested interests, and from foreign rivals.

37

Their most vulnerable point was the one where the opposition of old and new tended to coincide : in the autonomist movements of the remoter or the least firmly controlled provinces or colonies. Thus in the Habsburg monarchy the reforms of Joseph II in the 1780s produced uproar in the Austrian Netherlands (the present Belgium) and a revolutionary movement which in 1789 joined naturally with that of the French. More commonly, communities of white settlers in the overseas colonies of European states resented the policy of their central government, which subordinated the colonial interests strictly to the metropolitan. In all parts of the Americas, Spanish, French and British, as well as in Ireland, such settler movements demanded autonomy – not always for régimes which represented economically more progressive forces than the metropolis – and several British colonies either won it peacefully for a time, like Ireland, or took it by revolution, like the USA. Economic expansion, colonial development and the tensions of the attempted reforms of 'enlightened absolutism' multiplied the occasions for such conflicts in the 1770s and 1780s.

In itself provincial or colonial dissidence was not fatal. Old-established monarchies could survive the loss of a province or two, and the main victim of colonial autonomism, Britain, did not suffer from the weaknesses of the old régimes and therefore remained as stable and dynamic as ever in spite of the American revolution. There were few regions in which the purely domestic conditions for a major transfer of power existed. What made the situation explosive was international rivalry.

For international rivalry, i.e. war, tested the resources of a state as nothing else did. When they could not pass this test, they shook, cracked, or fell. One major such rivalry dominated the European international scene for most of the eighteenth century, and lay at the core of its recurrent periods of general war : 1689–1713, 1740–8, 1756–63, 1776–83 and, overlapping into our period, 1792–1815. This was the conflict between Britain and France, which was also, in a sense, that between the old and the new régimes. For France, though rousing British hostility by the rapid expansion of its trade and colonial empire, was also the most powerful, eminent and influential, in a word the classical, aristocratic absolute monarchy. Nowhere is the superiority of the new to the old social order more vividly exemplified than in the conflict between these two powers. For the

British not only won, with varying degrees of decisiveness in all but one of these wars. They supported the effort of organizing, financing and waging them with relative ease. The French monarchy, on the other hand, though very much larger, more populous, and in terms of her potential resources, wealthier than Britain, found the effort too great. After its defeat in the Seven Years' War (1756–63) the revolt of the American colonies gave it the opportunity to turn the tables on its adversary. France took it. And indeed, in the subsequent international conflict Britain was badly defeated, losing the most important part of her American empire; and France, the ally of the new USA, was consequently victorious. But the cost was excessive, and the French government's difficulties led it inevitably into that period of domestic political crisis, out of which, six years later, the Revolution emerged.

VII

It remains to round off this preliminary survey of the world on the eve of the dual revolution with a glance at the relations between Europe (or more precisely North-western Europe) and the rest of the world. The complete political and military domination of the world by Europe (and her overseas prolongations, the white settler communities) was to be the product of the age of the dual revolution. In the late eighteenth century several of the great non-European powers and civilizations still confronted the white trader, sailor and soldier on apparently equal terms. The great Chinese empire, then at the height of its effectiveness under the Manchu (Ch'ing) dynasty, was nobody's victim. On the contrary, if anything the current of cultural influence ran from east to west, and European philosophers pondered the lessons of the very different but evidently high civilization, while artists and craftsmen embodied the often misunderstood motifs of the Far East in their works and adapted its new materials ('china') to European uses. The Islamic powers, though (like Turkey) periodically shaken by the military forces of neighbouring European states (Austria and above all Russia), were far from the helpless hulks they were to become in the nineteenth century. Africa remained virtually immune to European military penetration. Except for small areas round the Cape of Good Hope, the whites were confined to coastal trading posts.

Yet already the rapid and increasingly massive expansion of European trade and capitalist enterprise undermined their social order; in Africa through the unprecedented intensity of the awful traffic in slaves, around the Indian Ocean through the penetration of the rival colonizing powers, in the Near and Middle East through trade and military conflict. Already direct European conquest began to extend significantly beyond the area long since occupied by the pioneer colonization of the Spaniards and Portuguese in the sixteenth century, the white North American settlers in the seventeenth. The crucial advance was made by the British, who had already established direct territorial control over part of India (notably Bengal), virtually overthrowing the Mughal empire, a step which was to lead them in our period to become the rulers and administrators of all India. Already the relative feebleness of the non-European civilizations when confronted with the technological and military superiority of the west was predictable. What has been called 'the age of Vasco da Gama', the four centuries of world history in which a handful of European states and the European force of capitalism established a complete, though as is now evident, a temporary, domination of the entire world, was about to reach its climax. The dual revolution was to make European expansion irresistible, though it was also to provide the non-European world with the conditions and equipment for its eventual counter-attack.

NOTES

1 Saint-Just, *Oeuvres complètes*, II, p. 514.
2 A. Hovelacque, La taille dans un canton ligure. *Revue Mensuelle de l'Ecole d'Anthropologie* (Paris 1896).
3 L. Dal Pane, *Storia del Lavoro dagli inizi del secolo XVIII al 1815* (1958), p. 135. R. S. Eckers, The North-South Differential in Italian Economic Development, *Journal of Economic History*, XXI, 1961, p. 290.
4 Thus in 1823–7 townsmen in Brussels were on average 3 cm. taller than men from the surrounding rural communes, townsmen in Louvain 2 cm. There is a considerable body of military statistics on this point, though all from the nineteenth century.[5]
5 Quêtelet, qu. by Manouvrier, Sur la taille des Parisiens, *Bulletin de la Société Anthropologique de Paris*, 1888, p. 171.
6 H. Sée, *Esquisse d'une Histoire du Régime Agraire en Europe au XVIII et XIX siècles* (1921), p. 184, J. Blum, *Lord and Peasant in Russia* (1961), pp. 455–60.

7 Eighty estates of over (roughly) 25,000 acres (10,000 ha) were confiscated in Czechoslovakia after 1918, among them 500,000 acres each from the Schoenborns and the Schwarzenbergs, 400,000 from the Liechtensteins, 170,000 from the Kinskys.[8]

8 Th. Haebich, *Deutsche Latifundien* (1947), pp. 27 ff.

9 A. Goodwin ed. *The European Nobility in the Eighteenth Century* (1953), p. 52.

10 L. B. Namier, *1848, The Revolution of the Intellectuals* (1944); J. Vicens Vives, *Historia Economica de España* (1959).

11 Sten Carlsson, *Ståndssamhälle och ståndspersoner 1700–1865* (1949).

12 Pierre Lebrun *et al.*, La rivoluzione industriale in Belgio, *Studi Storici*, II, 3–4, 1961, pp. 564–5.

13 Also to some extent of the Far East, where they bought the tea, silks, china, etc. for which there was a growing European demand. But the political independence of China and Japan made this trade as yet a somewhat less piratical one.

14 Like Turgot (*Oeuvres* V, p. 244). 'Ceux qui connaissent la marche du commerce savent aussi que toute entreprise importante, de trafic ou d'industrie, exige le concours de deux espèces d'hommes, d'entrepreneurs . . . et des ouvriers qui travaillent pour le compte des premiers, moyennant un salaire convenu. Telle est la véritable origine de la distinction entre les entrepreneurs et les maîtres, et les ouvriers ou compagnons, laquelle est fondé sur la nature des choses.'

2

The Industrial Revolution

*Such works, however their operations, causes, and con-
sequences, have infinite merit, and do great credit to the
talents of this very ingenious and useful man, who will
have the merit, wherever he goes, of* setting men to think.
*... Get rid of that dronish, sleepy, and stupid indifference,
that lazy negligence, which enchains men in the exact
paths of their forefathers, without enquiry, without
thought, and without ambition, and you are sure of doing
good. What trains of thought, what a spirit of exertion,
what a mass and power of effort have sprung in every
path of life, from the works of such men as Brindley,
Watt, Priestley, Harrison, Arkwright. ... In what path of
life can a man be found that will not animate his pursuit
from seeing the steam-engine of Watt?*

Arthur Young, *Tours in England and Wales* [1]

*From this foul drain the greatest stream of human
industry flows out to fertilize the whole world. From this
filthy sewer pure gold flows. Here humanity attains its
most complete development and its most brutish, here
civilization works its miracles and civilized man is turned
almost into a savage.*

A. de Toqueville on Manchester in 1835 [2]

I

Let us begin with the Industrial Revolution, that is to say with
Britain. This is at first sight a capricious starting-point, for the repercussions of this revolution did not make themselves felt in an
obvious and unmistakable way – at any rate outside England – until
quite late in our period; certainly not before 1830, probably not
before 1840 or thereabouts. It is only in the 1830s that literature and
the arts began to be overtly haunted by that rise of the capitalist
society, that world in which all social bonds crumbled except the

implacable gold and paper ones of the cash nexus (the phrase comes from Carlyle). Balzac's *Comédie Humaine*, the most extraordinary literary monument of its rise, belongs to that decade. It is not until about 1840 that the great stream of official and unofficial literature on the social effects of the Industrial Revolution begins to flow : the major Bluebooks and statistical enquiries in England, Villermé's *Tableau de l'état physique et moral des ouvriers*, Engels' *Condition of the Working Class in England*, Ducpetiaux's work in Belgium, and scores of troubled or appalled observers from Germany to Spain and the USA. It was not until the 1840s that the proletariat, that child of the Industrial Revolution, and Communism, which was now attached to its social movements – the spectre of the Communist Manifesto – walked across the continent. The very name of the Industrial Revolution reflects its relatively tardy impact on Europe. The thing existed in Britain before the word. Not until the 1820s did English and French socialists – themselves an unprecedented group –invent it, probably by analogy with the political revolution of France.[3]

Nevertheless it is as well to consider it first, for two reasons. First, because in fact it 'broke out' – to use a question-begging phrase – before the Bastille was stormed; and second because without it we cannot understand the impersonal groundswell of history on which the more obvious men and events of our period were borne; the uneven complexity of its rhythm.

What does the phrase 'the Industrial Revolution broke out' mean? It means that some time in the 1780s, and for the first time in human history, the shackles were taken off the productive power of human societies, which henceforth became capable of the constant, rapid and up to the present limitless multiplication of men, goods and services. This is now technically known to the economists as the 'take-off into self-sustained growth'. No previous society had been able to break through the ceiling which a pre-industrial social structure, defective science and technology, and consequently periodic breakdown, famine and death, imposed on production. The 'take-off' was not, of course, one of those phenomena which, like earthquakes and large meteors, take the non-technical world by surprise. Its pre-history in Europe can be traced back, depending on the taste of the historian and his particular range of interest, to about AD 1000, if not before, and earlier attempts to leap into the air, clumsy as the

43

experiments of young ducklings, have been flattered with the name of 'industrial revolution' – in the thirteenth century, in the sixteenth, in the last decades of the seventeenth. From the middle of the eighteenth century the process of gathering speed for the take-off is so clearly observable that older historians have tended to date the Industrial Revolution back to 1760. But careful enquiry has tended to lead most experts to pick on the 1780s rather than the 1760s as the decisive decade, for it was then that, so far as we can tell, all the relevant statistical indices took that sudden, sharp, almost vertical turn upwards which marks the 'take-off'. The economy became, as it were, airborne.

To call this process the Industrial Revolution is both logical and in line with a well-established tradition, though there was at one time a fashion among conservative historians – perhaps due to a certain shyness in the presence of incendiary concepts – to deny its existence, and substitute instead platitudinous terms like 'accelerated evolution'. If the sudden, qualitative and fundamental transformation, which happened in or about the 1780s, was not a revolution then the word has no commonsense meaning. The Industrial Revolution was not indeed an episode with a beginning and an end. To ask when it was 'complete' is senseless, for its essence was that henceforth revolutionary change became the norm. It is still going on; at most we can ask when the economic transformations had gone far enough to establish a substantially industrialized economy, capable of producing, broadly speaking, anything it wanted within the range of the available techniques, a 'mature industrial economy' to use the technical term. In Britain, and therefore in the world, this period of initial industrialization probably coincides almost exactly with the period with which this book deals, for if it began with the 'take-off' in the 1780s, it may plausibly be said to be concluded with the building of the railways and the construction of a massive heavy industry in Britain in the 1840s. But the Revolution itself, the 'take-off period', can probably be dated with as much precision as is possible in such matters, to some time within the twenty years from 1780 to 1800 : contemporary with, but slightly prior to, the French Revolution.

By any reckoning this was probably the most important event in world history, at any rate since the invention of agriculture and cities. And it was initiated by Britain. That this was not fortuitous, is evident. If there was to be a race for pioneering the Industrial Revolution in the eighteenth century, there was really only one starter. There was plenty of industrial and commercial advance, fostered by the intelligent and economically far from naïve ministers and civil servants of every enlightened monarchy in Europe, from Portugal to Russia, all of whom were at least as much concerned with 'economic growth' as present-day administrators. Some small states and regions did indeed industrialize quite impressively for example, Saxony and the bishopric of Liège, though their industrial complexes were too small and localized to exert the world-revolutionary influence of the British ones. But it seems clear that even before the revolution Britain was already a long way ahead of her chief potential competitor in *per capita* output and trade, even if still comparable to her in total output and trade.

Whatever the British advance was due to, it was not scientific and technological superiority. In the natural sciences the French were almost certainly ahead of the British; an advantage which the French Revolution accentuated very sharply, at any rate in mathematics and physics, for it encouraged science in France while reaction suspected it in England. Even in the social sciences the British were still far from that superiority which made – and largely kept – economics a pre-eminently Anglo-Saxon subject; but here the Industrial Revolution put them into unquestioned first place. The economist of the 1780s would read Adam Smith, but also – and perhaps more profitably – the French physiocrats and national income accountants, Quesnay, Turgot, Dupont de Nemours, Lavoisier, and perhaps an Italian or two. The French produced more original inventions, such as the Jacquard loom (1804) – a more complex piece of apparatus than any devised in Britain – and better ships. The Germans possessed institutions of technical training like the Prussian *Bergakademie* which had no parallel in Britain, and the French Revolution created that unique and impressive body, the *Ecole Polytechnique*. English education was a joke in poor taste, though its deficiencies were somewhat offset by the dour village schools and the austere, turbulent, democratic universities of Calvinist Scotland which sent a stream of brilliant, hard-working, career-seeking and rationalist young men into the south country : James Watt, Thomas Telford, Loudon McAdam, James Mill. Oxford and Cambridge, the only two English universities, were intellectually null, as were the somnolent public or grammar schools, with the exception of the Academies founded by

45

the Dissenters who were excluded from the (Anglican) educational system. Even such aristocratic families as wished their sons to be educated, relied on tutors or Scottish universities. There was no system of primary education whatever before the Quaker Lancaster (and after him his Anglican rivals) established a sort of voluntary mass-production of elementary literacy in the early nineteenth century, incidentally saddling English education forever after with sectarian disputes. Social fears discouraged the education of the poor.

Fortunately few intellectual refinements were necessary to make the Industrial Revolution.[4] Its technical inventions were exceedingly modest, and in no way beyond the scope of intelligent artisans experimenting in their workshops, or of the constructive capacities of carpenters, millwrights and locksmiths : the flying shuttle, the spinning jenny, the mule. Even its scientifically most sophisticated machine, James Watt's rotary steam-engine (1784), required no more physics than had been available for the best part of a century – the proper *theory* of steam engines was only developed *ex post facto* by the Frenchman Carnot in the 1820s – and could build on several generations of practical employment for steam engines, mostly in mines. Given the right conditions, the technical innovations of the Industrial Revolution practically made themselves, except perhaps in the chemical industry. This does not mean that early industrialists were not often interested in science and on the look-out for its practical benefits.[5]

But the right conditions were visibly present in Britain, where more than a century had passed since the first king had been formally tried and executed by his people, and since private profit and economic development had become accepted as the supreme objects of government policy. For practical purposes the uniquely revolutionary British solution of the agrarian problem had already been found. A relative handful of commercially-minded landlords already almost monopolized the land, which was cultivated by tenant-farmers employing landless or smallholders. A good many relics of the ancient collective economy of the village still remained to be swept away by Enclosure Acts (1760–1830) and private transactions, but we can hardly any longer speak of a 'British peasantry' in the same sense that we can speak of a French, German or Russian peasantry. Farming was already predominantly for the market; manufacture had long been diffused throughout an unfeudal countryside. Agriculture was already prepared to carry out its three fundamental functions in an era of industrialization : to increase production and productivity, so as to feed a rapidly rising non-agricultural population; to provide a large and rising surplus of potential recruits for the towns and industries; and to provide a mechanism for the accumulation of capital to be used in the more modern sectors of the economy. (Two other functions were probably less important in Britain : that of creating a sufficiently large market among the agricultural population – normally the great mass of the people – and of providing an export surplus which helps to secure capital imports.) A considerable volume of social overhead capital – the expensive general equipment necessary for the entire economy to move smoothly ahead – was already being created, notably in shipping, port facilities, and the improvement of roads and waterways. Politics were already geared to profit. The businessman's specific demands might encounter resistance from other vested interests; and as we shall see, the agrarians were to erect one last barrier to hold up the advance of the industrialists between 1795 and 1846. On the whole, however, it was accepted that money not only talked, but governed. All the industrialist had to get to be accepted among the governors of society was enough money.

The businessman was undoubtedly in the process of getting more money, for the greater part of the eighteenth century was for most of Europe a period of prosperity and comfortable economic expansion; the real background to the happy optimism of Voltaire's Dr Pangloss. It may well be argued that sooner or later this expansion, assisted by a gentle inflation, would have pushed some country across the threshold which separates the pre-industrial from the industrial economy. But the problem is not so simple. Much of eighteenth-century industrial expansion did not in fact lead immediately, or within the foreseeable future, to industrial *revolution*, i.e. to the creation of a mechanized 'factory system' which in turn produces in such vast quantities and at such rapidly diminishing cost, as to be no longer dependent on existing demand, but to create its own market.[6] For instance the building trade, or the numerous small scale industries producing domestic metal goods – nails, pots, knives, scissors, etc. – in the British Midlands and Yorkshire, expanded very greatly in this period, but always as a function of the existing market. In 1850, while producing far more than in 1750, they produced in substantially the old manner. What was needed was not any kind of expansion, but the special kind of expansion which produced Manchester rather than Birmingham.

Moreover, the pioneer industrial revolutions occurred in a special historical situation, in which economic growth emerges from the criss-crossing decisions of countless private entrepreneurs and investors, each governed by the first commandment of the age, to buy in the cheapest market and to sell in the dearest. How were they to discover that maximum profit was to be got out of organizing industrial revolution rather than out of more familiar (and in the past more profitable) business activities? How were they to learn, what nobody could as yet know, that industrial revolution would produce an unexampled acceleration in the expansion of their markets? Given that the main social foundations of an industrial society had already been laid, as they almost certainly had in the England of the later eighteenth century, they required two things : first, an industry which already offered exceptional rewards for the manufacturer who could expand his output quickly, if need be by reasonably cheap and simple innovations, and second, a *world* market largely monopolized by a single producing nation.[7]

These considerations apply in some ways to all countries in our period. For instance, in all of them the lead in industrial growth was taken by the manufacturers of goods of mass consumption – mainly, but not exclusively, textiles[9] – because the mass market for such goods already existed, and businessmen could clearly see its possibilities of expansion. In other ways, however, they apply to Britain alone. For the pioneer industrialists have the most difficult problems. Once Britain had begun to industrialize, other countries could begin to enjoy the benefits of the rapid economic expansion which the pioneer industrial revolution stimulated. Moreover, British success proved what could be achieved by it, British technique could be imitated, British skill and capital imported. The Saxon textile industry, incapable of making its own inventions, copied the English ones, sometimes under the supervision of English mechanics; Englishmen with a taste for the continent, like the Cockerills, established themselves in Belgium and various parts of Germany. Between 1789 and 1848 Europe and America were flooded with British experts, steam engines, cotton machinery and investments.

Britain enjoyed no such advantages. On the other hand it possessed an economy strong enough and a state aggressive enough to capture the markets of its competitors. In effect the wars of 1793–1815, the last and decisive phase of a century's Anglo-French duel, virtually eliminated all rivals from the non-European world, except to some extent the young USA. Moreover, Britain possessed an industry admirably suited to pioneering industrial revolution under capitalist conditions, and an economic conjuncture which allowed it to : the cotton industry, and colonial expansion.

II

The British, like all other cotton industries, had originally grown up as a by-product of overseas trade, which produced its raw material (or rather one of its raw materials, for the original product was *fustian*, a mixture of cotton and linen), and the Indian cotton goods or *calicoes* which won the markets that the European manufacturers were to attempt to capture with their own imitations. To begin with they were not very successful, though better able to reproduce the cheap and coarse goods competitively than the fine and elaborate ones. Fortunately, however, the old-established and powerful vested interest of the woollen trade periodically secured import prohibitions of Indian calicoes (which the purely mercantile interest of the East India Company sought to export from India in the largest possible quantities, and thus gave the native cotton industry's substitutes a chance. Cheaper than wool, cotton and cotton mixtures won themselves a modest but useful market at home. But their major chances of rapid expansion were to lie overseas.

Colonial trade had created the cotton industry, and continued to nourish it. In the eighteenth century it developed in the hinterland of the major colonial ports, Bristol, Glasgow but especially Liverpool, the great centre of the slave trades. Each phase of this inhuman but rapidly expanding commerce stimulated it. In fact, during the entire period with which this book is concerned slavery and cotton marched together. The African slaves were bought, in part at least, with Indian cotton goods; but when the supply of these was interrupted by war or revolt in and about India, Lancashire was able to leap in. The plantations of the West Indies, where the slaves were taken, provided the bulk of the raw cotton for the British industry, and in return the planters bought Manchester cotton checks in appreciable quantities. Until shortly before the 'take-off' the overwhelming bulk of Lancashire cotton exports went to the combined African and American markets.[10] Lancashire was later to repay its debt to slavery by preserving it; for after the 1790s the slave plantations of the Southern United States were extended and maintained by the insatiable and rocketing demands of the Lancashire mills, to which they supplied the bulk of their raw cotton.

The cotton industry was thus launched, like a glider, by the pull of the colonial trade to which it was attached; a trade which promised not only great, but rapid and above all unpredictable expansion, which encouraged the entrepreneur to adopt the revolutionary techniques required to meet it. Between 1750 and 1769 the export of British cottons increased more than ten times over. In such situations the rewards for the man who came into the market first with the most cotton checks were astronomical and well worth the risks of leaps into technological adventure. But the overseas market, and especially within it the poor and backward 'under-developed areas', not only expanded dramatically from time to time, but expanded constantly without apparent limit. Doubtless any given section of it, considered in isolation, was small by industrial standards, and the competition of the different 'advanced economies' made it even smaller for each. But, as we have seen, supposing any one of the advanced economies managed, for a sufficiently long time, to monopolize *all* or almost all of it, then its prospects really were limitless. This is precisely what the British cotton industry succeeded in doing, aided by the aggressive support of the British Government. In terms of sales, the Industrial Revolution can be described except for a few initial years in the 1780s as the triumph of the export market over the home : by 1814 Britain exported about four yards of cotton cloth for every three used at home, by 1850 thirteen for every eight.[11] And within this expanding export market, in turn, the semi-colonial and colonial markets, long the main outlets for British goods abroad, triumphed. During the Napoleonic Wars, when the European markets were largely cut off by wars and blockades, this was natural enough. But even after the wars they continued to assert themselves. In 1820 Europe, once again open to free British imports, took 128 million yards of British cotton; America outside the USA, Africa and Asia took 80 millions; but by 1840 Europe took 200 million yards, while the 'under-developed' areas took 529 millions.

For within these areas British industry had established a monopoly by means of war, other people's revolutions and her own imperial rule. Two regions deserve particular notice. *Latin America* came to depend virtually entirely on British imports during the Napoleonic Wars, and after it broke with Spain and Portugal (see pp. 139–291 below) it became almost an economic dependency of Britain, being cut off from any political interference by Britain's potential European competitors. By 1820 this impoverished continent already took more than a quarter as much of British cotton cloths as Europe; by 1840 it took almost half as much again in Europe. The East Indies had been, as we have seen, the traditional exporter of cotton goods, encouraged by the East India Company. But as the industrialist vested interest prevailed in Britain, the East India mercantile interests (not to mention the Indian ones) were pressed back. India was systematically deindustrialized and became in turn a market for Lancashire cottons : in 1820 the subcontinent took only 11 million yards; but by 1840 it already took 145 million yards. This was not merely a gratifying extension of Lancashire's markets. It was a major landmark in world history. For since the dawn of time Europe had always imported more from the East than she had sold there; because there was little the Orient required from the West in return for the spices, silks, calicoes, jewels, etc., which it sent there. The cotton shirtings of the Industrial Revolution for the first time reversed this relationship, which had been hitherto kept in balance by a mixture of bullion exports and robbery. Only the conservative and self-satisfied Chinese still refused to buy what the West, or western-controlled economies offered, until between 1815 and 1842 western traders, aided by western gun-boats, discovered an ideal commodity which could be exported *en masse* from India to the East : opium.

Cotton therefore provided prospects sufficiently astronomical to tempt private entrepreneurs into the adventure of industrial revolution, and an expansion sufficiently sudden to require it. Fortunately it also provided the other conditions which made it possible. The new inventions which revolutionized it – the spinning jenny, the water-frame, the mule in spinning, a little later the power-loom in weaving – were sufficiently simple and cheap, and paid for themselves almost immediately in terms of higher output. They could be

51

installed, if need be piecemeal, by small men who started off with a few borrowed pounds, for the men who controlled the great accumulations of eighteenth-century wealth were not greatly inclined to invest large amounts in industry. The expansion of the industry could be financed easily out of current profits, for the combination of its vast market conquests and a steady price inflation produced fantastic rates of profit. 'It was not five per cent or ten per cent,' a later English politician was to say, with justice, 'but hundreds per cent and thousands per cent that made the fortunes of Lancashire.' In 1789 an ex-draper's assistant like Robert Owen could start with a borrowed £100 in Manchester; by 1809 he bought out his partners in the New Lanark Mills for £84,000 *in cash*. And his was a relatively modest story of business success. It should be remembered that around 1800 less than 15 per cent of British families had an income of more than £50 per year, and of these only one-quarter earned more than £200 a year.[12]

But the cotton manufacture had other advantages. All its raw material came from abroad, and its supply could therefore be expanded by the drastic procedures open to white men in the colonies – slavery and the opening of new areas of cultivation – rather than by the slower procedures of European agriculture; nor was it hampered by the vested interests of European agriculturalists.[13] From the 1790s on British cotton found its supply, to which its fortunes remained linked until the 1860s, in the newly-opened Southern States of the USA. Again, at crucial points of manufacture (notably spinning) cotton suffered from a shortage of cheap and efficient labour, and was therefore pushed into mechanization. An industry like *linen*, which had initially rather better chances of colonial expansion than cotton, suffered in the long run from the very ease with which cheap, non-mechanized production could be expanded in the impoverished peasant regions (mainly in Central Europe, but also in Ireland) in which it mainly flourished. For the *obvious* way of industrial expansion in the eighteenth century, in Saxony and Normandy as in England, was not to construct factories, but to extend the so-called 'domestic' or 'putting-out' system, in which workers – sometimes former independent craftsmen, sometimes former peasants with time on their hands in the dead season – worked up the raw material in their own homes, with their own or rented tools, receiving it from and delivering it back to merchants who were in the process of becoming employers.[14] Indeed, both in Britain and in the rest of the economically progressive world, the bulk of expansion in the initial period of industrialization continued to be of this kind. Even in the cotton industry such processes as weaving were expanded by creating hosts of domestic handloom weavers to serve the nuclei of mechanized spinneries, the primitive handloom being a rather more efficient device than the spinning-wheel. Everywhere weaving was mechanized a generation after spinning, and everywhere, incidentally, the handloom weavers died a lingering death, occasionally revolting against their awful fate, when industry no longer had any need for them.

III

The traditional view which has seen the history of the British Industrial Revolution primarily in terms of cotton is thus correct. Cotton was the first industry to be revolutionized, and it is difficult to see what other could have pushed a host of private entrepreneurs into revolution. As late as the 1830s cotton was the only British industry in which the factory or 'mill' (the name was derived from the most widespread pre-industrial establishment employing heavy power-operated machinery) predominated; at first (1780–1815) mainly in spinning, carding and a few ancillary operations, after 1815 increasingly also in weaving. The 'factories' with which the new Factory Acts dealt were, until the 1860s, assumed to be exclusively textile factories and predominantly cotton mills. Factory production in other textile branches was slow to develop before the 1840s, and in other manufactures was negligible. Even the steam engine, though applied to numerous other industries by 1815, was not used in any quantity outside mining, which had pioneered it. In 1830 'industry' and 'factory' in anything like the modern sense still meant almost exclusively the cotton areas of the United Kingdom.

This is not to underestimate the forces which made for industrial innovation in other consumer goods, notably in other textiles,[15] in food and drink, in pottery and other household goods, greatly stimulated by the rapid growth of cities. But in the first place these employed far fewer people : no industry remotely approached the million-and-a-half people directly employed by or dependent on employment in cotton in 1833.[17] In the second place their power to

53

transform was much smaller : *brewing*, which was in most respects a technically and scientifically much more advanced and mechanized business, and one revolutionized well before cotton, hardly affected the economy around it, as may be proved by the great Guinness brewery in Dublin, which left the rest of the Dublin and Irish economy (though not local tastes) much as it was before its construction.[18] The demand derived from cotton – for more building and all activities in the new industrial areas, for machines, for chemical improvements, for industrial lighting, for shipping and a number of other activities – is itself enough to account for a large proportion of the economic growth in Britain up to the 1830s. In the third place, the expansion of the cotton industry was so vast and its weight in the foreign trade of Britain so great, that it dominated the movements of the entire economy. The quantity of raw cotton imported into Britain rose from 11 million lb. in 1785 to 588 million lb. in 1850; the output of cloth from 40 million to 2,025 million yards.[19] Cotton manufactures formed between 40 and 50 per cent of the annual declared value of *all* British exports between 1816 and 1848. If cotton flourished, the economy flourished; if it slumped, so did the economy. Its price movements determined the balance of the nation's trade. Only agriculture had a comparable power, and that was visibly declining.

Nevertheless, though the expansion of the cotton industry and the cotton-dominated industrial economy 'mocks all that the most romantic imagination could have previously conceived possible under any circumstances',[20] its progress was far from smooth, and by the 1830s and early 1840s produced major problems of growth, not to mention revolutionary unrest unparalleled in any other period of recent British history. This first general stumbling of the industrial capitalist economy is reflected in a marked slowing down in the growth, perhaps even in a decline, in the British national income at this period.[21] Nor was this first general capitalist crisis a purely British phenomenon.

Its most serious consequences were social : the transition to the new economy created misery and discontent, the materials of social revolution. And indeed, social revolution in the form of spontaneous risings of the urban and industrial poor did break out, and made the revolution of 1848 on the continent, the vast Chartist movement in Britain. Nor was discontent confined to the labouring poor. Small and inadaptable businessmen, petty-bourgeois, special sections of the economy, were also the victims of the Industrial Revolution and of its ramifications. Simple-minded labourers reacted to the new system by smashing the machines which they thought responsible for their troubles; but a surprisingly large body of local businessmen and farmers sympathized profoundly with these Luddite activities of their labourers, because they too saw themselves as victims of a diabolical minority of selfish innovators. The exploitation of labour which kept its incomes at subsistence level, thus enabling the rich to accumulate the profits which financed industrialization (and their own ample comforts), antagonized the proletarian. However, another aspect of this diversion of national income from the poor to the rich, from consumption to investment, also antagonized the small entrepreneur. The great financiers, the tight community of home and foreign 'fund-holders' who received what all paid in taxes (cf. chapter on War) – something like 8 per cent of the entire national income[22] – were perhaps even more unpopular among small businessmen, farmers and the like than among labourers, for these knew enough about money and credit to feel a personal rage at their disadvantage. It was all very well for the rich, who could raise all the credit they needed, to clamp rigid deflation and monetary orthodoxy on the economy after the Napoleonic Wars; it was the little man who suffered, and who, in all countries and at all times in the nineteenth century de-manded easy credit and financial unorthodoxy.[23] Labour and the disgruntled petty-bourgeois on the verge of toppling over into the unpropertied abyss, therefore shared common discontents. These in turn united them in the mass movements of 'radicalism', 'democracy' or 'republicanism' of which the British Radicals, the French Repub-licans and the American Jacksonian Democrats were the most for-midable between 1815 and 1848.

From the point of view of the capitalists, however, these social problems were relevant to the progress of the economy only if, by some horrible accident, they were to overthrow the social order. On the other hand there appeared to be certain inherent flaws of the economic process which threatened its fundamental motive-force : profit. For if the rate of return on capital fell to nothing, an economy in which men produced for profit only must slow down into that 'stationary state' which the economists envisaged and dreaded.[24]

The three most obvious of these flaws were the trade cycle of boom

55

and slump, the tendency of the rate of profit to decline, and (what amounted to the same thing) the shortage of profitable investment opportunities. The first of these was not regarded as serious, except by the critics of capitalism as such, who were the first to investigate it and to consider it as an integral part of the capitalist economic process and as a symptom of its inherent contradictions.[25] Periodic crises of the economy leading to unemployment, falls in production, bankruptcies, etc. were well known. In the eighteenth century they generally reflected some agrarian catastrophe (harvest failures, etc.) and on the continent of Europe, it has been argued, agrarian disturbances remained the primary cause of the most widespread depressions until the end of our period. Periodic crises in the small manufacturing and financial sectors of the economy were also familiar, in Britain at least from 1793. After the Napoleonic Wars the periodic drama of boom and collapse – in 1825–6, in 1836–7, in 1839–42, in 1846–8 – clearly dominated the economic life of a nation at peace. By the 1830s, that crucial decade in our period of history, it was vaguely recognized that they were regular periodic phenomena, at least in trade and finance.[26] However, they were still commonly regarded by businessmen as caused either by particular mistakes – e.g. overspeculation in American stocks – or by outside interference with the smooth operations of the capitalist economy. They were not believed to reflect any fundamental difficulties of the system.

Not so the falling margin of profit, which the cotton industry illustrated very clearly. Initially this industry benefited from immense advantages. Mechanization greatly increased the productivity (i.e. reduced the cost per unit produced) of its labour, which was in any case abominably paid, since it consisted largely of women and children.[27] Of the 12,000 operatives in the cotton mills of Glasgow in 1833, only 2,000 earned an average of over 11s. a week. In 131 Manchester mills average wages were less than 12s., in only twenty-one were they higher.[28] And the building of factories was relatively cheap : in 1846 an entire weaving plant of 410 machines, including the cost of ground and buildings, could be constructed for something like £11,000.[29] But above all the major cost, that of raw material, was drastically cut by the rapid expansion of cotton cultivation in the Southern USA after the invention of Eli Whitney's cotton-gin in 1793. If we add that entrepreneurs enjoyed the bonus of a profit-inflation (i.e. the general tendency for prices to be higher when they sold their product than when they made it), we shall understand why the manufacturing classes felt buoyant.

After 1815 these advantages appeared increasingly offset by the narrowing margin of profit. In the first place industrial revolution and competition brought about a constant and dramatic fall in the price of the finished article but not in several of the costs of production.[30] In the second place after 1815 the general atmosphere of prices was one of deflation and not inflation, that is to say profits, so far from enjoying an extra boost, suffered from a slight lag. Thus, while in 1784 the selling-price of a pound of spun yarn had been 10s. 11d., the cost of its raw material 2s. (margin, 8s. 11d.), in 1812 its price was 2s. 6d., its raw material cost 1s. 6d. (margin 1s.) and in 1832 its price 11¼d., its raw material cost 7½d., and the margin for other costs and profits therefore only 4d.[31] Of course the situation, which was general throughout British – and indeed all advanced – industry, was not too tragic. 'Profits are still sufficient', wrote the champion and historian of cotton in 1835, in extreme understatement, 'to allow of a great accumulation of capital in the manufacture.'[32] As the total sales soared upwards, so did the total of profits even at their diminishing rate. All that was needed was continued and astronomic expansion. Nevertheless, it seemed that the shrinking of profit-margins had to be arrested or at least slowed down. This could only be done by cutting costs. And of all the costs *wages* – which McCulloch reckoned at three times the amount per year of the raw material – were the most compressible.

They could be compressed by direct wage-cutting, by the substitution of cheaper machine-tenders for dearer skilled workers, and by the competition of the machine. This last reduced the average weekly wage of the handloom weaver in Bolton from 33s. in 1795 to 14s. in 1815 to 5s. 6d. (or more precisely a net income of 4s. 1½d.) in 1829–34.[33] And indeed money wages fell steadily in the post-Napoleonic period. But there was a physiological limit to such reductions, unless the labourers were actually to starve, as of course the 500,000 handloom weavers did. Only if the cost of living fell could wages also fall beyond that point. The cotton manufacturers shared the view that it was kept artificially high by the monopoly of the landed interest, made even worse by the heavy protective tariffs which a Parliament of landlords had wrapped around British farming after the wars – the *Corn Laws*. These, moreover, had the additional disadvantage of threatening the essential growth of British exports. For if the rest of the not yet industrialized world was prevented from selling its agrarian products, how was it to pay for the manufactured goods which Britain alone could – and had to – supply? Manchester business therefore became the centre of militant and increasingly desperate opposition to landlordism in general and the Corn Laws in particular, and the backbone of the Anti-Corn Law League of 1838–46. But the Corn Laws were not abolished until 1846, their abolition did not immediately lead to a fall in the cost of living, and it is doubtful whether before the age of railways and steamers even free food-imports would have greatly lowered it.

The industry was thus under immense pressure to mechanize (i.e. to lower costs by labour-saving), to rationalize and to expand its production and sales, thus making up by the mass of small profits per unit for the fall in the margins. Its success was variable. As we have seen, the actual rise in production and exports was gigantic; so, after 1815, was the mechanization of hitherto manual or partly-mechanized occupations, notably weaving. This took the form chiefly of the general adoption of existing or slightly improved machinery rather than of further technological revolution. Though the pressure for technical innovation increased significantly – there were thirty-nine new patents in cotton spinning, etc. in 1800–20, fifty-one in the 1820s, eighty-six in the 1830s and a hundred and fifty-six in the 1840s [34] – the British cotton industry was technologically stabilized by the 1830s. On the other hand, though the production per operative increased in the post-Napoleonic period, it did not do so to any revolutionary extent. The really substantial speed-up of operations was to occur in the second half of the century.

There was comparable pressure on the rate of interest on capital, which contemporary theory tended to assimilate to profit. But consideration of this takes us to the next phase of industrial development – the construction of a basic capital-goods industry.

IV

It is evident that no industrial economy can develop beyond a certain point until it possesses adequate capital-goods capacity. This is why even today the most reliable single index of any country's industrial potential is the quantity of its iron and steel production. But it is also evident that under conditions of private enterprise the extremely costly capital investment necessary for much of this development is not likely to be undertaken for the same reasons as the industrialization of cotton or other consumer goods. For these a mass market already exists, at least potentially : even very primitive men wear shirts or use household equipment and foodstuffs. The problem is merely how to put a sufficiently vast market sufficiently quickly within the purview of businessmen. But no such market exists, e.g. for heavy iron equipment such as girders. It only comes into existence in the course of an industrial revolution (and not always then), and those who lock up their money in the very heavy investments required even by quite modest ironworks (compared to quite large cotton-mills) before it is visibly there, are more likely to be speculators, adventurers and dreamers than sound businessmen. In fact in France a sect of such speculative technological adventurers, the Saint-Simonians (cf. pp. 216, 293), acted as chief propagandists of the kind of industrialization which needed heavy and long-range investment.

These disadvantages applied particularly to metallurgy, especially of iron. Its capacity increased, thanks to a few simple innovations such as that of puddling and rolling in the 1780s, but the non-military demand for it remained relatively modest, and the military, though gratifyingly large thanks to a succession of wars between 1756 and 1815, slackened off sharply after Waterloo. It was certainly not large enough to make Britain into an outstandingly large producer of iron. In 1790 she out-produced France by only forty per cent or so, and even in 1800 her output was considerably less than half of the combined continental one, and amounted to the, by later standards, tiny figure of a quarter of a million tons. If anything, the British share of world iron output tended to sink in the next decades.

Fortunately they applied less to mining, which was chiefly the mining of *coal*. For coal had the advantage of being not merely the major source of industrial power in the nineteenth century, but also a major form of domestic fuel, thanks largely to the relative shortage of forests in Britain. The growth of cities, and especially of London, had caused coal mining to expand rapidly since the late sixteenth century. By the early eighteenth it was substantially a primitive modern industry, even employing the earliest steam engines (devised

59

for similar purposes in non-ferrous metal mining, mainly in Cornwall) for pumping. Hence coal mining hardly needed or underwent major technological revolution in our period. Its innovations were improvements rather than transformations of production. But its capacity was already immense and, by world standards, astronomic. In 1800 Britain may have produced something like ten million tons of coal, or about 90 per cent of the world output. Its nearest competitor, France, produced less than a million.

This immense industry, though probably not expanding fast enough for really massive industrialization on the modern scale, was sufficiently large to stimulate the basic invention which was to transform the capital goods industries : the railway. For the mines not only required steam engines in large quantities and of great power, but also required efficient means of transporting the great quantities of coal from coalface to shaft and especially from pithead to the point of shipment. The 'tramway' or 'railway' along which trucks ran was an obvious answer; to pull these trucks by stationary engines was tempting; to pull them by moving engines would not seem too impractical. Finally, the costs of overland transport of bulk goods were so high that it was likely to strike coal-owners in inland fields that the use of these short-term means of transport could be profitably extended for long-term haulage. The line from the inland coalfield of Durham to the coast (Stockton–Darlington 1825) was the first of the modern railways. Technologically the railway is the child of the mine, and especially the northern English coalmine. George Stephenson began life as a Tyneside 'engineman', and for years virtually all locomotive drivers were recruited from his native coalfield.

No innovation of the Industrial Revolution has fired the imagination as much as the railway, as witness the fact that it is the only product of nineteenth-century industrialization which has been fully absorbed into the imagery of popular and literate poetry. Hardly had they been proved technically feasible and profitable in England (c. 1825–30), before plans to build them were made over most of the Western world, though their execution was generally delayed. The first short lines were opened in the USA in 1827, in France in 1828 and 1835, in Germany and Belgium in 1835 and even in Russia by 1837. The reason was doubtless that no other invention revealed the power and speed of the new age to the layman as dramatically; a revelation made all the more striking by the remarkable technical maturity of even the very earliest railways. (Speeds of up to sixty miles per hour, for instance, were perfectly practicable in the 1830s, and were not substantially improved by later steam-railways.) The iron road, pushing its huge smoke-plumed snakes at the speed of wind across countries and continents, whose embankments and cuttings, bridges and stations, formed a body of public building beside which the pyramids and the Roman aqueducts and even the Great Wall of China paled into provincialism, was the very symbol of man's triumph through technology.

In fact, from an economic point of view, its vast expense was its chief advantage. No doubt in the long run its capacity to open up countries hitherto cut off by high transport costs from the world market, the vast increase in the speed and bulk of overland communication it brought for men and goods, were to be of major importance. Before 1848 they were economically less important : outside Britain because railways were few, in Britain because for geographical reasons transport problems were much less intractable than in large landlocked countries.[35] But from the perspective of the student of economic development the immense appetite of the railways for iron and steel, for coal, for heavy machinery, for labour, for capital investment, was at this stage more important. For it provided just that massive demands which was needed if the capital goods industries were to be transformed as profoundly as the cotton industry had been. In the first two decades of the railways (1830–50) the output of iron in Britain rose from 680,000 to 2,250,000, in other words it trebled. The output of coal between 1830 and 1850 also trebled from 15 million tons to 49 million tons. That dramatic rise was due primarily to the railway, for on average each mile of line required 300 tons of iron merely for track.[36] The industrial advances which for the first time made the mass production of steel possible followed naturally in the next decades.

The reason for this sudden, immense, and quite essential expansion lay in the apparently irrational passion with which businessmen and investors threw themselves into the construction of railways. In 1830 there were a few dozen miles of railways in all the world – chiefly consisting of the line from Liverpool to Manchester. By 1840 there were over 4,500 miles, by 1850 over 23,500. Most of them were projected in a few bursts of speculative frenzy known as the 'railway manias' of 1835-7 and especially in 1844-7; most of them were built in large part with British capital, British iron, machines and know-how.[37] These investment booms appear irrational, because in fact few railways were much more profitable to the investor than other forms of enterprise, most yielded quite modest profits and many none at all: in 1855 the average interest on capital sunk in the British railways was a mere 3·7 per cent. No doubt promoters, speculators and others did exceedingly well out of them, but the ordinary investor clearly did not. And yet by 1840 £28 millions, by 1850 £240 millions had been hopefully invested in them.[39]

Why? The fundamental fact about Britain in the first two generations of the Industrial Revolution was that the comfortable and rich classes accumulated income so fast and in such vast quantities as to exceed all available possibilities of spending and investment. (The annual investable surplus in the 1840s was reckoned at about £60 millions.[40]) No doubt feudal and aristocratic societies would have succeeded in throwing a great deal of this away in riotous living, luxury building and other uneconomic activities.[41] Even in Britain the sixth Duke of Devonshire, whose normal income was princely enough, succeeded in leaving his heir £1,000,000 of debts in the mid-nineteenth century (which he paid off by borrowing another £1,500,000 and going in for the development of real estate values).[42] But the bulk of the middle classes, who formed the main investing public, were still savers rather than spenders, though by 1840 there are many signs that they felt sufficiently wealthy to spend *as well as* to invest. Their wives began to turn into 'ladies', instructed by the handbooks of etiquette which multiply about this period, their chapels began to be rebuilt in ample and expensive styles, and they even began to celebrate their collective glory by constructing those shocking town halls and other civic monstrosities in Gothic and Renaissance imitations, whose exact and Napoleonic costs their municipal historians recorded with pride.[43]

Again, a modern socialist or welfare society would no doubt have distributed some of these vast accumulations for social purposes. In our period nothing was less likely. Virtually untaxed, the middle classes therefore continued to accumulate among the hungry populace, whose hunger was the counterpart of their accumulation. And as they were not peasants, content to hoard their savings in woollen stockings or as golden bangles, they had to find profitable investment for them. But where? Existing industries, for instance, had become far too cheap to absorb more than a fraction of the available surplus for investment : even supposing the size of the cotton industry to be doubled, the capital cost would absorb only a part of it. What was needed was a sponge large enough to hold all of it.[45]

Foreign investment was one obvious possibility. The rest of the world – mostly, to begin with, old governments seeking to recover from the Napoleonic Wars and new ones borrowing with their usual dash and abandon for indeterminate purposes – was only too anxious for unlimited loans. The English investor lent readily. But alas, the South American loans which appeared so promising in the 1820s, the North American ones which beckoned in the 1830s, turned only too often into scraps of worthless paper : of twenty-five foreign government loans sold between 1818 and 1831, sixteen (involving about half of the £42 millions at issue prices) were in default in 1831. In theory these loans should have paid the investor 7 or 9 per cent; in fact in 1831 he received an average of 3·1 per cent. Who would not be discouraged by experiences such as those with the Greek 5 per cent loans of 1824 and 1825 which did not begin to pay any interest at all until the 1870s?[46] Hence it is natural that the capital flooding abroad in the speculative booms of 1825 and 1835–7, should seek an apparently less disappointing employment.

John Francis, looking back on the mania from 1851, described the rich man who :

saw the accumulation of wealth, which with an industrial people always outstrips the ordinary modes of investment, legitimately and justly employed . . . He saw the money which in his youth had been thrown into war loans and in his manhood wasted on South American mines, forming roads, employing labour and increasing business. [The railway's] absorption of capital was at least an absorption, if unsuccessful, in the country that produced it. Unlike foreign mines and foreign loans, they could not be exhausted or utterly valueless.[47]

Whether it could have found other forms of home investment – for instance in building – is an academic question to which the answer is still in doubt. In fact it found the railways, which could not conceivably have been built as rapidly and on as large a scale without this torrent of capital flooding into them, especially in the middle 1840s. It was a lucky conjuncture, for the railways happened to solve virtually all the problems of the economy's growth at once.

V

To trace the impetus for industrialization is only one part of the historian's task. The other is to trace the mobilization and redeployment of economic resources, the adaptation of the economy, and the society which were required to maintain the new and revolutionary course.

The first and perhaps the most crucial factor which had to be mobilized and redeployed was *labour,* for an industrial economy means a sharp proportionate decline in the agricultural (i.e. rural) and a sharp rise in the non-agricultural (i.e. increasingly in the urban) population, and almost certainly (as in our period) a rapid general increase in population. It therefore implies in the first instance a sharp rise in the supply of food, mainly from home agriculture – i.e. an 'agricultural revolution'.[48]

The rapid growth of towns and non-agricultural settlements in Britain had naturally long stimulated agriculture, which is fortunately so inefficient in its pre-industrial forms that quite small improvements – a little rational attention to animal husbandry, crop-rotation, fertilization and the lay-out of farms, or the adoption of new crops – can produce disproportionately large results. Such agricultural change had preceded the industrial revolution and made possible the first stages of rapid population increases, and the impetus naturally continued, though British farming suffered heavily in the slump which followed the abnormally high prices of the Napoleonic Wars. In terms of technology and capital investment the changes of our period were probably fairly modest until the 1840s, the period when agricultural science and engineering may be said to have come of age. The vast increase in output which enabled British farming in the 1830s to supply 98 per cent of the grain for a population between two and three times the mid-eighteenth-century size,[49] was achieved by general adoption of methods pioneered in the earlier eighteenth century, by rationalization and by expansion of the cultivated area.

All these in turn were achieved by social rather than technological transformation. by the liquidation of medieval communal cultiva-

64

tion with its open field and common pasture (the 'enclosure movement'), of self-sufficient peasant farming, and of old-fashioned uncommercial attitudes towards the land. Thanks to the preparatory evolution of the sixteenth to eighteenth centuries this uniquely radical solution of the agrarian problem, which made Britain a country of a few large landowners, a moderate number of commercial tenant farmers and a great number of hired labourers, was achieved with a minimum of trouble, though intermittently resisted not only by the unhappy rural poor but by the traditionalist country gentry. The 'Speenhamland System' of poor relief, spontaneously adopted by gentlemen-justices in several counties in and after the hungry year of 1795, has been seen as the last systematic attempt to safeguard the old rural society against the corrosion of the cash nexus.[50] The Corn Laws with which the agrarian interest sought to protect farming against the post-1815 crisis, in the teeth of all economic orthodoxy, were in part a manifesto against the tendency to treat agriculture as an industry just like any other, to be judged by the criteria of profitability alone. But these were doomed rearguard actions against the final introduction of capitalism into the countryside; they were finally defeated in the wave of middle-class radical advance after 1830, by the new Poor Law of 1834 and the abolition of the Corn Laws in 1846.

In terms of economic productivity this social transformation was an immense success; in terms of human suffering, a tragedy, deepened by the agricultural depression after 1815 which reduced the rural poor to demoralizing destitution. After 1800 so enthusiastic a champion of enclosure and agricultural progress as Arthur Young was shaken by its social effects.[51] But from the point of view of industrialization these also were desirable consequences; for an industrial economy needs labour, and where else but from the former non-industrial sector was it to come from? The rural population at home or, in the form of (mainly Irish) immigration, abroad, were the most obvious sources supplemented by the miscellaneous petty producers and labouring poor.[52] Men must be attracted into the new occupations, or if – as was most probable – they were initially immune to these attractions and unwilling to abandon their traditional way of life[53] – they must be forced into it. Economic and social hardship was the most effective whip; the higher money wages and greater freedom of the town the supplementary carrot. For various reasons the forces

65

tending to prise men loose from their historic social anchorage were still relatively weak in our period, compared to the second half of the nineteenth century. It took a really sensational catastrophe such as the Irish hunger to produce the sort of massive emigration (one and a half millions out of a total population of eight and a half millions in 1835–50) which became common after 1850. Nevertheless, they were stronger in Britain than elsewhere. Had they not been, British industrial development might have been as hampered as that of France was by the stability and relative comfort of its peasantry and petty-bourgeoisie, which deprived industry of the required intake of labour.[54]

To acquire a sufficient number of labourers was one thing; to acquire sufficient labour of the right qualifications and skills was another. Twentieth-century experience has shown that this problem is as crucial and more difficult to solve. In the first place *all* labour had to learn how to work in a manner suited to industry, i.e. in a rhythm of regular unbroken daily work which is entirely different from the seasonal ups and downs of the farm, or the self-controlled patchiness of the independent craftsman. It had also to learn to be responsive to monetary incentives. British employers then, like South African ones now, constantly complained about the 'laziness' of labour or its tendency to work until it had earned a traditional week's living wage and then to stop. The answer was found in a draconic labour discipline (fines, a 'Master and Servant' code mobilizing the law on the side of the employer, etc.), but above all in the practice where possible of paying labour so little that it would have to work steadily all through the week in order to make a minimum income (cf. p. 242). In the factories, where the problem of labour discipline was more urgent, it was often found more convenient to employ the tractable (and cheaper) women and children : out of all workers in the English cotton mills in 1834–47 about one-quarter were adult men, over half women and girls and the balance boys below the age of eighteen.[55] Another common way of ensuring labour discipline, which reflected the small-scale, piecemeal process of industrialization in this early phase, was sub-contract or the practice of making skilled workers the actual employers of their unskilled helpers. In the cotton industry, for instance, about two-thirds of the boys and one-third of the girls were thus 'in the direct employ of operatives' and hence more closely watched, and outside the factories proper such arrangements were even more widespread. The sub-employer, of course, had a direct financial incentive to see that this hired help did not slack.

It was rather more difficult to recruit or train sufficient skilled or technically trained workers, for few pre-industrial skills were of much use in modern industry, though of course many occupations, like building, continued practically unchanged. Fortunately the slow semi-industrialization of Britain in the centuries before 1789 had built up a rather large reservoir of suitable skills, both in textile technique and in the handling of metals. Thus on the continent the locksmith, one of the few craftsmen used to precision work with metals, became the ancestor of the machine-builder and sometimes provided him with a name, whereas in Britain the millwright, and the 'engineer' or 'engineman' (already common in and around mines) did so. Nor is it accidental that the English word 'engineer' describes both the skilled metal-worker and the designer and planner; for the bulk of higher technologists could be, and was, recruited from among these mechanically skilled and self-reliant men. In fact, British industrialization relied on this unplanned supply of the higher skills, as continental industrialism could not. This explains the shocking neglect of general and technical education in this country, the price of which was to be paid later.

Beside such problems of labour supply, those of capital supply were unimportant. Unlike most other European countries, there was no shortage of immediately investable capital in Britain. The major difficulty was that those who controlled most of it in the eighteenth century – landlords, merchants, shippers, financiers, etc. – were reluctant to invest it in the new industries, which therefore had often to be started by small savings or loans and developed by the ploughing back of profits. Local capital shortage made the early industrialists – especially the self-made men – harder, thriftier and more grasping, and their workers therefore correspondingly more exploited; but this reflected the imperfect flow of the national investment surplus and not its inadequacy. On the other hand, the eighteenth-century rich were prepared to sink their money in certain enterprises which benefited industrialization; most notably in transport (canals, dock facilities, roads and later also railways) and in mines, from which landowners drew royalties even when they did not themselves manage them.

Nor was there any difficulty about the technique of trade and finance, private or public. Banks and banknotes, bills of exchange, stocks and shares, the technicalities of overseas and wholesale trade, and marketing, were familiar enough and men who could handle them or easily learn to do so, were in abundant supply. Moreover, by the end of the eighteenth century, government policy was firmly committed to the supremacy of business. Older enactments to the contrary (such as those of the Tudor social code) had long fallen into desuetude, and were finally abolished – except where they touched agriculture – in 1813–35. In theory the laws and financial or commercial institutions of Britain were clumsy and designed to hinder rather than help economic development; for instance, they made expensive 'private acts' of Parliament necessary almost every time men wished to form a joint-stock company. The French Revolution provided the French – and through their influence the rest of the continent – with far more rational and effective machinery for such purposes. In practice the British managed perfectly well, and indeed considerably better than their rivals.

In this rather haphazard, unplanned and empirical way the first major industrial economy was built. By modern standards it was small and archaic, and its archaism still marks Britain today. By the standards of 1848 it was monumental, though also rather shocking, for its new cities were uglier, its proletariat worse off, than else-where,[56] and the fog-bound, smoke-laden atmosphere in which pale masses hurried to and fro troubled the foreign visitor. But it har-nessed the power of a million horses in its steam-engines, turned out two million yards of cotton cloth per year on over seventeen million mechanical spindles, dug almost fifty million tons of coal, imported and exported £170 millions worth of goods in a single year. Its trade was twice that of its nearest competitor, France : in 1780 it had only just exceeded it. Its cotton consumption was twice that of the USA, four times the French. It produced more than half the total pig-iron of the economically developed world, and used twice as much per inhabitant as the next-most industrialized country (Belgium), three times as much as the USA, more than four times as much as France. Between £200 and £300 million of British capital investment – a quarter in the USA, almost a fifth in Latin America – brought back dividends and orders from all parts of the world.[58] It was, in fact, the 'workshop of the world'.

And both Britain and the world knew that the Industrial Revolution launched in these islands by and through the traders and entre-preneurs, whose only law was to buy in the cheapest markets and sell without restriction in the dearest, was transforming the world. Nothing could stand in its way. The gods and kings of the past were powerless before the businessmen and steam-engines of the present.

NOTES

1 Arthur Young, *Tours in England and Wales*, London School of Economics edition, p. 269.
2 A. de Toqueville, *Journeys to England and Ireland*, ed. J. P. Mayer (1958), pp. 107–8.
3 Anna Bezanson, The Early Uses of the Term Industrial Revolu-tion, *Quarterly Journal of Economics*, XXXVI, 1921–2, p. 343, G. N. Clark, *The Idea of the Industrial Revolution* (Glasgow 1953).
4 'On the one hand it is gratifying to see that the English derive a rich treasure for their political life, from the study of the ancient authors, however pedantically this might be conducted; so much so that parliamentary orators not infrequently cited the ancients to good purpose, a practice which was favourably received by, and not without effect upon, their Assembly. On the other hand it cannot but amaze us that a country in which the manufacturing tendencies are predominant, and hence the need to familiarize the people with the sciences and arts which advance these pursuits is evident; the absence of these subjects in the curriculum of youthful education is hardly noticed. It is equally astonishing how much is nevertheless achieved by men lacking any formal education for their professions.' W. Wachsmuth, *Europaeische Sittengeschichte 5, 2* (Leipzig 1839), p. 736.
5 cf. A. E. Musson & E. Robinson, Science and Industry in the late Eighteenth Century, *Economic History Review*, XIII. 2, Dec 1960, and R. E. Schofield's work on the Midland Industrialists and the Lunar Society *Isis* 47 (March 1956), 48 (1957), *Annals of Science* II (June 1956) etc.
6 The modern motor industry is a good example of this. It is not the demand for motor-cars existing in the 1890s which created an industry of the modern size, but the capacity to produce cheap cars which produced the modern mass demand for them.
7 Only slowly did purchasing power expand with population, in-come per head, transport costs and restraints on trade. But the market was expanding, and the vital question was when would a producer of some mass consumption goods capture enough of it to allow fast and continuous expansion of their production.[8]

8 K. Berrill, International Trade and the Rate of Economic Growth, *Economic History Review*, XII, 1960, p. 358.

9 W. G. Hoffmann, *The Growth of Industrial Economies* (Manchester 1958), p. 68.

10 A. P. Wadsworth & J. de L. Mann, *The Cotton Trade and Industrial Lancashire* (1931), chapter VII.

11 F. Crouzet, *Le Blocus Continental et l'Economie Britannique* (1958), p. 63, suggests that in 1805 it was up to two-thirds.

12 P. K. O'Brien, British Incomes and Property in the early Nineteenth Century, *Economic History Review*, XII, 2 (1959), p. 267.

13 Overseas supplies of wool, for instance, remained of negligible importance during our entire period, and only became a major factor in the 1870s.

14 The 'domestic system', which is a universal stage of manufacturing development on the road from home or craft production to modern industry, can take innumerable forms, some of which can come fairly close to the factory. If an eighteenth-century writer speaks of 'manufactures' this is almost invariably and in all western countries what he means.

15 In all countries possessing any kind of marketable manufactures, textiles tended to predominate : in Silesia (1800) they formed 74 per cent of the value of all manufacture.[16]

16 Hoffmann, op. cit., p. 73.

17 Baines, *History of the Cotton Manufacture in Great Britain* (London 1835). p. 431.

18 P. Mathias, *The Brewing Industry in England* (Cambridge 1959).

19 M. Mulhall, *Dictionary of Statistics* (1892), p. 158.

20 Baines, op. cit., p. 112.

21 cf. Phyllis Deane, Estimates of the British National Income, *Economic History Review* (April 1956 and April 1957).

22 O'Brien, op. cit., p. 267.

23 From the post-Napoleonic Radicalism in Britain to the Populists in the USA, all protest movements including farmers and small entrepreneurs can be recognized by their demand for financial unorthodoxy : they were all 'currency cranks'.

24 For the stationary state cf. J. Schumpeter, *History of Economic Analysis* (1954), pp. 570–1. The crucial formulation is John Stuart Mill's (*Principles of Political Economy*, Book IV, chapter iv) : 'When a country has long possessed a large production, and a large net income to make saving from, and when, therefore, the means have long existed of making a great annual addition to capital; it is one of the characteristics of such a country, that the rate of profit is habitually within, as it were, a hand's breadth of the minimum, and the country therefore on the very verge of the stationary state . . . The mere continuance of the present annual increase in capital if no circumstances occurred to counter its effect would suffice in a small number of years to reduce the net

rate of profit (to the minimum.)' However, when this was published (1848) the counteracting force – the wave of development induced by the railways – had already shown itself.

25 The Swiss Simonde de Sismondi, and the conservative and country-minded Malthus, were the first to argue along these lines, even before 1825. The new socialists made their crisis-theory into a keystone of their critique of capitalism.

26 By the radical John Wade, *History of the Middle and Working Classes*, the banker Lord Overstone, *Reflections suggested by the perusal of Mr J. Horsley Palmer's pamphlet on the causes and consequences of the pressure on the Money Market* (1837), the Anti-Corn Law campaigner J. Wilson, *Fluctuations of Currency, Commerce and Manufacture; referable to the Corn Laws* (1840); and in France by A. Blanqui (brother of the famous revolutionary) in 1837 and M. Briaune in 1840. Doubtless also by others.

27 E. Baines in 1835 estimated the average wages of all the spinning and weaving operatives at 10s. a week – allowing for two unpaid weeks holiday a year – and of the handloom weavers at 7s.

28 Baines, op. cit., p. 441. A. Ure & P. L. Simmonds, *The Cotton Manufacture of Great Britain* (1861 edition), p. 390 ff.

29 Geo. White, *A Treatise on Weaving* (Glasgow 1846), p. 272.

30 M. Blaug, The Productivity of Capital in the Lancashire Cotton Industry during the Nineteenth Century, *Economic History Review* (April 1961).

31 Thomas Ellison, *The Cotton Trade of Great Britain* (London 1886), p. 61.

32 Baines, op. cit., p. 356.

33 Baines, op. cit., p. 489.

34 Ure & Simmonds, op. cit., Vol. I, p. 317 ff.

35 No point in Britain is more than 70 miles from the sea, and all the chief industrial areas of the nineteenth century, with one exception, are either on the sea or within easy reach of it.

36 J. H. Clapham, *An Economic History of Modern Britain* (1926), p. 427 ff.; Mulhall, op. cit., pp. 121, 332, M. Robbins, *The Railway Age* (1962), p. 30–1.

37 In 1848 one third of the capital in the French railways was British.[38]

38 Rondo E. Cameron, *France and the Economic Development of Europe 1800–1914* (1961), p. 77.

39 Mulhall, op. cit., 501, 497.

40 L. H. Jenks, *The Migration of British Capital to 1875* (New York and London 1927), p. 126.

41 Of course such spending also stimulates the economy, but very inefficiently, and hardly at all in the direction of industrial growth.

42 D. Spring, The English Landed Estate in the Age of Coal and Iron, *Journal of Economic History*, (XI, I, 1951).

43 A few cities with eighteenth-century traditions never ceased

public building; but a typical new industrial metropolis like Bolton in Lancashire built practically no conspicuous and non-utilitarian structures before 1847-8.[44]

44 J. Clegg, *A chronological history of Bolton* (1876).

45 The total capital – fixed and working – of the cotton industry was estimated by McCulloch at £34 millions in 1833, £47 millions in 1845.

46 Albert M. Imlah, British Balance of Payments and Export of Capital, 1816–1913, *Economic History Review V* (1952, 2, p. 24).

47 John Francis, *A History of the English Railway* (1851), II, 136; see also H. Tuck, *The Railway Shareholder's Manual* (7th edition 1846), Preface, and T. Tooke, *History of Prices* II, pp. 275, 333–4 for the pressure of accumulated Lancashire surpluses into railways.

48 Before the age of railway and the steamship – i.e. before the end of our period – the possibility of importing vast quantities of food from abroad was limited, though Britain became on balance a net importer of food from the 1780s.

49 Mulhall, op. cit., p. 14.

50 Under it the poor were to be guaranteed a living wage by subsidies from the rates where necessary; the system, though well-intentioned, eventually led to even greater pauperization than before.

51 *Annals of Agric.* XXXVI, p. 214.

52 Another view holds that the labour supply comes not from such transfers, but from the rise in the total population, which as we know was increasing very rapidly. But this is to miss the point. In an industrial economy not only the numbers, but the *proportion* of the non-agricultural labour force must increase steeply. This means that men and women who would otherwise have stayed in the village as their forefathers did, *must* move elsewhere at some stage of their lives, for the towns grow faster than their own natural rate of increase, which in any case tended normally to be lower than the villages. This is so whether the farming population actually diminishes, holds its numbers, or even increases.

53 Wilbert Moore, *Industrialisation and Labour* (Cornell 1951).

54 Alternatively, like the USA, Britain would have to rely on massive immigration. In fact she did rely on the immigration of the Irish.

55 Blaug, loc. cit., p. 368. Children under 13, however, declined sharply in the 1830s.

56 'On the whole the condition of the working class seems distinctly worse in England than in France in 1830–48,' concludes a modern historian.[57]

57 H. Sée, *Histoire Economique de la France*, Vol. II, p. 189 n.

58 Mulhall, op. cit.; Imlah, loc. cit., II, 52, pp. 228–9. The precise date of this estimate is 1854.

3

The French Revolution

An Englishman not filled with esteem and admiration at the sublime *manner in which one of the most IMPORTANT REVOLUTIONS the world has ever seen is now effecting, must be dead to every sense of virtue and of freedom; not one of my countrymen who has had the* good fortune *to witness the transactions of the last three days in this great city, but will testify that my language is not hyperbolical.*

The *Morning Post* (July 21, 1789) on the fall of the Bastille

Soon the enlightened nations will put on trial those who have hitherto ruled over them. The kings shall flee into the deserts, into the company of the wild beasts whom they resemble; and Nature shall resume her rights.

Saint-Just. *Sur la Constitution de la France, Discours prononcé à la Convention 24 avril 1793*

I

If the economy of the nineteenth-century world was formed mainly under the influence of the British Industrial Revolution, its politics and ideology were formed mainly by the French. Britain provided the model for its railways and factories, the economic explosive which cracked open the traditional economic and social structures of the non-European world; but France made its revolutions and gave them their ideas, to the point where a tricolour of some kind became the emblem of virtually every emerging nation, and European (or indeed world) politics between 1789 and 1917 were largely the struggle for and against the principles of 1789, or the even more incendiary ones of 1793. France provided the vocabulary and the issues of liberal and radical-democratic politics for most of the world. France provided the first great example, the concept and the vocabulary of nationalism. France provided the codes of law, the model of scientific and technical organization, the metric system of measurement for most countries. The ideology of the modern world first penetrated the ancient civilizations which had hitherto resisted European ideas through French influence. This was the work of the French Revolution.[1]

The later eighteenth century, as we have seen, was an age of crisis for the old régimes of Europe and their economic systems, and its last decades were filled with political agitations sometimes reaching the point of revolt, of colonial movements for autonomy sometimes reaching that of secession : not only in the USA (1776–83), but also in Ireland (1782–4), in Belgium and Liège (1787–90), in Holland (1783–7), in Geneva, even – it has been argued – in England (1779). So striking is this clustering of political unrest that some recent historians have spoken of an 'age of democratic revolution' of which the French was only one; though the most dramatic and far-reaching.[2]

Insofar as the crisis of the old régime was not purely a French phenomenon, there is some weight in such observations. Just so it may be argued that the Russian Revolution of 1917 (which occupies a position of analogous importance in our century) was merely the most dramatic of a whole cluster of similar movements, such as those which – some years before 1917 – finally ended the age-old Turkish and Chinese empires. Yet this is to miss the point. The French Revolution may not have been an isolated phenomenon, but it was far more fundamental than any of the other contemporary ones and its consequences were therefore far more profound. In the first place, it occurred in the most powerful and populous state of Europe (leaving Russia apart). In 1789 something like one European out of every five was a Frenchman. In the second place it was, alone of all the revolutions which preceded and followed it, a mass *social* revolution, and immeasurably more radical than any comparable upheaval. It is no accident that the American revolutionaries, and the British 'Jacobins' who migrated to France because of their political sympathies, found themselves moderates in France. Tom Paine was an extremist in Britain and America; but in Paris he was among the most moderate of the Girondins. The results of the American revolutions were, broadly speaking, countries carrying on much as before, only minus the political control of the British, Spaniards and Portuguese. The result of the French Revolution was that the age of Balzac replaced the age of Mme Dubarry.

In the third place, alone of all the contemporary revolutions, the French was ecumenical. Its armies set out to revolutionize the world; its ideas actually did so. The American Revolution has remained a crucial event in American history, but (except for the countries directly involved in and by it) it has left few major traces elsewhere. The French Revolution is a landmark in all countries. Its repercussions rather than those of the American Revolution, occasioned the risings which led to the liberation of Latin America after 1808. Its direct influence radiated as far as Bengal, where Ram Mohan Roy was inspired by it to found the first Hindu reform movement, the ancestor of modern Indian nationalism. (When he visited England in 1830, he insisted on travelling in a French ship to demonstrate his enthusiasm for its principles.) It was, as has been well said, 'the first great movement of ideas in Western Christendom that had any real effect on the world of Islam',[3] and that almost immediately. By the middle of the nineteenth century the Turkish word 'vatan', hitherto merely describing a man's place of birth or residence, had begun to turn under its influence into something like 'patrie'; the term 'liberty', before 1800 primarily a legal term denoting the opposite to 'slavery', had begun to acquire a new political content. Its indirect influence is universal, for it provided the pattern for all subsequent revolutionary movements, its lessons (interpreted according to taste) being incorporated into modern socialism and communism.[4]

The French Revolution thus remains *the* revolution of its time, and not merely one, though the most prominent, of its kind. And its origins must therefore be sought not merely in the general conditions of Europe, but in the specific situation of France. Its peculiarity is perhaps best illustrated in international terms. Throughout the eighteenth century France was the major international economic rival of Britain. Her foreign trade, which multiplied fourfold between 1720 and 1780, caused anxiety; her colonial system was in certain areas (such as the West Indies) more dynamic than the British. Yet France was not a power like Britain, whose foreign policy was already determined substantially by the interests of capitalist expansion. She was the most powerful and in many ways the most typical of the old aristocratic absolute monarchies of Europe. In other words, the conflict between the official framework and the vested interests of the old régime and the rising new social forces was more acute in France than elsewhere.

The new forces knew fairly precisely what they wanted. Turgot, the physiocrat economist, stood for an efficient exploitation of the land, for free enterprise and trade, for a standardized, efficient administration of a single homogeneous national territory, and the abolition of all restrictions and social inequalities which stood in the way of the development of national resources and rational, equitable administration and taxation. Yet his attempt to apply such a programme as the first minister of Louis XVI in 1774–6 failed lamentably, and the failure is characteristic. Reforms of this character, in modest doses, were not incompatible with or unwelcome to absolute monarchies. On the contrary, since they strengthened their hand, they were, as we have seen, widely propagated at this time among the so-called 'enlightened despots'. But in most of the countries of 'enlightened despotism' such reforms were either inapplicable, and therefore mere theoretical flourishes, or unlikely to change the general character of their political and social structure; or else they failed in the face of the resistance of the local aristocracies and other vested interests, leaving the country to relapse into a somewhat tidied-up version of its former state. In France they failed more rapidly than elsewhere, for the resistance of the vested interests was more effective. But the results of this failure were more catastrophic for the monarchy; and the forces of bourgeois change were far too strong to relapse into inactivity. They merely transformed their hopes from an enlightened monarchy to the people or 'the nation'.

Nevertheless, such a generalization does not take us far towards an understanding of why the revolution broke out when it did, and why it took the remarkable road it did. For this it is most useful to consider the so-called 'feudal reaction' which actually provided the spark to explode the powder-barrel of France.

The 400,000 or so persons who, among the twenty-three million Frenchmen, formed the nobility, the unquestioned 'first order' of the nation, though not so absolutely safeguarded against the intrusion of lesser orders as in Prussia and elsewhere, were secure enough. They enjoyed considerable privileges, including exemption from several taxes (but not from as many as the better-organized clergy), and the right to receive feudal dues. Politically their situation was less brilliant. Absolute monarchy, while entirely aristocratic and even feudal in its *ethos*, had deprived the nobles of political independence and responsibility and cut down their old representative institutions – estates and *parlements* – so far as possible. The fact continued to rankle among the higher aristocracy and among the more recent *noblesse de robe* created by the kings for various purposes, mostly finance and administration; an ennobled government middle class which expressed the double discontent of aristocrats and bourgeois so far as it could through the surviving law-courts and estates. Economically the nobles' worries were by no means negligible. Fighters rather than earners by birth and tradition – nobles were even formally debarred from exercising a trade or profession – they depended on the income of their estates, or, if they belonged to the favoured minority of large or court nobles, on wealthy marriages, court pensions, gifts and sinecures. But the expenses of noble status were large and rising, their incomes – since they were rarely businesslike managers of their wealth, if they managed it at all – fell. Inflation tended to reduce the value of fixed revenues such as rents.

It was therefore natural that the nobles should use their one main asset, the acknowledged privileges of the order. Throughout the eighteenth century, in France as in many other countries, they encroached steadily upon the official posts which the absolute monarchy had preferred to fill with technically competent and politically harmless middle class men. By the 1780s four quarterings of nobility were needed even to buy a commission in the army, all bishops were nobles and even the keystone of royal administration, the intendancies, had been largely recaptured by them. Consequently the nobility not merely exasperated the feelings of the middle class by their successful competition for official posts; they also undermined the state itself by an increasing tendency to take over provincial and central administration. Similarly they – and especially the poorer provincial gentlemen who had few other resources – attempted to counteract the decline in their income by squeezing the utmost out of their very considerable feudal rights to exact money (or more rarely service) from the peasantry. An entire profession, the *feudists*, came into existence to revive obsolete rights of this kind or to maximize the yield of existing ones. Its most celebrated member, Gracchus Babeuf, was to become the leader of the first communist revolt in modern history in 1796. Consequently the nobility exasperated not only the middle class but also the peasantry.

The position of this vast class, comprising perhaps 80 per cent of all Frenchmen, was far from brilliant. They were indeed in general free, and often landowners. In actual quantity noble estates covered only one-fifth of the land, clerical estates perhaps another 6 per cent with regional variations.[5] Thus in the diocese of Montpellier the peasants already owned 38 to 40 per cent of the land, the bourgeoisie 18 to 19, the nobles 15 to 16, the clergy 3 to 4, while one-fifth was common land.[6] In fact, however, the great majority were landless or with insufficient holdings, a deficiency increased by the prevailing technical backwardness; and the general land-hunger was intensified by the rise in population. Feudal dues, tithes and taxes took a large and rising proportion of the peasant's income, and inflation reduced the value of the remainder. For only the minority of peasants who had a constant surplus for sale benefited from the rising prices; the rest, in one way or another, suffered from them, especially in times of bad harvest, when famine prices ruled. There is little doubt that in the twenty years preceding the Revolution the situation of the peasants grew worse for these reasons.

The financial troubles of the monarchy brought matters to a head. The administrative and fiscal structure of the kingdom was grossly obsolete, and, as we have seen, the attempt to remedy this by the reforms of 1774–6 failed, defeated by the resistance of vested interests headed by the *parlements*. Then France became involved in the American War of Independence. Victory over England was gained at the cost of final bankruptcy, and thus the American Revolution can claim to be the direct cause of the French. Various expedients were tried with diminishing success, but nothing short of a fundamental reform, which mobilized the real and considerable taxable capacity of the country could cope with a situation in which expenditure outran revenue by at least 20 per cent, and no effective economies were possible. For though the extravagance of Versailles has often been blamed for the crisis, court expenditure only amounted to 6 per cent of the total in 1788. War, navy and diplomacy made up one-quarter, the service of the existing debt one-half. War and debt – the American War and its debt – broke the back of the monarchy.

The government's crisis gave the aristocracy and the *parlements* their chance. They refused to pay without an extension of their privileges. The first breach in the front of absolutism was a hand-picked but nevertheless rebellious 'assembly of notables' called in 1787 to grant the government's demands. The second, and decisive, was the desperate decision to call the States-General – the old feudal assembly of the realm, buried since 1614. The Revolution thus began as an aristocratic attempt to recapture the state. This attempt miscalculated for two reasons : it underestimated the independent intentions of the 'Third Estate' – the fictional entity deemed to represent all who were neither nobles nor clergy, but in fact dominated by the middle class – and it overlooked the profound economic and social crisis into which it threw its political demands.

The French Revolution was not made or led by a formed party or movement in the modern sense, nor by men attempting to carry out a systematic programme. It hardly even threw up 'leaders' of the kind to which twentieth-century revolutions have accustomed us, until the post-revolutionary figure of Napoleon. Nevertheless a striking consensus of general ideas among a fairly coherent social group gave the revolutionary movement effective unity. The group was the 'bourgeoisie'; its ideas were those of classical liberalism, as formulated by the 'philosophers' and 'economists' and propagated by free-masonry and in informal associations. To this extent 'the philosophers' can be justly made responsible for the Revolution. It would have occurred without them; but they probably made the difference between a mere breakdown of an old régime and the effective and rapid substitution of a new one.

In its most general form the ideology of 1789 was the masonic one expressed with such innocent sublimity in Mozart's *Magic Flute* (1791), one of the earliest of the great propagandist works of art of an age whose highest artistic achievements so often belonged to propaganda. More specifically, the demands of the *bourgeois* of 1789 are laid down in the famous Declaration of the Rights of Man and Citizens of that year. This document is a manifesto against the hierarchical society of noble privilege, but not one in favour of democratic or egalitarian society. 'Men are born and live free and equal under the laws,' said its first article; but it also provides for the existence of social distinctions, if 'only on grounds of common utility'. Private property was a natural right, sacred, inalienable and inviolable. Men were equal before the law and careers were equally open to talent; but if the race started without handicaps, it was

79

equally assumed that the runners would not finish together. The declaration laid down (as against the noble hierarchy or absolutism) that 'all citizens have a right to co-operate in the formation of the law'; but 'either personally or through their representatives'. And the representative assembly which it envisaged as the fundamental organ of government was not necessarily a democratically elected one, or the régime it implied one which eliminated kings. A constitutional monarchy based on a propertied oligarchy expressing itself through a representative assembly was more congenial to most bourgeois liberals than the democratic republic which might have seemed a more logical expression of their theoretical aspirations; though there were some who did not hesitate to advocate this also. But on the whole the classical liberal bourgeois of 1789 (and the liberal of 1789–1848) was not a democrat but a believer in constitutionalism, a secular state with civil liberties and guarantees for private enterprise, and government by tax-payers and property-owners.

Nevertheless officially such a régime would express not simply his class interests, but the general will of 'the people', which was in turn (a significant identification) 'the French nation'. The king was no longer Louis, by the Grace of God, King of France and Navarre, but Louis, by the Grace of God and the constitutional law of the state, King of the French. 'The source of all sovereignty,' said the Declaration, 'resides essentially in the nation.' And the nation, as Abbé Siéyès put it, recognized no interest on earth above its own, and accepted no law or authority other than its own – neither that of humanity at large nor of other nations. No doubt the French nation, and its subsequent imitators, did not initially conceive of its interests clashing with those of other peoples, but on the contrary saw itself as inaugurating, or taking part in, a movement of the general liberation of peoples from tyranny. But in fact national rivalry (for instance that of French businessmen with British businessmen) and national subordination (for instance that of conquered or liberated nations to the interests of *la grande nation*) were implicit in the nationalism to which the bourgeois of 1789 gave its first official expression. 'The people' identified with 'the nation' was a revolutionary concept; more revolutionary than the bourgeois-liberal programme which purported to express it. But it was also a double-edged one.

Since the peasants and labouring poor were illiterate, politically modest or immature and the process of election indirect, 610 men, mostly of this stamp, were elected to represent the Third Estate. Most were lawyers who played an important economic role in provincial France; about a hundred were capitalists and businessmen. The middle class had fought bitterly and successfully to win a representation as large as that of the nobility and clergy combined, a moderate ambition for a group officially representing 95 per cent of the people. They now fought with equal determination for the right to exploit their potential majority votes by turning the States General into an assembly of individual deputies voting as such, instead of the traditional feudal body deliberating and voting by 'orders', a situation in which nobility and clergy could always outvote the Third. On this issue the first revolutionary break-through occurred. Some six weeks after the opening of the States-General, the Commons, anxious to forestall action by king, nobles and clergy, constituted themselves and all who were prepared to join them on their own terms a National Assembly with the right to recast the constitution. An attempt at counter-revolution led them to formulate their claims virtually in terms of the English House of Commons. Absolutism was at an end as Mirabeau, a brilliant and disreputable ex-noble, told the King : 'Sire, you are a stranger in this assembly, you have not the right to speak here.' [7]

The Third Estate succeeded, in the face of the united resistance of the king and the privileged orders, because it represented not merely the views of an educated and militant minority, but of far more powerful forces : the labouring poor of the cities, and especially of Paris, and shortly, also, the revolutionary peasantry. For what turned a limited reform agitation into a revolution was the fact that the calling of the States-General coincided with a profound economic and social crisis. The later 1780s had been, for a complexity of reasons, a period of great difficulties for virtually all branches of the French economy. A bad harvest in 1788 (and 1789) and a very difficult winter made this crisis acute. Bad harvests hurt the peasantry, for while they meant that large producers could sell grain at famine prices, the majority of men on their insufficient holdings might well have to eat up their seed-corn, or buy food at such prices, especially in months immediately preceding the new harvest (i.e. May–July). They obviously hurt the urban poor, whose cost of living – bread was the staple food – might well double. It hurt them all the more as the impoverishment of the countryside reduced the market for manufacturers and therefore also produced an industrial depression. The country poor were therefore desperate and restless with riot and banditry; the urban poor were doubly desperate as work ceased at the very moment that the cost of living soared. Under normal circumstances little more than blind-rioting might have occurred. But in 1788 and 1789 a major convulsion in the kingdom, a campaign of propaganda and election, gave the people's desperation a political perspective. They introduced the tremendous and earth-shaking idea of *liberation* from gentry and oppression. A riotous people stood behind the deputies of the Third Estate.

Counter-revolution turned a potential mass rising into an actual one. Doubtless it was only natural that the old régime should have fought back, if necessary with armed force; though the army was no longer wholly reliable. (Only unrealistic dreamers can suggest that Louis XVI might have accepted defeat and immediately turned himself into a constitutional monarch, even if he had been a less negligible and stupid man than he was, married to a less chicken-brained and irresponsible woman, and prepared to listen to less disastrous advisers.) In fact counter-revolution mobilized the Paris masses, already hungry, suspicious and militant. The most sensational result of their mobilization was the capture of the Bastille, a state prison symbolizing royal authority, where the revolutionaries expected to find arms. In times of revolution nothing is more powerful than the fall of symbols. The capture of the Bastille, which has rightly made July 14th into the French national day, ratified the fall of despotism and was hailed all over the world as the beginning of liberation. Even the austere philosopher Immanuel Kant of Koenigsberg, it is said, whose habits were so regular that the citizens of that town set their watches by him, postponed the hour of his afternoon stroll when he received the news, thus convincing Koenigsberg that a world-shaking event had indeed happened. What is more to the point, the fall of the Bastille spread the revolution to the provincial towns and the countryside.

Peasant revolutions are vast, shapeless, anonymous, but irresistible movements. What turned an epidemic of peasant unrest into an irreversible convulsion was a combination of provincial town risings and a wave of mass panic, spreading obscurely but rapidly across vast stretches of the country : the so-called *Grande Peur* of late July and early August 1789. Within three weeks of July 14th the social structure of French rural feudalism and the state machine of royal France lay in fragments. All that remained of state power was a scattering of doubtfully reliable regiments, a National Assembly without coercive force, and a multiplicity of municipal or provincial middle class administrations which soon set up bourgeois armed 'National Guards' on the model of Paris. Middle class and aristocracy immediately accepted the inevitable : all feudal privileges were officially abolished though, when the political situation had settled, a stiff price for their redemption was fixed. Feudalism was not finally abolished until 1793. By the end of August the Revolution had also acquired its formal manifesto, the Declaration of the Rights of Man and Citizen. Conversely, the king resisted with his usual stupidity, and sections of the middle class revolutionaries, frightened by the social implications of the mass upheaval, began to think that the time for conservatism had come.

In brief, the main shape of French and all subsequent bourgeois-revolutionary politics were by now clearly visible. This dramatic dialectical dance was to dominate the future generations. Time and again we shall see moderate middle class reformers mobilizing the masses against die-hard resistance or counter-revolution. We shall see the masses pushing beyond the moderates' aims to their own social revolutions, and the moderates in turn splitting into a conservative group henceforth making common cause with the reactionaries, and a left wing group determined to pursue the rest of the as yet unachieved moderate aims with the help of the masses, even at the risk of losing control over them. And so on through repetitions and variations of the pattern of resistance – mass mobilization – shift to the left – split-among-moderates-and-shift-to-the-right – until the bulk of the middle class either passed into the henceforth conservative camp, or was defeated by social revolution. In most subsequent bourgeois revolutions the moderate liberals were to pull back, or transfer into the conservative camp, at a very early stage. Indeed in the nineteenth century we increasingly find (most notably in Germany) that they became unwilling to begin revolution at all, for fear of its incalculable consequences, preferring a compromise with king and aristocracy. The peculiarity of the French Revolution is that one section of the liberal middle class was prepared to remain revolutionary up to and indeed beyond the brink of anti-bourgeois revolution : these were the Jacobins, whose name came to stand for 'radical revolution' everywhere.

Why? Partly, of course, because the French bourgeoisie had not yet, like subsequent liberals, the awful memory of the French Revolution to be frightened of. After 1794 it would be clear to moderates that the Jacobin régime had driven the Revolution too far for bourgeois comfort and prospects, just as it would be clear to revolutionaries that 'the sun of 1793', if it were to rise again, would have to shine on a non-bourgeois society. Again, the Jacobins could afford radicalism because in their time no class existed which could provide a coherent social alternative to theirs. Such a class only arose in the course of the industrial revolution, with the 'proletariat' or, more precisely, with the ideologies and movements based on it. In the French Revolution the working class – and even this is a misnomer for the aggregate of hired, but mostly non-industrial, wage-earners – as yet played no significant independent part. They hungered, they rioted, perhaps they dreamed; but for practical purposes they followed non-proletarian leaders. The peasantry never provides a political alternative to anyone; merely, as occasion dictates, an almost irresistible force or an almost immovable object. The only alternative to bourgeois radicalism (if we except small bodies of ideologues or militants powerless when deprived of mass support) were the 'Sansculottes', a shapeless, mostly urban movement of the labouring poor, small craftsmen, shopkeepers, artisans, tiny entrepreneurs and the like. The Sansculottes were organized, notably in the 'sections' of Paris and the local political clubs, and provided the main striking-force of the revolution – the actual demonstrators, rioters, constructors of barricades. Through journalists like Marat and Hébert, through local spokesmen, they also formulated a policy, behind which lay a vaguely defined and contradictory social ideal, combining respect for (small) private property with hostility to the rich, government-guaranteed work, wages and social security for the poor man, an extreme, egalitarian and libertarian democracy, localized and direct. In fact the Sansculottes were one branch of that universal and important political trend which sought to express the interests of the great mass of 'little men' who existed between the poles of the 'bourgeois' and the 'proletarian', often perhaps rather nearer the latter than the former because they were, after all, mostly poor. We can observe it in the United States (as Jeffersonianism and Jacksonian democracy, or populism) in Britain (as 'radicalism'), in

France (as the ancestors of the future 'republicans' and radical-socialists), in Italy (as Mazzinians and Garibaldians), and elsewhere. Mostly it tended to settle down, in post-revolutionary ages, as a left-wing of middle-class liberalism, but one loth to abandon the ancient principle that there are no enemies on the left, and ready, in times of crisis, to rebel against 'the wall of money' or 'the economic royalists' or 'the cross of gold crucifying mankind'. But Sansculottism provided no real alternative either. Its ideal, a golden past of villages and small craftsmen or a golden future of small farmers and artisans undisturbed by bankers and millionaires, was unrealizable. History moved dead against them. The most they could do – and this they achieved in 1793–4 – was to erect roadblocks in its path, which have hampered French economic growth from that day almost to this. In fact Sansculottism was so helpless a phenomenon that its very name is largely forgotten, or remembered only as a synonym of Jacobinism, which provided it with leadership in the year II.

II

Between 1789 and 1791 the victorious moderate bourgeoisie, acting through what had now become the Constituent Assembly, set about the gigantic rationalization and reform of France which was its object. Most of the lasting institutional achievements of the Revolution date from this period, as do its most striking international results, the metric system and the pioneer emancipation of the Jews. Economically the perspectives of the Constituent Assembly were entirely liberal : its policy for the peasantry was the enclosure of common lands and the encouragement of rural entrepreneurs, for the working-class, the banning of trade unions, for the small crafts, the abolition of guilds and corporations. It gave little concrete satisfaction to the common people, except, from 1790, by means of the secularization and sale of church lands (as well as those of the emigrant nobility) which had the triple advantage of weakening clericalism, strengthening the provincial and peasant entrepreneur, and giving many peasants a measurable return for their revolutionary activity. The Constitution of 1791 fended off excessive democracy by a system of constitutional monarchy based on an admittedly rather wide property-franchise of 'active citizens'. The passive, it was hoped, would live up to their name.

85

In fact, this did not happen. On the one hand the monarchy, though now strongly supported by a powerful ex-revolutionary bourgeois faction, could not resign itself to the new régime. The Court dreamed of and intrigued for a crusade of royal cousins to expel the governing rabble of commoners and restore God's anointed, the most Catholic king of France, to his rightful place. The Civil Constitution of the Clergy (1790), a misconceived attempt to destroy, not the Church, but the Roman absolutist allegiance of the Church, drove the majority of the clergy and of their faithful into opposition, and helped to drive the king into the desperate, and as it proved suicidal, attempt to flee the country. He was recaptured at Varennes (June 1791) and henceforth republicanism became a mass force; for traditional kings who abandon their peoples lose the right to loyalty. On the other hand, the uncontrolled free enterprise economy of the moderates accentuated the fluctuations in the level of food-prices, and consequently the militancy of the urban poor, especially in Paris. The price of bread registered the political temperature of Paris with the accuracy of a thermometer; and the Paris masses were the decisive revolutionary force: not for nothing was the new French tricolour constructed by combining the old royal white with the red-and-blue colours of Paris.

The outbreak of war brought matters to a head; that is to say it led to the second revolution of 1792, the Jacobin Republic of the Year II, and eventually to Napoleon. In other words it turned the history of the French Revolution into the history of Europe.

Two forces pushed France into a general war: the extreme right and the moderate left. For the king, the French nobility and the growing aristocratic and ecclesiastical emigration, camped in various West German cities, it was evident that only foreign intervention could restore the old régime.[8] Such intervention was not too easily organized, given the complexities of the international situation, and the relative political tranquillity of other countries. However, it was increasingly evident to nobles and divinely appointed rulers elsewhere that the restoration of Louis XVI's power was not merely an act of class solidarity, but an important safeguard against the spread of the appalling ideas propagated from France. Consequently the forces for the reconquest of France gathered abroad.

At the same time the moderate liberals themselves, most notably the group of politicians clustering round the deputies from the mercantile Gironde department, were a bellicose force. This was partly because every genuine revolution tends to be ecumenical. For Frenchmen, as for their numerous sympathisers abroad, the liberation of France was merely the first instalment of the universal triumph of liberty; an attitude which led easily to the conviction that it was the duty of the fatherland of revolution to liberate all peoples groaning under oppression and tyranny. There was a genuinely exalted and generous passion to spread freedom among the revolutionaries, moderate and extreme; a genuine inability to separate the cause of the French nation from that of all enslaved humanity. Both the French and all other revolutionary movements were to accept this view, or to adapt it, henceforth until at least 1848. All plans for European liberation until 1848 hinged on a joint rising of peoples under the leadership of the French to overthrow European reaction; and after 1830 other movements of national and liberal revolt, such as the Italian or Polish, also tended to see their own nations in some sense as Messiahs destined by their own freedom to initiate everyone else's.

On the other hand, considered less idealistically, war would also help to solve numerous domestic problems. It was tempting and obvious to ascribe the difficulties of the new régime to the plots of emigrés and foreign tyrants, and to divert popular discontents against these. More specifically, businessmen argued that the uncertain economic prospects, the devaluation of the currency and other troubles could only be remedied if the threat of intervention were dispersed. They and their ideologists might reflect, with a glance at the record of Britain, that economic supremacy was the child of systematic aggressiveness. (The eighteenth century was not one in which the successful businessman was at all wedded to peace.) Moreover, as was soon to appear, war could be made to produce profit. For all these reasons the majority of the new Legislative Assembly, except for a small right wing and a small left wing under Robespierre, preached war. For these reasons also, when war came, the conquests of the revolution were to combine liberation, exploitation and political diversion.

War was declared in April 1792. Defeat, which the people (plausibly enough) ascribed to royal sabotage and treason, brought radicalization. In August–September the monarchy was overthrown, the Republic one and indivisible established, a new age in human history proclaimed with the institution of the Year I of the revolutionary calendar, by the armed action of the Sansculotte masses of Paris. The iron and heroic age of the French Revolution began among the massacres of the political prisoners, the elections to the National Convention – probably the most remarkable assembly in the history of parliamentarism – and the call for total resistance to the invaders. The king was imprisoned, the foreign invasion halted by an undramatic artillery duel at Valmy.

Revolutionary wars impose their own logic. The dominant party in the new Convention were the Girondins, bellicose abroad and moderate at home, a body of parliamentary orators of charm and brilliance representing big business, the provincial bourgeoisie and much intellectual distinction. Their policy was utterly impossible. For only states waging limited campaigns with established regular forces could hope to keep war and domestic affairs in watertight compartments, as the ladies and gentlemen in Jane Austen's novels were just then doing in Britain. The Revolution waged neither a limited campaign nor had it established forces; for its war oscillated between the maximum victory of world revolution and the maximum defeat which meant total counter-revolution, and its army – what was left of the old French army – was ineffective and unreliable. Dumouriez, the Republic's leading general, was shortly to desert to the enemy. Only unprecedented and revolutionary methods could win in such a war, even if victory were to mean merely the defeat of foreign intervention. In fact, such methods were found. In the course of its crisis the young French Republic discovered or invented total war : the total mobilization of a nation's resources through conscription, rationing and a rigidly controlled war economy, and virtual abolition, at home or abroad, of the distinction between soldiers and civilians. How appalling the implications of this discovery are has only become clear in our own historic epoch. Since the revolutionary war of 1792–4 remained an exceptional episode, most nineteenth-century observers could make no sense of it, except to observe (until in the fatness of later Victorian times even this was forgotten) that wars lead to revolutions, and revolutions win otherwise unwinnable wars. Only today can we see how much about the Jacobin Republic and the 'Terror' of 1793–4 makes sense in no other terms than those of a modern total war effort.

The Sansculottes welcomed a revolutionary war government, not only because they rightly argued that counter-revolution and foreign intervention could only thus be defeated, but also because its methods mobilized the people and brought social justice nearer. (They overlooked the fact that no effective modern war effort is compatible with the decentralized voluntarist direct democracy which they cherished.) The Gironde, on the other hand, was afraid of the political consequences of the combination of mass revolution and war which they unleashed. Nor were they equipped for competition with the left. They did not want to try or execute the king, but had to compete with their rivals, 'the Mountain' (the Jacobins), for this symbol of revolutionary zeal; the Mountain gained prestige, not they. On the other hand, they did want to extend the war into a general ideological crusade of liberation and a direct challenge to the great economic rival, Britain. They succeeded in this object. By March 1793 France was at war with most of Europe, and had begun foreign annexations (legitimized by the newly-invented doctrine of France's right to her 'natural frontiers'). But the expansion of the war, all the more as it went badly, only strengthened the hands of the left, which alone could win it. Retreating and outmanoeuvred, the Gironde was finally driven to ill-judged attacks against the left, which were soon to turn into organized provincial revolt against Paris. A rapid coup by the Sansculottes overthrew it on June 2, 1793. The Jacobin Republic had come.

III

When the educated layman thinks of the French Revolution it is the events of 1789 but especially the Jacobin Republic of the Year II which chiefly comes to his mind. The prim Robespierre, the huge and whoring Danton, the icy revolutionary elegance of Saint-Just, the gross Marat, committee of public safety, revolutionary tribunal and guillotine are the images which we see most clearly. The very names of the moderate revolutionaries who come between Mirabeau and Lafayette in 1789 and the Jacobin leaders in 1793, have lapsed from all but the memory of historians. The Girondins are remembered only as a group, and perhaps for the politically negligible but romantic women attached to them – Mme Roland or Charlotte Corday. Who, outside the expert field, knows even the names of Brissot, Vergniaud, Gaudet and the rest? Conservatives have created a lasting image of The Terror, dictatorship and hysterical bloodlust unchained, though by twentieth-century standards, and indeed by the standards of conservative repressions of social revolution such as the massacres after the Paris Commune of 1871, its mass killings were relatively modest, 17,000 official executions in fourteen months.[10] Revolutionaries, especially in France, have seen it as the first people's republic, the inspiration of all subsequent revolt. For all it was an era not to be measured by everyday human criteria.

That is true. But for the solid middle class Frenchman who stood behind The Terror, it was neither pathological nor apocalyptic, but first and foremost the only effective method of preserving their country. This the Jacobin Republic did, and its achievement was superhuman. In June 1793 sixty out of the eighty departments of France were in revolt against Paris; the armies of the German princes were invading France from the north and east; the British attacked from the south and west : the country was helpless and bankrupt. Fourteen months later all France was under firm control, the invaders had been expelled, the French armies in turn occupied Belgium and were about to enter on twenty years of almost unbroken and effortless military triumph. Yet by March 1794 an army three times as large as before was run at half the cost of March 1793, and the value of the French currency (or rather of the paper *assignats* which had largely replaced it) was kept approximately stable, in marked contrast to both past and future. No wonder Jeanbon St André, the Jacobin member of the Committee of Public Safety who, though a firm republican, later became one of Napoleon's most efficient prefects, looked at imperial France with contempt as it staggered under the defeats of 1812-3. The Republic of the Year II had coped with worse crises, and with fewer resources [11]

For such men, as indeed for the majority of the National Convention which at bottom retained control throughout this heroic period, the choice was simple : either The Terror with all its defects from the middle class point of view, or the destruction of the Revolution, the disintegration of the national state, and probably – was there not the example of Poland? – the disappearance of the country. Very likely, but for the desperate crisis of France, many among them would have preferred a less iron régime and certainly a less firmly controlled economy : the fall of Robespierre led to an epidemic of economic decontrol and corrupt racketeering which, incidentally, culminated in galloping inflation and the national bankruptcy of 1797. But even from the narrowest point of view, the prospects of the French middle class depended on those of a unified strong centralized national state. And anyway, could the Revolution which had virtually created the terms 'nation' and 'patriotism' in their modern senses, abandon the '*grande nation*'?

The first task of the Jacobin régime was to mobilize mass support against the dissidence of the Gironde and the provincial notables, and to retain the already mobilized mass support of the Paris Sans-culottes, some of whose demands for a revolutionary war-effort – general conscription (the 'levée en masse'), terror against the 'traitors' and general price-control (the 'maximum') – in any case coincided with Jacobin common sense, though their other demands were to prove troublesome. A somewhat radicalized new constitution, hitherto delayed by the Gironde, was proclaimed. According to this noble but academic document the people were offered universal suffrage, the right of insurrection, work or maintenance, and – most significant of all – the official statement that the happiness of all was the aim of government and the people's rights were to be not merely available but operative. It was the first genuinely democratic constitution proclaimed by a modern state. More concretely, the Jacobins abolished all remaining feudal rights without indemnity, improved the small buyer's chance to purchase the forfeited land of emigrés, and – some months later – abolished slavery in the French colonies, in order to encourage the Negroes of San Domingo to fight for the Republic against the English. These measures had the most far-reaching results. In America they helped to create the first independent revolutionary leader of stature in Toussaint-Louverture.[12] In France they established that impregnable citadel of small and middle peasant proprietors, small craftsmen and shopkeepers, econ-omically retrogressive but passionately devoted to Revolution and Republic, which has dominated the country's life ever since. The capitalist transformation of agriculture and small enterprise, the essential condition for rapid economic development, was slowed to a crawl; and with it the speed of urbanization, the expansion of the home market, the multiplication of the working-class and, incident-ally, the ulterior advance of proletarian revolution. Both big business and the labour movement were long doomed to remain minority phenomena in France, islands surrounded by a sea of corner grocers, peasant smallholders and café proprietors (cf. below Chapter 9).

The centre of the new government, representing as it did an alliance of Jacobin and Sansculotte, therefore shifted perceptibly to the left. This was reflected in the reconstructed Committee of Public Safety, which rapidly became the effective war-cabinet of France. It lost Danton, a powerful, dissolute, probably corrupt, but immensely talented revolutionary more moderate than he looked (he had been a minister in the last royal administration) and gained Maximilien Robespierre, who became its most influential member. Few historians have been dispassionate about this dandyish, thin-blooded, fanatical lawyer with his somewhat excessive sense of private monopoly in virtue, because he still incarnates the terrible and glorious year II about which no man is neutral. He was not an agreeable individual; even those who think he was right nowadays tend to prefer the shining mathematical rigour of that architect of Spartan paradises, the young Saint-Just. He was not a great man and often a narrow one. But he is the only individual thrown up by the Revolution (other than Napoleon) about whom a cult has grown up. This is because for him, as for history, the Jacobin Republic was not a war-winning device but an ideal : the terrible and glorious reign of justice and virtue when all good citizens were equal in the sight of the nation and the people smote the traitors. Jean-Jacques Rousseau (cf. below p. 300) and the crystalline conviction of rightness gave him his strength. He had no formal dictatorial powers or even office, being merely one member of the Committee of Public Safety, which was in turn merely one sub-committee – the most powerful, though never all-powerful – of the Convention. His power was that of the people – the Paris masses; his terror theirs. When they abandoned him he fell.

The tragedy of Robespierre and the Jacobin Republic was that they were themselves obliged to alienate this support. The régime was an alliance between middle class and labouring masses; but for the middle class Jacobins, Sansculotte concessions were tolerable only because, and as far as, they attached the masses to the régime without terrifying property-owners; and within the alliance the middle class Jacobins were decisive. Moreover, the very needs of the war obliged any government to centralize and discipline, at the expense of the free, local, direct democracy of club and section, the casual voluntarist militia, the free argumentative elections on which the

Sansculottes thrived. The process which, during the Spanish Civil War of 1936–9, strengthened Communists at the expense of Anarchists, strengthened Jacobins of Saint-Just's stamp at the expense of Sansculottes of Hébert's. By 1794 government and politics were monolithic and run in harness by direct agents of Committee or Convention – through delegates *en mission* – and a large body of Jacobin officers and officials in conjunction with local party organizations. Lastly, the economic needs of the war alienated popular support. In the towns price-control and rationing benefited the masses; but the corresponding wage-freeze hurt them. In the countryside the systematic requisitioning of food (which the urban Sansculottes had been the first to advocate) alienated the peasantry.

The masses therefore retired into discontent or into a puzzled and resentful passivity, especially after the trial and execution of the Hébertists, the most vocal spokesmen of the Sansculotterie. Meanwhile more moderate supporters were alarmed by the attack on the right-wing opposition, now headed by Danton. This faction had provided a refuge for numerous racketeers, speculators, black market operators and other corrupt though capital-accumulating elements, all the more readily as Danton himself embodied the a-moral, Falstaffian, free loving and free spending which always emerges initially in social revolutions until overpowered by the hard puritanism that invariably comes to dominate them. The Dantons of history are always defeated by the Robespierres (or by those who pretended to behave like Robespierres) because hard narrow dedication can succeed where bohemianism cannot. However, if Robespierre won moderate support for eliminating corruption, which was after all in the interests of the war-effort, the further restrictions of freedom and money-making were more disconcerting to the businessman. Finally, no large body of opinion liked the somewhat fanciful ideological excursions of the period – the systematic dechristianization campaigns (due to Sansculotte zeal) and Robespierre's new civic religion of the Supreme Being, complete with ceremonies, which attempted to counteract the atheists and carry out the precepts of the divine Jean-Jacques. And the steady hiss of the guillotine reminded all politicians that no one was really safe.

By April 1794, both right and left had gone to the guillotine and the Robespierrists were therefore politically isolated. Only the war-crisis maintained them in power. When, late in June 1794, the new armies of the Republic proved their firmness by decisively defeating the Austrians at Fleurus and occupying Belgium, the end was at hand. On the Ninth Thermidor by the revolutionary calendar (July 27, 1794) the Convention overthrew Robespierre. The next day he, Saint-Just and Couthon were executed, and so a few days later were eighty-seven members of the revolutionary Paris Commune.

IV

Thermidor is the end of the heroic and remembered phase of the Revolution : the phase of ragged Sansculottes and correct red-bonneted citizens who saw themselves as Brutus and Cato, of the grandiloquent classical and generous, but also of the mortal phrases : 'Lyon n'est plus', 'Ten thousand soldiers lack shoes. You will take the shoes of all the aristocrats in Strasbourg and deliver them ready for transport to headquarters by tomorrow ten a.m.'[13] It was not a comfortable phase to live through, for most men were hungry and many afraid; but it was a phenomenon as awful and irreversible as the first nuclear explosion, and all history has been permanently changed by it. And the energy it generated was sufficient to sweep away the armies of the old régimes of Europe like straw.

The problem which faced the French middle class for the remainder of what is technically described as the revolutionary period (1794–9) was how to achieve political stability and economic advance on the basis of the original liberal programme of 1789–91. It has never solved this problem adequately from that day to this, though from 1870 on it was to discover a workable formula for most times in the parliamentary republic. The rapid alternations of régime – Directory (1795–9), Consulate (1799–1804), Empire (1804–14), restored Bourbon Monarchy (1815–30), Constitutional Monarchy (1830–48), Republic (1848–51), and Empire (1852–70) – were all attempts to maintain a bourgeois society while avoiding the double danger of the Jacobin democratic republic and the old régime.

The great weakness of the Thermidorians was that they enjoyed no political support but at most toleration, squeezed as they were between a revived aristocratic reaction and the Jacobin-Sansculotte Paris poor who soon regretted the fall of Robespierre. In 1795 they devised an elaborate constitution of checks and balances to safeguard themselves against both, and periodic shifts to right and left main-

94

tained them precariously in balance; but increasingly they had to rely on the army to disperse the opposition. It was a situation curiously similar to the Fourth Republic, and its conclusion was similar : the rule of a general. But the Directory depended on the army for more than the suppression of periodic coups and plots (various ones in 1795, Babeuf's conspiracy in 1796, Fructidor in 1797, Floréal in 1798, Prairial in 1799).[14] Inactivity was the only safe guarantee of power for a weak and unpopular régime, but initiative and expansion was what the middle class needed. The army solved this apparently insoluble problem. It conquered; it paid for itself; more than this, its loot and conquests paid for the government. Was it surprising that eventually the most intelligent and able of the army leaders, Napoleon Bonaparte, should have decided that the army could dispense altogether with the feeble civilian régime?

This revolutionary army was the most formidable child of the Jacobin Republic. From a 'levée en masse' of revolutionary citizens it soon turned into a force of professional fighters, for there was no call-up between 1793 and 1798, and those who had no taste or talent for soldiering deserted en masse. It therefore retained the characteristics of the Revolution and acquired those of the vested interest; the typical Bonapartist mixture. The Revolution gave it its unprecedented military superiority, which Napoleon's superb generalship was to exploit. It always remained something of an improvised levy, in which barely trained recruits picked up training and morale from old sweats, formal barrack-discipline was negligible, soldiers were treated as men and the absolute rule of promotion by merit (which meant distinction in battle) produced a simple hierarchy of courage. This and the sense of arrogant revolutionary mission made the French army independent of the resources on which more orthodox forces depended. It never acquired an effective supply system, for it lived off the country. It was never backed by an armaments industry faintly adequate to its nominal needs; but it won its battles so quickly that it needed few arms : in 1806 the great machine of the Prussian army crumbled before an army in which an entire corps fired a mere 1,400 cannon shots. Generals could rely on unlimited offensive courage and a fair amount of local initiative. Admittedly it also had the weakness of its origins. Apart from Napoleon and a very few others, its generalship and staff-work was poor, for the revolutionary general or Napoleonic marshal was most likely a tough sergeant-major or company-officer type promoted for bravery and leadership rather than brains : the heroic but very stupid Marshal Ney was only too typical. Napoleon won battles; his marshals alone tended to lose them. Its sketchy supply system sufficed in the rich and lootable countries where it had been developed : Belgium, North Italy, Germany. In the waste spaces of Poland and Russia, as we shall see, it collapsed. Its total absence of sanitary services multiplied casualties : between 1800 and 1815 Napoleon lost 40 per cent of his forces though about one-third of this through desertion); but between 90 and 98 per cent of these losses were men who died not in battle but of wounds, sickness, exhaustion and cold. In brief, it was an army which conquered all Europe in short sharp bursts not only because it could, but because it had to.

On the other hand the army was a career like any other of the many the bourgeois revolution had opened to talent; and those who succeeded in it had a vested interest in internal stability like any other bourgeois. That is what made the army, in spite of its built-in Jacobinism, a pillar of the post-Thermidorian government, and its leader Bonaparte a suitable person to conclude the bourgeois revolution and begin the bourgeois régime. Napoleon Bonaparte himself, though of gentlemanly birth by the standards of his barbarous island-home of Corsica, was himself a typical careerist of this kind. Born in 1769 he made his way slowly in the artillery, one of the few branches of the royal army in which technical competence was indispensable, ambitious, discontented and revolutionary. Under the Revolution, and especially under the Jacobin dictatorship which he supported strongly, he was recognized by a local commissar on a crucial front – a fellow Corsican incidentally, which can hardly have harmed his prospects – as a soldier of splendid gifts and promise. The Year II made him a general. He survived the fall of Robespierre, and a gift for cultivating useful connections in Paris helped him forward after this difficult moment. He seized his opportunities in the Italian campaign of 1796 which made him the unchallenged first soldier of the Republic, who acted virtually in independence of the civilian authorities. Power was half-thrust upon him, half grasped by him when the foreign invasions of 1799 revealed the Directory's feebleness and his own indispensability. He became First Consul; then Consul for life; then Emperor. And with his arrival, as by a miracle, the insoluble problems of the Directory became soluble. Within a few years France had a Civil Code, a concordat with the Church and even, most striking symbol of bourgeois stability, a National Bank. And the world had its first secular myth.

Older readers or those in old-fashioned countries will know the Napoleonic myth as it existed throughout the century when no middle-class cabinet was complete without his bust, and pamphleteering wits could argue, even for a joke, that he was not a man but a sun-god. The extraordinary power of this myth can be adequately explained neither by Napoleonic victories nor by Napoleonic propaganda, nor even by Napoleon's own undoubted genius. As a man he was unquestionably very brilliant, versatile, intelligent and imaginative, though power made him rather nasty. As a general he had no equal; as a ruler he was a superbly efficient planner, chief and executive and sufficient of an all-round intellectual to understand and supervise what his subordinates were doing. As an individual he appears to have radiated a sense of greatness; but most of those who testify to this – like Goethe – saw him at the peak of his fame, when the myth already enveloped him. He was, without any question, a very great man, and – perhaps with the exception of Lenin – his picture is the one which most reasonably educated men would, even today, recognize most readily in the portrait gallery of history, if only by the triple trade-mark of the small size, the hair brushed forward over the forehead and the hand pushed into the half-open waistcoat. It is perhaps pointless to measure him against twentieth-century candidates for greatness.

For the Napoleonic myth is based less on Napoleon's merits than on the facts, then unique, of his career. The great known world-shakers of the past had begun as kings like Alexander or patricians like Julius Caesar; but Napoleon was the 'little corporal' who rose to rule a continent by sheer personal talent. (This was not strictly true, but his rise was sufficiently meteoric and high to make the description reasonable.) Every young intellectual who devoured books, as the young Bonaparte had done, wrote bad poems and novels, and adored Rousseau could henceforth see the sky as his limit, laurels surrounding his monogram. Every businessman henceforth had a name for his ambition : to be – the clichés themselves say so – a 'Napoleon of finance' or industry. All common men were thrilled by the sight, then unique, of a common man who became greater than those born to wear crowns. Napoleon gave ambition a personal name at the moment when the double revolution had opened the world to men of ambition. Yet he was more. He was the civilized man of the eighteenth century, rationalist, inquisitive, enlightened, but with sufficient of the disciple of Rousseau about him to be also the romantic man of the nineteenth. He was the man of the Revolution, and the man who brought stability. In a word, he was the figure every man who broke with tradition could identify himself with in his dreams.

For the French he was also something much simpler: the most successful ruler in their long history. He triumphed gloriously abroad; but at home he also established or re-established the apparatus of French institutions as they exist to this day. Admittedly most – perhaps all – of his ideas were anticipated by Revolution and Directory; his personal contribution was to make them rather more conservative, hierarchical and authoritarian. But his predecessors anticipated: he carried out. The great lucid monuments of French law, the Codes which became models for the entire non-Anglo-Saxon bourgeois world, were Napoleonic. The hierarchy of officials, from the prefects down, of courts, of university and schools, was his. The great 'careers' of French public life, army, civil service, education, law still have their Napoleonic shapes. He brought stability and prosperity to all except the quarter-of-a-million Frenchmen who did not return from his wars; and even to their relatives he brought glory. No doubt the British saw themselves fighting for liberty against tyranny; but in 1815 most Englishmen were probably poorer and worse off than they had been in 1800, while most Frenchmen were almost certainly better off; nor had any except the still negligible wage-labourers lost the substantial economic benefits of the Revolution. There is little mystery about the persistence of Bonapartism as an ideology of non-political Frenchmen, especially the richer peasantry, after his fall. It took a second and smaller Napoleon to dissipate it between 1851 and 1870.

He had destroyed only one thing: the Jacobin Revolution, the dream of equality, liberty and fraternity, and of the people rising in its majesty to shake off oppression. It was a more powerful myth than his, for after his fall it was this, and not his memory, which inspired the revolutions of the nineteenth century, even in his own country.

1 This difference between the British and French influences should not be pushed too far. Neither centre of the dual revolution confined its influence to any special field of human activity, and the two were complementary rather than competitive. However, even when both converged most clearly – as in *socialism*, which was almost simultaneously invented and named in both countries – they converged from somewhat different directions.

2 See R. R. Palmer, *The Age of Democratic Revolution* (1959); J. Godechot, *La Grande Nation* (1956), Vol. I, Chapter 1.

3 B. Lewis, The Impact of the French Revolution on Turkey, *Journal of World History*, I (1953–4, p. 105).

4 This is not to underestimate the influence of the American Revolution. It undoubtedly helped to stimulate the French, and in a narrower sense provided constitutional models – in competition and sometimes alternation with the French – for various Latin American states, and inspiration for democratic-radical movements from time to time.

5 H. Sée, *Esquisse d'une Histoire du Régime Agraire* (1931), pp. 16–17.

6 A. Soboul, *Les Campagnes Montpelliéraines à la fin de l'Ancien Régime* (1958).

7 A. Goodwin, *The French Revolution* (1959 ed.), p. 70.

8 Something like 300,000 Frenchmen emigrated between 1789 and 1795.[9]

9 C. Bloch, L'émigration francaise au XIX siècle, *Etudes d'Histoire Moderne & Contemp.* I (1947), p. 137; D. Greer, *The Incidence of the Emigration during the French Revolution* (1951) however, suggests a very much smaller figure.

10 D. Greer, *The Incidence of the Terror* (Harvard 1935).

11 'Do you know what kind of government (was victorious)? . . . A government of the Convention. A government of passionate Jacobins in red bonnets, wearing rough woollen cloth, wooden shoes, who lived on simple bread and bad beer and went to sleep on mattresses laid on the floor of their meeting-halls, when they were too tired to wake and deliberate further. That is the kind of men who saved France. I was one of them, gentlemen. And here, as in the apartments of the Emperor which I am about to enter, I glory in the fact.' Quoted J. Savant, *Les Prefets de Napoléon* (*1958*), 111–2.

12 The failure of Napoleonic France to recapture Haiti was one of the main reasons for liquidating the entire remaining American Empire, which was sold by the Louisiana Purchase (1803) to the

USA. Thus a further consequence of spreading Jacobinism to America was to make the USA a continent-wide power.

13 *Oeuvres Complètes de Saint Just*, Vol. II, p. 147 (ed. C. Vellay, Paris 1908).

14 The names are those of months in the revolutionary calendar.

4

War

*In a time of innovation, all that is not new is pernicious.
The military art of the monarchy no longer suits us, for
we are different men and have different enemies. The
power and conquests of peoples, the splendour of their
politics and warfare, have always depended on a single
principle, a single powerful institution. . . . Our nation
has already a national character of its own. Its military
system must be different from its enemies'. Very well
then: if the French nation is terrible because of our
ardour and skill, and if our enemies are clumsy, cold and
slow, then our military system must be impetuous.*

Saint-Just, *Rapport présenté à la Convention
Nationale au nom du Comité de Salut Public, 19 du
premier mois de l'an II* (October 10, 1793)

It is not true that war is divinely ordained; *it is not
true that* the earth thirsts for blood. *God himself curses
war and so do the men who wage it, and who hold it in
secret horror.*

Alfred de Vigny, *Servitude et grandeur militaires.*

I

From 1792 until 1815 there was almost uninterrupted war in Europe,
combined or coincident with occasional war outside : in the West
Indies, the Levant and India in the 1790s and early 1800s, in
occasional naval operations abroad thereafter, in the USA in 1812–
14. The consequences of victory or defeat in these wars were considerable, for they transformed the map of the world. We must
therefore consider them first. But we shall also have to consider a
less tangible problem. What were the consequences of the actual
process of warfare, the military mobilization and operations, the
political and economic measures consequent upon them?

Two very different kinds of belligerents confronted one another during those twenty-odd years: powers and systems. France as a state, with its interests and aspirations confronted (or was in alliance with) other states of the same kind, but on the other hand France as the Revolution appealed to the peoples of the world to overthrow tyranny and embrace liberty, and the forces of conservatism and reaction opposed her. No doubt after the first apocalyptic years of revolutionary war the difference between these two strands of conflict diminished. By the end of Napoleon's reign the element of imperial conquest and exploitation prevailed over the elements of liberation, whenever French troops defeated, occupied or annexed some country, and international warfare was therefore much less mixed with international (and in each country domestic) civil war. Conversely, the anti-revolutionary powers were resigned to the irreversibility of much of the revolution's achievement in France, and consequently ready to negotiate (within certain reservations) peace-terms as between normally functioning powers rather than as between light and darkness. They were even, within a few weeks of Napoleon's first defeat, prepared to readmit France as an equal player into the traditional game of alliance, counter-alliance, bluff, threat and war in which diplomacy regulated the relationships between the major states. Nevertheless, the dual nature of the wars as a conflict, both between states and between social systems, remained.

Socially speaking, the belligerents were very unevenly divided. Apart from France itself, there was only one state of importance whose revolutionary origins and sympathy with the Declarations of the Rights of Man might give it an ideological inclination to the French side: the United States of America. In fact, the USA did lean to the French side, and on at least one occasion (1812–14) fought a war, if not in alliance with the French, then at least against a common enemy, the British. However, the USA remained neutral for the most part and its friction with the British requires no ideological explanation. For the rest the ideological allies of France were parties and currents of opinion within other states rather than state powers in their own right.

In a very broad sense virtually every person of education, talent and enlightenment sympathized with the Revolution, at all events until the Jacobin dictatorship, and often for very much longer. (It was not until Napoleon had made himself Emperor that Beethoven revoked the dedication of the Eroica Symphony to him.) The list of European talent and genius which supported the Revolution initially can only be compared with the similar and almost universal sympathy for the Spanish Republic in the 1930s. In Britain it included the poets – Wordsworth, Blake, Coleridge, Robert Burns, Southey – scientists, the chemist Joseph Priestley and several members of the distinguished Birmingham Lunar Society,[1] technologists and industrialists like Wilkinson the ironmaster and Thomas Telford the engineer, and Whig or Dissenting intellectuals in general. In Germany it included the philosophers Kant, Herder, Fichte, Schelling and Hegel, the poets Schiller, Hoelderlin, Wieland and the aged Klopstock and the musician Beethoven, in Switzerland the educationalist Pestalozzi, the psychologist Lavater and the painter Fuessli (Fuseli), in Italy virtually all persons of anticlerical opinions. However, though the Revolution was charmed by such intellectual support, and honoured eminent foreign sympathizers and those whom it believed to stand for its principles by granting them honorary French citizenship,[2] neither a Beethoven nor a Robert Burns were of much political or military importance in themselves.

Serious political philo-Jacobinism or pro-French sentiment existed in the main in certain areas adjoining France, where social conditions were comparable or cultural contacts permanent (the Low Countries, the Rhineland, Switzerland and Savoy), in Italy, and for somewhat different reasons in Ireland and Poland. In Britain 'Jacobinism' would undoubtedly have been a phenomenon of greater political importance, even after The Terror, if it had not clashed with the traditional anti-French bias of popular English nationalism, compounded equally of John Bull's beef-fed contempt for the starveling continentals (all French in the popular cartoons of the period are as thin as matchsticks) and of hostility to what was, after all, England's 'hereditary enemy', though also Scotland's hereditary ally.[2] British Jacobinism was unique in being primarily an artisan or working-class phenomenon, at least after the first general enthusiasm had passed. The *Corresponding Societies* can claim to be the first independent political organizations of the labouring class. But it found a voice of unique force in Tom Paine's *Rights of Man* (which may have sold a million copies), and some political backing from Whig interests, themselves immune to persecution by reason of their wealth and social position, who were prepared to defend the traditions of British civil liberty and the desirability of a negotiated peace with France. Nevertheless, the real weakness of British Jacobinism is indicated by the fact that the very fleet at Spithead, which mutinied at a crucial stage of the war (1797), clamoured to be allowed to sail against the French once their economic demands had been met.

In the Iberian peninsula, in the Habsburg dominions, Central and Eastern Germany, Scandinavia, the Balkans and Russia, philo-Jacobinism was a negligible force. It attracted some ardent young men, some illuminist intellectuals and a few others who, like Ignatius Martinovics in Hungary or Rhigas in Greece, occupy the honoured places of precursors in the history of their countries' struggle for national or social liberation. But the absence of any mass support for their views among the middle and upper classes, let alone their isolation from the bigoted illiterate peasantry, made Jacobinism easy to suppress even when, as in Austria, it ventured on a conspiracy. A generation would have to pass before the strong and militant Spanish liberal tradition was to emerge from the few tiny student conspiracies or Jacobin emissaries of 1792–5.

The truth was that for the most part Jacobinism abroad made its direct ideological appeal to the educated and middle classes and that its political force therefore depended on their effectiveness or willingness to use it. Thus in Poland the French Revolution made a profound impression. France had long been the chief foreign power in whom Poles hoped to find backing against the joint greed of the Prussians, Russians and Austrians, who had already annexed vast areas of the country and were soon to divide it among themselves entirely. France also provided a model of the kind of profound internal reform which, as all thinking Poles agreed, could alone enable their country to resist its butchers. Hence it is hardly surprising that the Reform constitution of 1791 was consciously and profoundly influenced by the French Revolution; it was the first of the modern constitutions to show this influence.[4] But in Poland the reforming nobility and gentry had a free hand. In Hungary, where the endemic conflict between Vienna and the local autonomists provided an analogous incentive for country gentlemen to interest themselves in theories of resistance (the county of Gömör demanded the abolition of censorship as being contrary to Rousseau's *Social Contract*), they had not. Consequently 'Jacobinism' was both much weaker and much less effective. Again in Ireland, national and agrarian discontent gave 'Jacobinism' a political force far in excess of the actual support for the free-thinking, masonic ideology of the leaders of the 'United Irishmen'. Church services were held in that most catholic country for the victory of the godless French, and Irishmen were prepared to welcome the invasion of their country by French forces, not because they sympathized with Robespierre but because they hated the English and looked for allies against them. In Spain, on the other hand, where both Catholicism and poverty were equally prominent, Jacobinism failed to gain a foothold for the opposite reason : no foreigners oppressed the Spaniards, and the only ones likely to do so were the French.

Neither Poland nor Ireland were typical examples of philo-Jacobinism, for the actual programme of the Revolution made little appeal there. It did in countries of similar social and political problems to those of France. These fall into two groups : states in which native 'Jacobinism' stood a reasonable chance of bidding for political power, and those in which only French conquest could push them forward. The Low Countries, parts of Switzerland, and possibly one or two Italian states belong to the first group, most of West Germany and Italy to the second. Belgium (the Austrian Netherlands) was already in revolt in 1789 : it is often forgotten that Camille Desmoulins called his journal *'Les Révolutions de France et de Brabant'*. The pro-French element of the revolutionaries (the democratic *Vonckists*) was no doubt weaker than the conservative *Statists*, but strong enough to produce genuine revolutionary support for the French conquest of their country, which they favoured. In the United Provinces the 'patriots', seeking an alliance with France, were powerful enough to consider a revolution, though doubtful whether it could succeed without external aid. They represented the lesser middle class, and others rallied against the dominant oligarchies of big merchant patricians. In Switzerland the left wing elements in certain Protestant cantons had always been strong, and the attraction of France had always been powerful. Here too French conquest supplemented rather than created the local revolutionary forces.

In West Germany and Italy this was not so. French invasion was welcomed by the German Jacobins, notably in Mainz and the southwest, but nobody would claim that they were within measurable distance of even causing their governments much trouble on their own.[5] In Italy the prevalence of illuminism and Masonry made the

Revolution immensely popular among the educated, but local Jacobinism was probably powerful only in the kingdom of Naples, where it captured virtually all the enlightened (i.e. anticlerical) middle class and a part of the gentry, and was well organized in the secret lodges and societies which flourished so well in the South Italian atmosphere. But even there it suffered from its total failure to make contact with the social-revolutionary masses. A Neapolitan republic was easily proclaimed as news of the French advance came, but equally easily overthrown by a social revolution of the right, under the banner of Pope and King; for the peasants and the Neapolitan *lazzaroni*, with some justification, defined a Jacobin as 'a man with a coach'.

Broadly speaking, therefore, the military value of foreign philo-Jacobinism was chiefly that of an auxiliary to French conquest, and a source of politically reliable administrators of conquered territories. And indeed, the tendency was for the areas with local Jacobin strength to be turned into satellite republics and thereafter, where convenient, to be annexed to France. Belgium was annexed in 1795; the Netherlands became the Batavian Republic in the same year and eventually a family kingdom of the Bonapartes. The left bank of the Rhine was annexed, and under Napoleon satellite states (like the Grand Duchy of Berg – the present Ruhr area – and the kingdom of Westphalia) and direct annexation extended further across Northwest Germany. Switzerland became the Helvetic Republic in 1798 and was eventually annexed. In Italy a string of republics were set up – the Cisalpine (1797), the Ligurian (1797), the Roman (1798), the Partenopean (1798) which eventually became partly French territory, but predominantly satellite states (the kingdom of Italy, the kingdom of Naples).

Foreign Jacobinism had some military importance, and foreign Jacobins within France played a significant part in the formation of Republican strategy, as notably the Saliceti group, which is incidentally more than a little responsible for the rise of the Italian Napoleon Bonaparte within the French army, and his subsequent fortunes in Italy. But few would claim that it or they were decisive. One foreign pro-French movement alone might have been decisive, had it been effectively exploited : the Irish. A combination of Irish revolution and French invasion, particularly in 1797–8 when Britain was temporarily the only belligerent left in the field against France, might well have forced Britain to make peace. But the technical problems of invasion across so wide a stretch of sea were difficult, the French efforts to do so hesitant and ill-conceived, and the Irish rising of 1798, though enjoying massive popular support, poorly organized and easily suppressed. To speculate about the theoretical possibilities of Franco-Irish operations is therefore idle.

But if the French enjoyed the support of revolutionary forces abroad, so did the anti-French. For the spontaneous movements of popular resistance against French conquest cannot be denied their social-revolutionary component, even when the peasants who waged them expressed it in terms of militant church-and-king conservatism. It is significant that the military tactic which in our century has become most completely identified with revolutionary warfare, the guerrilla or partisan, was between 1792 and 1815 the almost exclusive preserve of the anti-French side. In France itself the Vendée and the *chouans* of Brittany carried on royalist guerrilla war from 1793, with interruptions, until 1802. Abroad, the bandits of Southern Italy in 1798–9 probably pioneered anti-French popular guerrilla action. The Tyrolese under the publican Andreas Hofer in 1809, but above all the Spaniards from 1808, and to some extent the Russians in 1812–13, practised it with considerable success. Paradoxically, the military importance of this revolutionary tactic for the anti-French was almost certainly greater than the military importance of foreign Jacobinism was for the French. No area beyond the borders of France itself maintained a pro-Jacobin government for a moment after the defeat or withdrawal of French troops; but Tyrol, Spain, and to some extent Southern Italy, presented a more serious military problem to the French after the defeat of their formal armies and rulers than before. The reason is obvious : these were peasant movements. Where anti-French nationalism was not based on the local peasantry, its military importance was negligible. Retrospective patriotism has created a German 'war of liberation' in 1813–14, but it can safely be said that, insofar as this is supposed to have been based on popular resistance to the French, it is a pious fiction.[6] In Spain the people held the French in check when the armies had failed; in Germany orthodox armies defeated them in a wholly orthodox manner.

Socially speaking, then, it is not too much of a distortion to speak of the war as one of France and its border territories against the rest. In terms of old-fashioned power relations, the line-up was more complex. The fundamental conflict here was that between France and Britain, which had dominated European international relations for the best part of a century. From the British point of view this was almost wholly economic. They wished to eliminate their chief competitor on the way to achieving total predominance of their trade in the European markets, the total control of the colonial and overseas markets, which in turn implied the control of the high seas. In fact, they achieved something not much less than this as the result of the wars. In Europe this objective implied no territorial ambitions, except for the control of certain points of maritime importance, or the assurance that these would not fall into the hands of states strong enough to be dangerous. For the rest of Britain was content with any continental settlement in which any potential rival was held in check by other states. Abroad it implied the wholesale destruction of other people's colonial empires and considerable annexations to the British.

This policy was in itself sufficient to provide the French with some potential allies, for all maritime, trading and colonial states regarded it with misgivings or hostility. In fact their normal posture was one of neutrality, for the benefits of trading freely in wartime are considerable; but the British tendency to treat neutral shipping (quite realistically) as a force helping the French rather than themselves, drove them into conflict from time to time, until the French blockade policy after 1806 pushed them in the opposite direction. Most maritime powers were too weak, or, being in Europe, too cut off, to cause the British much trouble; but the Anglo-American war of 1812–14 was the outcome of such a conflict.

The French hostility to Britain was somewhat more complex, but the element in it which, like the British, demanded a *total* victory was greatly strengthened by the Revolution, which brought to power a French bourgeoisie whose appetites were, in their way, as limitless as those of the British. At the very least victory over the British required the destruction of British commerce, on which Britain was correctly believed to be dependent; and a safeguard against future British recovery, its permanent destruction. (The parallel between the Franco-British and the Rome-Carthage conflict was much in the minds of the French, whose political imagery was largely classical.) In a more ambitious mood, the French bourgeosie could hope to offset the evident economic superiority of the British only by its own political and military resources : e.g. by creating for itself a vast captive market from which its rivals were excluded. Both these considerations lent the Anglo-French conflict a persistence and stubbornness unlike any other. Neither side was really – a rare thing in those days, though a common one today – prepared to settle for less than total victory. The one brief spell of peace between the two (1802–3) was brought to an end by the reluctance of both to maintain it. This was all the more remarkable, since the purely military situation imposed a stalemate : it was clear from the later 1790s that the British could not effectively get at the continent and the French could not effectively break out of it.

The other anti-French powers were engaged in a less murderous kind of struggle. They all hoped to overthrow the French Revolution, though not at the expense of their own political ambitions, but after 1792–5 this was clearly no longer practicable. Austria, whose family links with the Bourbons were reinforced by the direct French threat to her possessions and areas of influence in Italy, and her leading position in Germany, was the most consistently anti-French, and took part in every major coalition against France. Russia was intermittently anti-French, entering the war only in 1795–1800, 1805–7 and 1812. Prussia was torn between a sympathy for the counter-revolutionary side, a mistrust of Austria, and her own ambitions in Poland and Germany, which benefited from the French initiative. She therefore entered the war occasionally and in a semi-independent fashion in 1792–5, 1806–7 (when she was pulverized) and 1813. The policy of the remainder of the states which from time to time entered anti-French coalitions, shows comparable fluctuations. They were against the Revolution but, politics being politics, they had other fish to fry also, and nothing in their state interests imposed a permanent unwavering hostility to France, especially to a victorious France which determined the periodic redistributions of European territory.

These permanent diplomatic ambitions and interests of the European states also supplied the French with a number of potential allies; for in every permanent system of states in rivalry and tension with one another, the enmity of A implies the sympathy of anti-A. The most reliable of these were those lesser German princes whose interest it had long been – normally in alliance with France – to weaken the power of the Emperor (i.e. Austria) over the principalities, or who suffered from the growth of Prussian power. The Southwestern German states – Baden, Wurtemberg, Bavaria, who became the nucleus of the Napoleonic Confederation of the Rhine (1806) – and Prussia's old rival and victim, Saxony, were the most important of these. Saxony, indeed, was the last and most loyal ally of Napoleon, a fact also partly explicable by her economic interests, for as a highly developed manufacturing centre she benefited from the Napoleonic 'continental system'.

Still, even allowing for the divisions on the anti-French side and the potential of allies on which the French might draw, on paper the anti-French coalitions were invariably much stronger than the French, at any rate initially. Yet the military history of the wars is one of almost unbroken and breath-taking French victory. After the initial combination of foreign attack and domestic counter-revolution had been beaten off (1793–4) there was only one short period, before the end, when the French armies were seriously on the defensive : in 1799 when the second coalition mobilized the formidable Russian army under Suvorov for its first operations in Western Europe. For all practical purposes the list of campaigns and land battles between 1794 and 1812 is one of virtually uninterrupted French triumph. The reason lies in the Revolution in France. Its political radiation abroad was not, as we have seen, decisive. At most we might claim that it prevented the population of the reactionary states from resisting the French, who brought them liberty; but in fact the military strategy and tactics of orthodox eighteenth-century states neither expected nor welcomed civilian participation in warfare : Frederick the Great had firmly told his loyal Berliners, who offered to resist the Russians, to leave war to the professionals to whom it belonged. But it transformed the warfare of the French and made them immeasurably superior to the armies of the old régime. Technically the old armies were better trained and disciplined, and where these qualities were decisive, as in naval warfare, the French were markedly inferior. They were good privateers and hit-and-run raiders, but could not compensate for the lack of sufficient trained seamen and above all competent naval officers, a class decimated by the Revolution, for it came largely from the royalist Norman and Breton gentry, and which could not be rapidly improvised. In six major and eight minor naval engagements between the British and the French, the French losses in men were something like ten times those of the British.[7] But where improvised organization, mobility, flexibility and above all sheer offensive courage and morale counted, the French had no rivals. These advantages did not depend on any man's military genius, for the military record of the French before Napoleon took charge was striking enough, and the average quality of French generalship was not exceptional. But it may well have depended in part on the rejuvenation of the French cadres at home or abroad, which is one of the chief consequences of any revolution. In 1806 out of 142 generals in the mighty Prussian army, seventy-nine were over sixty years of age, as were a quarter of all regimental commanders.[8] But in 1806 Napoleon (who had been a general at the age of twenty-four), Murat (who had commanded a brigade at twenty-six), Ney (who did so at twenty-seven) and Davout, were all between twenty-six and thirty-seven years old.

II

The relative monotony of French success makes it unnecessary to discuss the military operations of the war on land in any great detail. In 1793–4 the French preserved the Revolution. In 1794–5 they occupied the Low Countries, the Rhineland, parts of Spain, Switzerland and Savoy (and Liguria). In 1796 Napoleon's celebrated Italian campaign gave them all Italy and broke the first coalition against France. Napoleon's expedition to Malta, Egypt and Syria (1797–9) was cut off from its base by the naval power of the British, and in his absence the second coalition expelled the French from Italy and threw them back to Germany. The defeat of the allied armies in Switzerland (battle of Zurich, 1799) saved France from invasion, and soon after Napoleon's return and seizure of power the French were on the offensive again. By 1801 they had imposed peace on the remaining continental allies, by 1802 even on the British. Thereafter French supremacy in the regions conquered or controlled in 1794–8 remained unquestioned. A renewed attempt to launch war against them, in 1805–7, merely brought French influences to the borders of Russia. Austria was defeated in 1805 at the battle of Austerlitz in Moravia and peace was imposed on her. Prussia, which entered separately and late, was destroyed at the battles of Jena and Auerstaedt in 1806, and dismembered. Russia, though defeated at Austerlitz, mauled at Eylau (1807) and defeated again at Friedland (1807), remained intact as a military power. The Treaty of Tilsit (1807) treated her with justifiable respect, though establishing French hegemony over the rest of the continent, omitting Scandinavia and the Turkish Balkans. An Austrian attempt to shake free in 1809 was defeated at the battles of Aspern-Essling and Wagram. However, the revolt of the Spaniards in 1808, against the imposition of Napoleon's brother Joseph as their king, opened up a field of operations for the British, and maintained constant military activity in the Peninsula, unaffected by the periodic defeats and retreats of the British (e.g. in 1809–10).

On the sea, however, the French were by this time completely defeated. After the battle of Trafalgar (1805) any chance, not merely of invading Britain across the channel but of maintaining contact overseas, disappeared. No way of defeating Britain appeared to exist except economic pressure, and this Napoleon attempted to exert effectively through the Continental System (1806). The difficulties of imposing this blockade effectively undermined the stability of the Tilsit settlement and led to the break with Russia, which was the turning-point of Napoleon's fortunes. Russia was invaded and Moscow occupied. Had the Tsar made peace, as most of Napoleon's enemies had done under similar circumstances, the gamble would have come off. But he did not, and Napoleon faced either endless further war without a clear prospect of victory, or retreat. Both were equally disastrous. The French army's methods as we have seen assumed rapid campaigns in areas sufficiently wealthy and densely peopled for it to live off the land. But what worked in Lombardy or the Rhineland, where such procedures had been first developed, and was still feasible in central Europe, failed utterly in the vast, empty and impoverished spaces of Poland and Russia. Napoleon was defeated not so much by the Russian winter as by his failure to keep the Grand Army properly supplied. The retreat from Moscow destroyed the Army. Of the 610,000 men who had at one time or another crossed the Russian frontier, 100,000 or so recrossed it.

Under these circumstances the final coalition against the French was joined not only by her old enemies and victims, but by all those anxious to be on what was now clearly going to be the winning side; only the king of Saxony left his adhesion too late. A new, and largely raw, French army was defeated at Leipzig (1813), and the allies advanced inexorably into France, in spite of the dazzling manœuvres of Napoleon, while the British advanced into it from the Peninsula. Paris was occupied and the Emperor resigned on the 6th of April 1814. He attempted to restore his power in 1815, but the battle of Waterloo (June 1815) ended it.

III

In the course of these decades of war the political frontiers of Europe were redrawn several times. Here we need consider only those changes which, in one way or another, were sufficiently permanent to outlast the defeat of Napoleon.

The most important of these was a general rationalization of the European political map, especially in Germany and Italy. In terms of political geography, the French Revolution ended the European middle ages. The characteristic modern state, which had been evolving for several centuries, is a territorially coherent and unbroken area with sharply defined frontiers, governed by a single sovereign authority and according to a single fundamental system of administration and law. Since the French Revolution it has also been assumed that it should represent a single 'nation' or linguistic group, but at this stage a sovereign territorial state did not yet imply this.) The characteristic European feudal state, though it could sometimes look like this, as for instance in medieval England, made no such requirements. It was patterned much more on the 'estate'. Just as the term 'the estates of the Duke of Bedford' implies neither that they should all be in a single block, nor that they should all be directly managed by their owner, or held on the same tenancies or terms, nor that sub-tenancies should be excluded, so the feudal state of Western Europe did not exclude a complexity which would appear wholly intolerable today. By 1789 these complexities were already felt to be troublesome. Foreign enclaves found themselves deep in some state's territory, like the papal city of Avignon in France. Territories within one state found themselves, for historical reasons, also dependent on another lord who now happened to be part of another state and therefore, in modern terms, under dual sovereignty.[9] 'Frontiers' in the form of customs-barriers ran between different provinces of the same state. The empire of the Holy Roman Emperor contained his private principalities, accumulated over the centuries and never adequately standardized or unified – the head of the House of Habsburg did not even have a single title to describe his rule over all his territories until 1804 [10] – and imperial authority over a variety of territories, ranging from great powers in their own right like the kingdom of Prussia (itself not fully unified as such until 1807), through principalities of all sizes, to independent city-state republics and 'free imperial knights' whose estates, often no bigger than a few acres, happened to have no superior lord. Each of these in turn, if large enough, showed the same lack of territorial unity and standardization, depending on the vagaries of a long history of piecemeal acquisition and the divisions and reunifications of the family heritage. The complex of economic, administrative, ideological and power-considerations which tend to impose a mimimum size of territory and population on the modern unit of government, and make us today vaguely uneasy at the thought of, say, UN membership for Liechtenstein, did not yet apply to any extent. Consequently, especially in Germany and Italy, small and dwarf states abounded.

The Revolution and the consequent wars abolished a good many of these relics, partly from revolutionary zeal for territorial unification and standardization, partly by exposing the small and weak states to the greed of their larger neighbours repeatedly and for an unusually long period. Such formal survivals of an earlier age as the Holy Roman Empire, and most city-states and city-empires, disappeared. The Empire died in 1806, the ancient Republics of Genoa and Venice went in 1797 and by the end of the war the German free cities had been reduced to the four. Another characteristic medieval survival, the independent ecclesiastical state, went the same way : the episcopal principalities, Cologne, Mainz, Treves, Salzburg and the rest, went; only the Papal states in central Italy survived until 1870. Annexation, peace-treaties, and the Congresses in which the French systematically attempted to reorganize the German political map (in 1797–8 and 1803) reduced the 234 territories of the Holy Roman Empire – not counting free imperial knights and the like – to forty; in Italy, where generations of jungle warfare had already simplified the political structure – dwarf states existed only at the confines of North and Central Italy – the changes were less drastic. Since most of these changes benefited some soundly monarchial state, Napoleon's defeat merely perpetuated them. Austria would no more have thought of restoring the Venetian Republic, because she had originally acquired its territories through the operation of the French Revolutionary armies, than she would have thought of giving up Salzburg (which she acquired in 1803) merely because she respected the Catholic Church.

Outside Europe, of course, the territorial changes of the wars were the consequence of the wholesale British annexation of other people's colonies and the movements of colonial liberation inspired by the French Revolution (as in San Domingo) or made possible, or imposed, by the temporary separation of colonies from their metropolis (as in Spanish and Portuguese America). The British domination of the seas ensured that most of these changes should be irreversible, whether they had taken place at the expense of the French or (more often) of the anti-French.

Equally important were the institutional changes introduced directly or indirectly by French conquest. At the peak of their power (1810), the French directly governed, as part of France, all Germany left of the Rhine, Belgium, the Netherlands and North Germany eastwards to Luebeck, Savoy, Piedmont, Liguria and Italy west of the Apennines down to the borders of Naples, and the Illyrian provinces from Carinthia down to and including Dalmatia. French family or satellite kingdoms and duchies covered Spain, the rest of Italy, the rest of Rhineland-Westphalia, and a large part of Poland. In all these territories (except perhaps the Grand Duchy of Warsaw) the institutions of the French Revolution and the Napoleonic Empire were automatically applied, or were the obvious models for local administration : feudalism was formally abolished, French legal codes applied and so on. These changes proved far less reversible than the shifting of frontiers. Thus the Civil Code of Napoleon remained, or became once again, the foundation of local law in Belgium, in the Rhineland (even after its return to Prussia) and in Italy. Feudalism, once officially abolished, was nowhere re-established.

Since it was evident to the intelligent adversaries of France that they had been defeated by the superiority of a new political system, or at any rate by their own failure to adopt equivalent reforms, the wars produced changes not only through French conquest but in reaction against it; in some instances – as in Spain – through both agencies. Napoleon's collaborators, the *afrancesados* on one side, the liberal leaders of the anti-French Junta of Cadiz on the other, envisaged substantially the same type of Spain, modernized along the lines of the French Revolutionary reforms; and what the ones failed to achieve, the others attempted. A much clearer case of reform by reaction – for the Spanish liberals were reformers first and anti-French only as it were by historical accident – was Prussia. There a form of peasant liberation was instituted, an army with elements of the *levée en masse* organized, legal, economic and educational reforms carried through entirely under the impact of the collapse of the Frederician army and state at Jena and Auerstaedt, and with the overwhelmingly predominant purpose of reversing that defeat.

In fact, it can be said with little exaggeration that no important continental state west of Russia and Turkey and south of Scandinavia emerged from these two decades of war with its domestic institutions wholly unaffected by the expansion or imitation of the French Revolution. Even the ultra-reactionary Kingdom of Naples did not actually re-establish legal feudalism once it had been abolished by the French.

But changes in frontiers, laws and government institutions were as nothing compared to a third effect of these decades of revolutionary war : the profound transformation of the political atmosphere. When the French Revolution broke out, the governments of Europe regarded it with relative sangfroid : the mere fact that institutions changed suddenly, that insurrections took place, that dynasties were deposed or kings assassinated and executed did not in itself shock eighteenth-century rulers, who were used to it, and who considered such changes in other countries primarily from the point of view of their effect on the balance of power and the relative position of their own. 'The insurgents I expel from Geneva,' wrote Vergennes, the famous French foreign minister of the old régime, 'are agents of England, whereas the insurgents in America hold out the prospects of long friendship. My policy towards each is determined not by their political systems, but by their attitude towards France. That is my reason of state.' [11] But by 1815 a wholly different attitude towards revolution prevailed, and dominated the policy of the powers.

It was now known that revolution in a single country could be a European phenomenon; that its doctrines could spread across the frontiers and, what was worse, its crusading armies could blow away the political systems of a continent. It was now known that social revolution was possible; that nations existed as something independent of states, peoples as something independent of their rulers, and even that the poor existed as something independent of the ruling classes. 'The French Revolution,' De Bonald had observed in 1796, 'is a unique event in history.' [12] The phrase is misleading : it was a universal event. No country was immune from it. The French soldiers who campaigned from Andalusia to Moscow, from the Baltic to Syria – over a vaster area than any body of conquerors since the Mongols, and certainly a vaster area than any previous single military force in Europe except the Norsemen – pushed the universality of their revolution home more effectively than anything else could have done. And the doctrines and institutions they carried with them, even under Napoleon, from Spain to Illyria, were universal doctrines, as the governments knew, and as the peoples themselves were soon to know also. A Greek bandit and patriot expressed their feelings completely :

'According to my judgment,' said Kolokotrones, 'the French Revolution and the doings of Napoleon opened the eyes of the world. The nations knew nothing before, and the people thought that kings were gods upon the earth and that they were bound to say that whatever they did was well done. Through this present change it is more difficult to rule the people.' [13]

IV

We have seen the effects of the twenty-odd years of war on the political structure of Europe. But what were the consequences of the actual process of warfare, the military mobilizations and operations, the political and economic measures consequent upon them?

Paradoxically these were the greatest where least concerned with the actual shedding of blood; except for France itself which almost certainly suffered higher casualties and indirect population losses than any other country. The men of the revolutionary and Napoleonic period were lucky enough to live between two periods of barbaric warfare – that of the seventeenth century and that of our own – which had the capacity to lay countries waste in a really sensational manner. No area affected by the wars of 1792–1815, not even in the Iberian peninsula, where military operations were more prolonged than anywhere else and popular resistance and reprisal made them more savage, was devastated as parts of Central and Eastern

Europe were in the Thirty Years' and Northern Wars of the seventeenth century, Sweden and Poland in the early eighteenth, or large parts of the world in war and civil war in the twentieth. The long period of economic improvement which preceded 1789 meant that famine and its companion, plague and pestilence, did not add excessively to the ravages of battle and plunder; at any rate until after 1811. (The major period of famine occurred *after* the wars, in 1816–17.) The military campaigns tended to be short and sharp, and the armaments used – relatively light and mobile artillery – not very destructive by modern standards. Sieges were uncommon. Fire was probably the greatest hazard to dwellings and the means of production, and small houses or farms were easily rebuilt. The only material destruction really difficult to make good quickly in a pre-industrial economy is that of timber, fruit- or olive-groves, which take many years to grow, and there does not seem to have been much of that.

Consequently the sheer human losses due to these two decades of war do not appear to have been, by modern standards, frighteningly high; though in fact no government made any attempt to calculate them, and all our modern estimates are vague to the point of guesswork, except those for the French and a few special cases. One million war dead for the entire period [14] compares favourably with the losses of any single major belligerent in the four and a half years of World War I, or for that matter with the 600,000 or so dead of the American Civil War of 1861–5. Even two millions would not, for more than two decades of general warfare, appear particularly murderous, when we remember the extraordinary killing capacity of famines and epidemics in those days : as late as 1865 a cholera epidemic in Spain is reported as having claimed 236,744 victims.[15] In fact, no country claims a significant slowing down of the rate of population growth during this period, except perhaps France.

For most inhabitants of Europe other than the combatants, the war probably did not mean more than an occasional direct interruption of the normal tenor of life, if it meant even that. Jane Austen's country families went about their business as though it were not there. Fritz Reuter's Mecklenburgers recalled the time of foreign occupation as one of small anecdote rather than drama; old Herr Kuegelgen, remembering his childhood in Saxony (one of the 'cockpits of Europe' whose geographical and political situation attracted armies and battles as only Belgium and Lombardy did besides), merely recalled the odd weeks of armies marching into or quartered in Dresden. Admittedly the number of armed men involved was much higher than had been common in earlier wars, though it was not extraordinary by modern standards. Even conscription did not imply the call-up of more than a fraction of the men affected : the Côte d'Or department of France in Napoleon's reign supplied only 11,000 men out of its 350,000 inhabitants, or 3·15 per cent, and between 1800 and 1815 no more than 7 per cent of the total population of France were called up, as against 21 per cent in the much shorter period in the first world war.[16] Still, in absolute figures this was a very large number. The *levée en masse* of 1793–4 put perhaps 630,000 men under arms (out of a theoretical call-up of 770,000); Napoleon's peacetime strength in 1805 was 400,000 or so, and at the outset of the campaign against Russia in 1812 the Grande Armée comprised 700,000 men (300,000 of them non-French), without counting the French troops in the rest of the continent, notably in Spain. The permanent mobilizations of the adversaries of France were very much smaller, if only because (with the exception of Britain) they were much less continuously in the field, as well as because financial troubles and organizational difficulties often made full mobilization difficult, e.g. for the Austrians who in 1813 were entitled under the peace treaty of 1809 to 150,000 men, but had only 60,000 actually ready for a campaign. The British, on the other hand, kept a surprisingly large number of men mobilized. At their peak (1813–14), with enough money voted for 300,000 in the regular army and 140,000 seamen and marines, they may well have carried a proportionately heavier load on their manpower than the French did for most of the war.[17, 18]

Losses were heavy, though once again not excessively so by the murderous standards of our century; but curiously few of them were actually due to the enemy. Only 6 or 7 per cent of the British sailors who died between 1793 and 1815 succumbed to the French; 80 per cent died from disease or accident. Death on the battlefield was a small risk; only 2 per cent of the casualties at Austerlitz, perhaps 8 or 9 per cent of those at Waterloo, were actually killed. The really frightening risk of war was neglect, filth, poor organization, defective medical services and hygienic ignorance, which massacred the wounded, the prisoners, and in suitable climatic conditions (as in the tropics) practically everybody.

Actual military operations killed people, directly and indirectly, and destroyed productive equipment, but, as we have seen, they did neither to an extent which seriously interfered with the normal tenor of a country's life and development. The economic requirements of war, and economic warfare, had more far-reaching consequences.

By the standards of the eighteenth century, the revolutionary and Napoleonic wars were expensive beyond precedent; and indeed their cost in money impressed contemporaries perhaps even more than their cost in lives. Certainly the fall in the financial burden of war in the generation after Waterloo was far more striking than the fall in the human cost : it is estimated that while wars between 1821 and 1850 cost an average of less than 10 per cent per year of the equivalent figure for 1790–1820, the annual average of war deaths remained at a little less than 25 per cent of the earlier period.[19] How was this cost to be paid? The traditional method had been a combination of monetary inflation (the issue of new currency to pay the government's bills), loans, and the minimum of special taxation, for taxes created public discontent and (where they had to be granted by parliaments or estates) political trouble. But the extraordinary financial demands and conditions of the wars broke or transformed all these.

In the first place they familiarized the world with unconvertible paper money.[20] On the continent the ease with which pieces of paper could be printed, to pay government obligations, proved irresistible. The French *Assignats* (1789) were at first simply French Treasury bonds (*bons de trésor*) with 5 per cent interest, designed to anticipate the proceeds of the eventual sale of church lands. Within a few months they had been transformed into currency, and each successive financial crisis caused them to be printed in greater quantity, and to depreciate more steeply, aided by the increasing lack of confidence of the public. By the outbreak of war they had depreciated about 40 per cent, by June 1793 about two-thirds. The Jacobin régime maintained them fairly well, but the orgy of economic decontrol after Thermidor reduced them progressively to about one three-hundredth of their face value, until official state bankruptcy in 1797 put an end to a monetary episode which prejudiced the French against any kind of banknote for the better part of a century. The paper currencies of other countries had less catastrophic careers, though by 1810 the Russian had fallen to 20 per cent of face value and the Austrian (twice devalued, in 1810 and 1815) to 10 per cent. The British avoided this particular form of financing war and were familiar enough with banknotes not to shy away from them, but even so the Bank of England could not resist the double pressure of the vast government demand – largely sent abroad as loans and subsidies – the private run on its bullion and the special strain of a famine year. In 1797 gold payments to private clients were suspended and the inconvertible banknote became, *de facto*, the effective currency : the £1 note was one result. The 'paper pound' never depreciated as seriously as continental currencies – its lowest mark was 71 per cent of face value and by 1817 it was back to 98 per cent – but it did last very much longer than had been anticipated. Not until 1821 were cash payments fully resumed.

The other alternative to taxation was loans, but the dizzying rise in the public debt produced by the unexpectedly heavy and prolonged expenditure of war frightened even the most prosperous, wealthy and financially sophisticated countries. After five years of financing the war essentially by loans, the British Government was forced into the unprecedented and portentous step of paying for the war out of direct taxation, introducing an income tax for this purpose (1799–1816). The rapidly increasing wealth of the country made this perfectly feasible, and the cost of the war henceforth was essentially met out of current income. Had adequate taxation been imposed from the beginning, the National Debt would not have risen from £228 millions in 1793 to £876 millions in 1816, and the annual debt charge from £10 millions in 1792 to £30 millions in 1815, which was *greater than the total government outlay in the last pre-war year*. The social consequences of such indebtedness were very great, for in effect it acted as a funnel for diverting increasingly large amounts of the tax revenue paid by the population at large into the pockets of the small class of rich 'fund-holders' against whom spokesmen of the poor and the small businessmen and farmers, like William Cobbett, launched their journalistic thunderbolts. Abroad loans were mainly raised (at least on the anti-French side) from the British Government, which had long followed a policy of subsidizing military allies : between 1794 and 1804 it raised £80 millions for this purpose. The main direct beneficiaries were the international financial houses – British or foreign, but operating increasingly through London, which became the main centre of international financing – like the Barings and the

House of Rothschild, who acted as intermediaries in these transactions. (Meyer Amschel Rothschild, the founder, sent his son Nathan from Frankfurt to London in 1798.) The great age of these international financiers came after the wars, when they financed the major loans designed to help old régimes recover from war and new ones to stabilize themselves. But the foundation of the era when the Barings and the Rothschilds dominated world finance, as nobody since the great German banks of the sixteenth century had done, was constructed during the wars.

However, the technicalities of wartime finance are less important than the general economic effect of the great diversion of resources from peacetime to military uses, which a major war entails. It is clearly wrong to regard the war-effort as entirely drawn from, or at the expense of, the civilian economy. The armed forces may to some extent mobilize only men who would otherwise be unemployed, or even unemployable within the limits of the economy.[21] War industry, though in the short run diverting men and materials from the civilian market, may in the long run stimulate developments which ordinary considerations of profit in peacetime would have neglected. This was proverbially the case with the iron and steel industries which, as we have seen (see chapter 2), enjoyed no possibilities of rapid expansion comparable to the cotton textiles, and therefore traditionally relied for their stimulus on government and war. 'During the eighteenth century,' Dionysius Lardner wrote in 1831, 'iron foundery became almost identified with the casting of cannon.'[22] We may well therefore regard part of the diversion of capital resources from peacetime uses as in the nature of long-term investment in capital goods industries and technical development. Among the technological innovations thus created by the revolutionary and Napoleonic wars were the beet-sugar industry on the continent (as a replacement for imported cane-sugar from the West Indies), and the canned food industry (which arose from the British navy's search for foodstuffs which could be indefinitely preserved on shipboard). Nevertheless, making all allowances, a major war does mean a major diversion of resources, and might even, under conditions of mutual blockade, mean that the wartime and peacetime sector of the economy competed directly for the same scarce resources.

An obvious consequence of such competition is inflation, and we know that in fact the period of war pushed the slope of the slowly rising eighteenth-century price-level steeply upwards in all countries though some of this was due to monetary devaluation. This in itself implies, or reflects, a certain redistribution of incomes, which has economic consequences; for instance, towards businessmen and away from wage-earners (since wages normally lag behind prices), and towards agriculture, which proverbially welcomes the high prices of wartime, and away from manufactures. Conversely, the end of the wartime demand, which releases a mass of resources – including men – hitherto employed by war, on to the peacetime market, brought, as always, correspondingly more intense problems of readjustment. To take an obvious example : between 1814 and 1818 the strength of the British army was cut by about 150,000 men, or more than the contemporary population of Manchester, and the level of wheat prices fell from 108·5 shillings a quarter in 1813 to 64·2 shillings in 1815. In fact we know the period of post-war adjustment to have been one of abnormal economic difficulties all over Europe; intensified moreover by the disastrous harvests of 1816–17.

We ought, however, to ask a more general question. How far did the diversion of resources due to the war impede or slow down the economic development of different countries? Clearly this question is of particular importance for France and Britain, the two major economic powers, and the two carrying the heaviest economic burden. The French burden was due not so much to the war in its later stages, for this was designed largely to pay for itself at the expense of the foreigners whose territories the conquering armies looted or requisitioned, and on whom they imposed levies of men, materials and money. About half the Italian tax revenue went to the French in 1805–12.[23] It probably did not do so, but it was also clearly much cheaper – in real as well as monetary terms – than it would otherwise have been. The real disruption of the French economy was due to the decade of revolution, civil war and chaos, which, for instance, reduced the turnover of the Seine-Inférieure (Rouen) manufactures from 41 to 15 millions between 1790 and 1795, and the number of their workers from 246,000 to 86,000. To this must be added the loss of overseas commerce due to the British control of the seas. The British burden was due to the cost of carrying not only the country's own war effort but, through the traditional subsidies to continental allies, some of that for other states. In monetary terms the British carried by far the heaviest load during the war : it cost them between three and four times as much as it did the French.

The answer to the general question is easier for France than for Britain, for there is little doubt that the French economy remained relatively stagnant, and the French industry and commerce would almost certainly have expanded further and faster but for the revolution and the wars. Though the country's economy advanced very substantially under Napoleon, it could not compensate for the regression and the lost impetus of the 1790s. For the British the answer is less obvious, for their expansion was meteoric, and the only question is whether, but for the war, it would have been more rapid still. The generally accepted answer today is that it would.[24] For the other countries the question is generally of less importance where economic development was slow, or fluctuating as in much of the Habsburg Empire, and where the quantitative impact of the war-effort was relatively small.

Of course such bald statements beg the question. Even the frankly economic wars of the British in the seventeenth and eighteenth centuries were not supposed to advance economic development by themselves or by stimulating the economy, but by victory : by eliminating competitors and capturing new markets. Their 'cost' in disrupted business, diversion of resources and the like was measured against their 'profit', which was expressed in the relative position of the belligerent competitors after the war. By these standards the wars of 1793–1815 clearly more than paid for themselves. At the cost of a slight slowing down of an economic expansion which nevertheless remained gigantic, Britain decisively eliminated her nearest possible competitor and became the 'workshop of the world' for two generations. In terms of every industrial or commercial index, Britain was very much further ahead of all other states (with the possible exception of the USA) than she had been in 1789. If we believe that the temporary elimination of her rivals and the virtual monopoly of maritime and colonial markets were an essential precondition of Britain's further industrialization, the price of achieving it was modest. If we argue that by 1789 her head start was already sufficient to ensure British economic supremacy without a long war, we may still hold that the cost of defending it against the French threat to recover by political and military means the ground lost in economic competition was not excessive.

NOTES

1 James Watt's son actually went to France, to his father's alarm.
2 To wit Priestley, Bentham, Wilberforce, Clarkson (the anti-slavery agitator), James Mackintosh, David Williams from Britain, Klopstock, Schiller, Campe and Anarcharsis Cloots from Germany, Pestalozzi from Switzerland, Kosciusko from Poland, Gorani from Italy, Cornelius de Pauw from the Netherlands, Washington, Hamilton, Madison, Tom Paine and Joel Barlow from the USA. Not all of these were sympathizers with the Revolution.
3 This may not be unconnected with the fact that Scottish Jacobinism was a very much more powerful popular force.
4 As Poland was essentially a Republic of the nobility and gentry, the constitution was 'jacobin' only in the most superficial sense : the rule of the nobles was reinforced rather than abolished.
5 The French even failed to establish a satellite Rhineland Republic.
6 Cf. e.g. W. von Groote, *Die Entstehung d. Nationalbewusssteins in Nordwestdeutschland 1790–1830* (1952).
7 M. Lewis, *A Social History of the Navy, 1793–1815* (1960), pp. 370, 373.
8 Gordon Craig, *The Politics of the Prussian Army 1640–1945* (1955), p. 26.
9 A lone European survivor of this genus is the republic of Andorra, which is under the dual suzerainty of the Spanish Bishop of Urgel and the President of the French Republic.
10 He was merely, in his single person, Duke of Austria, King of Hungary, King of Bohemia, Count of Tyrol, etc.
11 A. Sorel, *L'Europe et la révolution francaise*, I (1922 ed.), p. 66.
12 *Considérations sur la France*, Chapter IV.
13 Quoted in L. S. Stavrianos, Antecedents to Balkan Revolutions, *Journal of Modern History*, XXIX, 1957, p. 344.
14 G. Bodart, *Losses of Life in Modern Wars* (1916), p. 133.
15 J. Vicens Vives ed. *Historia Social de España y América* (1956), IV, ii, p. 15.
16 G. Bruun, *Europe and the French Imperium* (1938), p. 72.
17 As these figures are based on the money authorized by Parliament, the number of men raised was certainly smaller.
18 J. Leverrier, *La Naissance de l'armée nationale, 1789–94* (1939), p. 139; G. Lefebvre, *Napoléon* (1936), pp. 198, 527; M. Lewis, op. cit., p. 119; *Parliamentary Papers* XVII, 1859, p. 15.
19 Mulhall, *Dictionary of Statistics* : War.
20 In actual fact any kind of paper money, whether exchangeable

upon demand for bullion or not, was relatively uncommon before the end of the eighteenth century.

21 This was the basis of the strong tradition of emigration for mercenary military service in overpopulated mountain regions like Switzerland.

22 *Cabinet Cyclopedia*, I, pp. 55–6 ('Manufactures in Metal').

23 E. Tarlé, *Le blocus continental et le royaume d'Italie* (1928), pp. 3–4, 25–31; H. Sée, *Histoire Economique de la France*, II, p. 52; Mulhall, loc. cit.

24 Gayer, Rostow and Schwartz, *Growth and Fluctuation of the British Economy, 1790–1850* (1953), pp. 646–9; F. Crouzet, *Le blocus continental et l'économie Britannique* (1958), p. 868 ff.

5

Peace

> The existing concert (of the Powers) is their only per-
> fect security against the revolutionary embers more or less
> existing in every state of Europe; and ... true wisdom is
> to keep down the petty contentions of ordinary times, and
> to stand together in support of the established principles
> of social order.
>
> Castlereagh [1]

> L'empereur de Russie est de plus le seul souverain par-
> faitement en état de se porter dès à présent aux plus vastes
> entreprises. Il est à la téte de la seule armée vraiment
> disponible qui soit aujourd'hui formée en Europe.
>
> Gentz, March 24, 1818 [2]

After more than twenty years of almost unbroken war and revolution, the victorious old régimes faced problems of peace-making and
peace-preservation which were particularly difficult and dangerous.
The debris of two decades had to be cleared away, the territorial loot
redistributed. What was more, it was evident to all intelligent statesmen that no major European war was henceforth tolerable; for such
a war would almost certainly mean a new revolution, and consequently the destruction of the old régimes. 'In Europe's present state
of social illness,' said King Leopold of the Belgians (Queen Victoria's
wise if somewhat boring uncle), à propos of a later crisis, 'it would be
unheard-of to let loose ... a general war. Such a war ... would certainly bring a conflict of principles, (and) from what I know of
Europe, I think that such a conflict would change her form and
overthrow her whole structure.' [3] Kings and statesmen were neither
wiser nor more pacific than before. But they were unquestionably
more frightened.

They were also unusually successful. There was, in fact, no general
European war, nor any conflict in which one great power opposed

another on the battlefield, between the defeat of Napoleon and the Crimean War of 1854–6. Indeed, apart from the Crimean War, there was no war involving more than two great powers between 1815 and 1914. The citizen of the twentieth century ought to appreciate the magnitude of this achievement. It was all the more impressive, because the international scene was far from tranquil, the occasions for conflict abundant. The revolutionary movements (which we shall consider in chapter 6) destroyed the hard-won international stability time and again : in the 1820s, notably in Southern Europe, the Balkans and Latin America, after 1830 in Western Europe (notably Belgium), and again on the eve of the 1848 Revolution. The decline of the Turkish Empire, threatened both by internal dissolution and the ambitions of rival great powers – mainly Britain, Russia and to a lesser extent France – made the so-called 'Eastern Question' a permanent cause of crisis : in the 1820s it cropped up over Greece, in the 1830s over Egypt, and though it calmed down after a particularly acute conflict in 1839–41, it remained as potentially explosive as before. Britain and Russia were on the worst of terms over the Near East and the no-man's land between the two empires in Asia. France was far from reconciled to a position so much more modest than the one she had occupied before 1815. Yet in spite of all these shoals and whirlpools, the diplomatic vessels navigated a difficult stretch of water without collision.

Our generation, which has failed so much more spectacularly in the fundamental task of international diplomacy, that of avoiding general wars, has therefore tended to look back upon the statesmen and methods of 1815–48 with a respect that their immediate successors did not always feel. Talleyrand, who presided over French foreign policy from 1814 to 1835, remains the model for the French diplomat to this day. Castlereagh, George Canning and Viscount Palmerston, who were Britain's foreign secretaries respectively in 1812–22, 1822–7 and all non-Tory administrations from 1830 to 1852 [4] have acquired a misleading and retrospective stature of diplomatic giants. Prince Metternich, the chief minister of Austria throughout the entire period from Napoleon's defeat to his own overthrow in 1848, is today seen less often as a mere rigid enemy of all change and more often as a wise maintainer of stability than used to be the case. However, even the eye of faith has been unable to detect foreign ministers worth idealizing in the Russia of Alexander I

(1801–25) and Nicholas I (1825–55) and in the relatively unimportant Prussia of our period.

In a sense the praise is justified. The settlement of Europe after the Napoleonic Wars was no more just and moral than any other, but given the entirely anti-liberal and anti-national (i.e. anti-revolutionary) purpose of its makers, it was realistic and sensible. No attempt was made to exploit the total victory over the French, who must not be provoked into a new bout of Jacobinism. The frontiers of the defeated country were left a shade better than they had been in 1789, the financial indemnity was not unreasonable, the occupation by foreign troops short-lived, and by 1818 France was readmitted as a full member of the 'concert of Europe'. (But for Napoleon's unsuccessful return in 1815 these terms would have been even more moderate.) The Bourbons were restored, but it was understood that they had to make concessions to the dangerous spirit of their subjects. The major changes of the Revolution were accepted, and that inflammatory device, a constitution, was granted to them – though of course in an extremely moderate form – under the guise of a Charter 'freely conceded' by the returned absolute monarch, Louis XVIII.

The map of Europe was redrawn without concern for either the aspirations of the peoples or the rights of the numerous princes dispossessed at one time or another by the French, but with considerable concern for the balance of the five great powers which emerged from the wars : Russia, Britain, France, Austria and Prussia. Only the first three of these really counted. Britain had no territorial ambitions on the continent, though she preferred to keep control or a protective hand over points of maritime and commercial importance. She retained Malta, the Ionian Islands and Heligoland, maintained a careful eye on Sicily, and benefited most evidently by the transfer of Norway from Denmark to Sweden, which prevented a single state from controlling the entry to the Baltic Sea, and the union of Holland and Belgium (the former Austrian Netherlands) which put the mouth of the Rhine and Scheldt in the hands of a harmless state, but one strong enough – especially when assisted by the barrier fortresses in the south – to resist the well-known French appetite for Belgium. Both arrangements were deeply unpopular with Belgians and Norwegians, and the latter only lasted until the 1830 Revolution. It was then replaced, after some Franco-British friction, by a small permanently neutralized kingdom under a prince of British choice. Outside Europe, of course, British territorial ambitions were much greater, though the total control of all seas by the British navy made it largely irrelevant whether any territory was actually under the British flag or not, except on the north-western confines of India, where only weak or chaotic principalities or regions separated the British and the Russian Empires. But the rivalry between Britain and Russia hardly affected the area which had to be resettled in 1814–15. In Europe British interests merely required no power to be too strong.

Russia, the decisive military power on land, satisfied her limited territorial ambitions by the acquisition of Finland (at the expense of Sweden), Bessarabia (at the expense of Turkey), and of the greater part of Poland, which was granted a degree of autonomy under the local faction that had always favoured a Russian alliance. (After the rising of 1830–1 this autonomy was abolished.) The remainder of Poland was distributed between Prussia and Austria, with the exception of the city republic of Cracow, which in turn did not survive the rising of 1846. For the rest Russia was content to exercise a remote, but far from ineffectual, hegemony over all absolute principalities east of France, her main interest being that revolution should be avoided. Tsar Alexander sponsored a Holy Alliance for this purpose, which Austria and Prussia joined, but Britain did not. From the British point of view this virtual Russian hegemony over most of Europe was perhaps a less than ideal arrangement, but it reflected the military realities, and could not be prevented except by allowing France a rather greater degree of power than any of her former adversaries were prepared for or at the intolerable cost of war. France's status as a great power was clearly recognized, but that was as far as anyone was as yet prepared to go.

Austria and Prussia were really great powers by courtesy only; or so it was believed – rightly – in view of Austria's well-known weakness in times of international crisis and – wrongly – in view of Prussia's collapse in 1806. Their chief function was to act as European stabilizers. Austria received back her Italian provinces plus the former Venetian territories in Italy and Dalmatia, and the protectorate over the lesser principalities of North and Central Italy, mostly ruled by Habsburg relatives (except for Piedmont-Sardinia, which swallowed the former Genoese Republic to act as a more efficient buffer between Austria and France). If 'order' was to be kept anywhere in Italy,

Austria was the policeman on duty. Since her only interest was stability – anything else risked her disintegration – she could be relied upon to act as a permanent safeguard against any attempts to unsettle the continent. Prussia benefited by the British desire to have a reasonably strong power in Western Germany, a region whose principalities had long tended to fall in with France, or which could be dominated by France, and received the Rhineland, whose immense economic potentialities aristocratic diplomats failed to allow for. She also benefited by the conflict between Britain and Russia over what the British considered excessive Russian expansion in Poland. The net result of complex negotiations punctuated with threats of war was that she yielded part of her former Polish territories to Russia, but received instead half of wealthy and industrial Saxony. In territorial and economic terms Prussia gained relatively more from the 1815 settlement than any other power, and in fact became for the first time a European great power in terms of real resources; though this did not become evident to the politicians until the 1860s. Austria, Prussia and the herd of lesser German states, whose main international function was to provide good breeding-stock for the royal houses of Europe, watched each other within the German Confederation, though Austrian seniority was not challenged. The main international function of the Confederation was to keep the lesser states outside the French orbit into which they traditionally tended to gravitate. In spite of nationalist disclaimers, they had been far from unhappy as Napoleonic satellites.

The statesmen of 1815 were wise enough to know that no settlement, however carefully carpentered, would in the long run withstand the strain of state rivalries and changing circumstance. Consequently they set out to provide a mechanism for maintaining peace – i.e. settling all outstanding problems as they arose – by means of regular congresses. It was of course understood that the crucial decisions in these were played by the 'great powers' (the term itself is an invention of this period). The 'concert of Europe' – another term which came into use then – did not correspond to a United Nations, but rather to the permanent members of the UN's Security Council. However, regular congresses were only held for a few years – from 1818, when France was officially readmitted to the concert, to 1822.

The congress system broke down, because it could not outlast the years immediately following the Napoleonic wars, when the famine of 1816–17 and business depressions maintained a lively but unjustified fear of social revolution everywhere, including Britain. After the return of economic stability about 1820 every disturbance of the 1815 settlement merely revealed the divergences between the interests of the powers. Faced with a first bout of unrest and insurrection in 1820–22 only Austria stuck to the principle that all such movements must be immediately and automatically put down in the interests of the social order (and of Austrian territorial integrity). Over Germany, Italy and Spain the three monarchies of the 'Holy Alliance' and France agreed, though the latter, exercising the job of international policeman with gusto in Spain (1823), was less interested in European stability than in widening the scope of her diplomatic and military activities, particularly in Spain, Belgium and Italy where the bulk of her foreign investments lay.[5] Britain stood out. This was partly because – especially after the flexible Canning replaced the rigid reactionary Castlereagh (1822) – it was convinced that political reforms in absolutist Europe were sooner or later inevitable, and because British politicians had no sympathy for absolutism, but also because the application of the policing-principle would merely have brought rival powers (notably France) into Latin America, which was, as we have seen, a British economic colony and a very vital one at that. Hence the British supported the independence of the Latin American states, as also did the USA in the Monroe Declaration of 1823, a manifesto which had no practical value – if anything protected Latin American independence it was the British navy – but considerable prophetic interest. Over Greece the powers were even more divided. Russia, with all its dislike of revolutions, could not but benefit from the movement of an Orthodox people, which weakened the Turks and must rely largely on Russian help. (Moreover, she had a treaty right to intervene in Turkey in defence of Orthodox Christians.) Fear of unilateral Russian intervention, philhellene pressure, economic interests and the general conviction that the disintegration of Turkey could not be prevented, but could at best be organized, eventually led the British from hostility through neutrality to an informal pro-hellenic intervention. Greece thus (1829) won her independence through both Russian and British help. The international damage was minimized by turning the country into a kingdom under one of the many available small German princes, which would not be a mere Russian satellite. But the permanence of the 1815 settlement, the congress system, and the principle of suppressing all revolutions lay in ruins.

The revolutions of 1830 destroyed it utterly, for they affected not merely small states but a great power itself, France. In effect they removed all Europe west of the Rhine from the police-operations of the Holy Alliance. Meanwhile the 'Eastern Question' – the problem of what to do about the inevitable disintegration of Turkey – turned the Balkans and the Levant into a battlefield of the powers, notably of Russia and Britain. The 'Eastern Question' disturbed the balance of forces, because everything conspired to strengthen the Russians, whose main diplomatic object, then as later, was to win control of the straits between Europe and Asia Minor which controlled her access to the Mediterranean. This was a matter not merely of diplomatic and military importance, but with the growth of Ukrainian grain exports, of economic urgency also. Britain, concerned as usual about the approaches to India, was deeply worried about the southward march of the one great power which could reasonably threaten it. The obvious policy was to shore up Turkey against Russian expansion at all costs. (This had the additional advantage of benefiting British trade in the Levant, which increased in a very satisfactory manner in this period.) Unfortunately such a policy was wholly impracticable. The Turkish Empire was by no means a helpless hulk, at least in military terms, but it was at best capable of fighting delaying actions against internal rebellion (which it could still beat fairly easily) and the combined force of Russia and an unfavourable international situation (which it could not). Nor was it yet capable of modernizing itself, or showed much readiness to do so; though the beginnings of modernization were made under Mahmoud II (1809–39) in the 1830s. Consequently only the direct diplomatic and military support of Britain (i.e. the threat of war) could prevent the steady increase in Russian influence and the collapse of Turkey under her various troubles. This made the 'Eastern Question' the most explosive issue in international affairs after the Napoleonic Wars, the only one likely to lead to a general war and the only one which in fact did so in 1854–6. However, the very situation which loaded the international dice in favour of Russia and against Britain, also made Russia inclined to compromise. She could achieve her diplomatic objectives in two ways : either by the defeat and partition of Turkey and an eventual Russian occupation of Constantinople and the Straits, or by a virtual protectorate over a weak and sub-servient Turkey. But one or the other would always be open. In other words, Constantinople was never worth a major war to the Tsar. Thus in the 1820s the Greek war fitted in with the policy of partition and occupation. Russia failed to get as much out of this as she might have hoped, but was unwilling to press her advantage too far. Instead, she negotiated an extraordinarily favourable treaty at Unkiar Skelessi (1833) with a hard-pressed Turkey, which was now keenly aware of the need for a powerful protector. Britain was out-raged: the 1830s saw the genesis of a mass Russophobia which created the image of Russia as a sort of hereditary enemy of Britain.[6] Faced with British pressure, the Russians in turn retreated, and in the 1840s reverted to proposals for the partition of Turkey.

Russo-British rivalry in the East was therefore in practice much less dangerous than the public sabre-rattling (especially in Britain) suggested. Moreover, the much greater British fear of a revival of France reduced its importance in any case. In fact the phrase 'the great game', which later came to be used for the cloak-and-dagger activities of the adventurers and secret agents of both powers who operated in the oriental no-man's land between the two empires, expresses it rather well. What made the situation really dangerous was the unpredictable course of the liberation movements within Turkey and the intervention of other powers. Of these Austria had a considerable passive interest in the matter, being itself a ram-shackle multinational empire, threatened by the movements of the very same peoples who also undermined Turkish stability – the Balkan Slavs, and notably the Serbs. However, their threat was not immediate, though it was later to provide the immediate occasion for World War I. France was more troublesome, having a long record of diplomatic and economic influence in the Levant, which it periodically attempted to restore and extend. In particular, since Napoleon's expedition to Egypt, French influence was powerful in that country, whose Pasha, Mohammed Ali, a virtually independent ruler, could more or less disrupt or hold together the Turkish Empire at will. Indeed, the crises of the Eastern Question in the 1830s (1831–3 and 1839–41) were essentially crises in Mohammed Ali's re-lations with his nominal sovereign, complicated in the latter case by French support for Egypt. However, if Russia was unwilling to make war over Constantinople, France neither could nor wanted to. There were diplomatic crises. But in the end, apart from the Crimean episode, there was no war over Turkey at any time in the nineteenth century.

It is thus clear from the course of international disputes in this period that the inflammable material in international relations was simply not explosive enough to set off a major war. Of the great powers the Austrians and the Prussians were too weak to count for much. The British were satisfied. They had by 1815 gained the most complete victory of any power in the entire history of the world, having emerged from the twenty years of war against France as the *only* industrialized economy, the *only* naval power – the British navy in 1840 had almost as many ships as all other navies put together – and virtually the only colonial power in the world. Nothing appeared to stand in the way of the only major expansionist interest of British foreign policy, the expansion of British trade and investment. Russia, while not as satiated, had only limited territorial ambitions, and nothing which could for long – or so it appeared – stand in the way of her advance. At least nothing which justified a socially dangerous general war. France alone was a 'dissatisfied' power, and had the capacity to disrupt the stable international order. But France could do so only under one condition : that she once again mobilized the revolutionary energies of Jacobinism at home and of liberalism and nationalism abroad. For in terms of orthodox great-power rivalry she had been fatally weakened. She would never again be able, as under Louis XIV or the Revolution, to fight a coalition of two or more great powers on equal terms, relying merely on her domestic population and resources. In 1780 there were 2·5 Frenchmen to every Englishman, but in 1830 less than three to every two. In 1780 there had been almost as many Frenchmen as Russians, but in 1830 there were almost half as many Russians again as French. And the pace of French economic evolution lagged fatally behind the British, the American, and very soon the German.

But Jacobinism was too high a price for any French government to pay for its international ambitions. In 1830 and again in 1848 when France overthrew its régime and absolutism was shaken or destroyed elsewhere, the powers trembled. They could have saved themselves sleepless nights. In 1830–1 the French moderates were unprepared even to lift a finger for the rebellious Poles, with whom all French (as well as European liberal) opinion sympathized. 'And

Poland?' wrote the old but enthusiastic Lafayette to Palmerston in 1831. 'What will you do, what shall we do for her?' [7] The answer was nothing. France could have readily reinforced her own resources with those of the European revolution; as indeed all revolutionaries hoped she would. But the implications of such a leap into revolutionary war frightened moderate liberal French governments as much as Metternich. No French government between 1815 and 1848 would jeopardize general peace in its own state interests.

Outside the range of the European balance, of course, nothing stood in the way of expansion and bellicosity. In fact, though extremely large, the actual territorial acquisitions of white powers were limited. The British were content to occupy points crucial to the naval control of the world and to their world-wide trading interests, such as the southern tip of Africa (taken from the Dutch during the Napoleonic wars), Ceylon, Singapore (which was founded at this period) and Hong Kong, and the exigencies of the campaign against the slave-trade – which satisfied both humanitarian opinion at home and the strategic interests of the British navy, which used it to reinforce its global monopoly – led them to maintain footholds along the African coasts. But on the whole, with one crucial exception, their view was that a world lying open to British trade and safeguarded by the British navy from unwelcome intrusion was more cheaply exploited without the administrative costs of occupation. The crucial exception was India and all that pertained to its control. India had to be held at all costs, as the most anti-colonialist free traders never doubted. Its market was of growing importance (cf. above pp. 49–51), and would certainly, it was held, suffer if India were left to herself. It was the key to the opening-up of the Far East, to the drug traffic and such other profitable activities as European businessmen wished to undertake. China was thus opened up in the Opium War of 1839–42. Consequently between 1814 and 1849 the size of the British Indian empire increased by two-thirds of the subcontinent, as the result of a series of wars against Mahrattas, Nepalese, Burmans, Rajputs, Afghans, Sindis and Sikhs, and the net of British influence was drawn more closely round the Middle East, which controlled the direct route to India, organized from 1840 by the steamers of the P & O line, supplemented by a land-crossing of the Suez Isthmus.

Though the reputation of the Russians for expansionism was far greater (at least among the British), their actual conquests were more modest. The Tsar in this period merely managed to acquire some large and empty stretches of Kirghiz steppe east of the Urals and some bitterly-contested mountain areas in the Caucasus. The USA on the other hand acquired virtually its entire west, south of the Oregon border, by insurrection and war against the hapless Mexicans. The French, on the other hand, had to confine their expansionist ambitions to Algeria, which they invaded on a trumped-up excuse in 1830 and attempted to conquer in the next seventeen years. By 1847 they had broken the back of its resistance.

One provision of the international peace settlement must, however, be mentioned separately : the abolition of the international slave-trade. The reasons for this were both humanitarian and economic : slavery was horrifying, and extremely inefficient. Moreover, from the point of view of the British who were the chief international champions of this admirable movement among the powers, the economy of 1815–48 no longer rested, like that of the eighteenth century, on the sale of men and of sugar, but on that of cotton goods. The actual abolition of slavery came more slowly (except, of course, where the French Revolution had already swept it away). The British abolished it in their colonies – mainly the West Indies – in 1834, though soon tending to replace it, where large-scale plantation agriculture survived, by the import of indentured labourers from Asia. The French did not officially abolish it again until the revolution of 1848. In 1848 there was still a very great deal of slavery, and consequently of (illegal) slave-trading left in the world.

NOTES

1 Castlereagh, *Correspondence*, Third Series, XI, p. 105.
2 Gentz, *Depêches inédites*, I, p. 371.
3 J. Richardson, *My Dearest Uncle, Leopold of the Belgians* (1961), p. 165.
4 i.e. throughout the period except for a few months in 1834–5 and in 1841–6.
5 R. Cameron, op. cit., p. 85.
6 In fact Anglo-Russian relations, based on economic complementarity, had been traditionally most amiable, and only began to deteriorate seriously after the Napoleonic wars.
7 F. Ponteil, *Lafayette et la Pologne* (1934).

6

Revolutions

Liberty, that nightingale with the voice of a giant, rouses the most profound sleepers. . . . How is it possible to think of anything today except to fight for or against freedom? Those who cannot love humanity can still be great as tyrants. But how can one be indifferent?
        Ludwig Boerne, February 14, 1831 [1]

The governments, having lost their balance, are frightened, intimidated and thrown into confusion by the cries of the intermediary class of society, which, placed between the Kings and their subjects, breaks the sceptre of the monarchs and usurps the cry of the people.
        Metternich to the Tsar, 1820 [2]

I

Rarely has the incapacity of governments to hold up the course of history been more conclusively demonstrated than in the generation after 1815. To prevent a second French Revolution, or the even worse catastrophe of a general European revolution on the French model, was the supreme object of all the powers which had just spent more than twenty years in defeating the first; even of the British, who were not in sympathy with the reactionary absolutisms which re-established themselves all over Europe and knew quite well that reforms neither could nor ought to be avoided, but who feared a new Franco-Jacobin expansion more than any other international contingency. And yet, never in European history and rarely anywhere else, has revolutionism been so endemic, so general, so likely to spread by spontaneous contagion as well as by deliberate propaganda.

There were three main waves of revolution in the western world between 1815 and 1848. (Asia and Africa as yet remained immune:

Asia's first major revolutions, the 'Indian Mutiny' and the 'Taiping Rebellion', only occurred in the 1850s.) The first occurred in 1820-4. In Europe it was confined mainly to the Mediterranean, with Spain (1820), Naples (1820) and Greece (1821) as its epicentres. Except for the Greek, all these risings were suppressed. The Spanish Revolution revived the liberation movement in Latin America, which had been defeated after an initial effort occasioned by Napoleon's conquest of Spain in 1808 and reduced to a few remote refugees and bands. The three great liberators of Spanish South America, Simon Bolivar, San Martin and Bernardo O'Higgins, established the independence respectively of 'Great Colombia' (which included the present republics of Colombia, Venezuela and Ecuador), of the Argentine but minus the inland areas of what is now Paraguay and Bolivia and the pampas across the River Plate where the cowboys of the Banda Oriental (now Uruguay) fought Argentines and Brazilians, and of Chile. San Martin, aided by the Chilean fleet under the British radical nobleman – the original of C. S. Forester's *Captain Hornblower* – Cochrane, liberated the last stronghold of Spanish power, the viceroyalty of Peru. By 1822 Spanish South America was free, and San Martin, a moderate and far-seeing man of rare self-abnegation, left it to Bolivar and republicanism and retired to Europe, living out his noble life in what was normally a refuge for debt-harried Englishmen, Boulogne-sur-Mer, on a pension from O'Higgins. Meanwhile the Spanish general sent against the surviving peasant guerillas in Mexico, Iturbide, made common cause with them under the impact of the Spanish Revolution and in 1821 permanently established Mexican independence. In 1822 Brazil quietly separated from Portugal under the regent left behind by the Portuguese royal family on its return from Napoleonic exile to Europe. The USA recognized the most important of the new states almost immediately; the British soon after, taking care to conclude commercial treaties with them, the French in effect before the 1820s were out.

The second wave of revolutionism occurred in 1829-34, and affected all Europe west of Russia and the North American continent; for the great reforming age of President Andrew Jackson (1829-37), though not directly connected with the European upheavals, must count as part of it. In Europe the overthrow of the Bourbons in France stimulated various other risings. Belgium (1830) won independence from Holland, Poland (1830-1) was suppressed only after considerable military operations, various parts of Italy and Germany were agitated, liberalism prevailed in Switzerland – a much less pacific country then than now – while a period of civil war between liberals and clericals opened in Spain and Portugal. Even Britain was affected, thanks in part to the threatened eruption of its local volcano, Ireland, which secured Catholic Emancipation (1829) and the re-opening of the reform agitation. The Reform Act of 1832 corresponds to the July Revolution of 1830 in France, and had indeed been powerfully stimulated by the news from Paris. This period is probably the only one in modern history when political events in Britain ran parallel with those on the continent, to the point where something not unlike a revolutionary situation might have developed in 1831–2 but for the restraint of both Whig and Tory parties. It is the only period in the nineteenth century when the analysis of British politics in such terms is not wholly artificial.

The revolutionary wave of 1830 was therefore a much more serious affair than that of 1820. In effect, it marks the definitive defeat of aristocratic by bourgeois power in Western Europe. The ruling class of the next fifty years was to be the 'grande bourgeoisie' of bankers, big industrialists and sometimes top civil servants, accepted by an aristocracy which effaced itself or agreed to promote primarily bourgeois policies, unchallenged as yet by universal suffrage, though harassed from outside by the agitations of the lesser or unsatisfied businessmen, the petty-bourgeoisie and the early labour movements. Its political system, in Britain, France and Belgium, was fundamentally the same : liberal institutions safeguarded against democracy by property or educational qualifications for the voters – there were, initially, only 168,000 of them in France – under a constitutional monarch; in fact, something very like the institutions of the first and most moderately bourgeois phase of the French Revolution, the constitution of 1791.[3] In the USA, however, Jacksonian democracy marks a step beyond this : the defeat of the non-democratic propertied oligarchs whose role corresponded to what was now triumphing in Western Europe, by the unlimited political democracy swept into power with the votes of the frontiersmen, the small farmers, the urban poor. It was a portentous innovation, and those thinkers of moderate liberalism, realistic enough to know that extensions of the franchise would probably be inevitable sooner or later, scrutinized it closely and anxiously; notably Alexis de Toqueville, whose *Democracy in Ame-*

rica (1835) came to gloomy conclusions about it. But as we shall see, 1830 marks an even more radical innovation in politics : the emergence of the working-class as an independent and self-conscious force in politics in Britain and France, and of nationalist movements in a great many European countries.

Behind these major changes in politics lay major changes in economic and social development. Whichever aspect of social life we survey, 1830 marks a turning-point in it; of all the dates between 1789 and 1848 it is the most obviously memorable. In the history of industrialization and urbanization on the continent and in the USA, in the history of human migrations, social and geographical, in that of the arts and or ideology, it appears with equal prominence. And in Britain and Western Europe in general it dates the beginning of those decades of crisis in the development of the new society which conclude with the defeat of the 1848 revolutions and the gigantic economic leap forward after 1851.

The third and biggest of the revolutionary waves, that of 1848, was the product of this crisis. Almost simultaneously revolution broke out and (temporarily) won in France, the whole of Italy, the German states, most of the Habsburg Empire and Switzerland (1847). In a less acute form the unrest also affected Spain, Denmark and Rumania, in a sporadic form Ireland, Greece and Britain. There has never been anything closer to the world-revolution of which the insurrectionaries of the period dreamed than this spontaneous and general conflagration, which concludes the era discussed in this volume. What had been in 1789 the rising of a single nation was now, it seemed, 'the springtime of peoples' of an entire continent.

II

Unlike the revolutions of the late eighteenth century, those of the post-Napoleonic period were intended or even planned. For the most formidable legacy of the French Revolution itself was the set of models and patterns of political upheaval which it established for the general use of rebels anywhere. This is not to say that the revolutions of 1815–48 were the mere work of a few disaffected agitators, as the spies and policemen of the period – a very fully employed species – purported to tell their superiors. They occurred because the political systems reimposed on Europe were profoundly, and in a period of rapid social change increasingly inadequate for the political conditions of the continent, and because economic and social discontents were so acute as to make a series of outbreaks virtually inevitable. But the political models created by the Revolution of 1789 served to give discontent a specific object, to turn unrest into revolution, and above all to link all Europe in a single movement – or perhaps it would be better to say current – of subversion.

There were several such models, though all stemmed from the experience of France between 1789 and 1797. They corresponded to the three main trends of post-1815 opposition : the moderate liberal (or, in social terms, that of the upper middle classes and liberal aristocracy), the radical-democratic (or, in social terms, that of the lower middle class, part of the new manufacturers, the intellectuals and the discontented gentry) and the socialist (or, in social terms, the 'labouring poor' or the new industrial working classes). Etymologically, by the way, all of them reflect the internationalism of the period : 'liberal' is Franco-Spanish in origin, 'radical' British, 'socialist' Anglo-French. 'Conservative' is also partly French in origin; another proof of the uniquely close correlation of British and continental politics in the Reform Bill period. The inspiration of the first was the Revolution of 1789–91, its political ideal the sort of quasi-British constitutional monarchy with a property-qualified, and therefore oligarchic, parliamentary system which the Constitution of 1791 introduced, and which, as we have seen, became the standard type of constitution in France, Britain and Belgium after 1830–32. The inspiration of the second could best be described as the Revolution of 1792–3, and its political ideal, a democratic republic with a bias towards a 'welfare state' and some animus against the rich, corresponds to the ideal Jacobin constitution of 1793. But just as the social groups which stood for radical democracy were a confused and oddly assorted collection, so also it is hard to attach a precise label to its French Revolutionary model. Elements of what would in 1792–3 have been called Girondism, Jacobinism and even Sansculottism were combined in it, though perhaps the Jacobinism of the constitution of 1793 represented it best. The inspiration of the third was the Revolution of the Year II and the post-Thermidorian risings, above all Babeuf's Conspiracy of the Equals, that significant rising of extreme Jacobins and early communists which marks the birth of the modern communist tradition in politics. It was the child of Sansculottism and the left wing of Robespierrism, though deriving little but its strong hatred of the middle classes and the rich from the former. Politically the Babouvist revolutionary model was in the tradition of Robespierre and Saint-Just.

From the point of view of the absolutist governments all these movements were equally subversive of stability and good order, though some seemed more consciously devoted to the propagation of chaos than others, and some more dangerous than others, because more likely to inflame the ignorant and impoverished masses. (Metternich's secret police in the 1830s therefore paid what seems to us a disproportionate amount of attention to the circulation of Lamennais' *Paroles d'un Croyant* [1834], for, in speaking the Catholic language of the unpolitical, it might appeal to subjects unaffected by frankly atheistic propaganda.)[4] In fact, however, the opposition movements were united by little more than their common detestation of the régimes of 1815 and the traditional common front of all opposed, for whatever reason, to absolute monarchy, church and aristocracy. The history of the period from 1815–48 is that of the disintegration of that united front.

III

During the Restoration period (1815–30) the blanket of reaction covered all who dissented equally, and in the darkness under it the differences between Bonapartists and Republicans, moderates and radicals, could hardly be seen. There were as yet no self-conscious working-class revolutionaries or socialists, at any rate in politics, except in Britain, where an independent proletarian trend in politics and ideology emerged under the aegis of Owenite 'co-operation' towards 1830. Most non-British mass discontent was as yet non-political, or ostensibly legitimist and clerical, a dumb protest against the new society which appeared to bring nothing but evil and chaos. With few exceptions, therefore, political opposition on the continent was confined to tiny groups of the rich or the educated, which still meant very much the same thing, for even in so powerful a stronghold of the left as the *Ecole Polytechnique* only one-third of the students – a notably subversive group – came from the petty-bourgeoisie (mostly via the lower échelons of the army and civil service) and only 0·3 per cent from the 'popular classes'. Such of the poor as were consciously on the left accepted the classical slogans of middle class revolution, though in the radical-democratic rather than the moderate version, but as yet without much more than a certain overtone of social challenge. The classical programme around which the British labouring poor rallied time and again was one of simple parliamentary reform as expressed in the 'Six Points' of the People's Charter.[5] In substance this programme was no different from the 'Jacobinism' of Paine's generation, and entirely compatible (but for its association with an increasingly self-conscious working class) with the political radicalism of the Benthamite middle-class reformers, as put forward say by James Mill. The only difference in the Restoration period was that the labouring radicals already preferred to hear it preached by men who spoke to them in their own terms – rhetorical windbags like Orator Hunt (1773–1835), or brilliant and energetic stylists like William Cobbett (1762–1835) and, of course, Tom Paine (1737–1809) – rather than by the middle class reformers themselves.

Consequently in this period neither social nor even national distinctions as yet significantly divided the European opposition into mutually incomprehensible camps. If we omit Britain and the USA, where a regular form of mass politics was already established (though in Britain it was inhibited by anti-Jacobin hysteria until the early 1820s), the political prospects looked very much alike to oppositionists in all European countries, and the methods of achieving revolution – the united front of absolutism virtually excluded peaceful reform over most of Europe – were very much the same. All revolutionaries regarded themselves, with some justification, as small élites of the emancipated and progressive operating among, and for the eventual benefit of, a vast and inert mass of the ignorant and misled common people, which would no doubt welcome liberation when it came, but could not be expected to take much part in preparing it. All of them (at any rate west of the Balkans) saw themselves fighting against a single enemy, the union of absolutist princes under the leadership of the Tsar. All of them therefore conceived of revolution as unified and indivisible : a single European phenomenon rather than an aggregate of national or local liberations. All of them tended to adopt the same type of revolutionary organization, or even the same organization : the secret insurrectionary brotherhood.

Such brotherhoods, each with a highly-coloured ritual and hierarchy derived or copied from masonic models, sprang up towards the end of the Napoleonic period. The best-known, because the most international, were the 'good cousins' or *Carbonari*. They appear to descend from masonic or similar lodges in Eastern France via anti-Bonapartist French officers in Italy, took shape in Southern Italy after 1806 and, with other similar groups, spread north and across the Mediterranean world after 1815. They, or their derivatives or parallels, are found as far afield as Russia, where such bodies bound together the *Decembrists,* who made the first insurrection of modern Russian history in 1825, but especially in Greece. The carbonarist era reached its climax in 1820–1, most of the brotherhoods being virtually destroyed by 1823. However, carbonarism (in the generic sense) persisted as the main stem of revolutionary organization, perhaps held together by the congenial task of assisting Greek freedom (philhellenism), and after the failure of the 1830 revolutions the political emigrants from Poland and Italy spread it still further afield.

Ideologically the Carbonari and their like were a mixed lot, united only by a common detestation of reaction. For obvious reasons the radicals, among them the left-wing Jacobins and Babouvists, being the most determined of revolutionaries, increasingly influenced the brotherhoods. Filippo Bounarroti, Babeuf's old comrade in arms, was their ablest and indefatigable conspirator, though his doctrines were probably very much to the left of most brethren or cousins.

Whether their efforts were ever co-ordinated to produce simultaneous international revolution is still a matter for debate, though persistent attempts to link all secret brotherhoods, at least at their highest and most initiated levels, into international super-conspiracies were made. Whatever the truth of the matter, a crop of insurrections of the Carbonarist type occurred in 1820–1. They failed utterly in France, where the political conditions for revolution were quite absent and the conspirators had no access to the only effective levers of insurrection in a situation not otherwise ripe for it, a disaffected army. The French army, then and throughout the nineteenth century, was a part of the civil service, that is to say it carried out the orders of whatever government was the official one. They succeeded completely, but temporarily in some Italian states and especially in Spain, where the 'pure' insurrection discovered its most effective formula, the military *pronunciamento*. Liberal colonels organized in their own secret officers' brotherhoods ordered their regiments to follow them into insurrection, and they did so. (The Decembrist conspirators in Russia tried to do the same with their guards regiments in 1825 but failed owing to fear of going too far.) The officers' brotherhood – often of a liberal tendency, since the new armies provided careers for non-aristocratic young men – and the *pronunciamento* henceforth became regular features of the Iberian and Latin American political scenes, and one of the most lasting and doubtful political acquisitions of the Carbonarist period. It may be observed in passing that the ritualized and hierarchical secret society, like Freemasonry, appealed very strongly to military men, for understandable reasons. The new Spanish liberal régime was overthrown by a French invasion backed by European reaction in 1823.

Only one of the 1820–2 revolutions maintained itself, thanks partly to its success in launching a genuine people's insurrection and partly to a favourable diplomatic situation : the Greek rising of 1821.[6] Greece therefore became the inspiration of international liberalism, and 'philhellenism', which included organized support for the Greeks and the departure of numerous volunteer fighters, played an analogous part in rallying the European left wing in the 1820s as the support for the Spanish Republic was to play in the later 1930s.

The revolutions of 1830 changed the situation entirely. As we have seen they were the first products of a very general period of acute and widespread economic and social unrest and rapidly quickening social change. Two chief results followed from this. The first was that mass politics and mass revolution on the 1789 model once again became possible and the exclusive reliance on secret brotherhoods therefore less necessary. The Bourbons were overthrown in Paris by a characteristic combination of crisis in what passed for the politics of the Restoration monarchy, and popular unrest induced by economic depression. So far from mass inactivity, the Paris of July 1830 showed the barricades springing up in greater number and in more places than ever before or after. (In fact 1830 made the barricade into the symbol of popular insurrection. Though its revolutionary history in Paris goes back to at least 1588, it played no important part in 1789–94.) The second result was that, with the progress of capitalism, 'the people' and 'the labouring poor' – i.e. the men who built barricades – could be increasingly identified with the new industrial proletariat as 'the working class'. A proletarian-socialist revolutionary movement therefore came into existence.

The 1830 revolutions also introduced two further modifications of left wing politics. They split moderates from radicals and they created a new international situation. In doing so they helped to split the movement not only into different social but into different national segments.

Internationally, the revolutions split Europe into two major regions. West of the Rhine they broke the hold of the united reactionary powers for good. Moderate liberalism triumphed in France, Britain and Belgium. Liberalism (of a more radical type) did not entirely triumph in Switzerland and the Iberian Peninsula, where popularly based liberal and anti-liberal catholic movements confronted each other, but the Holy Alliance could no longer intervene in these regions, as it still did everywhere east of the Rhine. In the Portuguese and Spanish civil wars of the 1830s the absolutist and moderate liberal powers each backed their side, though the liberal ones slightly more energetically, and with the assistance of some foreign radical volunteers and sympathizers, which faintly foreshadowed the philo-hispanism of the 1930s.[7] But at bottom the issue in these countries was left to be decided by the local balance of forces. That is to say it remained undecided, fluctuating between short periods of liberal victory (1833–7, 1840–3) and conservative recovery.

East of the Rhine the situation remained superficially as before 1830, for all the revolutions were suppressed, the German and Italian risings by or with the support of the Austrians, the Polish rising, much the most serious, by the Russians. Moreover, in this region the national problem continued to take precedence over all others. All peoples lived under states which were either too small or too large by national criteria : as members of disunited nations split into small principalities or none (Germany, Italy, Poland), as members of multinational empires (the Habsburg, the Russian and the Turkish), or in both capacities. We need not trouble about the Dutch and Scandinavians who, though belonging broadly to the non-absolutist zone, lived a relatively tranquil life outside the dramatic events of the rest of Europe.

A great deal remained in common between the revolutionaries of both regions, as witness the fact that the 1848 revolutions occurred in both, though not in all sections of both. However within each a marked difference in revolutionary ardour emerged. In the west Britain and Belgium ceased to follow the general revolutionary rhythm, while Spain, Portugal, and to a lesser extent Switzerland, were now involved in their endemic civil struggles, whose crises no longer coincided with those elsewhere except by accident (as in the Swiss civil war of 1847). In the rest of Europe a sharp difference between the actively 'revolutionary' nations and the passive or unenthusiastic ones emerged. Thus the secret services of the Habsburgs were constantly troubled by the problem of the Poles, the Italians and the (non-Austrian) Germans, as well as by the perennially obstreperous Hungarians, while reporting no dangers from the alpine lands or the other Slav ones. The Russians had as yet only the Poles to worry about, while the Turks could still rely on most of the Balkan Slavs to remain tranquil.

These differences reflected the variations in the tempo of evolution and in the social conditions in different countries which became increasingly evident in the 1830s and 1840s, and increasingly important for politics. Thus the advanced industrialization of Britain changed the rhythm of British politics : while most of the continent had its most acute period of social crises in 1846-8, Britain had its equivalent, a purely industrial depression, in 1841-2. (See also chapter 9.) Conversely, while in the 1820s groups of young idealists might plausibly hope that a military *putsch* could ensure the victory of freedom in Russia as in Spain or France, after 1830, the fact that the social and political conditions in Russia were far less ripe for revolution than in Spain could hardly be overlooked.

Nevertheless the problems of revolution were comparable in East and West, though not of the same kind : they led to increased tension between the moderates and the radicals. In the west the moderate liberals moved out of the common Restoration front of opposition (or out of close sympathy with it) into the world of government or potential government. Moreover, having gained power by the efforts of the radicals – for who else fought on the barricades? – they immediately betrayed them. There was to be no truck with anything as dangerous as democracy or the republic. 'There is no longer legitimate cause,' said Guizot, opposition liberal under the Restoration, Prime Minister under the July Monarchy, 'nor specious pretext for the maxims and the passions so long placed under the banner of democracy. What was formerly democracy, would now be anarchy; the democratic spirit is now and long will be nothing but the revolutionary spirit.'[8]

More than this : after a short interval of toleration and zeal, the liberals tended to moderate their enthusiasm for further reform and to suppress the radical left, and especially the working-class revolutionaries. In Britain the Owenite 'General Union' of 1834–5 and the Chartists faced the hostility both of the men who had opposed the Reform Act and of many who had advocated it. The commander of the armed forces deployed against the Chartists in 1839 sympathized with many of their demands as a middle-class radical, but he held them in check nevertheless. In France the suppression of the republican rising of 1834 marked the turning-point; in the same year the terrorization of six honest Wesleyan labourers who had tried to form an agricultural workers union (the 'Tolpuddle Martyrs') marked the equivalent offensive against the working-class movement in Britain. Radicals, republicans and the new proletarian movements therefore moved out of alignment with the liberals; the moderates, when still in opposition, were haunted by the 'democratic and social republic' which now became the slogan of the left.

In the rest of Europe no revolutions had won. The split between moderates and radicals and the emergence of the new social-revolutionary trend arose out of the inquest on defeat and the analysis of the prospects of victory. The moderates – whiggish landowners and such of the middle class as existed – placed their hopes in reform by suitably impressionable governments and in the diplomatic support of the new liberal powers. Suitably impressionable governments were rare. Savoy in Italy remained sympathetic to liberalism and increasingly attracted a body of moderate support which looked toward it for help in the country's eventual unification. A group of liberal catholics, encouraged by the curious and short-lived phenomenon of a 'liberal papacy' under the new Pope Pius IX (1846), dreamed, quite fruitlessly, of mobilizing the force of the Church for the same purpose. In Germany no state of importance was other than hostile to liberalism. This did not prevent some moderates – fewer than Prussian historical propaganda has suggested – from looking towards Prussia, which had at least a German Customs Union (1834) to its credit, and all to dream of suitably converted princes rather than barricades. In Poland, where the prospect of moderate reform with the support of the Tsar no longer encouraged the magnate faction which had always pinned its hopes to it (the Czartoryskis), moderates could at least hope against hope for Western diplomatic intervention. None of these prospects were in the least realistic, as things stood between 1830 and 1848.

The radicals were equally disappointed by the failure of the French to play the part of international liberators assigned to them by the Great Revolution and by revolutionary theory. Indeed, this disappointment, together with the growing nationalism of the 1830s (cf. Chapter 7) and the new awareness of the differences in the revolutionary prospects of each country, shattered the unified internationalism the revolutionaries had aspired to during the Restoration. The strategic prospects remained the same. A neo-Jacobin France, and perhaps (as Marx thought) a radically interventionist Britain, still remained almost indispensable for European liberation, short of the unlikely prospect of a Russian revolution.[9] Nevertheless, a nationalist reaction against the Franco-centric internationalism of the Carbonarist period gained ground, an emotion which fitted well into the new fashion of romanticism (cf. Chapter 14) which captured much of the left after 1830 : there is no sharper contrast than that between the reserved eighteenth-century music-master and rationalist Buonarroti and the woolly and ineffective self-dramatizer Giuseppe Mazzini (1805–72) who became the apostle of this anti-Carbonarist reaction, forming various national conspiracies ('Young Italy', 'Young Germany', 'Young Poland', etc.) linked together as 'Young Europe'. In one sense this decentralization of the revolutionary movement was realistic, for in 1848 the nations did indeed rise separately, spontaneously, and simultaneously. In another it was not : the stimulus for their simultaneous eruption still came from France, and French reluctance to play the role of liberator wrecked them.

Romantic or not, the radicals rejected the moderates' trust in princes and powers for practical as well as ideological reasons. The peoples must be prepared to win their liberation themselves for nobody else would do it for them; a sentiment also adapted for use by the proletarian-socialist movements at the same time. They must do so by direct action. This was still largely conceived in the Carbonarist fashion, at all events while the masses remained passive. It was consequently not very effective, though there was a world of difference between ridiculous efforts like Mazzini's attempted invasion of Savoy and the serious and continued attempts by the Polish demo-

crats to maintain or revive partisan warfare in their country after the
defeat of 1831. But the very determination of the radicals to take
power without or against the established forces introduced yet another split in their ranks. Were they or were they not prepared to do
so at the price of social revolution?

IV

The question was inflammatory everywhere except in the USA,
where nobody could any longer take or refrain from the decision to
mobilize the common people in politics, because Jacksonian democracy had already done so.[10] But, in spite of the appearance of a *Work-
ingmen's Party* in the USA in 1828–9, social revolution of the European kind was not a serious issue in that vast and rapidly expanding
country, though sectional discontents were. Nor was it inflammatory
in Latin America, where nobody in politics, except perhaps in
Mexico, dreamed of mobilizing the Indians (i.e. peasants or rural
labourers), the Negro slaves, or even the 'mixed breeds' (i.e. small
farmers, craftsmen and urban poor) for any purpose whatever. But
in Western Europe where social revolution by the urban poor was a
real possibility, and in the large European zone of agrarian revolution, the question whether or not to appeal to the masses was urgent
and unavoidable.

The growing disaffection of the poor – especially the urban poor –
in Western Europe was visible everywhere. Even in imperial Vienna
it was reflected in that faithful mirror of plebeian and petty-bourgeois attitudes, the popular suburban theatre. In the Napoleonic
period its plays had combined *Gemuetlichkeit* with a naïve Habsburg loyalty. Its greatest writer in the 1820s, Ferdinand Raimund,
filled the stage with fairy-tales, sadness, and nostalgia for the lost
innocence of the simple, traditional, uncapitalist community. But
from 1835 it was dominated by a star (Johann Nestroy) who was
primarily a social and political satirist, a bitter and dialectical wit,
a destroyer who, characteristically, became an enthusiastic revolutionary in 1848. Even German emigrants, passing through Le Havre,
gave as their reason for going to the USA, which in the 1830s began
to be the poor European's dream country, that 'there's no king
there'.[11]

Urban discontent was universal in the West. A proletarian and socialist movement was chiefly visible in the countries of the dual revolution, Britain and France (Cf. also chapter 11). In Britain it emerged round 1830 and took the extremely mature form of a mass movement of the labouring poor which regarded the whigs and liberals as its probable betrayers and the capitalists as its certain enemies. The vast movement for the *People's Charter*, which reached its peak in 1839–42 but retained great influence until after 1848, was its most formidable achievement. British socialism or 'co-operation' was very much weaker. It began impressively in 1829–34 by recruiting perhaps the bulk of working-class militants to its doctrines (which had been propagated, mainly among artisans and skilled workers, since the early 1820s), and by ambitious attempts to set up national 'general unions' of the working class which, under Owenite influence, even made attempts to establish a general co-operative economy bypassing the capitalist. Disappointment after the Reform Act of 1832 caused the bulk of the labour movement to look towards these Owenites, co-operators, primitive revolutionary syndicalists, etc., for leadership, but their failure to develop an effective political strategy and leadership, and systematic offensive by employers and government, destroyed the movement in 1834–6. This failure reduced the socialists to propagandist and educational groups standing somewhat outside the main stream of labour agitation or to pioneers of the more modest consumers' co-operation, in the form of the co-operative shop, pioneered in Rochdale, Lancashire, from 1844. Hence the paradox that the peak of the revolutionary mass movement of the British labouring poor, Chartism, was ideologically somewhat less advanced, though politically more mature, than the movement of 1829–34. But this did not save it from defeat through the political incapacity of its leaders, local and sectional differences, and an inability for concerted national action other than the preparation of monster petitions.

In France no comparable mass movement of the industrial labouring poor existed : the militants of the French 'working-class movement' in 1830–48 were in the main old-fashioned urban craftsmen and journeymen, mostly in the skilled trades, and centres of traditional domestic and putting-out industry such as the Lyons silk trade. (The arch-revolutionary *canuts* of Lyons were not even wage-workers but a form of small masters.) Moreover, the various brands of the new 'utopian' socialism – the followers of Saint-Simon, Fourier, Cabet and the rest were uninterested in political agitation, though in fact their little conventicles and groups – notably the Fourierists – were to act as nuclei of working-class leadership and mobilizers of mass action at the outset of the 1848 revolution. On the other hand France possessed the powerful and politically highly developed tradition of left wing Jacobinism and Babouvism, a crucial part of which after 1830 became communist. Its most formidable leader was Auguste Blanqui (1805–1881), a pupil of Buonarroti.

In terms of social analysis and theory Blanquism had little to contribute to socialism except the assertion of its necessity, and the decisive observation that the proletariat of exploited wage-workers was to be its architect and the middle class (no longer the upper) its main enemy. In terms of political strategy and organization, it adapted the traditional organ of revolutionism, the secret conspiratorial brotherhood to proletarian conditions – incidentally stripping it of much of its Restoration ritualism and fancy dress – and the traditional method of Jacobin revolution, insurrection and centralized popular dictatorship to the cause of the workers. From the Blanquists (who in turn derived it from Saint-Just, Babeuf and Buonarroti) the modern socialist revolutionary movement acquired the conviction that its object must be the seizure of political power, followed by the 'dictatorship of the proletariat'; the term is of Blanquist coinage. The weakness of Blanquism was in part that of the French working class. In the absence of a large mass movement it remained, like its Carbonarist predecessors, an élite which planned its insurrections somewhat in the void, and therefore often failed – as in the attempted rising of 1839.

Working class or urban revolution and socialism therefore appeared very real dangers in Western Europe, though in fact in the most industrialized countries like Britain and Belgium, government and employing classes regarded them with relative – and justified – placidity : there is no evidence that the British Government was seriously troubled by the threat to public order of the huge, but divided, ill-organized, and abysmally led Chartists.[12] On the other hand, the rural population offered little to encourage the revolutionaries or frighten the rulers. In Britain the government had a moment's panic when a wave of rioting and machine-breaking rapidly propagated itself among the starving farm-labourers of Southern and Eastern England at the end of 1830. The influence of the French

Revolution of July 1830 was detected in this spontaneous, wide-spread, but rapidly subsiding 'last labourers' revolt',[13] which was punished with far greater savagery than the Chartist agitation; as was perhaps to be expected in view of the much tenser political situation during the Reform Bill period. However, agrarian unrest soon relapsed into politically less frightening forms. In the rest of the economically advanced areas, except to some extent in Western Germany, no serious agrarian revolutionism was expected or envisaged; and the entirely urban outlook of most revolutionaries held little attraction for the peasantry. In all Western Europe (leaving aside the Iberian peninsula) only Ireland contained a large and endemic movement of agrarian revolution, organized in secret and widespread terrorist societies such as the *Ribbonmen* and *Whiteboys*. But socially and politically Ireland belonged to a different world from its neighbour.

The issue of social revolution therefore split the middle class radicals, i.e. those groups of discontented businessmen, intellectuals and others who still found themselves in opposition to the moderate liberal governments of 1830. In Britain it divided the 'middle class radicals' into those who were prepared to support Chartism, or to make common cause with it (as in Birmingham or in the Quaker Joseph Sturge's Complete Suffrage Union) and those who insisted, like the Manchester Anti-Corn-Law Leaguers, on fighting both aristocracy and Chartism. The intransigents prevailed, confident in the greater homogeneity of their class consciousness, in their money, which they spent in vast quantities, and in the effectiveness of the propagandist and advertising organization which they set up. In France the weakness of the official opposition to Louis Philippe and the initiative of the revolutionary Paris masses swung the decision the other way. 'So we have become republicans again,' wrote the radical poet Béranger after the February Revolution of 1848. 'Perhaps it has been a little too soon and a little too fast. . . . I should have preferred a more cautious procedure, but we have chosen neither the hour nor marshalled the forces, nor determined the route of the march.'[14] The break of the middle class radicals with the extreme left here was to occur only after the revolution.

For the discontented petty-bourgeoisie of independent artisans, shopkeepers, farmers and the like who (together with a mass of skilled workers) probably formed the main corps of Radicalism in Western

Europe, the problem was less taxing. As little men they sympathized with the poor against the rich, as men of small property with the rich against the poor. But the division of their sympathies led them into hesitation and doubt rather than into a major change of political allegiance. When it came to the point they were, however feebly, Jacobins, republicans and democrats. A hesitant component of all popular fronts, they were nevertheless an invariable component, until potential expropriators were actually in power.

V

In the rest of revolutionary Europe, where the discontented lesser country gentry and the intellectuals formed the core of radicalism, the problem was far more serious. For the masses were the peasantry; often a peasantry belonging to a different nation from its landlords and townsmen – Slavonic and Rumanian in Hungary, Ukrainian in Eastern Poland, Slavonic in parts of Austria. And the poorest and least efficient landlords, who could least afford to abandon the status which gave them their income, were often the most radically nationalist. Admittedly while the bulk of the peasantry remained sunk in ignorance and political passivity, the question of its support for the revolution was less immediate than it might have been; but not less burning. And in the 1840s even this passivity could no longer be taken for granted. The serf rising in Galicia in 1846 was the greatest jacquerie since the days of the French Revolution of 1789.

Burning as the question was, it was also to some extent rhetorical. Economically, the modernization of backward areas, such as those of Eastern Europe, demanded agrarian reform; or at the very least the abolition of serfdom which still persisted in the Austrian, Russian and Turkish empires. Politically, once the peasantry reached the threshold of activity, nothing was more certain than that something would have to be done to meet its demands, at any rate in countries where revolutionaries fought against foreign rule. For if they did not attract the peasants to their side, the reactionaries would; legitimate kings, emperors and churches in any case held the tactical advantage that traditionalist peasants trusted them more than lords and were still in principle prepared to expect justice from them. And monarchs were perfectly prepared to play peasants against gentry, if necessary : the Bourbons of Naples had done so without hesitation against the Neapolitan Jacobins in 1799. 'Long live Radetsky,' the Lombard peasants were to shout in 1848, cheering the Austrian general who overthrew the nationalist rising : 'death to the lords'.[15] The question before the radicals in under-developed countries was not whether to seek alliance with the peasantry, but whether they would succeed in obtaining it.

The radicals in such countries therefore fell into two groups : the democrats and the extreme left. The former (represented in Poland by the Polish Democratic Society, in Hungary by Kossuth's followers, in Italy by the Mazzinians) recognized the need to attract the peasantry to the revolutionary cause, where necessary by the abolition of serfdom and the grant of property rights to small cultivators, but hoped for some sort of peaceful coexistence between a nobility voluntarily renouncing its feudal rights – not without compensation – and a national peasantry. However, where the wind of peasant rebellion had not reached gale force or the fear of its exploitation by princes was not great (as in much of Italy) the democrats in practice neglected to provide themselves with a concrete agrarian, or indeed with any social programme, preferring to preach the generalities of political democracy and national liberation.

The extreme left frankly conceived of the revolutionary struggle as one of the masses against both foreign rulers and domestic exploiters. Anticipating the national-cum-social revolutionaries of our century, they doubted the capacity of the nobility and of the weak middle class, with its frequent vested interest in imperial rule, to lead the new nation into independence and modernization. Their own programme was thus powerfully influenced by the nascent socialism of the west, though, unlike most pre-Marxist 'utopian' socialists, they were political revolutionaries as well as social critics. The short-lived Republic of Cracow in 1846 thus abolished all peasant burdens and promised its urban poor 'national workshops'. The most advanced of the south Italian Carbonari adopted the Babouvist-Blanquist platform. Except perhaps in Poland this current of thought was relatively weak, and its influence was further diminished by the failure of movements substantially composed of schoolboys, students, declassed intellectuals of gentry or plebeian origins and a few idealists to mobilize the peasantry which they so earnestly sought to recruit.[16]

The radicals of under-developed Europe therefore never effectively solved their problem, partly through the reluctance of their supporters to make adequate or timely concessions to the peasantry, partly through the political immaturity of the peasants. In Italy the revolutions of 1848 were conducted substantially over the heads of an inactive rural population, in Poland (where the rising of 1846 had rapidly developed into a peasant rebellion against the Polish gentry, encouraged by the Austrian government) no revolution took place at all in 1848, except in Prussian Poznania. Even in the most advanced of revolutionary nations, Hungary, the qualifications of a gentry-operated land reform were to make it impossible fully to mobilize the peasantry for the war of national liberation. And over most of Eastern Europe the Slav peasants in imperial soldiers' uniforms were the effective suppressors of German and Magyar revolutionaries.

VI

Nevertheless, though now divided by differences in local conditions, by nationality, and by class, the revolutionary movements of 1830–48 maintained a good deal in common. In the first place, as we have seen, they remained to a great extent minority organizations of middle class and intellectual conspirators, often in exile, or confined to the relatively small world of the literate. (When revolutions broke out, of course, the common people came into its own. Of the 350 dead in the Milan insurrection of 1848 only a dozen or so were students, clerks or from landowning families. Seventy-four were women and children and the rest artisans or workmen.) [17] In the second place, they retained a common pattern of political procedure, strategic and tactical ideas, etc. derived from the experience and heritage of the Revolution of 1789, and a strong sense of international unity.

The first factor is easily explicable. A long-established tradition of mass agitation and organization as part of normal (and not immediately pre- or post-revolutionary) social life hardly existed except in the USA and Britain, or perhaps Switzerland, the Netherlands and Scandinavia; nor were the conditions for it present outside Britain and the USA. For a newspaper to have a weekly circulation of over 60,000 and a much vaster number of readers, like the Chartist *Northern Star* in April 1839,[18] was altogether unthinkable elsewhere; 5,000 seems to have been a more common circulation for newspapers, though semi-official ones or – from the 1830s – entertainment journals could probably exceed 20,000 in a country like France.[19] Even in constitutional countries like Belgium and France, the legal agitation of the extreme left was only intermittently allowed, and its organizations were often illegal. Consequently, while a simulacrum of democratic politics existed among the restricted classes who formed the *pays légal*, some of which had its repercussions among the unprivileged, the fundamental devices of mass politics – public campaigns to put pressure on governments, mass organizations, petitions, itinerant oratory addressed to the common people and the like – were only rarely possible. Outside Britain nobody would have seriously thought of achieving universal parliamentary franchise by a mass campaign of signatures and public demonstrations or to abolish an unpopular law by a mass advertising and pressure campaign, as Chartism and the Anti-Corn-Law League tried respectively to do. Major constitutional changes mean a break with legality, and so *a fortiori* did major social changes.

Illegal organizations are naturally smaller than legal ones, and their social composition is far from representative. Admittedly the evolution of general Carbonarist secret societies into proletarian-revolutionary ones, such as the Blanquist, brought about a relative decline in their middle-class and a rise in their working-class membership, i.e. in the number of craftsmen and skilled journeymen. The Blanquist organizations of the later 1830s and 1840s were said to be strongly lower-class.[20] So was the German League of the Outlaws (which in turn became the League of the Just and the Communist League of Marx and Engels), whose backbone consisted of expatriate German journeymen. But this was a rather exceptional case. The bulk of the conspirators consisted, as before, of men from the professional classes or the lesser gentry, students and schoolboys, journalists and the like; though perhaps with a smaller component (outside the Iberian countries) of young officers than in the Carbonarist heyday.

Moreover, up to a point the entire European and American left continued to fight the same enemies, to share common aspirations and a common programme. 'We renounce, repudiate and condemn all hereditary inequalities and distinctions of "caste",' wrote the Fraternal Democrats (composed of 'natives of Great Britain, France, Germany, Scandinavia, Poland, Italy, Switzerland, Hungary and other countries') in their Declaration of Principles, 'consequently we regard kings, aristocracies and classes monopolizing privileges in virtue of their possession of property, as usurpers. Governments elected by and responsible to the entire people is our political creed.'[21] What radical or revolutionary would have disagreed with them? If bourgeois, he would favour a state in which property, while not enjoying political privilege as such (as in the constitutions of 1830–2 which made the vote dependent on a property qualification), would have economic elbow-room; if socialist or communist, that it must be socialized. No doubt the point would be reached – in Britain it already had by the time of Chartism – when the former allies against king, aristocracy and privilege would turn against each other and the fundamental conflict would be that between bourgeois and workers. But before 1848 that point had not yet been reached anywhere else. Only the *grande bourgeoisie* of a few countries was as yet officially in the government camp. Even the most conscious proletarian communists still saw themselves and acted as the extreme left wing of the general radical and democratic movement; and normally regarded the achievement of the 'bourgeois-democratic' republic as the indispensable preliminary for the further advance of socialism. Marx and Engels' Communist Manifesto is a declaration of future war against the bourgeoisie but – at least for Germany – of present alliance. The most advanced German middle class, the Rhineland industrialists, not merely asked Marx to edit their radical organ the *Neue Rheinische Zeitung* in 1848; he accepted and edited it not simply as a communist organ, but as the spokesman and leader of German radicalism.

More than a merely common outlook, the European left shared a common picture of what the revolution would be like, derived from 1789 with touches of 1830. There would be a crisis in the political affairs of the state, leading to insurrection. (The Carbonarist idea of an élite *putsch* or rising organized without reference to the general political or economic climate was increasingly discredited, except in Iberian countries, notably by the abject failure of various attempts of the kind in Italy – e.g. in 1833–4, 1841–5 – and of *putsches* such as that attempted by Napoleon's nephew Louis Napoleon in 1836.) Barricades would go up in the capital; the revolutionaries would make for the palace, parliament or (among extremists who recalled 1792) the city hall, hoist whichever tricolour was theirs and proclaim the republic and a Provisional Government. The country would then accept the new régime. The decisive importance of the capitals was universally accepted, though it was not until after 1848 that governments began to replan them in order to facilitate the operation of troops against revolutionaries.

A National Guard of armed citizens would be organized, democratic elections for a Constituent Assembly would be held, the provisional government would become a definitive government and the new Constitution would come into force. The new régime would then give brotherly aid to the other revolutions which, almost certainly, would have also occurred. What happened thereafter belonged to the post-revolutionary era, for which the events of France in 1792–9 also provided fairly concrete models of what to do and what to avoid. The minds of the most Jacobin among the revolutionaries would naturally turn readily to the problems of safeguarding the revolution against overthrow by foreign or domestic counter-revolutionaries. On the whole it can also be said that the more left wing the politician, the more he was likely to favour the (Jacobin) principle of centralization and a strong executive against the (Girondin) principles of federalism, decentralization or the division of powers.

This common outlook was strongly reinforced by the strong tradition of internationalism, which survived even among those separatist nationalists who refused to accept the automatic leadership of any country – i.e. of France, or rather Paris. The cause of all nations was the same, even without considering the obvious fact that the liberation of most European ones appeared to imply the defeat of Tsarism. National prejudices (which had, as the Fraternal Democrats held, 'been, in all ages, taken advantage of by the people's oppressors') would disappear in the world of fraternity. Attempts to set up international revolutionary bodies never ceased, from Mazzini's *Young Europe* – designed as a counter to the old Carbonarist-masonic internationals – to the *Democratic Association for the Unification of All Countries* of 1847. Among the nationalist movements such internationalism tended to decline in importance, as countries won their independence and the relations between peoples proved to be less fraternal than had been supposed. Among the social-revolutionary ones, increasingly accepting the proletarian orientation, it grew in strength. The *International*, as an organization and as a song, was to become an integral part of socialist movements later in the century.

One accidental factor which reinforced the internationalism of 1830–48 was exile. Most political militants of the continental left were expatriates for some time, many for decades, congregating in the relatively few zones of refuge or asylum : France, Switzerland, to a lesser extent Britain and Belgium. (The Americas were too far for temporary political emigration, though they attracted some.) The largest contingent of such exiles was that of the great Polish emigration of between five and six thousand,[22] driven from their country by the defeat of 1831, the next largest the Italian and German (both reinforced by the important non-political emigré or locally settled communities of their nationalities in other countries). By the 1840s a small colony of Russian intellectuals of wealth had also absorbed Western revolutionary ideas on study tours abroad or sought an atmosphere more congenial than that of Nicholas I's combination of the dungeon and the drill-square. Students and wealthy residents from small or backward countries were also to be found in the two cities which formed the cultural suns of Eastern Europe, Latin America and the Levant : Paris and, a long way after, Vienna.

In the centres of refuge the emigrés organized, argued, quarrelled, frequented and denounced one another, and planned the liberation of their countries, or in the meantime that of other countries. The Poles and to a lesser extent the Italians (Garibaldi in exile fought for the liberty of various Latin-American countries) became in effect international corps of revolutionary militants. No rising or war of liberation anywhere in Europe between 1831 and 1871 was to be complete without its contingent of Polish military experts or fighters; not even (it has been held) the only armed rising in Britain during the Chartist period, in 1839. However, they were not the only ones. A fairly typical expatriate liberator of peoples, Harro Harring of (as he claimed) Denmark, successively fought for Greece (in 1821), for Poland (in 1830-1), as member of Mazzini's *Young Germany*, *Young Italy* and the somewhat more shadowy *Young Scandinavia*, across the oceans in the struggle for a projected United States of Latin America and in New York, before returning for the 1848 Revolution; meanwhile publishing works with such titles as 'The Peoples', 'Drops of Blood', 'Words of a Man' and 'Poetry of a Scandinavian'.[23]

A common fate and a common ideal bound these expatriates and travellers together. Most of them faced the same problems of poverty and police surveillance, of illegal correspondence, espionage and the ubiquitous agent-provocateur. Like fascism in the 1930s, absolutism in the 1830s and 1840s bound its common enemies together. Then as a century later communism, which purported to explain and provide solutions for the social crisis of the world, attracted the militant and the mere intellectually curious to its capital – Paris – thus adding a serious attraction to the lighter charms of the city. ('If it were not for the French women, life would not be worth living. *Mais tant qu'il y a des grisettes, va!*)[24] In these centres of refuge the emigrés formed that provisional, but so often permanent community of exile while they planned the liberation of mankind. They did not always like or approve of each other, but they knew each other, and that their fate was the same. Together they prepared for and awaited the European revolution which came– and failed – in 1848.

NOTES

1 Luding Boerne, *Gesammelte Schriften*, III, pp. 130–1.
2 *Memoirs of Prince Metternich*, III, p. 468.
3 Only in practice with a much more restricted franchise than in 1791.
4 Vienna, Verwaltungsarchiv : Polizeihofstelle H 136/1834, *passim*.
5 (1) Manhood Suffrage, (2) Vote by Ballot, (3) Equal Electoral Districts, (4) Payment of Members of Parliament, (5) Annual Parliaments, (6) Abolition of property qualification for candidates.
6 For Greece see also chapter 7.
7 Englishmen had been interested in Spain by the liberal Spanish refugees with whom they came into contact in the 1820s. British anti-catholicism also played a certain part in turning the striking vogue for Spain – immortalized in George Borrow's *Bible in Spain* and Murray's famous *Handbook of Spain* – into an anti-Carlist direction.
8 Guizot, *Of Democracy in Modern Societies* (London 1838), p. 32.
9 The most lucid discussion of this general revolutionary strategy is contained in Marx's articles in the *Neue Rheinische Zeitung* during the 1848 revolution.
10 Except, of course, for the slaves of the South.
11 M. L. Hansen, *The Atlantic Migration* (1945), p. 147.
12 F. C. Mather, The Government and the Chartists, in A. Briggs ed. *Chartist Studies* (1959).
13 cf. *Parliamentary Papers*, XXXIV, of 1834; answers to question 53 (causes and consequences of the agricultural riots and burning of 1830 and 1831), e.g. Lambourn, Speen (Berks), Steeple Claydon (Bucks), Bonington (Glos), Evenley (Northants).
14 R. Dautry, *1848 et la Deuxième République* (1848), p. 80.
15 St. Kiniewicz, La Pologne et l'Italie à l'époque du printemps des peuples. *La Pologne au Xe Congrés International Historique*, 1955, p. 245.

16 However, in a few areas of small peasant property, tenancy or share-cropping, such as the Romagna, or parts of South-western Germany, radicalism of the Mazzinian type succeeded in establishing a fair degree of mass support in and after 1848.

17 D. Cantimori in F. Fejtö ed., *The Opening of an Era: 1848* (1948), p. 119.

18 D. Read, *Press and People* (1961), p. 216.

19 Irene Collins, *Government and Newspaper Press in France, 1814–81* (1959).

20 cf. E. J. Hobsbawm, *Primitive Rebels* (1959), pp. 171–2; V. Volguine, Les idées socialiste et communistes dans les sociétés secrètes (*Questions d'Histoire*, II, 1954, pp. 10–37); A. B. Spitzer, *The Revolutionary Theories of Auguste Blanqui* (1957), pp. 165–6.

21 G. D. H. Cole and A. W. Filson, *British Working Class Movements. Select Documents* (1951), p. 402.

22 J. Zubrzycki, Emigration from Poland, *Population Studies*, VI, (1952–3), p. 248.

23 He was unlucky enough to attract the hostility of Marx, who spared some of his formidable gifts of satirical invective to preserve him for posterity, in his *Die Grossen Maenner des Exils* (Marx-Engels *Werke*, Berlin 1960, vol. 8, 292–8).

24 Engels to Marx, March 9, 1847.

7

Nationalism

> *Every people has its special mission, which will co-*
> *operate towards the fulfilment of the general mission of*
> *humanity. That mission constitutes its* nationality.
> *Nationality is sacred.*
>
> Act of Brotherhood of *Young Europe, 1834*

> *The day will come . . . when sublime Germania shall*
> *stand on the bronze pedestal of liberty and justice, bear-*
> *ing in one hand the torch of enlightenment, which shall*
> *throw the beam of civilization into the remotest corners of*
> *the earth, and in the other the arbiter's balance. The*
> *people will beg her to settle their disputes; those very*
> *people who now show us that might is right, and kick us*
> *with the jackboot of scornful contempt.*
>
> From Siebenpfeiffer's speech at the Hambach Festi-
> val, 1832

I

After 1830, as we have seen, the general movement in favour of revolution split. One product of this split deserves special attention : the self-consciously nationalist movements.

The movements which best symbolize this development are the 'Youth' movements founded or inspired by Giuseppe Mazzini shortly after the 1830 revolution : *Young Italy, Young Poland, Young Switzerland, Young Germany* and *Young France* (1831–6) and the analogous *Young Ireland* of the 1840s, the ancestor of the only last- ing and successful revolutionary organization on the model of the early nineteenth-century conspiracy brotherhoods, the Fenians or Irish Republican Brotherhood, better known through its executive arm of the Irish Republican Army. In themselves these movements were of no great importance; the mere presence of Mazzini would have been enough to ensure their total ineffectiveness. Symbolically they are of extreme importance, as is indicated by the adoption in subsequent nationalist movements of such labels as 'Young Czechs' or 'Young Turks'. They mark the disintegration of the European revolutionary movement into national segments. Doubtless each of these segments had much the same political programme, strategy and tactics as the others, and even much the same flag – almost invariably a tricolour of some kind. Its members saw no contradiction between their own demands and those of other nations, and indeed envisaged a brotherhood of all, simultaneously liberating themselves. On the other hand each now tended to justify its primary concern with its own nation by adopting the role of a Messiah for all. Through Italy (according to Mazzini), through Poland (according to Mickiewicz) the suffering peoples of the world were to be led to freedom; an attitude readily adaptable to conservative or indeed imperialist policies, as witness the Russian Slavophiles with their championship of Holy Russia, the Third Rome, and the Germans who were subsequently to tell the world at some length that it would be healed by the German spirit. Admittedly this ambiguity of nationalism went back to the French Revolution. But in those days there had been only *one* great and revolutionary nation and it made sense (as indeed it still did) to regard it as the headquarters of all revolutions, and the necessary prime mover in the liberation of the world. To look to Paris was rational; to look to a vague 'Italy', 'Poland' or 'Germany' (represented in practice by a handful of conspirators and emigrés) made sense only for Italians, Poles and Germans.

If the new nationalism had been confined only to the membership of the national-revolutionary brotherhoods, it would not be worth much more attention. However, it also reflected much more powerful forces, which were emerging into political consciousness in the 1830s as the result of the double revolution. The most immediately powerful of these were the discontent of the lesser landowners or gentry and the emergence of a national middle and even lower middle class in numerous countries; the spokesmen for both being largely professional intellectuals.

The revolutionary role of the lesser gentry is perhaps best illustrated in Poland and Hungary. There, on the whole, the large landed magnates had long found it possible and desirable to make terms with absolutism and foreign rule. The Hungarian magnates were in general Catholic and had long been accepted as pillars of Viennese court society; very few of them were to join the revolution of 1848. The memory of the old *Rzeczpospolita* made even Polish magnates nationally minded; but the most influential of their quasi-national parties, the Czartoryski connection, now operating from the luxurious emigration of the Hotel Lambert in Paris, had always favoured the alliance with Russia and continued to prefer diplomacy to revolt. Economically they were wealthy enough to afford what they needed, short of really titanic dissipation, and even to invest enough in the improvement of their estates to benefit from the economic expansion of the age, if they chose to. Count Széchenyi, one of the few moderate liberals from this class and a champion of economic improvement, gave a year's income for the new Hungarian Academy of Sciences – some 60,000 florins. There is no evidence that his standard of life suffered from such disinterested generosity. On the other hand the numerous gentlemen who had little but their birth to distinguish them from other impoverished farmers – one in eight of the Hungarian population claimed gentlemanly status – had neither the money to make their holdings profitable nor the inclination to compete with Germans and Jews for middle class wealth. If they could not live decently on their rents, and a degenerate age deprived them of a soldier's chances, then they might, if not too ignorant, consider the law, administration or some intellectual position; but no bourgeois activity. Such gentlemen had long been the stronghold of opposition to absolutism, foreigners and magnate rule in their respective countries, sheltering (as in Hungary) behind the dual buttress of Calvinism and county organization. It was natural that their opposition, discontent, and aspiration for more jobs for local gentlemen should now fuse with nationalism.

The national business classes which emerged in this period were, paradoxically, a rather less nationalist element. Admittedly in disunited Germany and Italy the advantages of a large unified national market made sense. The author of *Deutschland über Alles* apostrophized

> Ham and scissors, boots and garters,
> Wool and soap and yarn and beer,[1]

because they had achieved, what the spirit of nationality had been unable to, a genuine sense of national unity through customs union.

However there is little evidence that, say, the shippers of Genoa (who were later to provide much of the financial backing for Garibaldi) preferred the possibilities of a national Italian market to the larger prosperity of trading all over the Mediterranean. And in the large multinational empires the industrial or trading nuclei which grew up in particular provinces might grumble about discrimination, but at bottom clearly preferred the great markets open to them now to the little ones of future national independence. The Polish industrialists, with all Russia at their feet, took little part as yet in Polish nationalism. When Palacky claimed on behalf of the Czechs that 'if Austria did not exist, it would have to be invented', he was not merely calling on the monarchy's support against the Germans, but also expressing the sound economic reasoning of the economically most advanced sector of a large and otherwise backward empire. Business interests were sometimes at the head of nationalism, as in Belgium, where a strong pioneer industrial community regarded itself, with doubtful reason, as disadvantaged under the rule of the powerful Dutch merchant community, to which it had been hitched in 1815. But this was an exceptional case.

The great proponents of middle-class nationalism at this stage were the lower and middle professional, administrative and intellectual strata, in other words the *educated* classes. (These are not, of course, distinct from the business classes, especially in backward countries where estate administrators, notaries, lawyers and the like are among the key accumulators of rural wealth.) To be precise, the advance guard of middle-class nationalism fought its battle along the line which marked the educational progress of large numbers of 'new men' into areas hitherto occupied by a small élite. The progress of schools and universities measures that of nationalism, just as schools and especially universities became its most conscious champions : the conflict of Germany and Denmark over Schleswig-Holstein in 1848 and again in 1864 was anticipated by the conflict of the universities of Kiel and Copenhagen on this issue in the middle 1840s.

That progress was striking, though the total number of the 'educated' remained small. The number of pupils in the French state *lycées* doubled between 1809 and 1842, and increased with particular rapidity under the July monarchy, but even so in 1842 it was only just under 19,000. (The total of all children receiving secondary education [2] then was about 70,000.) Russia, around 1850, had some

20,000 secondary pupils out of a total population of sixty-eight millions.[3] The number of university students was naturally even smaller, though it was rising. It is difficult to realize that the Prussian academic youth which was so stirred by the idea of liberation after 1806 consisted in 1805 of not much more than 1,500 young men all told; that the *Polytechnique*, the bane of the post-1815 Bourbons, trained a total of 1,581 young men in the entire period from 1815 to 1830, i.e. an annual intake of about one hundred. The revolutionary prominence of the students in the 1848 period makes us forget that in the whole continent of Europe, including the unrevolutionary British Isles, there were probably not more than 40,000 university students in all.[4] Still their numbers rose. In Russia it rose from 1,700 in 1825 to 4,600 in 1848. And even if they did not, the transformation of society and the universities (cf. chapter 15) gave them a new consciousness of themselves as a social group. Nobody remembers that in 1789 there were something like 6,000 students in the University of Paris, because they played no independent part in the Revolution.[5] But by 1830 nobody could possibly overlook such a number of young academics.

Small élites can operate in foreign languages; once the cadre of the educated becomes large enough, the national language imposes itself (as witness the struggle for linguistic recognition in the Indian states since the 1940s). Hence the moment when textbooks or newspapers in the national language are first written, or when that language is first used for some official purpose, measures a crucial step in national evolution. The 1830s saw this step taken over large areas of Europe. Thus the first major Czech works on astronomy, chemistry, anthropology, mineralogy and botany were written or completed in this decade; and so, in Rumania, were the first school textbooks substituting Rumanian for the previously current Greek. Hungarian was adopted instead of Latin as the official language of the Hungarian Diet in 1840, though Budapest University, controlled from Vienna, did not abandon Latin lectures until 1844. (However, the struggle for the use of Hungarian as an official language had gone on intermittently since 1790.) The Zagreb Gai published his *Croatian Gazette* (later: *Illyrian National Gazette*) from 1835 in the first literary version of what had hitherto been merely a complex of dialects. In countries which had long possessed an official national language, the change cannot be so easily measured, though it is interesting that after 1830 the number of German books published in Germany (as against Latin and French titles) for the first time consistently exceeded 90 per cent, the number of French ones after 1820 fell below 4 per cent.[6, 7] More generally the expansion of publishing gives us a comparable indication. Thus in Germany the number of books published remained much the same in 1821 as in 1800 – about 4,000 titles a year; but by 1841 it had risen to 12,000 titles.[8]

Of course the great mass of Europeans, and of non-Europeans, remained uneducated. Indeed, with the exception of the Germans, the Dutch, Scandinavians, Swiss and the citizens of the USA, no people can in 1840 be described as literate. Several can be described as totally illiterate, like the Southern Slavs, who had less than one-half per cent literacy in 1827 (even much later only one per cent of Dalmatian recruits to the Austrian army could read and write) or the Russians who had two per cent (1840), and a great many as almost illiterate, like the Spaniards, the Portuguese (who appear to have had barely 8,000 children in all *at school* after the Peninsular War) and, except for the Lombards and Piedmontese, the Italians. Even Britain, France and Belgium were 40 to 50 per cent illiterate in the 1840s.[9] Illiteracy is no bar to political consciousness, but there is, in fact, no evidence that nationalism of the modern kind was a powerful mass force except in countries already transformed by the dual revolution : in France, in Britain, in the USA and – because it was an economic and political dependency of Britain – in Ireland.

To equate nationalism with the literate class is not to claim that the mass of, say, Russians, did not consider themselves 'Russian' when confronted with somebody or something that was not. However, for the masses in general the test of nationality was still religion : the Spaniard was defined by being Catholic, the Russian by being Orthodox. However, though such confrontations were becoming rather more frequent, they were still rare, and certain kinds of national feeling such as the Italian, were as yet wholly alien to the great mass of the people, which did not even speak the national literary language but mutually almost incomprehensible *patois*. Even in Germany patriotic mythology has greatly exaggerated the degree of national feeling against Napoleon. France was extremely popular in Western Germany, especially among soldiers, whom it employed freely.[10] Populations attached to the Pope or the Emperor might express resentment against their enemies, who happened to be the

French, but this hardly implied any feelings of national consciousness, let alone any desire for a national state. Moreover, the very fact that nationalism was represented by middle class and gentry was enough to make the poor man suspicious. The Polish radical-democratic revolutionaries tried earnestly – as did the more advanced of the South Italian Carbonari and other conspirators – to mobilize the peasantry even to the point of offering agrarian reform. Their failure was almost total. The Galician peasants in 1846 opposed the Polish revolutionaries even though these actually proclaimed the abolition of serfdom, perferring to massacre gentlemen and trust to the Emperor's officials.

The uprooting of peoples, which is perhaps the most important single phenomenon of the nineteenth century, was to break down this deep, age-old and localized traditionalism. Yet over most of the world up to the 1820s hardly anybody as yet migrated or emigrated, except under the compulsion of armies and hunger, or in the traditionally migratory groups such as the peasants from Central France who did seasonal building jobs in the north, or the travelling German artisans. Uprooting still meant, not the mild form of homesickness which was to become the characteristic psychological disease of the nineteenth century (reflected in innumerable sentimental popular songs), but the acute, killing *mal de pays* or *mal de coeur* which had first been clinically described by doctors among the old Swiss mercenaries in foreign lands. The conscription of the Revolutionary Wars revealed it, notably among the Bretons. The pull of the remote northern forests was so strong, that it could lead an Estonian servant-girl to leave her excellent employers the Kügelgens in Saxony, where she was free, and return home to serfdom. Migration and emigration, of which the migration to the USA is the most convenient index, increased notably from the 1820s, though it did not reach anything like major proportions until the 1840s, when one and three-quarter millions crossed the North Atlantic (a little less than three times the figure for the 1830s). Even so, the only major migratory nation outside the British Isles was as yet the German, long used to sending its sons as peasant settlers to Eastern Europe and America, as travelling artisans across the continent and as mercenaries everywhere.

We can in fact speak of only one western national movement organized in a coherent form before 1848 which was genuinely based on the masses, and even this enjoyed the immense advantage of identification with the strongest carrier of tradition, the Church. This was the Irish Repeal movement under Daniel O'Connell (1785–1847), a golden-voiced lawyer-demagogue of peasant stock, the first – and up to 1848 the only one – of those charismatic popular leaders who mark the awakening of political consciousness in hitherto backward masses. (The only comparable figures before 1848 were Feargus O'Connor (1794–1855), another Irishman, who symbolized Chartism in Britain, and perhaps Louis Kossuth (1802–1894), who may have acquired something of his subsequent mass prestige before the 1848 revolution, though in fact his reputation in the 1840s was made as a champion of the gentry, and his later canonization by nationalist historians makes it difficult to see his early career at all clearly.) O'Connell's Catholic Association, which won its mass support and the not wholly justified confidence of the clergy in the successful struggle for Catholic Emancipation (1829) was in no sense tied to the gentry, who were in any case Protestant and Anglo-Irish. It was a movement of peasants, and such elements of a native Irish lower-middle class as existed in that pauperized island. 'The Liberator' was borne into leadership by successive waves of a mass movement of agrarian revolt, the chief motive force of Irish politics throughout that appalling century. This was organized in secret terrorist societies which themselves helped to break down the parochialism of Irish life. However, his aim was neither revolution nor national independence, but a moderate middle class Irish autonomy by agreement or negotiation with the British Whigs. He was, in fact, not a nationalist and still less a peasant revolutionary but a moderate middle class autonomist. Indeed, the chief criticism which has been not unjustifiably raised against him by later Irish nationalists (much as the more radical Indian nationalists have criticised Gandhi, who occupied an analogous position in his country's history) was that he could have raised all Ireland against the British, and deliberately refused to do so. But this does not alter the fact that the movement he led was genuinely supported by the mass of the Irish nation.

II

Outside the zone of the modern bourgeois world there were, however, movements of popular revolt against alien rule (i.e. normally understood as meaning rule by a different religion rather than a different nationality) which sometimes appear to anticipate later national movements. Such were the rebellions against the Turkish Empire, against the Russians in the Caucasus, and the fight against the encroaching British raj in and on the confines of India. It is unwise to read too much modern nationalism into these, though in backward areas populated by armed and combative peasants and herdsmen, organized in clan groups and inspired by tribal chieftains, bandit-heroes and prophets, resistance to the foreign (or better, the unbelieving) ruler could take the form of veritable people's wars quite unlike the élite nationalist movements in less Homeric countries. In fact, however, the resistance of Mahrattas (a feudal-military Hindu group) and Sikhs (a militant religious sect) to the British in 1803–18 and 1845–49 respectively have little connection with subsequent Indian nationalism and produced none of their own.[11] The Caucasian tribes, savage, heroic and feud-ridden, found in the puritan Islamic sect of Muridism a temporary bond of unity against the invading Russians and in Shamyl (1797–1871) a leader of major stature; but there is not to this day a Caucasian nation, but merely a congeries of small mountain peoples in small Soviet republics. (The Georgians and Armenians, who have formed nations in the modern sense, were not involved in the Shamyl movement.) The Bedouin, swept by puritan religious sects like the Wahhabi in Arabia and the Senussi in what is today Libya, fought for the simple faith of Allah and the simple life of the herdsman and raider against the corruption of taxes, pashas and cities; but what we now know as Arab nationalism – a product of the twentieth century – has come out of the cities, not the nomadic encampments.

Even the rebellions against the Turks in the Balkans, especially among the rarely subdued mountain peoples of the south and west, should not be too readily interpreted in modern nationalist terms though the bards and braves of several – the two were often the same, as among the poet-warrior-bishops of Montenegro – recalled the glories of quasi-national heroes like the Albanian Skanderbeg and the tragedies like the Serbian defeat at Kossovo in the remote battles against the Turks. Nothing was more natural than to revolt, where necessary or desirable, against a local administration or a weakening Turkish Empire. However, little but a common economic backwardness united what we now know as the Yugoslavs, even those in the

Turkish Empire, and the very concept of Yugoslavia was the product of intellectuals in Austro-Hungary rather than those who actually fought for liberty.[12] The Orthodox Montenegrins, never subdued, fought the Turks; but with equal zest they fought the unbelieving Catholic Albanians and the unbelieving, but solidly Slav, Moslem Bosnians. The Bosnians revolted against the Turks, whose religion many of them shared, with as much readiness as the orthodox Serbs of the wooded Danube plain, and with more zest than the orthodox 'old Serbs' of the Albanian frontier-area. The first of the Balkan peoples to rise in the nineteenth century were the Serbs under a heroic pig-dealer and brigand Black George (1760–1817) but the initial phase of his rising (1804–7) did not even claim to be against Turkish rule, but on the contrary for the Sultan against the abuses of the local rulers. There is little in the early history of mountain rebellion in the Western Balkans to suggest that the local Serbs, Albanians, Greeks and others would not in the early nineteenth century have been satisfied with the sort of non-national autonomous principality which a powerful satrap, Ali Pasha 'the Lion of Jannina' (1741–1822), for a time set up in Epirus.

In one and only one case did the perennial fight of the sheep-herding clansmen and bandit-heroes against *any* real government fuse with the ideas of middle-class nationalism and the French Revolution : in the Greek struggle for independence (1821–30). Not unnaturally Greece therefore became the myth and inspiration of nationalists and liberals everywhere. For in Greece alone did an entire people rise against the oppressor in a manner which could be plausibly identified with the cause of the European left; and in turn the support of the European left, headed by the poet Byron who died there, was of very considerable help in the winning of Greek independence.

Most Greeks were much like the other forgotten warrior-peasantries and clans of the Balkan peninsula. A part, however, formed an international merchant and administrative class also settled in colonies or minority communities throughout the Turkish Empire and beyond, and the language and higher ranks of the entire Orthodox Church, to which most Balkan peoples belonged, were Greek, headed by the Greek Patriarch of Constantinople. Greek civil servants, transmuted into vassal princes, governed the Danubian principalities (the present Rumania). In a sense the entire educated and mercantile classes of the Balkans, the Black Sea area and the Levant, whatever their national origins, were hellenized by the very nature of their activities. During the eighteenth century this hellenization proceeded more powerfully than before, largely because of the marked economic expansion which also extended the range and contacts of the Greek diaspora. The new and thriving Black Sea grain trade took it into Italian, French and British business centres and strengthened its links with Russia; the expansion of Balkan trade brought Greek or Grecized merchants into Central Europe. The first Greek language newspapers were published in Vienna (1784–1812). Periodic emigration and resettlement of peasant rebels further reinforced the exile communities. It was among this cosmopolitan diaspora that the ideas of the French Revolution – liberalism, nationalism and the methods of political organization by masonic secret societies – took root. Rhigas (1760–98), the leader of an early obscure and possibly pan-Balkanist revolutionary movement, spoke French and adapted the *Marseillaise* to Hellenic conditions. The *Philiké Hetairía*, the secret patriotic society mainly responsible for the revolt of 1821, was founded in the great new Russian grain port of Odessa in 1814.

Their nationalism was to some extent comparable to the élite movements of the west. Nothing else explains the project of raising a rebellion for Greek independence in the Danube principalities under the leadership of local Greek magnates; for the only people who could be described as Greeks in these miserable serf-lands were lords, bishops, merchants and intellectuals. Naturally enough that rising failed miserably (1821). Fortunately, however, the Hetairía had also set out to enrol the anarchy of local brigand-heroes, outlaws and clan chieftains in the Greek mountains (especially in the Peloponnese), and with considerably greater success – at any rate after 1818 – than the South Italian gentlemen Carbonari, who attempted a similar proselytization of their local banditti. It is doubtful whether anything like modern nationalism meant much to these 'klephts', though many of them had their 'clerks' – a respect for and interest in book-learning was a surviving relic of ancient Hellenism – who composed manifestos in the Jacobin terminology. If they stood for anything it was for the age-old ethos of a peninsula in which the role of man was to become a hero, and the outlaw who took to the mountains to resist any government and to right the peasant's wrongs was the universal political ideal. To the rebellions of men like Kolokotrones, brigand and cattle-dealer, the nationalists of the Western type gave leadership and a pan-hellenic rather than a purely local scale. In turn they got from them that unique and awe-inspiring thing, the mass rising of an armed people.

The new Greek nationalism was enough to win independence, though the combination of middle-class leadership, klephtic disorganization and great power intervention produced one of those petty caricatures of the Western liberal ideal which were to become so familiar in areas like Latin America. But it also had the paradoxical result of narrowing hellenism to Hellas, and thus creating or intensifying the latent nationalism of the other Balkan peoples. While being Greek had been little more than the professional requirement of the literate Orthodox Balkan Christian, hellenization had made progress. Once it meant the political support for Hellas, it receded, even among the assimilated Balkan literate classes. In this sense Greek independence was the essential preliminary condition for the evolution of the other Balkan nationalisms.

Outside Europe it is difficult to speak of nationalism at all. The numerous Latin American republics which replaced the broken Spanish and Portuguese Empires (to be accurate, Brazil became and remained an independent monarchy from 1816 to 1889), their frontiers often reflecting little more than the distribution of the estates of the grandees who had backed one rather than another of the local rebellions, began to acquire vested political interests and territorial aspirations. The original pan-American ideal of Simon Bolivar (1783–1830) of Venezuela and San Martin (1778–1850) of the Argentine was impossible to realize, though it has persisted as a powerful revolutionary current throughout all the areas united by the Spanish language, just as pan-Balkanism, the heir of Orthodox unity against Islam, persisted and may still persist today. The vast extent and variety of the continent, the existence of independent foci of rebellion in Mexico (which determined Central America), Venezuela and Buenos Aires, and the special problem of the centre of Spanish colonialism in Peru, which was liberated from without, imposed automatic fragmentation. But the Latin American revolutions were the work of small groups of patricians, soldiers and gallicized évolués, leaving the mass of the Catholic poor white population passive and the Indians indifferent or hostile. Only in Mexico was independence won by the initiative of a popular agrarian, i.e. Indian, movement marching under the banner of the Virgin of Guadalupe, and Mexico has consequently ever since followed a different and politically more advanced road from the remainder of continental Latin America. However, even among the tiny layer of the politically decisive Latin Americans it would be anachronistic in our period to speak of anything more than the embryo of Colombian, Venezuelan, Ecuadorian, etc. 'national consciousness'.

Something like a proto-nationalism, however, existed in various countries of Eastern Europe, but paradoxically it took the direction of conservatism rather than national rebellion. The Slavs were oppressed everywhere, except in Russia and in a few wild Balkan strongholds; but in their immediate perspective the oppressors were, as we have seen, not the absolute monarchs, but the German or Magyar landlords and urban exploiters. Nor did the nationalism of these allow any place for Slav national existence : even so radical a programme as that of the German United States proposed by the republicans and democrats of Baden (in South-west Germany) envisaged the inclusion of an Illyrian (i.e. Croat and Slovene) republic with its capital in Italian Trieste, a Moravian one with its capital in Olomouc, and a Bohemian one led by Prague.[13] Hence the immediate hope of the Slav nationalists lay in the emperors of Austria and Russia. Various versions of Slav solidarity expressed the Russian orientation, and attracted Slav rebels – even the anti-Russian Poles – especially in times of defeat and hopelessness as after the failure of the risings in 1846. 'Illyrianism' in Croatia and moderate Czech nationalism expressed the Austrian trend, and both received deliberate support from the Habsburg rulers, two of whose leading ministers – Kolowrat and the chief of the police system, Sedlnitzky – were themselves Czechs. Croatian cultural aspirations were protected in the 1830s, and by 1840 Kolowrat actually proposed what was later to prove so useful in the 1848 revolution, the appointment of a Croat military *ban* as chief of Croatia, and with control over the military frontier with Hungary, as a counterweight to the obstreperous Magyars.[14] To be a revolutionary in 1848 therefore came to be virtually identical with opposition to Slav national aspirations; and the tacit conflict between the 'progressive' and the 'reactionary' nations did much to doom the revolutions of 1848 to failure.

Nothing like nationalism is discoverable elsewhere, for the social conditions for it did not exist. In fact, if anything the forces which were later to produce nationalism were at this stage opposed to the alliance of tradition, religion and mass poverty which produced the most powerful resistance to the encroachment of western conquerors and exploiters. The elements of a local bourgeoisie which grew up in Asian countries did so in the shelter of the foreign exploiters whose agents, intermediaries and dependants they largely were : The Parsee community of Bombay is an example. Even if the educated and 'enlightened' Asian was not a *compradore* or a lesser official of some foreign ruler or firm (a situation not dissimilar to that of the Greek diaspora in Turkey), his first political task was to Westernize – i.e. to introduce the ideas of the French Revolution and of scientific and technical modernization among his people against the united resistance of traditional rulers and traditional ruled (a situation not dissimilar to that of the gentleman-Jacobins of Southern Italy). He was therefore doubly cut off from his people. Nationalist mythology has often obscured this divorce, partly by suppressing the link between colonialism and the early native middle classes, partly lending to earlier anti-foreign resistance the colours of a later nationalist movement. But in Asia, in the Islamic countries, and even more in Africa, the junction between the évolués and nationalism, and between both and the masses, was not made until the twentieth century.

Nationalism in the East was thus the eventual product of Western influence and Western conquest. This link is perhaps most evident in the one plainly oriental country in which the foundations of what was to become the first modern colonial nationalist movement (other than the Irish) were laid : in Egypt. Napoleon's conquest introduced Western ideas, methods and techniques, whose value an able and ambitious local soldier, Mohammed Ali (Mehemet Ali), soon recognized. Having seized power and virtual independence from Turkey in the confused period which followed the withdrawal of the French, and with French support, Mohammed Ali set out to establish an efficient and Westernizing despotism with foreign (mainly French) technical aid. European leftwingers in the 1820s and 30s hailed this enlightened autocrat, and put their services at his disposal, when reaction in their own countries looked too dispiriting. The extraordinary sect of the Saint-Simonians, equally suspended between the advocacy of socialism and of industrial development by investment bankers and engineers, temporarily gave him their collective aid and prepared his plans of economic development. (For them, see p. 293). They thus also laid the foundation for the Suez Canal (built by the Saint-Simonian de Lesseps) and the fatal dependence of Egyptian rulers on vast loans negotiated by competing groups of European swindlers, which turned Egypt into a centre of imperialist rivalry and anti-imperialist rebellion later on. But Mohammed Ali was no more a nationalist than any other oriental despot. His Westernization, not his or his people's aspirations, laid the foundations for later nationalism. If Egypt acquired the first nationalist movement in the Islamic world and Morocco one of the last, it was because Mohammed Ali (for perfectly comprehensible geopolitical reasons) was in the main paths of Westernization and the isolated self-sealed Sherifian Empire of the Moslem far west was not, and made no attempts to be. Nationalism, like so many other characteristics of the modern world, is the child of the dual revolution.

NOTES

1 Hoffmann v. Fallersleben, Der Deutsche Zollverein, in *Unpolitische Lieder*.

2 G. Weill, *L'Enseigement Sécondaire en France 1802–1920* (1921), p. 72.

3 E. de Laveleye, *L'Instruction du Peuple* (1872), p. 278.

4 F. Paulsen, *Geschichte des Gelehrten Unterrichts* (1897), II, p. 703; A. Daumard, Les élèves de l'Ecole Polytechnique 1815–48 (*Rev. d'Hist. Mod. et Contemp* V, 1958); the total number of German and Belgian students in an average Semester of the early 1840s was about 14,000. J. Conrad, Die Frequenzverhältnisse der Universitäten der hauptsächlichen Kulturländer (*Jb. f. Nationalök. u. Statistik* LVI, 1895, pp. 376 ff.)

5 L. Liard, *L'Enseignement Supérieur en France 1789–1889* (1888), p. 11 ff.

6 In the early eighteenth century only about 60 per cent of all titles published in Germany were in the German language; since then the proportion had risen fairly steadily.

7 Paulsen, op. cit., II, pp. 690–1.

8 *Handwörterbuch d. Staabwissenschaften* (2nd ed.) art. Buchhandel.

9 Laveleye, op. cit., p. 264.

10 W. Wachsmuth, *Europäische Sittengeschichte*, V, 2 (1839), pp. 807–8.

11 The Sikh movement has remained largely *sui generis* to this day. The tradition of combative Hindu resistance in Maharashtra made that area an early centre of Indian nationalism, and pro-

vided some of its earliest – and highly traditionalist – leaders, notably B. G. Tilak; but this was at best a regional, and far from dominant strain in the movement. Something like Mahratta nationalism may exist today, but its social basis is the resistance of large Mahratta working class and underprivileged lower middle class to the economically and until recently linguistically dominant Gujeratis.

12 It is significant that the present Yugoslav régime has broken up what used to be classed as the Serb nation into the much more realistic sub-national republics and units of Serbia, Bosnia, Montenegro, Macedonia and Kossovo-Metohidja. By the linguistic standards of nineteenth-century nationalism most of these belonged to a single 'Serb' people, except the Macedonians, who are closer to the Bulgarians, and the Albanian minority in Kosmet. But in fact they have never developed a single Serb nationalism.

13 J. Sigmann, Les radicaux badois et l'idée nationale allemande en 1848. *Etudes d'Histoire Moderne et Contemporaine*, II, 1948, pp. 213–4.

14 J. Miskolczy, *Ungarn und die Habsburger-Monarchie* (1959), p. 85.

PART II
Results

8

Land

*I am your lord and my lord is the Tsar. The Tsar has a
right to give me orders and I must obey, but not to give
them to you. On my estate I am the Tsar, I am your god
on earth, and I must be responsible for you to God in
heaven. . . . First a horse must be curried ten times with
the iron curry-comb, then only can you brush it with the
soft brush. I shall have to curry you pretty roughly, and
who knows whether I shall ever get down to the brush.
God cleanses the air with thunder and lightning, and in
my village I shall cleanse with thunder and fire, whenever
I think it necessary.*

A Russian estate owner to his serfs.[1]

*The possession of a cow or two, with a hog, and a few
geese, naturally exalts the peasant, in his own conception,
above his brothers in the same rank of society. . . . In
sauntering after his cattle, he acquires a habit of indo-
lence. . . . Day labour becomes disgusting; the aversion
increases by indulgence; and at length the sale of a half-
fed calf, or hog, furnishes the means of adding intem-
perance to idleness. The sale of the cow frequently
succeeds, and its wretched and disappointed possessor,
unwilling to resume the daily and regular course of
labour, from whence he drew his former subsistence. . .
extracts from the poor's rate the relief to which he is in no
degree entitled.*

Survey of the Board of Agriculture for Somerset, 1798 [2]

I

What happened to the land determined the life and death of most
human beings in the years from 1789 to 1848. Consequently the

impact of the dual revolution on landed property, land tenure and agriculture was the most catastrophic phenomenon of our period. For neither the political nor the economic revolution could neglect land, which the first school of economists, the Physiocrats, considered the sole source of wealth, and whose revolutionary transformation all agreed to be the necessary precondition and consequence of bourgeois society, if not of all rapid economic development. The great frozen ice-cap of the world's traditional agrarian systems and rural social relations lay above the fertile soil of economic growth. It had at all costs to be melted, so that that soil could be ploughed by the forces of profit-pursuing private enterprise. This implied three kinds of changes. In the first place land had to be turned into a commodity, possessed by private owners and freely purchasable and saleable by them. In the second place it had to pass into the ownership of a class of men willing to develop its productive resources for the market and impelled by reason, i.e. enlightened self-interest and profit. In the third place the great mass of the rural population had in some way to be transformed, at least in part, into freely mobile wage-workers for the growing non-agricultural sector of the economy. Some of the more thoughtful or radical economists were also aware of a fourth desirable change, though one difficult if not impossible to achieve. For in an economy which assumed the perfect mobility of all factors of production land, a 'natural monopoly', did not quite fit. Since the size of the earth was limited, and its various pieces differed in fertility and accessibility, those who owned its more fertile parts must inevitably enjoy a special advantage and levy a rent on the rest. How this burden was to be removed or mitigated – e.g. by suitable taxation, by laws against the concentration of landownership or even by nationalization – was the subject of acute debate, especially in industrial England. (Such arguments also affected other 'natural monopolies' like railways whose nationalization was for this reason never considered incompatible with a private enterprise economy, and widely practised.[3]) However, these were problems of land in a bourgeois society. The immediate task was to install it.

Two major obstacles stood in the way of such an imposition, and both required a combination of political and economic action : precapitalist landlords and the traditional peasantry. On the other hand the task could be fulfilled in a variety of ways. The most radical were the British and the American, for both eliminated the peasantry and one the landlord altogether. The classical British solution produced a country in which perhaps 4,000 proprietors owned perhaps four-sevenths of the land [4] which was cultivated – I take the 1851 figures – by a quarter of a million farmers (three-quarters of the acreage being in farms of from 50 to 500 acres) who employed about one and a quarter million of hired labourers and servants. Pockets of small-holders persisted, but outside of the Scots highlands and parts of Wales only the pedant can speak of a British peasantry in the conti-nental sense. The classical American solution was that of the owner-occupying commercial farmer who made up for the shortage of a hired labour force by intensive mechanization. Obed Hussey's (1833) and Cyrus McCormick's (1834) mechanical reapers were the comple-ment to the purely commercial-minded farmers or land-speculating entrepreneurs who extended the American way of life westwards from the New England states, seizing their land or later by buying it at the most nominal prices from the government. The classical Prus-sian solution was socially the least revolutionary. It consisted in turning feudal landlords themselves into capitalist farmers and serfs into hired labourers. The Junkers retained control of their lean estates which they had long cultivated for the export market with servile labour; but they now operated with peasants 'liberated' from serfdom – and from land. The Pomeranian example, where later in the century some 2,000 large estates covered 61 per cent of the land, some 60,000 middle and small holdings the rest and the remainder of the population was landless, is doubtless extreme;[5] but it is a fact that a rural labouring class was too unimportant for the word 'labourer' even to be mentioned in Krüniz' *Encyclopaedia of Domes-tic and Agricultural Economy* of 1773, while in 1849 the number of landless or substantially wage-employed rural labourers in Prussia was estimated at almost two millions.[6] The only other systematic solution of the agrarian problem in a capitalist sense was the Danish, which also created a large body of small and medium commercial farmers. However, it was due in the main to the reforms of the period of enlightened despotism in the 1780s, and therefore falls somewhat outside the range of this volume.

The Northern American solution depended on the unique fact of a virtually unlimited supply of free land, and the absence of all relics of feudal relations or traditional peasant collectivism. Virtually the only obstacle to the extension of pure individualist farming was the slight one of the Red Indian tribes, whose lands – normally guaranteed by treaties with the British, French and American governments – were held in collectivity, often as hunting grounds. The total conflict between a view of society which regarded individual perfectly alienable property not merely as the only rational but the only *natural* arrangement and one which did not is perhaps most evident in the confrontation between Yankees and Indians. 'Amongst the most mischievous and fatal [of the causes which prevented the Indians from learning the benefits of civilization],' argued the Commissioner for Indian Affairs,[7] 'were *their possession of too great an extent of country held in common*, and the right to large money annuities; the one giving them ample scope for their indulgence in their unsettled and vagrant habits, and preventing their *acquiring a knowledge of individuality in property* and the advantage of settled homes; the other fostering idleness and want of thrift, and giving them means of gratifying their depraved tastes and appetites.' To deprive them of their lands by fraud, robbery and any other suitable kind of pressure was therefore as moral as it was profitable.

Nomadic and primitive Indians were not the only people who neither understood bourgeois-individualist rationalism on the land nor wished for it. In fact, with the exception of minorities of the enlightened, the acquisitive and the 'strong and sober' among the peasantry, the vast bulk of the rural population from the largest feudal lord down to the most poverty-stricken shepherd united in abominating it. Only a politico-legal revolution directed against both lords and traditional peasants could create the conditions in which the rational minority might become the rational majority. The history of agrarian relations over most of Western Europe and its colonies in our period is the history of this revolution though its full consequences were not felt until the second half of the century.

As we have seen, its first object was to turn land into a commodity. Entails and other prohibitions of sale or dispersal which rested on noble estates had to be broken and the landowner therefore subjected to the salutary penalty of bankruptcy for economic incompetence, which would allow economically more competent purchasers to take over. Above all in Catholic and Moslem countries (Protestant ones had long since done so), the great bloc of ecclesiastical land had to be taken out of the Gothic realm of non-economic superstition and opened to the market and rational exploitation. Secularization and sale awaited them. The equally vast blocks of collectively owned – and therefore badly utilized – lands of village and town communities, common fields, common pastures, woodlands, etc., had to be made accessible to individual enterprise. Division into individual lots and 'enclosure' awaited them. That the new purchasers would be the enterprising, strong and sober could hardly be doubted; and thus the second of the objects of the agrarian revolution would be achieved.

But only on condition that the peasantry, from whose ranks many of them would doubtless arise, was itself turned into a class freely capable of disposing of its resources; a step which would also automatically achieve the third object, the creation of a large 'free' labour force composed from those who failed to become bourgeois. The liberation of the peasant from non-economic bonds and duties (villeinage, serfdom, payments to lords, forced labour, slavery, etc.) was therefore also essential. This would have an additional and crucial advantage. For the free wage-labourer, open to the incentive of higher rewards, or the free farmer, could be shown, it was thought, to be a more efficient worker than the forced labourer, whether serf, peon or slave. Only one further condition had to be fulfilled. The very large number of those who now vegetated on the land to which all human history tied them, but who, if it were productively exploited, would be a mere surplus population,[8] had to be torn away from their roots and allowed to move freely. Only thus would they migrate into the towns and factories where their muscles were increasingly needed. In other words, the peasants had to lose their land together with their other bonds.

Over most of Europe this meant that the complex of traditional legal and political arrangements commonly known as 'feudalism' had to be abolished, where it was not already absent. Broadly speaking, in the period from 1789 to 1848 this was achieved – mostly by direct or indirect agency of the French Revolution – from Gibraltar to East Prussia, and from the Baltic to Sicily. The equivalent changes in Central Europe only took place in 1848, in Russia and Rumania in the 1860s. Outside Europe something nominally like them was achieved in the Americas, with the major exceptions of Brazil, Cuba and the Southern USA where slavery persisted until 1862–88. In a few colonial areas directly administered by European states, notably in parts of India and Algeria, similar legal revolutions were also introduced. So they were in Turkey and, for a brief period, in Egypt.[10]

Except for Britain and a few other countries in which feudalism in this sense had either been abolished already or had never really existed (though traditional peasant collectivities had), the actual methods of achieving this revolution were very similar. In Britain no legislation to expropriate large property was necessary or politically feasible, for the large landowners or their farmers were already attuned to a bourgeois society. Their resistance to the final triumph of bourgeois relations in the countryside – between 1795 and 1846 – was bitter. However, though it contained, in an inarticulate form, a sort of traditionalist protest against the destructive sweep of the pure individualist profit-principle, the cause of their most obvious discontents was much simpler : the desire to maintain the high prices and high rents of the revolutionary and Napoleonic wars in a period of post-war depression. Theirs was an agrarian pressure-group rather than a feudal reaction. The main cutting edge of the law was therefore turned against the relics of the peasantry, the cottagers and labourers. Some 5,000 'enclosures' under the private and general Enclosure Acts broke up some six million acres of common fields and common lands from 1760 onwards, transformed them into private holdings, and numerous less formal arrangements supplemented them. The *Poor Law* of 1834 was designed to make life so intolerable for the rural paupers as to force them to migrate to any jobs that offered. And indeed they soon began to do so. In the 1840s several counties were already on the verge of an *absolute* loss of population, and from 1850 land-flight became general.

The reforms of the 1780s abolished feudalism in *Denmark* though their main beneficiaries there were not landlords but peasant tenants and owners who were encouraged after the abolition of the open fields to consolidate their strips into individual holdings; a process analogous to 'enclosure' which was largely complete by 1800. Estates tended to be parcelled out and sold to their former tenants, though the post-Napoleonic depression, which small owners found harder to survive than tenants, slowed this process down between 1816 and about 1830. By 1865 Denmark was mainly a country of independent peasant owners. In *Sweden* similar but less drastic reforms had similar effects, so that by the second half of the nineteenth century traditional communal cultivation, the strip system had virtually disappeared. The formerly feudal areas of this country were assimilated to the rest of the country, in which the free peasantry had always been predominant, as it was overwhelmingly in *Norway* (after 1815 a part of Sweden, formerly of Denmark). A tendency to subdivide larger enterprises, in some regions, offset by one to consolidate holdings, made itself felt. The net result was that agriculture improved its productivity rapidly – in Denmark the number of cattle doubled in the last quarter of the eighteenth century [11] – but with the rapid rise in population a growing number of the rural poor found no employment. After the middle of the nineteenth century their hardship led to what was proportionately the most massive of all the century's movements of emigration (mostly to the American Midwest) from infertile Norway and a little later from Sweden, though less so from Denmark.

II

In France, as we have seen, the abolition of feudalism was the work of the revolution. Peasant pressure and Jacobinism pushed agrarian reform beyond the point where champions of capitalist development would have wished it to stop (cf. above pp. 66, 91–2). France as a whole therefore became neither a country of landlords and farm-labourers nor of commercial farmers, but largely of various types of peasant proprietors, who became the chief prop of all subsequent political régimes which did not threaten to take away their land. That the number of peasant owners increased by over 50 per cent – from four to six and a half millions – is an old, plausible, but not readily verifiable guess. All we know for certain is that the number of such proprietors did not diminish and in some areas increased more than in others; but whether the Moselle department, where it increased by 40 per cent between 1789 and 1801, is more typical than the Norman Eure department, where it remained unchanged,[12] must await further study. Conditions on the land were, on the whole, good. Even in 1847–8 there was no real hardship except among a section of the wage-labourers.[13] The flow of surplus labour from the village to town was therefore small, a fact which helped to retard French industrial development.

Over most of Latin Europe, the Low Countries, Switzerland and Western Germany the abolition of feudalism was the work of the

French conquering armies, determined to 'proclaim immediately in the name of the French nation . . . the abolition of tithes, feudality and seigneurial rights',[14] or of native liberals who co-operated with them or were inspired by them. By 1799 the legal revolution had thus conquered in the countries adjoining Eastern France and in Northern and Central Italy, often merely completing an evolution already far advanced. The return of the Bourbons after the abortive Neapolitan revolution of 1798–9 postponed it in continental Southern Italy until 1808; the British occupation kept it out of Sicily, though feudalism was formally abolished in that island between 1812 and 1843. In Spain the anti-French liberal Cortes of Cadiz in 1811 abolished feudalism and in 1813 certain entails, though, as usual outside the areas profoundly transformed by long incorporation into France, the return of the old régimes delayed the practical application of these principles. The French reforms therefore began or continued, rather than completed, the legal revolution in such areas as North-western Germany east of the Rhine and in the 'Illyrian Provinces' (Istria, Dalmatia, Ragusa, later also Slovenia and part of Croatia), which did not come under French rule or domination until after 1805.

The French Revolution was not, however, the only force making for a thorough revolution of agrarian relations. The sheer economic argument in favour of a rational utilization of the land had greatly impressed the enlightened despots of the pre-revolutionary period, and produced very similar answers. In the Habsburg Empire Joseph II had actually abolished serfdom and secularized much church land in the 1780s. For comparable reasons, and because of their persistent rebellions the serfs of Russian Livonia were formally restored to the status of peasant proprietors which they had enjoyed rather earlier under Swedish administration. It did not help them in the slightest, for the greed of the all-powerful landlords soon turned emancipation into a mere instrument of peasant expropriation. After the Napoleonic wars the peasants' few legal safeguards were swept away and between 1819 and 1850 they lost at least one-fifth of their land while the noble demesnes grew between 60 and 180 per cent.[15] A class of landless labourers now cultivated them.

These three factors – the influence of the French Revolution, the rational economic argument of civil servants, and the greed of the nobility, determined the emancipation of the peasants in Prussia between 1807 and 1816. The influence of the Revolution was clearly decisive; for its armies had just pulverized Prussia and thus demonstrated with dramatic force the helplessness of old régimes which did not adopt modern methods, i.e. those patterned on the French. As in Livonia, emancipation was combined with the abolition of the modest legal protection which the peasantry had previously enjoyed. In return for the abolition of forced labour and feudal dues and for his new property-rights the peasant was obliged, among other losses, to give his former lord one-third or one-half of his old holding or an equivalent and crippling sum of money. The long and complex legal process of transition was far from complete by 1848, but it was already evident that while the estate owners had benefited greatly and a smaller number of comfortable peasants somewhat, thanks to their new property-rights, the bulk of the peasantry were distinctly worse off and the landless labourers were increasing fast.[16]

Economically the result was beneficial in the long run, though the losses in the short run were – as often in major agrarian changes – serious. By 1830–31 Prussia had only just got back to the numbers of cattle and sheep of the beginning of the century, the landlords now owning a larger and the peasants a smaller share. On the other hand the area under tillage rose by well over a third and productivity by half in, roughly, the first half of the century.[18] The surplus rural population clearly grew rapidly; and since rural conditions were distinctly bad – the famine of 1846–8 was probably worse in Germany than anywhere else except Ireland and Belgium – it had plenty of incentive to migrate. And indeed of all peoples before the Irish Famine, the Germans provided the largest body of emigrants.

The actual legal steps to secure bourgeois systems of landed property were thus, as we have seen, taken mostly between 1789 and 1812. Their consequences, outside France and a few adjoining areas, made themselves felt much more slowly, mostly because of the strength of social and economic reaction after Napoleon's defeat. In general every further advance of liberalism pushed the legal revolutions a step further from theory to practice, every recovery of the old régimes delayed them, notably in Catholic countries where the secularization and sale of Church lands were among the most urgent of the liberal demands. Thus in Spain the temporary triumph of a liberal revolution in 1820 brough a new law of 'unfettering' (*Desvinculacion*) which allowed nobles to sell their lands freely; the restoration of absolutism abrogated it in 1823; the renewed victory of liberalism reaffirmed it in 1836 and so on. The actual volume of land transfers in our period, insofar as we can measure it, was therefore as yet modest, except in areas where an active body of middle class buyers and land-speculators stood ready to use their opportunities : on the plain of Bologna (North Italy) noble lands fell from 78 per cent of total value in 1789 through 66 per cent in 1804 to 51 per cent in 1835.[19] On the other hand in Sicily 90 per cent of all land continued to remain in noble hands until much later.[20] [21]

There was one exception to this : the lands of the church. These vast and almost invariably ill-utilised and ramshackle estates – it has been claimed that two-thirds of the land in the Kingdom of Naples around 1760 was ecclesiastical [23] – had few defenders and only too many wolves hovering round them. Even in the absolutist reaction in Catholic Austria after the collapse of Joseph II's enlightened despotism nobody suggested the return of the secularized and dissipated monastery lands. Thus in one commune in the Romagna (Italy) church lands fell from 42·5 per cent of the area in 1783 to 11·5 per cent in 1812; but the lost lands passed not only to bourgeois owners (who rose from 24 to 47 per cent) but also to nobles (who rose from 34 to 41 per cent).[24] Consequently it is not surprising that even in Catholic Spain the intermittent liberal governments managed by 1845 to sell off over half the church estates, most notably in the provinces in which ecclesiastical property was most concentrated or economic development was most advanced (in fifteen provinces over three-quarters of all church estates had been sold).[25]

Unfortunately for liberal economic theory this large scale redistribution of land did not produce that class of enterprising and progressive landlords or farmers which had been confidently expected. Why should even a middle-class purchaser – a city lawyer, merchant or speculator – in economically undeveloped and inaccessible areas saddle himself with the investment and trouble of transforming landed property into a soundly run business enterprise, instead of merely taking the place, from which he had been hitherto debarred, of the former noble or clerical landlord, whose powers he could now exercise with more regard for cash and less for tradition and custom? Throughout vast areas of Southern Europe a new and harsher set of 'barons' thus reinforced the old. The great latifundist concentrations were slightly diminished, as in continental Southern Italy, left untouched, as in Sicily, or even reinforced, as in Spain. In such régimes the legal revolution thus reinforced the old feudality by a new; all the more so as the small purchaser, and especially the peasant, hardly benefited at all from the land-sales. However, in most of Southern Europe the age-old social structure remained strong enough to make even the thought of mass migration impossible. Men and women lived where their ancestors had done, and, if they had to, starved there. The mass exodus from Southern Italy for instance was a half-century away.

But even where the peasantry actually received the land, or were confirmed in its possession, as in France, parts of Germany, or Scandinavia, they did not automatically, as hoped for, turn into the enterprising class of small farmers. And this for the simple reason that while the peasantry wanted land, it rarely wanted a bourgeois agrarian economy.

III

For the old traditional system, inefficient and oppressive as it had been, was also a system of considerable social certainty and, at a most miserable level, of some economic security; not to mention that it was hallowed by custom and tradition. The periodic famines, the burden of labour which made men old at forty and women at thirty, were acts of God; they only became acts for which men were held responsible in times of abnormal hardship or revolution. The legal revolution, from the peasant's point of view, gave nothing except some legal rights, but it took away much. Thus in Prussia emancipation gave him two-thirds or half the land he already tilled and freedom from forced labour and other dues; but it formally took away : his claim to assistance from the lord in times of bad harvest or cattle plague; his right to collect or buy cheap fuel from the lord's forest; his right to the lord's assistance in repairing or rebuilding his house; his right in extreme poverty to ask the lord's help in paying taxes; his right to pasture animals in the lord's forest. For the poor peasant it seemed a distinctly hard bargain. Church property might have been inefficient, but this very fact recommended it to the peasants, for on it their custom tended to become prescriptive right. The division and enclosure of common fields, pasture and forest merely withdrew from the poor peasant or cottager resources and reserves to which he felt he (or rather he as part of the community) had a right. The free land market meant that he probably had to sell his land; the creation of a rural class of entrepreneurs, that the most hard-hearted and hard-headed exploited him instead of, or in addition to, the old lords. Altogether the introduction of liberalism on the land was like some sort of silent bombardment which shattered the social structure he had always inhabited and left nothing in its place but the rich : a solitude called freedom.

Nothing was more natural than that the peasant poor or the entire rural population should resist as best it could, and nothing was more natural than that it should resist in the name of the age-old customary ideal of a stable and just society, i.e. in the name of church and legitimate king. If we except the peasant revolution of France (and even this was in 1789 neither generally anti-clerical nor anti-monarchical) virtually all important peasant movements in our period which were not directed against the *foreign* king or church, were ostensibly made for priest and ruler. The South Italian peasantry joined with the urban sub-proletariat to make a social counter-revolution against the Neapolitan Jacobins and the French in 1799 in the name of the Holy Faith and the Bourbons; and these also were the slogans of the Calabrian and Apulian brigand-guerrillas against the French occupation, as later against Italian unity. Priests and brigand-heroes led the Spanish peasantry in their guerrilla war against Napoleon. Church, king and a traditionalism so extreme as to be odd even in the early nineteenth century, inspired the Carlist guerrillas of the Basque country, Navarre, Castile, Leon and Aragon in their implacable warfare against the Spanish Liberals in the 1830s and 1840s. The Virgin of Guadalupe led the Mexican peasants in 1810. Church and Emperor fought the Bavarians and French under the lead of the publican Andreas Hofer in Tyrol in 1809. The Tsar and Holy Orthodoxy were what the Russians fought for in 1812–13. The Polish revolutionaries in Galicia knew that their only chance of raising the Ukrainian peasantry was through the Greek-Orthodox or Uniate priests; they failed, for the peasants preferred Emperor to gentleman. Outside France, where Republicanism or Bonapartism captured an important section of the peasantry between 1791 and 1815, and where the Church had in many regions withered away even before the Revolution, there were few areas – perhaps most obviously those in which the Church was a foreign and long-resented ruler, as in the Papal Romagna and Emilia – of what we would today call left-wing peasant agitation. And even in France Brittany and the Vendée remained fortresses of popular Bourbonism. The failure of the European peasantries to rise with Jacobin or Liberal, that is to say with lawyer, shopkeeper, estate administrator, official and landlord, doomed the revolutions of 1848 in those countries in which the French Revolution had not given them the land; and where it had, their conservative fear of losing it, or their contentment, kept them equally inactive.

Of course the peasants did not rise for the real king, whom they hardly knew, but for the ideal of the just king who, if only he knew, would punish the transgressions of his underlings and lords; though often they did rise for the real church. For the village priest was one of them, the saints were certainly theirs and nobody else's, and even the tumbledown ecclesiastical estates were sometimes more tolerable landlords than the grasping laymen. Where the peasantry had land and was free, as in Tyrol, Navarre, or (without a king) in the Catholic cantons of the original William Tell Switzerland, its traditionalism was a defence of relative liberty against the encroachment of liberalism. Where it had not, it was more revolutionary. Any call to resist the conquest of foreigner and bourgeois, whether launched by priest, king or anyone else, was likely to produce not only the sack of the houses of gentry and lawyers in the city, but the ceremonial march with drums and saints' banners to occupy and divide the land, the murder of landlords and the rape of their women, the burning of legal documents. For surely it was against the real wish of Christ and king that the peasant was poor and landless. It is this firm foundation of social revolutionary unrest which made peasant movements in the areas of serfdom and large estates, or in the areas of excessively small and sub-divided property, so unreliable an ally of reaction. All they needed to switch from a formally legitimist revolutionism to a formally left-wing one was the consciousness that king and church had gone over to the side of the local rich, and a revolutionary movement of men like themselves, speaking in their own terms. Garibaldi's populist radicalism was perhaps the first of such movements, and the Neapolitan brigands hailed him with enthusiasm, while continuing to hail Holy Church and the Bourbons. Marxism and Bakuninism were to be even more effective. But the transfer of peasant rebellion from the political right to the political left wing had hardly begun to occur before 1848, for the massive impact of the bourgeois economy on the land, which was to turn endemic peasant rebelliousness into an epidemic, only really began to make itself felt after the middle of the century, and especially during and after the great agrarian depression of the 1880s.

IV

For large parts of Europe, as we have seen, the legal revolution came as something imposed from outside and above, a sort of artificial earthquake rather than as the slide of long-loosened land. This was even more obviously the case where it was imposed on a wholly non-bourgeois economy conquered by a bourgeois one, as in Africa and Asia.

Thus in Algeria the conquering French came upon a characteristically medieval society with a firmly established and reasonably flourishing system of religious schools – it has been said that the French peasant soldiers were less literate than the people they conquered [26] – financed by the numerous pious foundations.[27] The schools, being regarded merely as nurseries of superstition were closed; the religious lands were allowed to be bought by Europeans who understood neither their purpose nor their legal inalienability; and the schoolmasters, normally members of the powerful religious fraternities, emigrated to the unconquered areas there to strengthen the forces of revolt under Abd-el-Kader. The systematic transfer of the land to simple alienable private property began, though its full effects were only to be felt much later. How indeed was the European liberal to understand the complex web of private and collective right and obligation which prevented, in a region like Kabylia, the land collapsing into an anarchy of minute patches and fragments of individually owned fig-trees?

Algeria had hardly been conquered by 1848. Vast areas of India had by then been directly administered by the British for more than a generation. Since no body of European settlers wished to acquire Indian land, no problem of simple expropriation arose. The impact of liberalism on Indian agrarian life was in the first instance a consequence of the British rulers' search for a convenient and effective method of land-taxation. It was their combination of greed and legal individualism which produced catastrophe. The land tenures of pre-British India were as complex as any in traditional but not unchanging societies periodically overrun by foreign conquest, but rested, speaking broadly, on two firm pillars; the land belonged – *de jure* or *de facto* – to self-governing collectivities (tribes, clans, village communes, brotherhoods etc.), and the government received a proportion of its produce. Though some land was in some sense alienable, and some agrarian relations could be construed as tenancies, some rural payments as rent, there were in fact neither landlords, tenants, individual landed property or rent in the English sense. It was a situation wholly distasteful and incomprehensible to the British administrators and rulers, who proceeded to invent the rural arrangement with which they were familiar. In Bengal, the first large area under direct British rule, the Mughal land tax had been collected by a species of tax-farmer or commission agent, the Zemindar. Surely these must be the equivalent of the British landlord, paying a tax assessed (as in the contemporary English land tax) on the whole of his estates, the class through which tax-collection ought to be organized, whose beneficent interest in the land must improve it, and whose political support of a foreign régime must give it stability? 'I consider,' wrote the subsequent Lord Teignmouth in the Minute of June 18, 1789, which outlined the 'Permanent Settlement' of Bengal land revenue, 'the Zemindars as the proprietors of the soil, to the property of which they succeed by right of inheritance. . . . The privilege of disposing of the land by sale or mortgage is derived from this fundamental right. . . .' [28] Varieties of this so-called Zemindari system were applied to about 19 per cent of the later area of British India.

Greed rather than convenience dictated the second type of revenue system, which eventually covered just over half of the area of British India, the *Ryotwari*. Here the British rulers, considering themselves the successors to an oriental despotism which in their not wholly ingenuous view was the supreme landlord of *all* the land, attempted the herculean task of making individual tax assessments of every peasant, considering him as a small landed proprietor or rather tenant. The principle behind this, expressed with the habitual clarity of the able official, was agrarian liberalism at its purest. It demanded, in the words of Goldsmid and Wingate, 'limitation of joint responsibility to a few cases where fields are held in common, or have been subdivided by coparceners; recognition of property in the soil; perfect freedom of management with regard to rent from sub-tenants, and sale, secured to its owners; facilities for effecting sales or transfers of land afforded, by the apportionment of the assessment on fields'.[24] The village community was entirely by-passed, in spite of the strong objections of the Madras Board of Revenue (1808–18), which rightly considered collective tax settlements with the village communities to be far more realistic, while also (and very typically) defending them as the best guarantee of private property. Doctrinairism and greed won, and 'the boon of private property' was conferred on the Indian peasantry.

Its disadvantages were so obvious that the land settlements of the subsequently conquered or occupied parts of North India (which covered about 30 per cent of the later area of British India) returned to a modified Zemindari system, but with some attempts to recognize the existing collectivities, most notably in the Punjab.

Liberal doctrine combined with disinterested rapacity to give another turn to the screw of compressing the peasantry : they sharply increased the weight of taxation. (The land revenue of Bombay was more than doubled within four years of the conquest of the province in 1817–18.) Malthus's and Ricardo's doctrine of Rent became the basis of Indian revenue theory, through the influence of the utilitarian chieftain James Mill. This doctrine regarded the revenue from landed property as a pure surplus, which had nothing to do with value. It simply arose because some lands were more fertile than others and was appropriated, with increasingly baneful results for the whole economy, by landlords. To confiscate all of it therefore had no effect on a country's wealth, except perhaps to prevent the growth of a landed aristocracy capable of holding sound businessmen to ransom. In a country such as Britain the political strength of the agrarian interest would have made so radical a solution – which amounted to a virtual nationalization of the land – impossible; but in India the despotic power of an ideological conqueror could impose it. Admittedly at this point two liberal lines of argument crossed. The whiggish administrators of the eighteenth century and the older business interests took the common-sense view that ignorant smallholders on the verge of subsistence would never accumulate agrarian capital and thus improve the economy. They therefore favoured 'Permanent Settlements' of the Bengal type, which encouraged a class of landlords, fixed tax-rates for ever (i.e. at a diminishing rate) and thus encouraged savings and improvement. The utilitarian administrators, headed by the redoubtable Mill, preferred land nationalization and a mass of small peasant-tenants to the danger of yet another landed aristocracy. Had India been in the least like Britain, the whig case would certainly have been overwhelmingly more persuasive, and after the Indian mutiny of 1857 it became so for political reasons. As it was, both views were equally irrelevant to Indian agriculture. Moreover, with the development of the Industrial Revolution at home the sectional interests of the old East India Company (which were, among other things, to have a reasonably flourishing colony to milk) were increasingly subordinated to the general interests of British industry (which was, above all things, to have India as a market, a source of income, but not as a competitor). Consequently the utilitarian policy which ensured strict British control and a markedly higher tax-yield, was preferred. The traditional pre-British limit of taxation was one-third of revenue; the standard basis for British assessment was one-half. Only after the doctrinaire utilitarianism had led to obvious impoverishment and the Revolt of 1857 was taxation reduced to a less extortionate rate.

The application of economic liberalism to the Indian land created neither a body of enlightened estate-owners nor a sturdy yeoman peasantry. It merely introduced another element of uncertainty, another complex web of parasites and exploiters of the village (e.g. the new officials of the British raj),[30] a considerable shift and concentration of ownership, a growth of peasant debt and poverty. In Cawnpore district (Uttar Pradesh) over 84 per cent of estates were owned by hereditary landowners at the time the East India Company took over. By 1840, 40 per cent of all estates had been purchased by their owners, by 1872, 62·6 per cent. Moreover, of the more than 3,000 estates or villages – roughly three-fifths of the total – transformed from the original owners in three districts of the North-west Provinces (Uttar Pradesh) by 1846–7, over 750 had been transferred to money-lenders.[31]

There is much to be said for the enlightened and systematic despotism of the utilitarian bureaucrats who built the British raj in this period. They brought peace, much development of public services, administrative efficiency, reliable law, and incorrupt government at the higher levels. But economically they failed in the most sensational manner. Of all the territories under the administration of European governments, or governments of the European type, even including Tsarist Russia, India continued to be haunted by the most gigantic and murderous famines; perhaps – though statistics are lacking for the earlier period – increasingly so as the century wore on.

The only other large colonial (or ex-colonial) area where attempts to apply liberal land law were made, was Latin America. Here the old feudal colonization of the Spaniards had never shown any prejudice against the fundamental collective and communal land-tenures of the Indians, so long as the white colonists got what land they wanted. The independent governments, however, proceeded to liberalize in the spirit of the French Revolutionary and Benthamite doctrines which inspired them. Thus Bolivar decreed the individualization of community land in Peru (1824) and most of the new republics abolished entails in the manner of the Spanish liberals. The liberation of noble lands may have led to some reshuffling and dispersion of estates, though the vast *hacienda* (*estancia, finca, fundo*) remained the dominant unit of landownership in most of the republics. The attack on communal property remained quite ineffective. Indeed, it was not really pressed seriously until after 1850. In fact, the liberalization of its political economy remained as artificial as the liberalization of its political system. In substance, parliaments, elections, land laws, etc., notwithstanding, the continent went on very much as before.

V

The revolution in land-tenure was the political aspect of the disruption of traditional agrarian society; its invasion by the new rural economy and the world market, its economic aspect. In the period from 1787 to 1848 this economic transformation was as yet imperfect, as can be measured by the very modest rates of migration. Railways and steamships had hardly yet begun to create a single agricultural world market until the great farming depression of the later nineteenth century. Local agriculture was therefore largely sheltered from international or even inter-provincial competition. Industrial competition had hardly as yet impinged much on the numerous village crafts and domestic manufactures, except perhaps to turn some of them to production for rather wider markets. New agricultural methods – outside the areas of successful capitalist agriculture – were slow to penetrate the village, though new industrial crops, notably sugar-beet, which spread in consequence of the Napoleonic discrimination against (British) cane-sugar and new food-crops, notably maize and potatoes, made striking advances. It took an extraordinary economic conjuncture, such as the immediate proximity of a highly industrial economy and the inhibition of normal development, to produce a real cataclysm in an agrarian society by purely economic means.

Such a conjuncture did exist, and such a cataclysm did occur in Ireland, and to a lesser extent, in India. What happened in India was simply the virtual destruction, within a few decades, of what had been a flourishing domestic and village industry which supplemented the rural incomes; in other words the deindustrialization of India. Between 1815 and 1832 the value of Indian cotton goods exported from the country fell from £1·3 millions to less than £100,000 while the import of British cotton goods increased sixteen times over. By 1840 an observer already warned against the disastrous effects of turning India into 'the agricultural farm of England; she is a manufacturing country, her manufactures of various descriptions have existed for ages, and have never been able to be competed with by any nation wherever fair play has been given to them. ... To reduce her now to an agricultural country would be an injustice to India.' [32] The description was misleading; for a leavening of manufacture had been, in India as in many other countries, an integral part of the agricultural economy in many regions. Consequently deindustrialization made the peasant village itself more dependent on the single, fluctuating fortune of the harvest.

The situation in Ireland was more dramatic. Here a population of small, economically backward, highly insecure tenants practising subsistence farming paid the maximum rent to a smallish body of foreign, non-cultivating, generally absentee landlords. Except in the north-east (Ulster) the country had long been deindustrialized by the mercantilist policy of the British government whose colony it was, and more recently by the competition of British industry. A single technical innovation – the substitution of the potato for the previously prevalent types of farming – had made a large increase in population possible; for an acre of land under potatoes can feed far more people than one under grass, or indeed under most other crops. The landlord's demand for the maximum number of rent-paying tenants, and later also for a labour-force to cultivate the new farms which exported food to the expanding British market, encouraged the multiplication

of tiny holdings : by 1841 in Connacht 64 per cent of all larger holdings were under five acres, without counting the unknown number of
dwarf holdings under one acre. Thus during the eighteenth and early
nineteenth centuries the population multiplied on such patches, living
on little except 1–2 lb. of potatoes per person per day and – at least
until the 1820s – some milk and an occasional taste of herring; a
population unparalleled in Western Europe for its poverty.[33]

Since there was no alternative employment – for industrialization
was excluded – the end of this evolution was mathematically predictable. Once the population had grown to the limits of the last potato
patch carved out of the last piece of just cultivable bog, there would
be catastrophe. Soon after the end of the French wars its advance
signs appeared. Food shortage and epidemic disease began once again
to decimate a people whose mass agrarian discontent is only too easily
explained. The bad harvests and crop diseases of the middle 1840s
merely provided the firing squad for an already condemned people.
Nobody knows, or will ever precisely know, the human cost of the
Great Irish Famine of 1847, which was by far the largest human
catastrophe in European history during our period. Rough estimates
suggest that something like one million people died of and through
hunger and another million emigrated from the stricken island between 1846 and 1851. In 1820 Ireland had just under seven million
inhabitants. In 1846 she had perhaps eight and a half. In 1851 she
was reduced to six and a half and her population has gone down
steadily through emigration since. *'Heu dira fames!'* wrote a parish
priest, reverting to the tones of chroniclers in the dark ages, *'Heu
saeva hujus memorabilis anni pestilentia!'* [34] in those months when
no children came to be christened in the parishes of Galway and
Mayo, because none were born.

India and Ireland were perhaps the worst countries to be a peasant
in between 1789 and 1848; but nobody who had the choice would
have wished to be a farm-labourer in England either. It is generally
agreed that the situation of this unhappy class deteriorated markedly
after the middle 1790s, partly through economic forces, partly
through the pauperizing 'Speenhamland System' (1795), a well-
meant but mistaken attempt to guarantee the labourer a minimum
wage by subsidizing wages out of poor rates. Its chief effect was to encourage farmers to lower wages, and to demoralize the labourers.
Their feeble and ignorant stirrings of revolt can be measured by the

increase in offences against the game laws in the 1820s, by arson and offences against property in the 1830s and 1840s, but above all by the desperate, helpless 'last labourers rising', an epidemic of riot which spread spontaneously from Kent through numerous counties at the end of 1830 and was savagely repressed. Economic liberalism proposed to solve the labourers' problem in its usual brisk and ruthless manner by forcing him to find work at an economic wage or to migrate. The *New Poor Law* of 1834, a statute of quite uncommon callousness, gave him poor relief only within the new workhouses (where he had to separate from wife and child in order to discourage the sentimental and unmalthusian habit of thoughtless procreation) and withdrawing the parish guarantee of a minimum livelihood. The cost of the poor law went down drastically (though at least a million Britons remained paupers up to the end of our period), and the labourers slowly began to move. Since agriculture was depressed their situation continued to be very miserable. It did not substantially improve until the 1850s.

Farm-labourers were indeed badly off everywhere, though perhaps in the most backward and isolated areas no worse off than usual. The unhappy discovery of the potato made it easy to depress their standard of life in large parts of Northern Europe, and substantial improvement in their situation did not occur, e.g. in Prussia, until the 1850s or 1860s. The situation of the self-sufficient peasant was probably rather better, though that of the smallholder was desperate enough in times of famine. A peasant country like France was probably less affected by the general agricultural depression after the boom of the Napoleonic wars than any other. Indeed a French peasant who looked across the Channel in 1840 and compared his situation and that of the English labourer with things in 1788 could hardly doubt which of the two had made the better bargain.[35] Meanwhile, from across the Atlantic, the American farmers observed the peasantry of the old world and congratulated themselves on their good fortune in not belonging to it.

NOTES

1 Haxthausen, Studien . . . ueber Russland (1847), II, p. 3.
2 J. Billingsley, *Survey of the Board of Agriculture for Somerset* (1798), p. 52.

3 Even in England it was seriously proposed in the 1840s.

4 The figures are based on the 'New Domesday Book' of 1871–3, but there is no reason to believe that they do not represent the situation in 1848.

5 *Handwörterbuch d. Staatswissenschaften* (Second Ed.), art. Grundbesitz.

6 Th. von der Goltz, *Gesch. d. Deutschen Landwirtschaft* (1903), II; Sartorius v. Waltershausen, *Deutsche Wirtschaftgeschichte 1815–1914* (1923), p. 132.

7 Quoted in L. A. White ed., *The Indian Journals of Lewis, Henry Morgan* (1959), p. 15.

8 Thus it was estimated in the early 1830s that the pool of surplus employable labour was 1 in 6 of the total population in urban and industrial England, 1 in 20 in France and Germany, 1 in 25 in Austria and Italy, 1 in 30 in Spain and 1 in 100 in Russia.[9]

9 L. V. A. de Villeneuve Bargemont, *Economie Politique Chrétienne* (1834), Vol. II, p. 3 ff.

10 C. Issawi, Egypt since 1800. *Journal of Economic History*, XXI, 1, 1961, p. 5.

11 B. J. Hovde, *The Scandinavian Countries 1720–1860* (1943), Vol. I, p. 279. For the increase in the average harvest from 6 million tons (1770) to 10 millions, see *Hwb. d. Staatswissenschaften*, art. Bauernbefreiung.

12 A. Chabert, *Essai sur les mouvements des prix et des revenus 1798–1820* (1949) II, p. 27 ff; l. l'Huillier, *Recherches sur l'Alsace Napoléonienne* (1945), p. 470.

13 e.g. G. Desert in E. Labrousse ed. *Aspects de la Crise . . . 1846–51* (1956), p. 58.

14 J. Godechot, *La Grande Nation* (1956), II, p. 584.

15 A. Agthe, *Ursprung u. Lage d. Landarbeiter in Livland* (1909), pp. 122–8.

16 The creation of large estates and landless labourers was encouraged by the lack of local industrial development and the production of one or two main export crops (chiefly grain). This lends itself easily to such organization. (In Russia at this time 90 per cent of commercial grain sales came from estates, only 10 per cent from peasant holdings.) On the other hand where local industrial development created a growing and *varied* market for town food near by, the peasant or small farmer had the advantage. Hence, while in Prussia the peasant emancipation expropriated the serf, in Bohemia the peasant emerged from liberation after 1848 into independence.[17]

17 For Russia, Lyashchenko, op. cit., p. 360; for comparison between Prussia and Bohemia, W. Stark, Niedergang und Ende d. Landwirtsch. Grossbetriebs in d. Boehm. Laendern (*Jb. f. Nat. Oek*, 146, 1937, p. 434 ff).

18 F. Luetge, Auswirkung der Bauernbefreiung, in *Jb. f. Nat. Oek.* 157, 1943, p. 353 ff.

19 R. Zangheri, *Prime Ricerche sulla distribuzione della proprietà fondiaria* (1957).

20 E. Sereni, *Il Capitalismo nelle Campagne* (1948), pp. 175–6.

21 It has been plausibly suggested that this powerful rural bourgeoisie which 'is in substance the social class guiding and regulating the march toward Italian unity', by its very agrarian orientation, tended towards doctrinaire free trade, which gained Italian unity much goodwill from Britain, but also held back Italian industrialization.[22]

22 cf. G. Mori, La storia dell'industria italiana contemporanea (*Annali dell'Instituto Giangiacomo Feltrinelli*, II, 1959, pp. 278–9); and the same author's 'Osservazioni sul libero-scambismo dei moderati nel Risorgimento' (*Rivista Storica del Socialismo*, III, 9, 1960).

23 Dal Pane, *Storia del Lavoro in Italia dagli inizi del secolo XVIII al 1815* (1958), p. 119.

24 R. Zangheri ed. *Le Campagne emiliane nell'epoca moderna* (1957), p. 73.

25 J. Vicens Vives, ed. *Historia Social y Economica de España y America* (1959), IVii, pp. 92, 95.

26 M. Emerit, L'état intellectuel et moral de l'Algérie en 1830, *Revue d'Histoire Moderne et Contemporaine*, I, 1954, p. 207.

27 These lands correspond to the lands given to the church for charitable or ritual purposes in medieval Christian countries.

28 R. Dutt, *The Economic History of India under early British Rule* (n.d. Fourth Ed.), p. 88.

29 R. Dutt, *India and the Victorian Age* (1904), pp. 56–7.

30 B. S. Cohn, The initial British impact on India (*Journal of Asian Studies*, 19, 1959–60, pp. 418–31) shows that in the Benares district (Uttar Pradesh) officials used their position to acquire land wholesale. Of 74 holders of large estates towards the end of the century, 23 owed the original title to the land to their connections with civil servants (p. 430).

31 Sulekh Chandra Gupta, Land Market in the North Western Provinces (Uttar Pradesh) in the first half of the nineteenth century (*Indian Economic Review*, IV, 2, August 1958). See also the same author's equally illuminating and pioneering Agrarian Background of 1857 Rebellion in the North-western Provinces (*Enquiry*, N. Delhi, Feb. 1959).

32 R. P. Dutt, *India Today* (1940), pp. 129–30.

33 K. H. Connell, Land and Population in Ireland, *Economic History Review*, II, 3, 1950, pp. 285, 288.

34 S. H. Cousens, Regional Death Rates in Ireland during the Great Famine. *Population Studies*, XIV, 1, 1960, p. 65.

35 'Having been much among the peasantry and labouring class

both at home and abroad, I must in truth say that a more civil, cleanly, industrious, frugal, sober or better-dressed people than the French peasantry, for persons in their condition . . . I have never known. In these respects they furnish a striking contrast with a considerable portion of the Scotch agricultural labourers, who are dirty and squalid to an excess; with many of the English, who are servile, broken-spirited and severely straitened in their means of living; with the poor Irish, who are half-clad and in a savage condition. . . .' H. Colman, *The Agricultural and Rural Economy of France, Belgium, Holland and Switzerland* (1848), 25-6.

9

Towards an Industrial World

These are indeed glorious times for the Engineers.
James Nasmyth, inventor of the steam hammer [1]

Devant de tels témoins, o secte progressive,
Vantez-nous le pouvoir de la locomotive,
Vantez-nous le vapeur et les chemins de fer.
A. Pommier [2]

I

Only one economy was effectively industrialized by 1848, the British, and consequently dominated the world. Probably by the 1840s the USA and a good part of Western and Central Europe had stepped across, or were on, the threshold of industrial revolution. It was already reasonably certain that the USA would eventually be considered – within twenty years, thought Richard Cobden in the middle 1830s [3] – a serious competitor to the British, and by the 1840s Germans, though perhaps no one else, already pointed to the rapid industrial advance of their countrymen. But prospects are not achievements, and by the 1840s the actual industrial transformations of the non-English-speaking world were still modest. There were, for instance, by 1850 a total of little more than a hundred miles of railway line in the whole of Spain, Portugal, Scandinavia, Switzerland and the entire Balkan peninsula, and (omitting the USA) less than this in all the non-European continents put together. If we omit Britain and a few patches elsewhere, the economic and social world of the 1840s can easily be made to look not so very different from that of 1788. Most of the population of the world, then as earlier, were peasants. In 1830 there was, after all, still only one western city of more than a million inhabitants (London), one of more than half a million (Paris) and – omitting Britain – only nineteen European cities of more than a hundred thousand.

This slowness of change in the non-British world meant that its economic movements continued, until the end of our period, to be controlled by the age-old-rhythm of good and bad harvests rather than by the new one of alternating industrial booms and slumps. The crisis of 1857 was probably the first that was both world-wide and caused by events other than agrarian catastrophe. This fact, incidentally, had the most far-reaching political consequences. The rhythm of change in industrial and non-industrial areas diverged between 1780 and 1848.[4]

The economic crisis which set fire to so much of Europe in 1846-8 was an old-style agrarian-dominated depression. It was in a sense the last, and perhaps worst, economic breakdown of the *ancien régime* in economics. Not so in Britain, where the worst breakdown of the period of early industrialism occurred between 1839 and 1842 for purely 'modern' reasons, and indeed coincided with fairly low corn-prices. The point of spontaneous social combustion in Britain was reached in the unplanned Chartist general strike of the summer of 1842 (the so-called 'plug riots'). By the time it was reached on the continent in 1848, Britain was merely suffering the first cyclical depression of the long era of Victorian expansion, as also was Belgium, the other more or less industrial economy of Europe. A continental revolution without a corresponding British movement, as Marx foresaw, was doomed. What he did not foresee was that the unevenness of British and Continental development made it inevitable that the continent should rise alone.

Nevertheless, what counts about the period from 1789 to 1848 is not that by later standards its economic changes were small, but that fundamental changes were plainly taking place. The first of these was demographic. World population – and especially the population of the world within the orbit of the dual revolution – had begun that unprecedented 'explosion' which has in the course of 150 years or so multiplied its numbers. Since few countries before the nineteenth century kept anything corresponding to censuses, and these in general far from reliable,[5] we do not know accurately how rapidly population rose in this period; it was certainly unparalleled, and greatest (except perhaps in underpopulated countries filling empty and hitherto under-utilized spaces such as Russia) in the economically most advanced areas. The population of the USA (swollen by immigration, encouraged by the unlimited spaces and resources of a continent) increased almost six times over from 1790 to 1850, from four to twenty-three millions. The population of the United King-

1 The absolute monarch:
Louis XVI of France, 1754–93

2 The middle classes: The Flacquer family (Spain) seen in the early nineteenth century

3 Aristocracy and gentry: German gentlemen out shooting rabbits, at the turn of the nineteenth century

4 The intellectuals:
revolutionary students in
the guard room of the Aula
of the University of Vienna

5 The financier:
Nathan Meyer Rothschild
(1777–1836), observed at
the Royal Exchange
by Dighton

6 and 7 The peasantry:
The agricultural labourer of the
nineteenth century

A peasant rising
in Moravia during the early
nineteenth century

8 The steel manufacturers of Sheffield, showing the
'Hull' or workshop of the razor grinders, and the
use of the fan

9 The new social order:
King Hudson, the railway magnate,
receives the homage of the old social hierarchy

10 The setting of noble life: the entrance hall
at Carlton House, which was built by John Nash
for the Prince Regent

11 The setting of middle-class life:
Biedemayer interior, Austria, from the 1830s

12 The slum: St Giles,
the notorious rookery,
in the 1840s

13 The industrial scene:
the Percy Pit from G. H. Harris' sketches
of coal mines in Northumberland and Durham

14 The French Revolution: the taking of the Bastille, July 14, 1789

15 Marie Antoinette on the way to execution, sketched by the Jacobin painter, Jean Louis David

16   The secular myth: David's idealization of Bonaparte
crossing the Alps, in the traces of Hannibal and
Charlemagne, turns man into superman

17 Apotheosis of the post-Napoleonic revolution: Delacroix's famous painting symbolizes not only the French Revolution of 1830, but the entire romantic conception and era of revolt

18 Polish insurgents, somewhat romanticized, forced into emigration after the defeat of the revolt of 1830-1

19 The people burning the throne at the foot of the July Column, 1848

20 An 'armed man of the people', Vienna, 1848

21 Neo-Gothic was the style of romantic architecture, conservative, medievalist and often religious. The Walter Scott Memorial, Edinburgh, commemorates this longing for a vanished or disappearing past

22 The dominant idiom of architecture, however, remained Classical. The townscape of Berlin, *Unter den Linden*, shaped by the neo-Classical genius of Schinkel

23 and 24 (*above*) The classical horse – suitably enough a race-horse, 'Molly Longlegs' owned by an English aristocrat and painted with accurate elegance by Stubbs – faces the romantic horse.

(*below*) Delacroix's animal is a force of nature, a symbol of boundless power, passion and freedom against a background of thunderstorm

25 The old contrasts with the new. Elegant mail coaches like the Brighton stage, here seen outside its London coach office (1814), were the last word in rapidity and ease of transport. They now ran on metalled roads constructed by great engineer road-builders like Telford and Macadam

26 The new railway made the mail coaches immediately obsolete. In the atmosphere of the Bay of Naples, not normally a cradle of technical progress, the first Italian railway from Naples to Portici was opened in 1849

27 The new technology made possible inspiring
triumphs, such as the construction of the Thames Tunnel
(1825–43) between Rotherhithe and Wapping. Like so
many other daring achievements, it was the work of
Isambard Kingdom Brunel

28   Michael Faraday demonstrating his discoveries
at a lecture at the Royal Institution in 1846

29   The revolutionary use of gaslight, first used for
streets in Pall Mall in 1805. This cartoon by Rowlandson
was drawn four years later, and shows the gaslamps
outside Carlton House Terrace

A PEEP AT THE GAS LIGHTS IN PALL-MALL.

dom almost doubled between 1800 and 1850, almost trebled between 1750 and 1850. The population of Prussia (1846 boundaries) almost doubled from 1800 to 1846, as did that of European Russia (without Finland). The populations of Norway, Denmark, Sweden, Holland, and large parts of Italy almost doubled between 1750 and 1850, but increased at a less extraordinary rate during our period; that of Spain and Portugal increased by a third.

Outside Europe we are less well-informed, though it would seem that the population of China increased at a rapid rate in the eighteenth and early nineteenth century, until European intervention and the traditional cyclical movement of Chinese political history produced the breakdown of the flourishing administration of the Manchu dynasty, which was at the peak of its effectiveness in this period.[6] In Latin America it probably increased at a rate comparable to Spain's.[7] There is no sign of any population explosion in other parts of Asia. Africa's population probably remained stable. Only certain empty spaces populated by white settlers increased at a really extraordinary rate, like Australia which in 1790 had virtually no white inhabitants but by 1851 had a half-million.

This remarkable increase in population naturally stimulated the economy immensely, though we ought to regard it as a consequence rather than an exogenous cause of the economic revolution; for without it so rapid a population growth could not have been maintained for more than a limited period. (Indeed, in Ireland, where is was not supplemented by constant economic revolution, it was not maintained.) It produced more labour, above all more *young* labour and more consumers. The world of our period was a far younger world than any previous one : filled with children, and with young couples or people in the prime of their lives.

The second major change was in communications. Railways were admittedly only in their infancy in 1848, though already of considerable practical importance in Britain, the USA, Belgium, France and Germany, but even before their introduction the improvement was, by former standards, breathtaking. The Austrian empire, for instance (omitting Hungary) added over 30,000 miles of road between 1830 and 1847, thus multiplying its highway mileage by two-and-a-third.[8] Belguim almost doubled its road network between 1830 and 1850, and even Spain, thanks largely to French occupation, almost doubled its tiny highway length. The USA, as usual more gigantic in its enterprises than any other country, multiplied its network of mail-coach roads more than eight times – from 21,000 miles in 1800 to 170,000 in 1850.[9] While Britain acquired her system of canals, France built 2,000 miles of them (1800–47), and the USA opened such crucial waterways as the Erie and the Chesapeake and Ohio. The total shipping tonnage of the western world more than doubled between 1800 and the early 1840s, and already steamships linked Britain and France (1822) and plied up and down the Danube. (There were in 1840 about 370,000 tons of steam shipping compared to nine million of sail, though in fact this may have already represented about one sixth of carrying capacity.) Here again the Americans outdid the rest of the world, racing even the British for the possession of the largest merchant fleet.[10]

Nor would we underestimate the sheer improvement in speed and carrying capacity thus achieved. No doubt the coach-service which drove the Tsar of all the Russias from St Petersburg to Berlin in four days (1834) was not available to lesser humans; but the new rapid mail (copied from the French and English), which after 1824 drove from Berlin to Magdeburg in fifteen hours instead of two and a half days, was. The railway and Rowland Hill's brilliant invention of the standardized charge for postal matter in 1839 (supplemented by the invention of the adhesive stamp in 1841) multiplied the mails; but even before both, and in countries less advanced than Britain, it increased rapidly : between 1830 and 1840 the number of letters annually sent in France rose from 64 to 94 millions. Sailing ships were not merely faster and more reliable : they were on average also bigger.[11]

Technically, no doubt, these improvements were not as deeply inspiring as the railways, though the ravishing bridges, curving freshly across the rivers, the great artificial waterways and docks, the splendid clipper-ships gliding like swans in full sail, and the elegant new mail-coaches were and remain some of the most beautiful products of industrial design. But as means of facilitating travel and transport, of linking town and country, poor and rich regions, they were admirably effective. The growth of population owed much to them; for what in pre-industrial times holds it back is not so much the high normal mortality of men, but the periodic catastrophes of – often very localized – famine and food shortage. If famine became less menacing in the western world in this period (except in years of almost universal harvest failure such as 1816–7 and 1846–8), it was primarily because of such improvements in transport, as well as, of course, the general improvement in the efficiency of government and administration (cf. Chapter 10).

The third major change was, naturally enough, in the sheer bulk of commerce and migration. No doubt not everywhere. There is, for instance, no sign that Calabrian or Apulian peasants were yet prepared to migrate, nor that the amount of goods annually brought to the great fair of Nijniy Novgorod increased to any startling extent.[12] But taking the world of the dual revolution as a whole, the movement of men and goods already had the momentum of a landslide. Between 1816 and 1850 something like five million Europeans left their native countries (almost four-fifths of them for the Americas), and within countries the currents of internal migration were far vaster. Between 1780 and 1840 the total international trade of the western world more than trebled; between 1780 and 1850 it multiplied more than fourfold. By later standards all this was no doubt very modest,[13] but by earlier ones – and these after all were what contemporaries compared their age with – they were beyond the wildest dreams.

II

What was more to the point, after about 1830 – the turning-point which the historian of our period cannot miss, whatever his particular field of interest – the rate of economic and social change accelerated visibly and rapidly. Outside Britain the period of the French Revolution and its wars brought relatively little immediate advance, except in the USA which leapt ahead after its own war of independence, doubling its cultivated area by 1810, multiplying its shipping seven-fold, and in general demonstrating its future capacities. (Not only the cotton-gin, but the steam-ship, the early development of assembly-line production – Oliver Evans' flour-mill on a conveyor-belt – are American advances of this period.) The foundations of a good deal of later industry, especially heavy industry, were laid in Napoleonic Europe, but not much survived the end of the wars, which brought crisis everywhere. On the whole the period from 1815 to 1830 was one of setbacks, or at the best of slow recovery. States put their finances in order – normally by rigorous deflation (the Russians were the last to do so in 1841). Industries tottered under the blows of crisis and foreign competition; the American cotton industry was very badly hit. Urbanization was slow: until 1828 the French rural population grew as fast as that of the cities. Agriculture languished, especially in Germany. Nobody observing the economic growth of this period, even outside the formidably expanding British economy, would be inclined to pessimism; but few would judge that any country other than Britain and perhaps the USA was on the immediate threshold of industrial revolution. To take an obvious index of the new industry: outside Britain, the USA and France the number of steam engines and the amount of steam power in the rest of the world in the 1820s was scarcely worth the attention of the statistician.

After 1830 (or thereabouts) the situation changed swiftly and drastically; so much so that by 1840 the characteristic social problems of industrialism – the new proletariat, the horrors of uncontrolled breakneck urbanization – were the commonplace of serious discussion in Western Europe and the nightmare of the politician and administrator. The number of steam engines in Belgium doubled, their horsepower almost trebled, between 1830 and 1838: from 354 (with 11,000 hp) to 712 (with 30,000). By 1850 the small, but by now very heavily industrialized, country had almost 2,300 engines of 66,000 horse-power,[14] and almost 6 million tons of coal production (nearly three times as much as in 1830). In 1830 there had been no joint-stock companies in Belgian mining; by 1841 almost half the coal output came from such companies.

It would be monotonous to quote analogous data for France, for German states, Austria or any other countries and areas in which the foundations of modern industry were laid in these twenty years: Krupps of Germany, for instance, installed their first steam engine in 1835, the first shafts of the great Ruhr coalfield were sunk in 1837, and the first coke-fired furnace was set up in the great Czech iron centre of Vítkovice in 1836, Falck's first rolling-mill in Lombardy in 1839–40. All the more monotonous as – with the exception of Belgium, and perhaps France – the period of really massive industrialization did not occur until after 1848. 1830–48 marks the birth of industrial areas, of famous industrial centres and firms whose names have become familiar from that day to this; but hardly even their adolescence, let alone their maturity. Looking back on the 1830s we know what that atmosphere of excited technical experiment, of discontented and innovating enterprise meant. It meant the opening of the American Middle West; but Cyrus McCormick's first mechanical reaper (1834) and the first 78 bushels of wheat sent eastwards from Chicago in 1838 only take their place in history because of what they led to after 1850. In 1846 the factory which risked manufacturing a hundred reapers was still to be congratulated on its daring : 'it was difficult indeed to find parties with sufficient boldness or pluck and energy, to undertake the hazardous enterprise of building reapers, and quite as difficult to prevail upon farmers to take their chances of cutting their grain with them, or to look favourably upon such innovation.' [15] It meant the systematic building of the railways and heavy industries of Europe, and incidentally, a revolution in the techniques of investment; but if the brothers Pereire had not become the great adventurers of industrial finance after 1851, we should pay little attention to the project of 'a *lending and borrowing office* where industry will borrow from all capitalists on the most favourable terms through the intermediary of the richest bankers acting as guarantors', which they vainly submitted to the new French government in 1830.[16]

As in Britain, consumer goods – generally textiles, but also sometimes foodstuffs – led these bursts of industrialization; but capital goods – iron, steel, coal, etc. – were already more important than in the first British industrial revolution : in 1846 17 per cent of Belgian industrial employment was in capital goods industries as against between 8 and 9 per cent in Britain. By 1850 three-quarters of all Belgian industrial steam-power was in mining and metallurgy.[17] As in Britain, the average new industrial establishment – factory, forge or mine – was rather small, surrounded by a great undergrowth of cheap, technically unrevolutionized domestic, putting-out or subcontracted labour, which grew with the demands of the factories and the market and would eventually be destroyed by the further advances of both. In Belgium (1846) the average number in a woollen, linen and cotton factory establishment was a mere 30, 35 and 43 workers, in Sweden (1838) the average per textile 'factory' was a mere 6 to 7.[18] On the other hand there are signs of rather heavier concentration than in Britain, as indeed one might expect where industry developed later, sometimes as an enclave in agrarian environments using the experience of the earlier pioneers, based on a more highly developed technology, and often enjoying greater planned support from government. In Bohemia (1841) three-quarters of all cotton-spinners were employed in mills with over 100 workers each, and almost half in fifteen mills with over 200 each.[19] (On the other hand virtually all weaving until the 1850s was done on hand-looms.) This was naturally even more so in the heavy industries which now came to the fore : the average Belgian foundry (1838) had 80 workers, the average Belgian coal-mine (1846) something like 150;[20] not to mention the industrial giants like Cockerill's of Seraing, which employed 2,000.

The industrial landscape was thus rather like a series of lakes studded with islands. If we take the country in general as the lake, the islands represent industrial cities, rural complexes (such as the networks of manufacturing villages so common in the central German and Bohemian mountains) or industrial areas : textile towns like Mulhouse, Lille or Rouen in France, Elberfeld-Barmen (the home of Frederick Engels' pious cotton-master family) or Krefeld in Prussia, southern Belgium or Saxony. If we take the broad mass of independent artisans, peasants turning out goods for sale in the winter season, and domestic or putting-out workers as the lake, the islands represent the mills, factories, mines and foundries of various sizes. The bulk of the landscape was still very much water; or – to adapt the metaphor a little more closely to reality – the reed-beds of small scale or dependent production which formed round the industrial and commercial centres. Domestic and other industries founded earlier as appendages of feudalism, also existed. Most of these – e.g. the Silesian linen-industry – were in rapid and tragic decline.[21] The great cities were hardly industrialized at all, though they maintained a vast population of labourers and craftsmen to serve the needs of consumption, transport and general services. Of the world's towns with over 100,000 inhabitants, apart from Lyon, only the British and American ones included obviously industrial centres : Milan, for instance, in 1841 had a mere two small steam engines. In fact the typical industrial centre – in Britain as well as on the continent – was a small or medium-sized provincial town or a complex of villages.

In one important respect, however, continental – and also to some extent American – industrialization, differed from the British. The pre-conditions for its spontaneous development by private enterprise were far less favourable. As we have seen, in Britain there was, after some 200 years of slow preparation, no real shortage of any of the factors of production and no really crippling institutional obstacle to full capitalist development. Elsewhere this was not so. In Germany, for instance, there was a distinct capital shortage; the very modesty of the standard of life among the German middle classes (beautifully transformed though it was into the charming austerities of Biedermayer interior decoration) demonstrates it. It is often forgotten that by contemporary German standards Goethe, whose house in Weimar corresponds to rather more – but not much more – than the standard of comfort of the modest bankers of the British Clapham sect, was a very wealthy man indeed. In the 1820s Court ladies and even princesses in Berlin wore simple *percale* dresses throughout the year; if they owned a silk dress, they saved it for special occasions.[22] The traditional guild system of master, journeyman and apprentice, still stood in the way of business enterprise, of the mobility of skilled labour, and indeed of all economic change : the obligation for a craftsman to belong to a guild was abolished in Prussia in 1811, though not the guilds themselves, whose members were, moreover, politically strengthened by the municipal legislation of the period. Guild production remained almost intact until the 1830s and 40s. Elsewhere the full introduction of *Gewerbefreiheit* had to wait until the 1850s.

A multiplicity of petty states, each with their controls and vested interests, still inhibited rational development. Merely to construct a general customs union (excluding Austria), as Prussia succeeded in doing in its own interest and by the pressure of its strategic position between 1818 and 1834, was a triumph. Each government, mercantilist and paternal, showered its regulations and administrative supervisions on the humble subject; to the benefit of social stability, but to the irritation of the private entrepreneur. The Prussian State controlled the quality and fair price of handicraft production, the activities of the Silesian domestic linen-weaving industry, and the operations of mine-owners on the right bank of the Rhine. Government permission was required before a man could open a mine, and could be withdrawn after he was in business.

Clearly under such circumstances (which can be paralleled in numerous other states), industrial development had to operate rather differently from the British way. Thus throughout the continent government took a much greater hand in it, not merely because it was already accustomed to, but because it had to. William I, King of the United Netherlands, in 1822 founded the *Société Générale pour favoriser l'Industrie Nationale des Pays Bas*, endowed with State land, with 40 per cent or so of its shares subscribed by the King and

5 per cent guaranteed to all other subscribers. The Prussian State continued to operate a large proportion of the country's mines. Without exception the new railway systems were planned by Governments and, if not actually built by them, encouraged by the grant of favourable concessions and the guarantee of investments. Indeed, to this day Britain is the only country whose railway system was built entirely by risk-bearing and profit-making private enterprise, unencouraged by bonuses and guarantees to investors and entrepreneurs. The earliest and best-planned of these networks was the Belgian, projected in the early 1830s, in order to detach the newly independent country from the (primarily waterborne) communication system based on Holland. Political difficulties and the reluctance of the conservative *grande bourgeoisie* to exchange safe for speculative investments postponed the systematic construction of the French network, which the Chamber had decided on in 1833; poverty of resources that of the Austrian, which the State decided to build in 1842, and the Prussian plans.

For similar reasons continental enterprise depended far more than the British on an adequately modernized business, commercial and banking legislation and financial apparatus. The French Revolution in fact provided both : Napoleon's legal codes, with their stress on legally guaranteed freedom of contract, their recognition of bills of exchange and other commercial paper, and their arrangements for joint-stock enterprise (such as the *société anonyme* and the *commandite*, adopted all over Europe except in Britain and Scandinavia) became the general model for the world for this reason. Moreover, the devices for financing industry which sprang from the fertile brain of those revolutionary young Saint-Simonians, the brothers Pereire, were welcomed abroad. Their greatest triumph had to await the world boom era of the 1850s; but already in the 1830s the Belgian *Société Générale* began to practise investment banking of the kind the Pereires envisaged and financiers in Holland (though not yet listened to by the bulk of businessmen) adopted the Saint-Simonian ideas. In essence these ideas aimed at mobilizing a variety of domestic capital resources which would not spontaneously have gone into industrial development, and whose owners would not have known where to invest them had they wanted to, through banks and investment trusts. After 1850 it produced the characteristic continental (especially German) phenomenon of the large bank acting as investor as much as banker, and thereby dominating industry and facilitating its early concentration.

III

However, the economic development of this period contains one gigantic paradox : France. On paper no country should have advanced more rapidly. It possessed, as we have seen, institutions ideally suited to capitalist development. The ingenuity and inventiveness of its entrepreneurs was without parallel in Europe. Frenchmen invented or first developed the department store, advertising, and, guided by the supremacy of French science, all manner of technical innovations and achievements – photography (with Nicephore Nièpce and Daguerre), the Leblanc soda process, the Berthollet chlorine bleach, electroplating, galvanization. French financiers were the most inventive of the world. The country possessed large capital reserves which it exported, aided by its technical expertise, all over the continent – and even, after 1850, with such things as the London General Omnibus Company, to Britain. By 1847 about 2,250 million francs had gone abroad [23] – a quantity second only to the British and astronomically bigger than any one else's. Paris was a centre of international finance lagging only a little behind London; indeed, in times of crisis such as 1847, stronger. French enterprise in the 1840s founded the gas companies of Europe – in Florence, Venice, Padua, Verona – and obtained charters to found them all over Spain, Algeria, Cairo and Alexandria. French enterprise was about to finance the railways of the European continent (except those of Germany and Scandinavia).

Yet in fact French economic development at the base was distinctly slower than that of other countries. Her population grew quietly, but it did not leap upwards. Her cities (with the exception of Paris) expanded only modestly; indeed in the early 1830s some contracted. Her industrial power in the later 1840s was no doubt larger than that of all other continental European countries – she possessed as much steam-power as the rest of the continent put together – but she had lost ground relatively to Britain and was about to lose it relatively to Germany. Indeed, in spite of her advantages and early start, France never became a major industrial power comparable to Britain, Germany and the USA.

The explanation of this paradox is, as we have seen (see above pp. 91–2), the French Revolution itself, which took away with the hand of Robespierre much of what it gave with the hand of the Constituent Assembly. The capitalist part of the French economy was a superstructure erected on the immovable base of the peasantry and petty-bourgeoisie. The landless free labourers merely trickled into the cities; the standardized cheap goods which made the fortunes of the progressive industrialist elsewhere lacked a sufficiently large and expanding market. Plenty of capital was saved, but why should it be invested in home industry? [24] The wise French entrepreneur made luxury goods and not goods for mass consumption; the wise financier promoted foreign rather than home industries. Private enterprise and economic growth go together only when the latter provides higher profits for the former than other forms of business. In France it did not, though through France it fertilized the economic growth of other countries.

At the opposite extreme from France stood the USA. The country suffered from a shortage of capital, but it was ready to import it in any quantities, and Britain stood ready to export it. It suffered from an acute shortage of manpower, but the British Isles and Germany exported their surplus population, after the great hunger of the middle forties, in millions. It lacked sufficient men of technical skill; but even these – Lancashire cotton workers, Welsh miners and ironmen – could be imported from the already industrialized sector of the world, and the characteristic American knack of inventing labour-saving and above all labour-simplifying machinery was already fully deployed. The USA lacked merely settlement and transport to open up its apparently endless territories and resources. The mere process of internal expansion was enough to keep its economy in almost unlimited growth, though American settlers, Governments, missionaries and traders already expanded overland to the Pacific or pushed their trade – backed by the most dynamic and second largest merchant fleet of the world – across the oceans, from Zanzibar to Hawaii. Already the Pacific and the Caribbean were the chosen fields of American empire.

Every institution of the new republic encouraged accumulation, ingenuity and private enterprise. A vast new population, settled in the seaboard cities and the newly occupied inland states, demanded the same standardized personal, household and farm goods and

equipment and provided an ideally homogeneous market. The rewards of invention and enterprise were ample : and the inventors
of the steamship (1807–13), the humble tack (1807), the screw-cutting
machine (1809), the artificial denture (1822), insulated wire (1827–31),
the revolver (1835), the idea of the typewriter and sewing machine
(1843–6), the rotary printing press (1846) and a host of pieces of farm
machinery, pursued them. No economy expanded more rapidly in
this period than the American, even though its really headlong rush
was only to occur after 1860.

Only one major obstacle stood in the way of the conversion of the
USA into the world economic power which it was soon to become :
the conflict between an industrial and farming north and a semi-
colonial south. For while the North benefited from the capital,
labour and skills of Europe – and notably Britain – as an independent
economy, the South (which imported few of these resources) was a
typical dependent economy of Britain. Its very success in supplying
the booming factories of Lancashire with almost all their cotton perpetuated its dependence, comparable to that which Australia was
about to develop on wool, the Argentine on meat. The South was
for free trade, which enabled it to sell to Britain and in return to buy
cheap British goods; the North, almost from the beginning (1816),
protected the home industrialist heavily against any foreigner – i.e.
the British – who would then have undersold him. North and South
competed for the territories of the West – the one for slave plantations and backward self-sufficient hill squatters, the other for mechanical reapers and mass slaughterhouses; and until the age of the
trans-continental railroad the South, which controlled the Missis-
sippi delta through which the Middle West found its chief outlet,
held some strong economic cards. Not until the Civil War of 1861–5
– which was in effect the unification of America by and under
Northern capitalism – was the future of the American economy
settled.

The other future giant of the world economy, Russia, was as yet
economically negligible, though forward-looking observers already
predicted that its vast size, population and resources must sooner or
later come into their own. The mines and manufactures created by
eighteenth-century Tsars with landlords or feudal merchants as employers, serfs as labourers, were slowly declining. The new industries
– domestic and small-scale textile works – only began a really notice-

able expansion in the 1860s. Even the export of corn to the west from the fertile black earth belt of the Ukraine made only moderate progress. Russian Poland was rather more advanced, but, like the rest of Eastern Europe, from Scandinavia in the north to the Balkan peninsula in the south, the age of major economic transformation was not yet at hand. Nor was it in Southern Italy and Spain, except for small patches of Catalonia and the Basque country. And even in Northern Italy, where economic changes were very much larger, they were far more obvious as yet in agriculture (always, in this region, a major outlet for capital investment and business enterprise) and in trade and shipping than in manufactures. But the development of these was handicapped all over Southern Europe by the acute shortage of what was then still the only important source of industrial power, coal.

One part of the world thus swept forward towards industrial power; another lagged. But the two phenomena are not unconnected with each other. Economic stagnation, sluggishness, or even regression was the product of economic advance. For how could the relatively backward economies resist the force – or in certain instances the attraction – of the new centres of wealth, industry and commerce? The English and certain other European areas could plainly undersell all competitors. To be the workshop of the world suited them. Nothing seemed more 'natural' than that the less advanced should produce food and perhaps minerals, exchanging these non-competitive goods for British (or other West-European) manufactures. 'The sun,' Richard Cobden told the Italians 'is your coal'.[25] Where local power was in the hands of large landowners or even progressive farmers or ranchers, the exchange suited both sides. Cuban plantation owners were quite happy to make their money by sugar, and to import the foreign goods which allowed the foreigners to buy sugar. Where local manufacturers could make their voice heard, or local governments appreciated the advantages of balanced economic development or merely the disadvantages of dependence, the disposition was less sunny. Frederick List, the German economist – as usual wearing the congenial costume of philosophic abstraction – rejected an international economy which in effect made Britain the chief or only industrial power and demanded protectionism; and so, as we have seen – minus the philosophy – did the Americans.

All this assumed that an economy was politically independent and strong enough to accept or reject the role for which the pioneer industrialization of one small sector of the world had cast it. Where it was not independent, as in colonies, it had no choice. India, as we have seen, was in the process of de-industrialization, Egypt provided an even more vivid illustration of the process. For there the local ruler, Mohammed Ali, had in fact systematically set out to turn his country into a modern, i.e. among other things an industrial, economy. Not only did he encourage the growing of cotton for the world market (from 1821), but by 1838 he had invested the very considerable sum of £12 millions in industry, which employed perhaps thirty to forty thousand workers. What would have happened had Egypt been left to herself, we do not know. For what did happen was that the Anglo-Turkish Convention of 1838 forced foreign traders on to the country, thus undermining the foreign trade monopoly through which Mohammed Ali had operated; and the defeat of Egypt by the West in 1839–41 forced him to reduce his army, and therefore removed most of the incentive which had led him to industrialize.[26] Not for the first or last time in the nineteenth century the gunboats of the west 'opened' a country to trade, i.e. to the superior competition of the industrialized sector of the world. Who, looking at Egypt in the time of the British protectorate at the end of the century, would have recognized the country which had, fifty years earlier – and to the disgust of Richard Cobden[27] – been the first non-white state to seek the modern way out of economic backwardness?

Of all the economic consequences of the age of dual revolution this division between the 'advanced' and the 'underdeveloped' countries proved to be the most profound and the most lasting. Roughly speaking by 1848 it was clear which countries were to belong to the first group, i.e. Western Europe (minus the Iberian peninsula), Germany, Northern Italy and parts of central Europe, Scandinavia, the USA and perhaps the colonies settled by English-speaking migrants. But it was equally clear that the rest of the world was, apart from small patches, lagging, or turning – under the informal pressure of western exports and imports or the military pressure of western gunboats and military expeditions – into the economic dependencies of the west. Until the Russians in the 1930s developed means of leaping this chasm between the 'backward' and the 'advanced', it would remain immovable, untraversed, and indeed growing wider, between the minority and the majority of the world's inhabitants. No fact has determined the history of the twentieth century more firmly than this.

NOTES

1 Quoted in W. Armytage, *A Social History of Engineering.* (1961), p. 126.
2 Quoted in R. Picard, *Le Romantisme Social,* (1944), pt. 2, cap. 6.
3 J. Morley, *Life of Richard Cobden* (1903 ed.), p. 108.
4 The world triumph of the industrial sector once more tended to make it converge, though in a different manner.
5 The first British census was that of 1801; the first reasonably adequate one, that of 1831.
6 The usual dynastic cycle in China lasted about 300 years; the Manchu came to power in the mid-seventeenth century.
7 R. Baron Castro, La poblacion hispano-americana, *Journal of World History,* V, 1959–60, pp. 339–40.
8 J. Blum, Transportation and Industry in Austria 1815–48, *Journal of Modern History* XV (1943), p. 27.
9 Mulhall, op. cit., Post Office.
10 They almost achieved their object by 1860, before the iron ship once again gave the British supremacy.
11 Mulhall, ibid.
12 P. A. Khromov, *Ekonomicheskoe Razvitie Rossii v XIX–XX Vekakh* (1950), Table 19, p. 482–3. But the amount of sales increased much faster. cf. also J. Blum, *Lord and Peasant in Russia,* p. 287.
13 Thus between 1850 and 1888 twenty-two million Europeans emigrated, and in 1889 total international trade amounted to nearly £3,400 million compared to less than £600 million in 1840.
14 R. E. Cameron, op. cit., p. 347.
15 Quoted in S. Giedion, *Mechanisation Takes Command* (1948), p. 152.
16 R. E. Cameron, op. cit., p. 115 ff.
17 R. E. Cameron, op. cit., p. 347; W. Hoffmann, *The Growth of Industrial Economies* (1958), p. 71.
18 W. Hoffmann, op. cit., p. 48; Mulhall, op. cit., p. 377.
19 J. Purs, The Industrial Revolution in the Czech Lands (*Historica,* II (1960), pp. 199–200).
20 R. E. Cameron, op. cit., p. 347; Mulhall, op. cit., p. 377.
21 H. Kisch, The Textile Industries in Silesia and the Rhineland, *Journal of Economic History,* XIX, December 1959.
22 O. Fischel and M. V. Boehn, *Die Mode, 1818–1842* (Munich 1924), p. 136.

23 R. E. Cameron, op. cit., pp. 79, 85.

24 The locus classicus of this discussion is G. Lefebvre, *La révolution francaise et les paysans* (1932), reprinted in *Etudes sur la révolution francaise* (1954).

25 G. Mori, Osservazioni sul liberoscambismo dei moderati nel Risorgimento, *Riv. Storic. del Socialismo*, III, 1960, p. 8.

26 C. Issawi, Egypt since 1800, *Journal of Economic History*. March 1961, XXI, p. 1.

27 'All this waste is going on with the best raw cotton, which ought to be sold to us. . . . This is not all the mischief, for the very hands that are driven into such manufactures are torn from the cultivation of the soil.' Morley, *Life of Cobden*, Chapter 3.

10

The Career Open to Talent

*One day I walked with one of these middle-class gen-
tlemen into Manchester. I spoke to him about the
disgraceful unhealthy slums and drew his attention to the
disgusting condition of that part of town in which the
factory workers lived. I declared that I had never seen so
badly built a town in my life. He listened patiently and
at the corner of the street at which we parted company, he
remarked: 'And yet there is a great deal of money made
here. Good morning, Sir!'*

      F. Engels, *Condition of the Working Class in England* [1]

*L'habitude prévalut parmi les nouveaux financiers de
faire publier dans les journaux le menu des diners et les
noms des convives.*

      M. Capefigue [2]

I

The formal institutions overthrown or founded by a revolution are
easily discernible, but they do not measure its effects. The chief result of the Revolution in France was to put an end to aristocratic
society. Not to 'aristocracy' in the sense of hierarchy of social status
distinguished by titles or other visible marks of exclusiveness, and
often modelling itself on the prototype of such hierarchies, nobility
'of blood'. Societies built on individual careerism welcome such
visible and established marks of success. Napoleon even recreated a
formal nobility of sorts, which joined the surviving old aristocrats
after 1815. Nor did the end of aristocratic society mean the end of
aristocratic influence. Rising classes naturally tend to see the symbols
of their wealth and power in terms of what their former superior
groups have established as the standards of comfort, luxury or pomp.
The wives of enriched Cheshire drapers would become 'ladies', instructed by the numerous books of etiquette and gracious living

which multiplied for this purpose from the 1840s, for the same reason as Napoleonic war-profiteers appreciated a baron's title, or that bourgeois salons were filled with 'velvet, gold, mirrors, some poor imitations of Louis XV chairs and other furniture . . . English styles for the servants and horses, but without the aristocratic spirit'. What could be prouder than the boast of some banker, sprung from who knows where, that 'When I appear in my box at the theatre, all *lorgnettes* are turned on me, and I receive an almost royal ovation?'[3]

Moreover, a culture as profoundly formed by court and aristocracy as the French would not lose the imprint. Thus the marked preoccupation of French prose literature with subtle psychological analyses of personal relationships (which can be traced back to the seventeenth-century aristocratic writers), or the formalized eighteenth-century pattern of sexual campaigning and advertised lovers or mistresses, became an integral part of 'Parisian' bourgeois civilization. Formerly kings had official mistresses; now successful stockjobbers joined them. Courtesans granted their well-paid favours to advertise the success of bankers, who could pay for them as well as young bloods who ruined their estates by them. Indeed in many ways the Revolution preserved aristocratic characteristics of French culture in an exceptionally pure form, for the same reason as the Russian Revolution has preserved classical ballet and the typical nineteenth-century bourgeois attitude to 'good literature' with exceptional fidelity. They were taken over by it, assimilated to it, as a desirable heritage from the past, and henceforth protected against the normal evolutionary erosion by it.

And yet the old régime was dead, even though the fishermen of Brest in 1832 regarded the cholera as a punishment by God for the deposition of the legitimate king. Formal republicanism among the peasantry was slow to spread beyond the Jacobin Midi and some long dechristianized areas, but in the first genuine universal election, that of May 1848, legitimism was already confined to the West and the poorer central departments. The political geography of modern rural France was already substantially recognizable. Higher up the social scale, the Bourbon Restoration did not restore the old régime; or, rather, when Charles X tried to do so he was thrown out. Restoration society was that of Balzac's capitalists and careerists, of Stendhal's Julien Sorel, rather than that of the returned emigré dukes. A geological epoch separates it from the 'sweetness of life' of the 1780s to which Talleyrand looked back. Balzac's Rastignac is far nearer to Maupassant's *Bel-Ami*, the typical figure of the 1880s, or even to Sammy Glick, the typical one of Hollywood in the 1940s, than to Figaro, the non-aristocratic success of the 1780s.

In a word the society of post-revolutionary France was bourgeois in its structure and values. It was the society of the parvenu, i.e. the self-made man, though this was not completely obvious except when the country was itself governed by parvenus, i.e. when it was republican or bonapartist. It may not seem excessively revolutionary to us, that half the French peerage in 1840 belonged to families of the old nobility, but to contemporary French bourgeois the fact that half had been commoners in 1789 was very much more striking; especially when they looked at the exclusive social hierarchies of the rest of continental Europe. The phrase 'when good Americans die, they go to Paris' expresses what Paris became in the nineteenth century, though it did not fully become the parvenu's paradise until the Second Empire. London, or even more Vienna, St Petersburg or Berlin, were capitals in which money could not yet buy everything, at any rate in the first generation. In Paris, there was very little worth buying that was beyond its reach.

This domination of the new society was not peculiar to France; but if we except the democratic USA it was in certain superficial respects both more obvious and more official in France, though not in fact more profound than in Britain or the Low Countries. In Britain the great chefs were still those who worked for noblemen, like Carême for the Duke of Wellington (he had previously served Talleyrand), or for the oligarchic clubs, like Alexis Soyer of the Reform Club. In France the expensive public restaurant, started by cooks of the nobility who lost their jobs during the Revolution, was already established. A change of world is implied in the title-page of the manual of classical French cookery which read 'by A. Beauvilliers, ancien officier de MONSIEUR, Comte de Provence ... et actuellement Restaurateur, rue de Richelieu no. 26, la Grande Taverne de Londres'.[4] The *gourmand* – a species invented during the Restoration and propagated by Brillat-Savarin's *Almanach des Gourmands* from 1817 – already went to the Café Anglais or the Café de Paris to eat dinners not presided over by hostesses. In Britain the press was still a vehicle of instruction, invective and political pressure. It was in

France that Emile Girardin (1836) founded the modern newspaper – *La Presse* – political but cheap, aimed at the accumulation of advertising revenue, and made attractive to its readers by gossip, serial novels, and various other stunts.[5] (French pioneering in these dubious fields is still recalled by the very words 'journalism' and 'publicity' in English, 'Reklame' and 'Annonce' in German.) Fashion, the department store, the public shop-window which Balzac hymned[7] were French inventions, the product of the 1820s. The Revolution brought that obvious career open to talents, the theatre, into 'good society' at a time when its social status in aristocratic Britain remained analogous to that of boxers and jockeys: at Maisons-Lafitte (named after a banker who made the suburb fashionable), Lablache, Talma and other theatrical people established themselves by the side of the Prince de la Moskowa's splendid house.

The effect of the Industrial Revolution on the structure of bourgeois society was superficially less drastic, but in fact far more profound. For it created new *blocs* of bourgeois which coexisted with the official society, too large to be absorbed by it except by a little assimilation at the very top, and too self-confident and dynamic to wish for absorption except on their own terms. In 1820 these great armies of solid businessmen were as yet hardly visible from Westminster, where peers and their relatives still dominated the unreformed Parliament, or from Hyde Park, where wholly unpuritan ladies like Harriete Wilson (unpuritan even in her refusal to pretend to being a broken blossom) drove their phaetons surrounded by dashing admirers from the armed forces, diplomacy and the peerage, not excluding the Iron and unbourgeois Duke of Wellington himself. The merchants, bankers and even the industrialists of the eighteenth century had been few enough to be assimilated into official society; indeed the first generation of cotton-millionaires, headed by Sir Robert Peel the elder, whose son was being trained for premiership, were fairly solidly Tory, though of a moderate kind. However, the iron plough of industrialization multiplied its hardfaced crops of businessmen under the rainy clouds of the North. Manchester no longer came to terms with London. Under the battle-cry 'What Manchester thinks today London will think tomorrow' it prepared to impose terms on the capital.

The new men from the provinces were a formidable army, all the more so as they became increasingly conscious of themselves as a *class* rather than a 'middle rank' bridging the gap between the upper and lower orders. (The actual term 'middle class' first appears around 1812.) By 1834 John Stuart Mill could already complain that social commentators 'revolved in their eternal circle of landlords, capitalists and labourers, until they seemed to think of the distinction of society into these three classes as though it were one of God's ordinances'.[8] Moreover, they were not merely a class, but a class army of combat, organized at first in conjunction with the 'labouring poor' (who must, they assumed, follow their lead[9]) against the aristocratic society, and later against both proletariat and landlords, most notably in that most class-conscious body the Anti-Corn-Law League. They were self-made men, or at least men of modest origins who owed little to birth, family or formal higher education. (Like Mr Bounderby in Dickens' *Hard Times*, they were not reluctant to advertise the fact.) They were rich and getting richer by the year. They were above all imbued with the ferocious and dynamic self-confidence of those whose own careers prove to them that divine providence, science and history have combined to present the earth to them on a platter.

'Political economy', translated into a few simple dogmatic propositions by self-made journalist-publishers who hymned the virtues of capitalism – Edward Baines of the *Leeds Mercury* (1774–1848), John Edward Taylor of the *Manchester Guardian* (1791–1844), Archibald Prentice of the *Manchester Times* (1792–1857), Samuel Smiles (1812–1904) – gave them intellectual certainty. Protestant dissent of the hard Independent, Unitarian, Baptist and Quaker rather than the emotional Methodist type gave them spiritual certainty and a contempt for useless aristocrats. Neither fear, anger, nor even pity moved the employer who told his workers :

'The God of Nature has established a just and equitable law which man has no right to disturb; when he ventures to do so it is always certain that he, sooner or later, meets with corresponding punishment . . . Thus when masters audaciously combine that by an union of power they may more effectually oppress their servants; by such an act, they insult the majesty of Heaven, and bring down the curse of God upon themselves, while on the other hand, when servants unite to extort from their employers that share of the profit which of right belongs to the master, they equally violate the laws of equity.'[10]

There was an order in the universe, but it was no longer the order of the past. There was only one God, whose name was steam and spoke in the voice of Malthus, McCulloch, and anyone who employed machinery.

The fringe of agnostic eighteenth-century intellectuals and self-made scholars and writers who spoke for them should not obscure the fact that most of them were far too busy making money to bother about anything unconnected with this pursuit. They appreciated their intellectuals, even when, like Richard Cobden (1804–1865) they were not particularly successful businessmen, so long as they avoided unpractical and excessively sophisticated ideas, for they were practical men whose own lack of education made them suspect anything that went much beyond empiricism. Charles Babbage the scientist (1792–1871) proposed his scientific methods to them in vain. Sir Henry Cole, the pioneer of industrial design, technical education and transport rationalization, gave them (with the inestimable help of the German Prince Consort) the most brilliant monument of their endeavours, the Great Exhibition of 1851. But he was forced out of public life nevertheless as a meddling busybody with a taste for bureaucracy, which, like all government interference, they detested, when it did not directly assist their profits. George Stephenson, the self-made colliery mechanic, dominated the new railways, imposing the gauge of the old horse and cart on them – he had never thought of anything else – rather than the imaginative, sophisticated and daring engineer Isambard Kingdom Brunel, who has no monument in the pantheon of engineers constructed by Samuel Smiles, except the damning phrase : 'measured by practical and profitable results the Stephensons were unquestionably the safer men to follow'.[11] The philosophic radicals did their best to construct a network of 'Mechanics' Institutes' – purged of the politically disastrous errors which the operatives insisted, against nature, on hearing in such places – in order to train the technicians of the new and scientifically based industries. By 1848 most of them were moribund, for want of any general recognition that such technological education could teach the Englishman (as distinct from the German or Frenchman) anything useful. There were intelligent, experimentally minded, and even cultured manufacturers in plenty, thronging to the meetings of the new British Association for the Advancement of Science; but it would be an error to suppose that they represented the norm of their class.

A generation of such men grew up in the years between Trafalgar and the Great Exhibition. Their predecessors, brought up in the social framework of cultured and rationalist provincial merchants and dissenting ministers and the intellectual framework of the whig century, were perhaps a less barbarous lot: Josiah Wedgwood the potter (1730–1795) was an FRS, a Fellow of the Society of Antiquaries, and a member of the Lunar Society with Matthew Boulton, his partner James Watt and the chemist and revolutionary Priestley. (His son Thomas experimented with photography, published scientific papers and subsidized the poet Coleridge.) The manufacturer of the eighteenth century naturally built his factories to the design of Georgian builders' books. Their successors, if not more cultured, were at least more prodigal, for by the 1840s they had made enough money to spend freely on pseudo-baronial residences, pseudo-gothic and pseudo-renaissance town-halls, and to rebuild their modest and utilitarian or classic chapels in the perpendicular style. But between the Georgian and the Victorian era there came what has been rightly called the bleak age of the bourgeoisie as well as of the working classes, whose lineaments Charles Dickens has forever caught in his *Hard Times*.

A pietistic protestantism, rigid, self-righteous, unintellectual, obsessed with puritan morality to the point where hypocrisy was its automatic companion, dominated this desolate epoch. 'Virtue', as G. M. Young said, 'advanced on a broad invincible front'; and it trod the unvirtuous, the weak, the sinful (i.e. those who neither made money nor controlled their emotional or financial expenditures) into the mud where they so plainly belonged, deserving at best only of their betters' charity. There was some capitalist economic sense in this. Small entrepreneurs had to plough back much of their profits into the business if they were to become big entrepreneurs. The masses of new proletarians had to be broken into the industrial rhythm of labour by the most draconic labour discipline, or left to rot if they would not accept it. And yet even today the heart contracts at the sight of the landscape constructed by that generation.[12]

You saw nothing in Coketown but what was severely workful. If the members of a religious persuasion built a chapel there – as the members of eighteen religious persuasions had done – they made it a pious warehouse of red brick, with sometimes (but this only in highly ornamented examples) a bell in a bird-cage on the top of it. . . . All the public inscriptions in the town were painted alike, in severe characters of black and white. The jail might have been the infirmary, the infirmary might have been the jail, the town-hall might have been either, or both, or anything else, for anything that appeared to the contrary in the graces of their construction. Fact, fact, fact, everywhere in the material aspect of the town; fact, fact, fact, everywhere in the immaterial. . . . Everything was fact between the lying-in hospital and the cemetery, and what you couldn't state in figures, or show to be purchaseable in the cheapest market and saleable in the dearest, was not and never should be, world without end, Amen.[13]

This gaunt devotion to bourgeois utilitarianism, which the evangelicals and puritans shared with the agnostic eighteenth-century 'philosophic radicals' who put it into logical words for them, produced its own functional beauty in railway lines, bridges and warehouses, and its romantic horror in the smoke-drenched endless greyblack or reddish files of small houses overlooked by the fortresses of the mills. Outside it the new bourgeoisie lived (if it had accumulated enough money to move), dispensing command, moral education and assistance to missionary endeavour among the black heathen abroad. Its men personified the money which proved their right to rule the world; its women, deprived by their husbands' money even of the satisfaction of actually doing household work, personified the virtue of their class : stupid ('be good sweet maid, and let who will be clever'), uneducated, impractical, theoretically unsexual, propertyless and protected. They were the only luxury which the age of thrift and self-help allowed itself.

The British manufacturing bourgeoisie was the most extreme example of its class, but all over the continent there were smaller groups of the same kind : Catholic in the textile districts of the French North or Catalonia, Calvinist in Alsace, Lutheran pietist in the Rhineland, Jewish all over central and eastern Europe. They were rarely quite as hard as in Britain, for they were rarely quite as divorced from older traditions of urban life and paternalism. Leon Faucher was painfully struck, in spite of his doctrinaire liberalism, by the sight of Manchester in the 1840s, as which continental observer was not?[14] But they shared with the English the confidence which came from steady enrichment – between 1830 and 1856 the marriage portions of the Dansette family in Lille increased from 15,000 to 50,000 francs [15] – the absolute faith in economic liberalism, and the rejection of non-economic activities. The spinners' dynasties of Lille maintained their total contempt for the career of arms until the First World War. The Dollfus of Mulhouse dissuaded their young Frédéric Engel from entering the famous Polytechnique, because they feared it might lead him into a military rather than a business career. Aristocracy and its pedigrees did not to begin with tempt them excessively : like Napoleon's marshals they were themselves ancestors.

II

The crucial achievement of the two revolutions was thus that they opened careers to talent, or at any rate to energy, shrewdness, hard work and greed. Not all careers, and not to the top rungs of the ladder, except perhaps in the USA. And yet, how extraordinary were the opportunities, how remote from the nineteenth century the static hierarchical ideal of the past ! Kabinettsrat von Schele of the Kingdom of Hanover, who refused the application of a poor young lawyer for a government post on the grounds that his father was a bookbinder, and he ought to have stuck to that trade, now appeared both vicious and ridiculous.[16] Yet he was doing no more than repeat the age-old proverbial wisdom of the stable pre-capitalist society, and in 1750 the son of a bookbinder would, in all probability, have stuck to his father's trade. Now he no longer had to. Four roads to the stars opened before him : business, education (which in turn led to the three goals of government service, politics and the free professions), the arts and war. The last, important enough in France during the revolutionary and Napoleonic period, ceased to be of much significance during the long generations of peace which succeeded, and perhaps for this reason also ceased to be very attractive. The third was new only insofar as the public rewards of an exceptional capacity to entertain or move the public were now much greater than ever before, as is shown by the rising social status of the stage, which was eventually to produce, in Edwardian Britain, the linked phenomena of the knighted actor and the nobleman marrying the chorus-girl. Even in the post-Napoleonic period they already produced the characteristic phenomena of the idolized singer (e.g. Jenny Lind, the 'Swedish Nightingale') or dancer (e.g. Fanny Elssler) and the deified concert artist (e.g. Paganini and Franz Liszt).

Neither business nor education were high roads open to everybody even among those who were sufficiently emancipated from the grip of custom and tradition to believe that 'people like us' would be admitted to them, to know how to operate in an individualist society, or to accept the desirability of 'bettering themselves'. A toll had to be paid by intending travellers: without *some* initial resources, however minimal, it was difficult to get started on the highway to success. This admission toll was unquestionably higher for those entering upon the education road than upon the business road, for even in the countries which had acquired a public educational system primary education was in general grossly neglected; and, even where it existed, was confined for political reasons to a minimum of literacy, arithmetic and moral obedience. However, at first sight paradoxically, the educational highway seemed more attractive than the business highway.

This was no doubt because it required a much smaller revolution in men's habits and ways of life. Learning, if only in the form of clerical learning, had its accepted and socially valued place in the traditional society; indeed a more eminent place than in the fully bourgeois society. To have a priest, minister or rabbi in the family was perhaps the greatest honour to which poor men could aspire, and well worth making titanic sacrifices for. This social admiration could be readily transferred, once such careers were open, to the secular intellectual, the official or teacher or, in the most marvellous cases, the lawyer and doctor. Moreover, learning was not antisocial as business so clearly seemed to be. The educated man did not automatically turn and rend his like as the shameless and selfish trader or employer would. Often indeed, especially as a teacher, he plainly helped to raise his fellows out of that ignorance and darkness which seemed responsible for their miseries. A general thirst for education was much easier to create than a general thirst for individual business success, and schooling more easily acquired than the strange arts of money-making. Communities almost wholly composed of small peasants, small traders and proletarians, like Wales, could simultaneously develop a hunger to push their sons into teaching and the ministry and a bitter social resentment against wealth and business as such.

Nevertheless in a sense education represented individualist competition, the 'career open to talent' and the triumph of merit over birth and connection quite as effectively as business, and this through the device of the competitive examination. As usual, the French Revolution produced its most logical expression, the parallel hierarchies of examinations which still progressively select from among the national body of scholarship winners the intellectual élite that administers and instructs the French people. Scholarships and competitive examination were also the ideal of the most self-consciously bourgeois school of British thinkers, the Benthamite philosophic radicals, who eventually – but not before the end of our period – imposed it in an extremely pure form on the higher British Home and Indian Civil Service, against the bitter resistance of aristocracy. Selection by merit, as determined in examination or other educational tests, became the generally accepted ideal of all except the most archaic European public services (such as the Papal or the British Foreign), or the most democratic, which tended – as in the USA – to prefer election to examination as a criterion of fitness for public posts. For, like other forms of individualist competition, examination-passing was a liberal, but not a democratic or egalitarian device.

The chief social result of opening education to talent was thus paradoxical. It produced not the 'open society' of free business competition but the 'closed society' of bureaucracy; but both, in their various ways, were characteristic institutions of the bourgeois-liberal era. The *ethos* of the nineteenth-century higher civil services was fundamentally that of the eighteenth-century enlightenment : Masonic and 'Josephinian' in Central and Eastern Europe, Napoleonic in France, liberal and anti-clerical in the other Latin countries, Benthamite in Britain. Admittedly competition was transformed into automatic promotion once the man of merit had actually won his place in the service; though how fast and how far a man was promoted would still depend (in theory) on his merits, unless corporate egalitarianism imposed pure promotion by seniority. At first sight therefore bureacracy looked very unlike the ideal of the liberal society. And yet, the public services were bound together by the consciousness of being selected by merit, by a prevailing atmosphere of incorruptibility, practical efficiency, and education, and by non-aristocratic origins. Even the rigid insistence on automatic promotion (which reached absurd lengths in that very middle-class organization, the British Navy) had at least the advantage of excluding the typically aristocratic or monarchical habit of favouritism. In societies where economic development lagged, the public service therefore provided an alternative focus for the rising middle classes.[17] It is no accident that in the Frankfurt Parliament of 1848, 68 per cent of all deputies were civil servants or other officials (as against only 12 per cent of the 'free professions' and 2·5 per cent of businessmen).[18]

It was thus fortunate for the intending careerist that the post-Napoleonic period was almost everywhere one of marked expansion in the apparatus and activity of government, though hardly large enough to absorb the growing supply of literate citizens. Between 1830 and 1850 public expenditure *per capita* increased by 25 per cent in Spain, by 40 per cent in France, by 44 per cent in Russia, by 50 per cent in Belgium, by 70 per cent in Austria, 75 per cent in the USA and by over 90 per cent in the Netherlands. (Only in Britain, the British colonies, Scandinavia and a few backward states did government expediture per head of the population remain stable or fall during this period, the heyday of economic liberalism.) [19] This was due not only to the obvious consumer of taxes, the armed forces, which remained much larger after the Napoleonic Wars than before, in spite of the absence of any major international wars : of the major states only Britain and France in 1851 had an army which was very much smaller than at the height of Napoleon's power in 1810 and several – e.g. Russia, various German and Italian states and Spain – were actually larger. It was due also to the development of old and the acquisition of new functions by states. For it is an elementary error (and one not shared by those logical protagonists of capitalism, the Benthamite 'philosophic radicals') to believe that liberalism was hostile to bureaucracy. It was merely hostile to inefficient bureaucracy, to public interference in matters better left to private enterprise and to excessive taxation. The vulgar-liberal slogan of a state reduced to the vestigial functions of the nightwatchman obscures the fact that the state shorn of its inefficient and interfering functions was a much more powerful and ambitious state than before. For instance, by 1848 it was a state which had acquired modern, often national, police-forces : in France from 1798, in Ireland from 1823, in England from 1829, and in Spain (the *Guardia Civil*) from 1844. Outside Britain it was normally a state which had a public educational system; outside Britain and the USA one which had or was about to have a public railway service; everywhere, one which had an increasingly large postal service to supply the rapidly expanding needs of business and private communication. The growth of population obliged it to maintain a larger judicial system; the growth of cities and urban social problems a larger system of municipal administration. Whether the government functions were old or new, they were increasingly conducted by a single national civil service of full-time career officials, the higher echelons of whom were freely transferred and promoted by central authority throughout each state. However, while an efficient service of this kind might well reduce the number of officials and the unit cost of administration by eliminating corruption and part-time service, it created a much more formidable government machine. The most elementary functions of the liberal state, such as the efficient assessment and collection of taxes by a body of salaried officials or the maintenance of a regular nationally organized rural constabulary, would have seemed beyond the wildest dreams of most pre-revolutionary absolutisms. So would the level of taxation, now actually sometimes a graduated income tax [20] which the subject of the liberal state tolerated : in 1840 government expenditure in liberal Britain was four times as high as in autocratic Russia.

Few of these new bureaucratic posts were really the equivalent of the officer's epaulette which the proverbial Napoleonic soldier carried in his knapsack as a first instalment towards his eventual marshal's baton. Of the 130,000 civil servants estimated for France in 1839 [21] the great bulk were postmen, teachers, lesser tax-collecting and legal officials and the like; and even the 450 officials of the Ministry of the Interior, the 350 of the Ministry of Foreign Affairs, consisted mainly of clerks; a brand of humanity which, as the literature from Dickens to Gogol makes only too clear, was hardly to be envied except perhaps for the privilege of public service, the security which allowed them to starve at an even rhythm all their lives. Officials who were really the social equivalent of a good middle-class career – financially no honest official could ever hope for more than decent comfort – were few. Even today the 'administrative class' of the entire British civil service, which was devised by the mid-nineteenth-century reformers as the equivalent of the middle classes in the bureaucratic hierarchy, consists of no more than 3,500 persons in all.

Yet, modest though the situation of the petty official or white-collar worker was, it was a mountain-range above the labouring poor. He did no physical work. Clean hands and the white collar put him, however symbolically, on the side of the rich. He normally carried with him the magic of public authority. Before him men and women had to queue for the documents which registered their lives; he waved them on or held them back; he told them what they could not do. In the more backward countries (as well as in the democratic USA) through him cousins and nephews might conceivably find jobs; in many not so backward countries he had to be bribed. For innumerable peasant or labouring families, for whom all other prospects of social ascent were dim, petty bureaucracy, teaching and the priest-hood were at least theoretically within reach, Himalayas which their sons might conceivably climb.

The free professions were hardly within their purview; for to become a doctor, a lawyer, a professor (which on the continent meant a secondary schoolmaster as well as a university teacher) or an 'other educated person following miscellaneous pursuits' [22] required long years of education or exceptional talent and opportunity. Britain in 1851 contained some 16,000 lawyers (not counting judges) and a mere 1,700 law students;[23] some 17,000 physicians and surgeons and 3,500 medical students and assistants, less than 3,000 architects, about 1,300 'editors and writers'. (The French term *Journalist* had not yet entered official cognizance.) Law and medicine were two of the great traditional professions. The third, the clergy, provided less of an opening than might have been expected if only because (except for the preachers of protestant sects) it was probably expanding rather more slowly than population. Indeed, thanks to the anti-clerical zeal of governments – Joseph II suppressed 359 abbeys and convents, the Spaniards in their liberal intervals did their best to suppress them all – certain parts of the profession were contracting rather than expanding.

Only one real opening existed : elementary school teaching by laymen and religious. The numbers of the teaching profession, which was in the main recruited from the sons of peasants, artisans, and other modest families, were by no means negligible in western states : in Britain some 76,000 men and women in 1851 described themselves as schoolmasters/mistresses or general teachers, not to mention the

20,000 or so governesses, the well-known last resource of penniless educated girls unable or unwilling to earn their living in less respectable ways. Moreover, teaching was not merely a large but an expanding profession. It was poorly paid; but outside the most philistine countries such as Britain and the USA, the elementary school teacher was a rightly popular figure. For if anyone represented the ideal of an age when for the first time common men and women looked above their heads and saw that ignorance could be dissipated, it was surely the man or the woman whose life and calling was to give children the opportunities which their parents had never had; to open the world to them; to imbue them with truth and morality.

Business, of course, was the most obvious career open to talent, and in a rapidly expanding economy business opportunities were naturally great. The small-scale nature of much enterprise, the prevalence of sub-contract, of modest buying and selling, made them relatively easy to take. Yet neither the material nor the social and cultural conditions were propitious for the poor. In the first place – – a fact frequently overlooked by the successful – the evolution of the industrial economy depended on creating wage-labourers faster than employers or the self-employed. For every man who moved up into the business classes, a greater number necessarily moved down. In the second place economic independence required technical qualifications, attitudes of mind, or financial resources (however modest) which were simply not in the possession of most men and women. Those who were lucky enough to possess them – for instance, members of religious minorities and sects, whose aptitude for such activities is well-known to the sociologist – might do well : the majority of those serfs of Ivanovo – the 'Russian Manchester' – who became textile manufacturers, belonged to the sect of the 'Old Believers'.[24] But it would have been entirely unrealistic to expect those who did not possess these advantages – for instance the majority of Russian peasants – to do the same, or even at this stage to think of emulating them.

III

No groups of the population welcomed the opening of the career to talent of whatever kind more passionately than those minorities who had hitherto been debarred from eminence not merely because they were not well-born, but because they suffered official and collective discrimination. The enthusiasm with which French protestants threw themselves into public life in and after the Revolution was exceeded only by the volcanic eruption of talent among the western Jews. Before the emancipation which eighteenth-century rationalism prepared and the French Revolution brought, only two roads to eminence were available to a Jew, commerce or finance and the interpretation of the sacred law; and both confined him to his own narrowly segregated ghetto community, from which only a handful of 'court Jews' or other men of wealth half-emerged, careful – even in Britain and Holland – not to step too far into the dangerous and unpopular light of celebrity. Nor was such emergence unpopular only among the brutal and drunken unbelievers who, on the whole, signally failed to welcome Jewish emancipation. Centuries of social compression had closed the ghetto in upon itself, rejecting any step outside its tight orthodoxies as unbelief and treason. The eighteenth-century pioneers of Jewish liberalization in Germany and Austria, notably Moses Mendelssohn (1729–1786), were reviled as deserters and atheists.

The great bulk of Judaism, which inhabited the rapidly growing ghettoes in the eastern part of the old kingdom of Poland and Lithuania, continued to live their self-contained and suspicious lives among the hostile peasantry, divided only in their allegiance between the learned intellectualist rabbis of the Lithuanian orthodoxy and the ecstatic and poverty-stricken Chassidim. It is characteristic that of forty-six Galician revolutionaries arrested by the Austrian authorities in 1834 only one was a Jew.[25] But in the smaller communities of the west the Jews seized their new opportunities with both hands, even when the price they had to pay for them was a nominal baptism, as in semi-emancipated countries it often still was, at any rate for official posts. The businessman did not even require this. The Rothschilds, kings of international Jewry, were not only rich. This they could also have been earlier, though the political and military changes of the period provided unprecedented opportunities for international finance. They could also now *be seen to be rich*, occupy a social position roughly commensurate to their wealth, and even aspire to the nobility which European princes actually began to grant them in 1816. (They became hereditary Habsburg barons in 1823.)

More striking than Jewish wealth was the flowering of Jewish talent in the secular arts, sciences and professions. By twentieth century standards it was as yet modest, though by 1848 the greatest Jewish mind of the nineteenth century and the most successful Jewish politician had both reached maturity : Karl Marx (1818–1883) and Benjamin Disraeli (1804–1881). There were no major Jewish scientists and only a few Jewish mathematicians of high but not supreme eminence. Meyerbeer (1791–1864) and Mendelssohn-Bartholdy (1809–1847) are not composers of the highest contemporary class, though among poets Heinrich Heine (1797–1856) survives rather better. There were as yet no Jewish painters of importance, no great Jewish executant musicians or conductors, and only one major theatrical figure, the actress Rachel (1821–1858). But in fact the production of genius is not the criterion of a people's emancipation, which is measured rather by the sudden abundance of less eminent Jewish participants in West European culture and public life, especially in France and above all in the German states, which provided the language and the ideology that gradually bridged the gap between medievalism and the nineteenth century for the immigrant Jews from the hinterland.

The dual revolution had given the Jews the nearest thing to equality they had ever enjoyed under Christianity. Those who seized their opportunity wished for nothing better than to 'assimilate' to the new society, and their sympathies were, for obvious reasons, overwhelmingly liberal. Yet the situation of the Jews was uncertain and uneasy, even though the endemic anti-semitism of the exploited masses, which could now often readily identify Jew and 'bourgeois',[26] was not seriously exploited by demagogic politicians. In France and Western Germany (but not yet elsewhere), some young Jews found themselves dreaming of an even more perfect society : there was a marked Jewish element in French Saint-Simonianism (Olinde Rodrigues, the brothers Pereire, Léon Halévy, d'Eichthal) and to a lesser extent in German communism (Moses Hess, the poet Heine, and of course Marx who, however, showed a total indifference to his Jewish origins and connections.)

The situation of the Jews made them exceptionally ready to assimilate to bourgeois society. They were a minority. They were already overwhelmingly urban, to the point of being largely immunized against the diseases of urbanization. In the cities their lower mortality and morbidity was already noted by the statisticians. They were

overwhelmingly literate and outside agriculture. A very large proportion of them were already in commerce or the professions. Their very
position constantly obliged them to consider new situations and ideas,
if only to detect the latent threat which they held. The great mass of
the world's peoples, on the other hand, found it much harder to adjust to the new society.

This was partly because the rock-ribbed armour of custom made it
almost impossible for them to understand what they were expected to
do in it; like the young Algerian gentlemen, transported to Paris to
gain a European education in the 1840s, who were shocked at the
discovery that they had been invited to the royal capital for anything
but the social commerce with king and nobility, which they knew to
be their due. Moreover, the new society did not make adjustment
easy. Those who accepted the evident blessings of middle-class civilization and middle-class manners could enjoy its benefits freely; those
who refused or were unable to, simply did not count. There was more
than mere political bias in the insistence on a property franchise which
characterized the moderate liberal governments of 1830; the man
who had not shown the ability to accumulate property was not a full
man, and could therefore hardly be a full citizen. The extremes of this
attitude occurred where the European middle class came into contact
with the unbelieving heathen, seeking to convert him through intellectually unsophisticated missionaries to the truths of Christianity,
commerce and the wearing of trousers (between which no sharp distinctions were drawn), or imposing on him the truths of liberal legislation. If he accepted these, liberalism (at all events among the
revolutionary French) was perfectly prepared to grant him full citizenship with all its rights, or the hope of being one day almost as good
as an Englishman, as among the British. The attitude is perfectly reflected in the *senatus-consulte* of Napoleon III which, a few years
after the end of our period but well within its spirit, opened citizenship to the native Algerian : *'Il peut, sur sa demande, être admis à
jouir des droits de citoyen français; dans ce cas il est régi par les lois
civiles et politiques de la France.'* [27] All he had to give up, in effect,
was Islam; if he did not want to do so – and few did – then he remained a subject and not a citizen.

The massive contempt of the 'civilized' for the 'barbarians'
(who included the bulk of labouring poor at home)[28] rested on this
feeling of demonstrated superiority. The middle-class world was

freely open to all. Those who failed to enter its gates therefore demonstrated a lack of personal intelligence, moral force or energy which automatically condemned them; or at best a historic or racial heritage which must permanently cripple them, or else they would already have made use of their opportunities. The period which culminated about the middle of the century was therefore one of unexampled callousness, not merely because the poverty which surrounded middle class respectability was so shocking that the native rich learned not to see it, leaving its horrors to make their full impact only on visiting foreigners (as the horrors of Indian slums today do), but because the poor, like the outer barbarians, were talked of as though they were not properly human at all. If their fate was to become industrial labourers, they were merely a mass to be forced into the proper disciplinary mould by sheer coercion, the draconic factory discipline being supplemented by the aid of the state. (It is characteristic that contemporary middle class opinion saw no incompatibility between the principle of equality before the law and the deliberately discriminatory labour codes, which, as in the British Master and Servant code of 1823, punished the workers by prison for breaches of contract and the employers merely by modest fines, if at all.) [29] They ought to be constantly on the verge of starvation, because otherwise they would not work, being inaccessible to 'human' motives. 'It is to the interest of the worker himself,' Villermé was told in the late 1830s by employers 'that he should be constantly harassed by need, for then he will not set his children a bad example, and his poverty will be a guarantee of good behaviour.' [30] There were nevertheless too many poor for their own good, but it was to be hoped that the operations of Malthus' law would starve off enough of them to establish a viable maximum; unless of course *per absurdum* the poor established their own rational checks on population by refraining from an excessive indulgence in procreation.

It was but a small step from such an attitude to the formal recognition of inequality which, as Henri Baudrillart argued in his inaugural lecture at the Collège de France in 1853, was one of the three pillars of human society, the other two being property and inheritance.[31] The hierarchical society was thus reconstructed on the foundations of formal equality. It had merely lost what made it tolerable in the old days, the general social conviction that men had duties and rights, that virtue was not simply the equivalent of money, and that the lower order, though low, had a right to their modest lives in the station to which God had called them.

NOTES

1 F. Engels, *Condition of the Working Class in England*, Chapter XII.
2 M. Capefigue, *Histoires des Grandes Operations Financières*, IV (1860), p. 255.
3 M. Capefigue, loc. cit., pp. 254, 248–9.
4 A. Beauvilliers, *L'Art du Cuisinier*, (Paris, 1814).
5 In 1835 the *Journal des Débats* (about 10,000 circulation) got about 20,000 francs per year from advertisements. In 1838 the fourth page of *La Presse* was rented at 150,000 francs a year, in 1845 at 300,000.[6]
6 H. Sée, *Histoire Economique de la France*, II, p. 216.
7 'Le grand poème de l'étalage chante ses strophes de couleur depuis la Madeleine jusqu'à la Porte Saint-Denis.'
8 A. Briggs, Middle Class Consciousness in English Politics 1780–1846, *Past and Present*, 9, April 1956, p. 68.
9 'The opinions of that class of people who are below the middle rank are formed and their minds directed by that intelligent and virtuous rank, who come the most immediately into contact with them.' James Mill, *An Essay on Government*, 1823.
10 Donald Read, *Press and People 1790–1850* (1961), p. 26.
11 S. Smiles, *Life of George Stephenson* (1881 ed.), p. 183.
12 Charles Dickens, *Hard Times*.
13 Cf. Leon Faucher, *Manchester in 1844* (1844), p. 24–5 : 'The town realises in a measure the utopia of Bentham. Everything is measured in its results by the standards of utility; and if the BEAUTIFUL, the GREAT, and the NOBLE ever take root in Manchester, they will be developed in accordance with this standard.'
14 Leon Faucher, *Etudes sur l'Angleterre*, I (1842), p. 322.
15 M. J. Lambert-Dansette, *Quelques familles du patronat textile de Lille-Armentières* (Lille 1954), p. 659.
16 Oppermann, *Geschichte d. Königreichs Hannover*, quoted in T. Klein, *1848, Der Vorkampf* (1914), p. 71.
17 All *fonctionnaires* in Balzac's novels appear to come from, or to be associated with, families of small entrepreneurs.
18 G. Schilfert, *Sieg u. Niederlage d. demokratischen Wahlrechts in d. deutschen Revolution 1848–9* (1952), pp. 404–5.
19 Mulhall, op. cit., p. 259.
20 In Britain this was temporarily imposed during the Napoleonic

Wars and permanently from 1842; no other country of importance had followed this lead before 1848.

21 W. R. Sharp, *The French Civil Service* (New York 1931), pp. 15–16.

22 *The Census of Great Britain in 1851* (London, Longman, Brown, Green and Longman 1854), p. 57.

23 On the continent the number and proportion of lawyers was often greater.

24 R. Portal, La naissance d'une bourgeoisie industrielle en Russie dans la première moitié du XIX siècle. *Bulletin de la Société d'Histoire Moderne*, Douzième série, II, 1959.

25 Vienna, *Verwaltungsarchiv*, Polizeihofstelle, H 136/1834.

26 The German brigand Schinderhannes (Johannes Bueckler 1777–1803) gained much popularity by concentrating on Jewish victims, and in Prague industrial unrest in the 1840s also took on an anti-Jewish note. (Vienna, Verwaltungsarchiv, Polizeihofstelle 1186–1845.)

27 A. Girault et L. Milliot, *Principes de Colonisation et de Législation Coloniale* (1938), p. 359.

28 Louis Chevalier, *Classes Laborieuses et Classes Dangereuses* (Paris 1958) III, pt. 2 discusses the use of the term 'barbarians', both by those hostile and by those friendly to the labouring poor in the 1840s.

29 D. Simon, Master and Servant in J. Saville ed., *Democracy and the Labour Movement* (1954).

30 P. Jaccard, *Histoire Sociale du Travail* (1960), p. 248.

31 P. Jaccard, op. cit., p. 249.

The Labouring Poor

> *Every manufacturer lives in his factory like the colonial planters in the midst of their slaves, one against a hundred, and the subversion of Lyon is a sort of insurrection of San Domingo. . . . The barbarians who menace society are neither in the Caucasus nor in the steppes of Tartary; they are in the suburbs of our industrial cities. . . . The middle class must clearly recognize the nature of the situation; it must know where it stands.*
>
> Saint-Marc Girardin in *Journal des Débats*,
> December 8, 1931

> *Pour gouverner il faut avoir*
> *Manteaux ou rubans en sautoir (bis).*
> *Nous en tissons pour vous, grands de la terre,*
> *Et nous, pauvres canuts, sans drap on nous enterre.*
> *C'est nous les canuts*
> *Nous sommes tout nus (bis).*
>
> *Mais quand notre règne arrive*
> *Quand votre règne finira.*
> *Alors nous tisserons le linceul du vieux monde*
> *Car on entend déjà le revolte qui gronde.*
> *C'est nous les canuts*
> *Nous n'irons plus tout nus.*
>
> Lyons silkweavers' song

I

Three possibilities were therefore open to such of the poor as found themselves in the path of bourgeois society, and no longer effectively sheltered in still inaccessible regions of traditional society. They could strive to become bourgeois; they could allow themselves to be ground down; or they could rebel.

The first course, as we have seen, was not merely technically difficult for those who lacked the minimum entrance fee of property or education, but profoundly distasteful. The introduction of a purely utilitarian individualist system of social behaviour, the theoretically justified jungle anarchy of bourgeois society with its motto 'every man for himself and the devil take the hindmost', appeared to men brought up in traditional societies as little better than wanton evil. 'In our times,' said one of the desperate Silesian hand-loom linenweavers who rioted vainly against their fate in 1844,[1] 'men have invented excellent arts to weaken and undermine one another's livelihood. But alas, nobody thinks any longer of the Seventh Commandment, which commands and forbids as follows : Thou shalt not steal. Nor do they bear in mind Luther's commentary upon it, in which he says : We shall love and fear the Lord, so that we may not take away our neighbour's property nor money, nor acquire it by false goods and trading, but on the contrary we should help him guard and increase his livelihood and property.' Such a man spoke for all who found themselves dragged into an abyss by what were plainly the forces of hell. They did not ask for much. ('The rich used to treat the poor with charity, and the poor lived simply, for in those days the lower orders needed much less for outward show in clothes and other expenses than they do today.') But even that modest place in the social order was now, it seemed, to be taken from them.

Hence their resistance against even the most rational proposals of bourgeois society, married as they were to inhumanity. Country squires introduced and labourers clung to the Speenhamland system, though the economic arguments against it were conclusive. As a means of alleviating poverty, Christian charity was worse than useless, as could be seen in the Papal states, which abounded in it. But it was popular not only among the traditionalist rich, who cherished it as a safeguard against the evil of equal rights (proposed by 'those dreamers who maintain that nature has created men with equal rights and that social distinctions should be founded purely on communal utility'[2]) but also among the traditionalist poor, who were profoundly convinced that they had a *right* to crumbs from the rich man's table. In Britain a chasm divided the middle class champions of Friendly Societies, who saw them entirely as a form of individual self-help and the poor, who treated them also, and often primarily, as *societies*, with convivial meetings, ceremonies, rituals and festivities; to the detriment of their actuarial soundness.

That resistance was only strengthened by the opposition of even the bourgeois to such aspects of pure individual free competition as did not actually benefit him. Nobody was more devoted to individualism than the sturdy American farmer and manufacturer, no Constitution more opposed than theirs – or so their lawyers believed until our own century – to such interferences with freedom as federal child labour legislation. But nobody was more firmly committed, as we have seen, to 'artificial' protection for their businesses. New machinery was one of the chief benefits to be expected from private enterprise and free competition. But not only the labouring Luddites arose to smash it : the smaller businessmen and farmers in their regions sympathized with them, because they also regarded innovators as destroyers of men's livelihoods. Farmers actually sometimes left their machines out for rioters to destroy, and the government had to send a sharply worded circular in 1830 to point out that 'machines are as entitled to the protection of the law as any other description of property'.[3] The very hesitation and doubt with which, outside the strongholds of bourgeois-liberal confidence, the new entrepreneur entered upon his historic task of destroying the social and moral order, strengthened the poor man's conviction.

There were of course labouring men who did their best to join the middle classes, or at least to follow the precepts of thrift, self-help and self-betterment. The moral and didactic literature of middle-class radicalism, temperance movements and protestant endeavour is full of the sort of men whose Homer was Samuel Smiles. And indeed such bodies attracted and perhaps encouraged the ambitious young man. The Royton Temperance Seminary, started in 1843 (confined to boys – mostly cotton operatives – who had taken the pledge of abstinence, refused to gamble and were of good moral character), had within twenty years produced five master cotton spinners, one clergyman, two managers of cotton mills in Russia 'and many others had obtained respectable positions as managers, overlookers, head mechanics, certified schoolmasters, or had become respectable shopkeepers'.[4] Clearly such phenomena were less common outside the Anglo-Saxon world, where the road out of the working class (except by migration) was very much narrower – it was not exceptionally broad even in

Britain – and the moral and intellectual influence of the Radical middle class on the skilled worker was less.

On the other hand there were clearly far more who, faced with a social catastrophe they did not understand, impoverished, exploited, herded into slums that combined bleakness and squalor, or into the expanding complexes of small-scale industrial villages, sank into demoralization. Deprived of the traditional institutions and guides to behaviour, how could many fail to sink into an abyss of hand-to-mouth expedients, where families pawned their blankets each week until pay-day [5] and where alcohol was 'the quickest way out of Manchester (or Lille or the Borinage). Mass alcoholism, an almost invariable companion of headlong and uncontrolled industrialization and urbanization, spread 'a pestilence of hard liquor' [6] across Europe. Perhaps the numerous contemporaries who deplored the growth of drunkenness, as of prostitution and other forms of sexual promiscuity, were exaggerating. Nevertheless, the sudden upsurge of systematic temperance agitations, both of a middle and working class character, in England, Ireland and Germany around 1840, shows that the worry about demoralization was neither academic nor confined to any single class. Its immediate success was shortlived, but for the rest of the century the hostility to hard liquor remained something which both enlightened employers and labour movements had in common. [7]

But of course the contemporaries who deplored the demoralization of the new urban and industrialized poor were not exaggerating. Everything combined to maximize it. Towns and industrial areas grew rapidly, without plan or supervision, and the most elementary services of city life utterly failed to keep pace with it : street-cleaning, water-supply, sanitation, not to mention working-class housing. [8] The most obvious consequence of this urban deterioration was the reappearance of mass epidemics of contagious (mainly waterborne) disease, notably of the *cholera*, which reconquered Europe from 1831 and swept the continent from Marseilles to St Petersburg in 1832 and again later. To take a single example : typhus in Glasgow 'did not arrest attention by any epidemic prevalence until 1818'. [9] Thereafter it increased. There were two major epidemics (typhus and cholera) in the city in the 1830s, three (typhus, cholera and relapsing fever) in the 1840s, two in the first half of the 1850s, until urban improvement caught up with a generation of neglect. The terrible effects of this neglect were all the greater, because the middle and ruling classes did not feel it. Urban development in our period was a gigantic process of class segregation, which pushed the new labouring poor into great morasses of misery outside the centres of government and business and the newly specialized residential areas of the bourgeoisie. The almost universal European division into a 'good' west end and a 'poor' east end of large cities developed in this period.[10] And what social institutions except the tavern and perhaps the chapel were provided in these new labourers' agglomerations except by the labourers' own initiative? Only after 1848, when the new epidemics sprung from the slums began to kill the rich also, and the desperate masses who grew up in them had frightened the powers-that-be by social revolution, was systematic urban rebuilding and improvement undertaken.

Drink was not the only sign of this demoralization. Infanticide, prostitution, suicide, and mental derangement have all been brought into relation with this social and economic cataclysm, thanks largely to the contemporary pioneering work of what we would today call social medicine.[12] And so has both the increase in crime and that growing and often purposeless violence which was a sort of blind personal assertion against the forces threatening to engulf the passive. The spread of apocalyptic, mystical or other sects and cults in this period (cf. chapter 12) indicates a similar incapacity to deal with the earthquakes of society which were breaking down men's lives. The cholera epidemics, for instance, provoked religious revivals in Catholic Marseilles as well as in Protestant Wales.

All these forms of distortions of social behaviour had one thing in common with one another, and incidentally with 'self-help'. They were attempts to escape the fate of being a poor labouring man, or at best to accept or forget poverty and humiliation. The believer in the second coming, the drunkard, the petty gangster, the lunatic, the tramp or the ambitious small entrepreneur, all averted their eyes from the collective condition and (with the exception of the last) were apathetic about the capacity of collective action. In the history of our period this massive apathy plays a much larger part than is often supposed. It is no accident that the least skilled, least educated, least organized and therefore least hopeful of the poor, then as later, were the most apathetic : at the 1848 elections in the Prussian town of Halle 81 per cent of the independent crafts masters and 71 per cent of the masons, carpenters and other skilled builders voted; but only

46 per cent of the factory and railway workers, the labourers, the domestic workers, etc.[13]

II

The alternative to escape or defeat was rebellion. And such was the situation of the labouring poor, and especially the industrial proletariat which became their nucleus, that rebellion was not merely possible, but virtually compulsory. Nothing was more inevitable in the first half of the nineteenth century than the appearance of labour and socialist movements, and indeed of mass social revolutionary unrest. The revolution of 1848 was its direct consequence.

That the condition of the labouring poor was appalling between 1815 and 1848 was not denied by any reasonable observer, and by 1840 there were a good many of these. That it was actually deteriorating was widely assumed. In Britain the Malthusian population theory, which held that the growth of population must inevitably outrun that of the means of subsistence, was based on such an assumption, and reinforced by the argument of Ricardian economists. Those who took a rosier view of working-class prospects were less numerous and less talented than those who took the gloomy view. In Germany in the 1830s the increasing pauperization of the people was the specific subject of at least fourteen different publications, and the question whether 'the complaints about increasing pauperization and food shortage' were justified was set for academic prize essays. (Ten of sixteen competitors thought they were and only two that they were not.)[14] The very prevalence of such opinions is itself evidence of the universal and apparently hopeless misery of the poor.

No doubt actual poverty was worst in the countryside, and especially among landless wage-labourers, rural domestic workers, and, of course, land-poor peasants, or those who lived on infertile land. A bad harvest, such as in 1789, 1795, 1817, 1832, 1847, still brought actual famine, even without the intervention of additional catastrophes such as the competition of British cotton goods, which destroyed the foundation of the Silesian cottage linen industry. After the ruined crop of 1813 in Lombardy many kept alive only by eating manure and hay, bread made from the leaves of bean plants and wild berries.[15] A bad year such as 1817 could, even in tranquil Switzerland, produce an actual excess of deaths over births.[16] The European hunger of 1846–8 pales beside the cataclysm of the Irish famine (cf. above pp. 201–2), but it was real enough. In East and West Prussia (1847) one-third of the population had ceased to eat bread, and relied only on potatoes.[17] In the austere, respectable, pauperized manufacturing villages of the middle German mountains, where men and women sat on logs and benches, owned few curtains or house-linen, and drank from earthenware or tin mugs for want of glass, the population had sometimes become so used to a diet of potatoes and thin coffee, that during famine-times the relief-workers had to teach it to eat the peas and porridge they supplied.[18] Hunger-typhus ravaged the countrysides of Flanders and Silesia, where the village linen-weaver fought his doomed battle against modern industry.

But in fact the misery – the increasing misery as so many thought – which attracted most attention, short of total catastrophe such as the Irish, was that of the cities and industrial areas where the poor starved less passively and less unseen. Whether their real incomes fell is still a matter of historical debate, though, as we have seen, there can be no doubt that the general situation of the poor in cities deteriorated. Variations between one region and another, between different types of workers and between different economic periods, as well as the deficiency of statistics, make such questions difficult to answer decisively, though any significant absolute general improvement can be excluded before 1848 (or in Britain perhaps 1844), and the gap between the rich and the poor certainly grew wider and more visible. The time when Baroness Rothschild wore one and a half million francs worth of jewellery at the Duke of Orléans' masked ball (1842) was the time when John Bright described the women of Rochdale: '2,000 women and girls passed through the streets singing hymns – it was a very singular and striking spectacle – approaching the sublime – they are dreadfully hungry – a loaf is devoured with greediness indescribable and if the bread is nearly covered with mud it is eagerly devoured'.[19]

It is in fact probable that there was some general deterioration over wide areas of Europe, for not only (as we have seen) urban institutions and social services failed to keep pace with headlong and un-planned expansion, and money (and often real) wages tended to fall after 1815, the production and transport of foodstuffs probably also fell behind in many large cities until the railway age.[20] It was on lags such as this that the contemporary Malthusians based their pessimism. But quite apart from such a lag, the mere change from the traditional diet of the pre-industrial man to the ignorant as well as impoverished free purchase of the urbanized and industrial one was likely to lead to worse feeding, just as the conditions of urban life and work were likely to lead to worse health. The extraordinary difference in health and physical fitness between the industrial and agricultural population (and of course between the upper, middle and working classes), on which the French and English statisticians fixed their attention, was clearly due to this. The average expectation of life at birth in the 1840s was twice as high for the labourers of rural Wiltshire and Rutland (hardly a pampered class) than for those of Manchester and Liverpool. But then – to take merely one example – 'till steam-power was introduced into the trade, towards the end of the last century, the grinder's disease was scarcely known in the Sheffield cutlery trades'. But in 1842 50 per cent of all razor-grinders in their thirties, 79 per cent of all in their forties, and 100 per cent of all razor-grinders over the age of fifty retched out their lungs with it.[21]

Moreover, the change in the economy shifted and displaced vast strata of labourers, sometimes to their benefit, but more often to their sorrow. Great masses of the population remained as yet unabsorbed by the new industries or cities as a permanent substratum of the pauperized and helpless, and even great masses were periodically hurled into unemployment by crises which were barely yet recognized as being temporary as well as recurrent. Two-thirds of the textile workers in Bolton (1842) or Roubaix (1847) would be thrown totally out of work by such a slump.[22] Twenty per cent of Nottingham, one-third of Paisley might be actually destitute.[23] A movement like Chartism in Britain would collapse, time and again, under its political weakness. Time and again sheer hunger – the intolerable burden which rested on millions of the labouring poor – would revive it.

In addition to these general storms, special catastrophes burst over the heads of particular kinds of the labouring poor. The initial phase of industrial revolution did not, as we have seen, push all labourers into mechanized factories. On the contrary, round the few mechanized and large-scale sectors of production, it multiplied the numbers of pre-industrial artisans, of certain types of skilled workers, and of the army of domestic and cottage labour, and often improved their condition, especially during the long years of labour shortage in the wars. In the 1820s and 1830s the iron and impersonal advance of machine and market began to throw them aside. At its mildest this turned independent men into dependent ones, persons into mere 'hands'. At its frequent harshest, it produced those multitudes of the declassed, the pauperized and the famished – hand-loom weavers, framework knitters etc. – whose condition froze the blood of even the most flinty economist. These were not unskilled and ignorant riff-raff. Such communities as those of the Norwich and the Dunfermline weavers which were broken and scattered in the 1830s, the London furniture-makers whose old-established negotiated 'price-lists' became scraps of paper as they sank into the morass of sweatshops, the continental journeymen who became itinerant proletarians, the artisans who lost their independence : these had been the most skilled, the most educated, the most self-reliant, the flower of the labouring people.[24] They did not know what was happening to them. It was natural that they should seek to find out, even more natural that they should protest.[25]

Materially the new factory proletariat was likely to be somewhat better off. On the other hand it was unfree; under the strict control and the even stricter discipline imposed by the master or his supervisors, against whom they had virtually no legal recourse and only the very beginnings of public protection. They had to work his hours or shifts; to accept his punishments and the fines with which he imposed his rules or increased his profits. In isolated areas or industries they had to buy in his shop, as often as not receiving their wages in *truck* (thus allowing the unscrupulous employer to swell his profits yet further), or live in the houses the master provided. No doubt the village boy might find such a life no more dependent and less impoverished than his parents'; and in continental industries with a strong paternalist tradition, the despotism of the master was at least partly balanced by the security, education and welfare services which he sometimes provided. But for the free man entry into the factory as a mere 'hand' was entry into something little better than slavery, and all but the most famished tended to avoid it, and even when in it to resist the draconic discipline much more persistently than the women and children, whom factory owners therefore tended to prefer. And, of course, in the 1830s and part of the 1840s even the material situation of the factory proletariat tended to deteriorate.

Whatever the actual situation of the labouring poor, there can be absolutely no doubt that every one of them who thought at all –

i.e. who did not accept the tribulations of the poor as part of fate and the eternal design of things – considered the labourer to be exploited and impoverished by the rich, who were getting richer while the poor became poorer. And the poor suffered *because* the rich benefited. The social mechanism of bourgeois society was in the profoundest manner cruel, unjust and inhuman. 'There can be no wealth without labour' wrote the *Lancashire Co-operator.* 'The workman is the source of all wealth. Who has raised all the food? The half-fed and impoverished labourer. Who built all the houses and warehouses, and palaces, which are possessed by the rich, who never labour or produce anything? The workman. Who spins all the yarn and makes all the cloth? The spinner and weaver.' Yet 'the labourer remains poor and destitute, while those who do not work are rich, and possess abundance to surfeiting'.[27] And the despairing rural labourer (echoed literally even today by the Negro gospel-singer) put it less clearly, but perhaps even more profoundly :

> If life was a thing that money could buy
> The rich would live and the poor might die.[28]

III

The labour movement provided an answer to the poor man's cry. It must not be confused with the mere collective revulsion against intolerable hardship, which occurs throughout recorded history, or even with the practice of striking and other forms of militancy which have since become characteristic of labour. These also have a history which goes back beyond the industrial revolution. What was new in the labour movement of the early nineteenth century was class consciousness and class ambition. The 'poor' no longer faced the 'rich'. A specific *class*, the labouring class, workers, or proletariat, faced another, the employers or capitalists. The French Revolution gave this new class confidence, the industrial revolution impressed on it the need for permanent mobilization. A decent livelihood could not be achieved merely by the occasional protest which served to restore the stable but temporarily disturbed balance of society. It required the eternal vigilance, organization and activity of the 'movement' – the trade union, the mutual or co-operative society, the working-class institute, newspaper or agitation. But the very novelty and rapidity of the social change which engulfed them encouraged the labourers to think in terms of an entirely changed society, based on their experience and ideas as opposed to their oppressors'. It would be co-operative and not competitive, collectivist and not individualist. It would be 'socialist'. And it would represent not the eternal dream of the free society, which poor men always have at the backs of their minds but think about only on the rare occasions of general social revolution, but a permanent, practicable alternative to the present system.

Working-class consciousness in this sense did not yet exist in 1789, or indeed during the French Revolution. Outside Britain and France it existed barely if at all even in 1848. But in the two countries which embody the dual revolution, it certainly came into existence between 1815 and 1848, more especially around 1830. The very word 'working class' (as distinct from the less specific 'the working classes') occurs in English labour writings shortly after Waterloo, and perhaps even earlier, and in French working-class writing the equivalent phrase becomes frequent after 1830.[29] In Britain the attempts to link all labouring men together in 'general trades' unions', i.e. to break through the sectional and local isolation of particular groups of workers to the national, perhaps even the universal solidarity of the labouring class, began in 1818 and were pursued with feverish intensity between 1829 and 1834. The pendant to the 'general union' was the general strike; and this too was formulated as a concept and a systematic tactic of the working class at this period, notably in William Benbow's *Grand National Holiday, and Congress of the Productive Classes* (1832), and was seriously discussed as a political method by the Chartists. Meanwhile, in both Britain and France intellectual discussion had produced both the concept and the word 'socialism' in the 1820s. It was immediately adopted by the workers, on a small scale in France (as by the Paris gilders of 1832) and on a much vaster scale by the British, who were soon to push Robert Owen into the leadership of a vast mass movement, for which he was singularly ill-suited. In brief, by the early 1830s proletarian class consciousness and social aspirations already existed. They were almost certainly feebler and much less effective than the middle class consciousness which their employers were acquiring or displaying at about the same time. But they were present.

Proletarian consciousness was powerfully combined with, and reinforced by, what may best be called Jacobin consciousness – the set of aspirations, experiences, methods and moral attitudes with which the French (and also before it the American) Revolution had imbued the thinking and confident poor. Just as the practical expression of the situation of the new working class was 'the labour movement' and its ideology 'the co-operative commonwealth', so that of the common people, proletarian or otherwise, whom the French Revolution pushed on to the stage of history as actors rather than merely as sufferers, was the democratic movement. 'Citizens of poor outward appearance and who in former times would not have dared show themselves in these places reserved for more elegant company, were going for walks along with the rich and holding their heads as high.'[30] They wanted respect, recognition and equality. They knew they could achieve it, for in 1793-4 they had done so. Not all such citizens were workers, but all conscious workers belonged to their sort.

Proletarian and Jacobin consciousness supplemented each other. Working-class experience gave the labouring poor the major institutions of everyday self-defence, the trade union and mutual aid society, and the major weapons of such collective struggle, solidarity and the strike (which in turn implied organization and discipline).[31] However, even where these were not as feeble, unstable and localized as they still usually were on the continent, their scope was strictly limited. The attempt to use a purely trade unionist or mutualist model not merely to win higher wages for organized sections of the workers, but to defeat the entire existing society and establish a new one, was made in Britain between 1829 and 1834, and again partly under Chartism. It failed, and this failure wrecked a remarkably mature and early proletarian socialist movement for a half-century. The attempts to turn trade unions into national unions of co-operative producers (as in the Operative Builders' Union with its 'builders' parliament' and 'builders' guild' – 1831-4) failed, and so did the attempt to set up national co-operative production and 'equitable labour exchanges' in other ways. The great all-embracing 'general unions', so far from proving stronger than the local and sectional societies, proved unwieldy and weak, though this was due less to the inherent drawbacks of general union than to the lack of discipline, organization and experience in leadership. The general strike proved inapplicable under Chartism, except (in 1842) as a spontaneously spreading hunger-riot.

Conversely the methods of political agitation which belonged to Jacobinism and radicalism in general, but not specifically to the working class, proved both their effectiveness and their flexibility : political campaigns, by means of newspapers and pamphlets, public meetings and demonstrations, and where necessary riot and insurrection. It is true that where such campaigns aimed too high, or frightened the ruling classes too much, they too failed. In the hysterical 1810s the tendency was to call out the armed forces against any serious demonstration (as at Spa Fields, London, in 1816, or 'Peterloo', Manchester, in 1819, when ten demonstrators were killed and several hundred injured). In 1834–48 the millions of signatures on the petitions did not bring the People's Charter any nearer. Nevertheless political campaigning on a narrower front *was* effective. Without it, there would have been no Catholic Emancipation in 1829, no Reform Act in 1832, and certainly no even modestly effective legislative control of factory conditions and working hours. Thus time and again we find a weakly organized working class compensating for its weakness by the agitational methods of political radicalism. The 'Factories Agitation' of the 1830s in the North of England compensated for the weakness of the local unions, just as the mass protest campaign against the exile of the 'Tolpuddle Martyrs' (cf. above p. 149) tried to save something from the wreck of the collapsing 'general unions' after 1834.

However, the Jacobin tradition in turn drew strength and an unprecedented continuity and massiveness from the cohesive solidarity and loyalty which were so characteristic of the new proletariat. They were not held together by the mere fact of being poor in the same place, but by the fact that working together in large numbers, co-operating in work, relying on each other, was their very life. Unbroken solidarity was their only weapon, for only thus could they demonstrate their single but decisive asset, collective indispensability. 'No strike-breaking' (or words to similar effect) was – and has remained – the first commandment in their moral code; the breaker of solidarity (described by the morally loaded adjective 'black' as in 'blackleg') was the Judas of their community. Once they had acquired even a flickering of political consciousness, their demonstrations were not the mere occasional eruptions of an exasperated 'mob', which easily relapsed into apathy. They were the stirrings of an army. Thus in a city like Sheffield, once the class struggle between middle and working class had become the main issue in local politics (in the early 1840s), a strong and stable proletarian bloc immediately appeared. By the end of 1847 there were eight Chartists on the town council, and the national collapse of Chartism in 1848 barely affected it in a city where between ten and twelve thousand hailed the Paris Revolution of that year : by 1849 Chartists held almost half the seats on the council.[32]

Below the working class and the Jacobin tradition there lay the substratum of an even older tradition which reinforced both : that of riot, or the occasional public protest by desperate men. The direct action or rioting, the smashing of machines, shops or the houses of the rich, had a long history. In general it expressed sheer hunger or the feelings of men at the end of their tether, as in the waves of machine-breaking which periodically engulfed declining hand-industries threatened by the machine (British textiles in 1810–11 and again in 1826, continental textiles in the mid-1830s and mid-1840s). Sometimes, as in England, it was a recognized form of collective pressure by organized workers, and implied no hostility to machines, as among miners, certain skilled textile operatives or the cutlers, who combined political moderation with systematic terrorism against non-unionist colleagues. Or else it expressed the discontent of the unemployed or the starving. At a time of ripening revolution such direct action by otherwise politically immature men and women could turn into a decisive force, especially if it occurred in capital cities or other politically sensitive spots. Both in 1830 and in 1848 such movements threw a gigantic weight behind otherwise quite minor expressions of discontent, turning protest into insurrection.

IV

The labour movement of this period was, therefore, neither in composition nor in its ideology and programme a strictly 'proletarian' movement, i.e. one of industrial and factory workers or even one confined to wage-earners. It was rather a common front of all forces and tendencies representing the (mainly urban) labouring poor. Such a common front had long existed, but even as late as the French Revolution its leadership and inspiration had come from the liberal and radical middle classes. As we have seen, 'Jacobinism' and not 'Sansculottism' (let alone the aspirations of the immature proletarians) had given such unity as it possessed to the Parisian popular tradition. The novelty of the situation after 1815 was, that the common front was increasingly directed against the liberal middle class as well as the kings and aristocrats, and that what gave it unity was the programme and ideology of the proletariat, even though the industrial and factory working class as yet barely existed, and was on the whole politically very much less mature than other sections of the labouring poor. Both the poor and the rich tended to assimilate the entire 'urban mass existing below the middle order of society' [33] politically to the 'proletariat' or 'the working class'. All who were troubled by the 'increasingly vivid and general sentiment that there is an internal disharmony in the present state of affairs, and that this state cannot last' [34] inclined to turn to socialism as the only considered and intellectually valid critique and alternative.

The leadership of the new movement reflected a similar state of affairs. The most active, militant and politically conscious of the labouring poor were not the new factory proletarians but the skilled craftsmen, independent artisans, small-scale domestic workers and others who lived and worked substantially as they had done before the Industrial Revolution, but under far greater pressure. The earliest trade unions were almost invariably those of printers, hatters, tailors and the like. The nucleus of leadership of Chartism in a city like Leeds – and this was typical – consisted of a joiner turned hand-loom weaver, a couple of journeymen printers, a bookseller, a wool-comber. The men who adopted Mr Owen's co-operative doctrines were in their majority such 'artisans', 'mechanics' and handworkers. The earliest German working-class communists were travelling journeymen craftsmen – tailors, joiners, printers. The men who rose against the bourgeoisie in the Paris of 1848 were still the inhabitants of the old artisan Faubourg Saint-Antoine, and not yet (as in the Commune of 1871) those of proletarian Belleville. Insofar as the advance of industry destroyed these very fortresses of 'working-class' consciousness, it fatally undermined the strength of these early labour movements. Between 1820 and 1850, for instance, the British movement created a dense network of institutions for working-class self-education and political education, the 'mechanics' institutes', Owenite 'Halls of Science' and others. By 1850 there were (not counting the more obviously political of these) 700 of them in Britain – 151 merely in the county of Yorkshire – with 400 newsrooms.[35] But they were already declining and within a few decades most would be either dead or somnolent.

There was only one exception. In Britain alone the new proletarians had already begun to organize and even to produce their own leaders : John Doherty, the Irish Owenite cotton spinner, Tommy Hepburn and Martin Jude, the miners. Not only the skilled artisans and the depressed domestic workers formed the battalions of Chartism; the factory workers were its fighters, and sometimes its leaders, too. But outside Britain the factory operatives and the miners were still in the main sufferers rather than agents. Not until the latter part of the century were they to take a hand themselves in the shaping of their fate.

The labour movement was an organization of self-defence, of protest, of revolution. But for the labouring poor it was more than a tool of struggle : it was also a way of life. The liberal bourgeoisie offered them nothing; history took them away from the traditional life which conservatives offered vainly to maintain or to restore. Neither had much to do with the sort of life into which they were increasingly drawn. But the movement had, or rather, the way of life which they hammered out for themselves, collective, communal, combative, idealist and isolated, implied the movement, for struggle was its very essence. And in return the movement gave it coherence and purpose. The liberal myth supposed that unions were composed of feckless labourers instigated by conscienceless agitators; but in reality the feckless were generally the least unionized, the most intelligent and competent workers the most firm in their support for union.

The most highly developed examples of such 'worlds of labour' in this period were probably still those of the old domestic industries. There was the community of the Lyons silk-workers, the ever-rebellious *canuts* – who rose in 1831 and again in 1834, and who, in Michelet's phrase, 'because this world would not do, made themselves another in the humid obscurity of their alleys, a moral paradise of sweet dreams and visions.[36] There were communities such as those of the Scottish linenweavers with their republican and Jacobin puritanism, their Swedenborgian heresies, their Tradesman's Library, savings bank, Mechanics Institute, Library and Scientific Club, their Drawing Academy, missionary meetings, temperance leagues and infant schools, their Florists' Society and literary magazine (the Dunfermline *Gasometer*) [37] – and of course their Chartism. Class consciousness, militancy, hatred and contempt for the oppressor belonged to this life as much as the looms on which men wove. They owed nothing to the rich except their wages. What they had in life was their own collective creation.

But this silent process of self-organization was not confined to workers of this older type. It is reflected in the 'union', often based on the local Primitive Methodist community, in the Northumberland and Durham mines. It is reflected in the dense concentration of workers' mutual and friendly societies in the new industrial areas, especially Lancashire.[38] Above all it is reflected in the serried thousands of men, women and children who streamed with torches on to the moors for Chartist demonstrations from the smaller industrial towns of Lancashire, in the rapidity with which the new Rochdale co-operative shops spread in the latter 1840s.

V

And yet, as we look back upon this period, there is a great and evident discrepancy between the force of the labouring poor, which the rich feared, the 'spectre of communism' which haunted them, and their actual organized force, let alone that of the new industrial proletariat. The public expression of their protest was, in the literal sense, a 'movement' rather than an organization. What linked even the most massive and comprehensive of their political manifestations – Chartism (1838–48) – together was little more than a handful of traditional and radical slogans, a few powerful orators and journalists who became the voices of the poor, like Feargus O'Connor (1794–1855), a few newspapers like the *Northern Star*. It was the common fate of being against the rich and the great which the old militants have recalled :

'We had a dog called Rodney. My grandmother disliked the name because she had a curious sort of notion that Admiral Rodney, having been elevated to the peerage, had been hostile to the people. The old lady, too, was careful to explain to me that Cobbett and Cobden were two different persons – that Cobbett was the hero, and that Cobden was just a middle class advocate. One of the pictures that I longest remember – it stood alongside samplers and stencilled drawings not far from a china statuette of George Washington – was a portrait of John Frost.[40] A line at the top of the picture indicated that it belonged to a series called the Portrait Gallery of People's Friends. Above the head was a laurel wreath, while below was a representation of Mr Frost appealing to Justice on behalf of ragged and wretched outcasts. . . . The most constant of our visitors was a crippled shoemaker . . . (who) made his appearance every Sunday morning as regular as clockwork, with a copy of the *Northern Star*, damp from the press, for the purpose of hearing some member of our household read out to him and others 'Feargus' letter'. The paper had first to be dried before the fire, and then carefully and evenly cut, so as not to damage a single line of the almost sacred production. This done, Larry, placidly smoking a cutty pipe, which he occasionally thrust into the grate, settled himself to listen with all the rapture of a devotee in a tabernacle to the message of the great Feargus.' [41]

There was little leadership or co-ordination. The most ambitious attempt to turn a movement into an organization, the 'general union' of 1834–5, broke down miserably and rapidly. At most – in Britain as on the continent – there was the spontaneous solidarity of the local labouring community, the men who, like the Lyons silk-workers, died as hard as they lived. What held this movement together was hunger, wretchedness, hatred and hope. And what defeated it, in Chartist Britain as on the revolutionary continent of 1848, was that the poor were hungry, numerous and desperate enough to rise, but lacked the organization and maturity which could have made their rebellion more than a momentary danger to the social order. By 1848 the movement of the labouring poor had yet to develop its equivalent to the Jacobinism of the revolutionary middle class of 1789–94.

NOTES

1 The weaver Hauffe, born 1807, quoted in Alexander Schneer, *Ueber die Noth der Leinen-Arbeiter in Schlelesien* . . . (Berlin 1844), p. 16.

2 The theologian P. D. Michele Augusti, *Della libertà ed eguaglianza degli uomini nell'ordine naturale e civile* (1790), quoted in A. Chérubini, *Dottrine e Metodi Assistenziali dal 1789 al 1848* (Milan 1958), p. 17.

3 E. J. Hobsbawm, The Machine Breakers, *Past and Present*, I, 1952.

4 'About some Lancashire Lads' in *The Leisure Hour* (1881). I owe this reference to Mr. A. Jenkin.

5 In 1855 60 per cent of all pledges with Liverpool pawnbrokers were 5*s*. or less in value, 27 per cent 2*s*. 6*d*. or less.

6 'die Schnapspest im ersten Drittel des Jahrhunderts', *Handwoerterbuch d. Staatswissenschaften* (Second ed.) art. 'Trunksucht'.

7 This is not true of hostility to beer, wine or other drinks forming part of men's habitual everyday diet. This was largely confined to Anglo-Saxon Protestant sectarians.

8 L. Chevalier, *Classes Laborieuses et Classes Dangereuses, passim*.

9 J. B. Russell, *Public Health Administration in Glasgow* (1903), p. 3.

10 'The circumstances which oblige the workers to move out of the centre of Paris have generally, it is pointed out, had deplorable effects on their behaviour and morality. In the old days they used to live on the higher floors of buildings whose lower floors were occupied by businessmen and other members of the relatively comfortable classes. A sort of solidarity grew up between the tenants of a single building. Neighbours helped each other in little ways. When sick or unemployed the workers might find much assistance within the house, while on the other hand a sort of feeling of human respect imbued working-class habits with a certain regularity.' The complacency is that of the Chamber of Commerce and the Police Prefecture from whose Report this is quoted; but the novelty of segregation is well brought out.[11]

11 Chevalier, op. cit., pp. 233–4.

12 The long list of doctors to whom we owe so much of our knowledge of the times – and of subsequent improvement – contrast vividly with the general complacency and hardness of bourgeois opinion. Villermé and the contributors to the *Annales d'Hygiène Publique*, which he founded in 1829, Kay, Thackrah, Simon, Gaskell and Farr in Britain, and several in Germany, deserve to be remembered more widely than in fact they are.

13 E. Neuss, *Entstehung u. Entwicklung d. Klasse d. besitzlosen Lohnarbeiter in Halle* (Berlin 1958), p. 283.

14 J. Kuczynski, *Geschichte der Lage der Arbeiter* (Berlin 1960), Vol. 9, p. 264 ff; Vol. 8 (1960), p. 109 ff.

15 R. J. Rath, The Habsburgs and the Great Depression in Lombardo-Venetia 1814–18. *Journal of Modern History*, XIII, p. 311.

16 M. C. Muehlemann, Les prix des vivres et le mouvement de la

population dans le canton de Berne 1782–1881. *IV Congrès International d'Hygiène* (1883).

17 F. J. Neumann, Zur Lehre von d. Lohngesetzen, *Jb.f.Nat.Oek.* 3rd ser. IV 1892, p. 374 ff.

18 R. Scheer, *Entwicklung d. Annaberger Posamentierindustrie im 19. Jahrhundert.* (Leipzig 1909), pp. 27–8, 33.

19 N. McCord, *The Anti-Corn Law League* (1958), p. 127.

20 'Par contre, il est sûr que la situation alimentaire, à Paris, s'est deteriorée peu à peu avec le XIX siècle, sans doute jusqu'au voisinage des années 50 ou 60.' R. Philippe in *Annales* 16, 3, 1961, 567. For analogous calculations for London, cf. E. J. Hobsbawm, The British Standard of Living, *Economic History Review*, X, 1, 1957. The total per capita meat consumption of France appears to have remained virtually unchanged from 1812 to 1840 (*Congrés Internationale d'Hygiène Paris 1878* (1880), vol. I, p. 432).

21 S. Pollard, *A History of Labour in Sheffield* (1960), pp. 62–3.

22 H. Ashworth in *Journal Stat. Soc.* V (1842), p. 74; E. Labrousse, ed. *Aspects de la Crise ... 1846–51* (1956), p. 107.

23 *Statistical Committee appointed by the Anti-Corn Law Conference ... March 1842* (n.d.), p. 45.

24 Of 195 Gloucestershire adult weavers in 1840 only fifteen could neither read nor write; but of the rioters arrested in the manufacturing areas of Lancashire, Cheshire and Staffordshire in 1842 only 13 per cent could read and write well, 32 per cent imperfectly.[25]

25 R. K. Webb in *English Historical Review*, LXV (1950), p. 333 ff.

26 'About one-third of our working population . . . consists of weavers and labourers, whose average earnings do not amount to a sum sufficient to bring up and maintain their families without parochial assistance. It is this portion of the community, for the most part decent and respectable in their lives, which is suffering most from the depression of wages, and the hardships of the times. It is to this class of my poor fellow-creatures in particular, that I desire to recommend the system of co-operation.' (F. Baker, *First Lecture on Co-operation*, Bolton, 1830.)

27 Quoted in A. E. Musson, The Ideology of Early Co-operation in Lancashire and Cheshire; *Transactions of the Lancashire and Cheshire Antiquarian Society*, LXVIII, 1958, p. 120.

28 A. Williams, *Folksongs of the Upper Thames* (1923), p. 105 prints a similar version rather more class conscious.

29 A. Briggs. The Language of 'class' in early nineteenth century England, in A. Briggs and J. Saville ed., *Essays in Labour History* (1960); E. Labrousse, *Le mouvement ouvrier et les Idées sociales*, III (Cours de la Sorbonne), pp. 168–9; E. Coornaert, La pensée ouvrière et la conscience de classe en France 1830–48, in *Studi*

in Onore di Gino Luzzato, III (Milan 1950), p. 28; G. D. H. Cole, *Attempts at General Union* (1953), p. 161.

30 A. Soboul, *Les Sansculottes de Paris en l'an II* (1958), p. 660.

31 The strike is so spontaneous and logical a consequence of working-class existence that most European languages have quite independent native words for it (e.g. *grève, huelga, sciopero, zabastovka*), whereas words for other institutions are often borrowed.

32 S. Pollard, op. cit., pp. 48–9.

33 Th. Mundt, *Der dritte Stand in Deutschland und Preussen . . .* (Berlin 1847), p. 4, quoted by J. Kuczynski, Gesch.d.Lage d. Arbeiter 9, p. 169.

34 Karl Biedermann, *Vorlesungen ueber Socialismus und sociale Fragen* (Leipzig 1847), quoted Kuczynski, op. cit., p. 71.

35 M. Tylecote, *The Mechanics' Institutes of Lancashire before 1851* (Manchester 1957), VIII.

36 Quoted in *Revue Historique* CCXXI (1959), p. 138.

37 Cf. T. L. Peacock, *Nightmare Abbey* (1818) : 'You are a philosopher,' said the lady, 'and a lover of liberty. You are the author of a treatise called "Philosophical Gas; or a Project for the General Illumination of the Human Mind".'

38 In 1821 Lancashire had by far the highest proportion of friendly societies' members to total population in the country (17 per cent); in 1845 almost half the lodges of the Oddfellows were in Lancashire and Yorkshire.[39]

39 P. Gosden, *The Friendly Societies in England 1815–75* (1961), pp. 23, 31.

40 Leader of the unsuccessful Chartist insurrection at Newport, 1839.

41 W. E. Adams, *Memoirs of a Social Atom*, I, pp. 163–5, (London 1903).

Ideology: Religion

> *Give me a people where boiling passions and worldly greed are calmed by faith, hope and charity; a people which sees this earth as a pilgrimage and the other life as its true fatherland; a people taught to admire and revere in Christian heroism its very poverty and its very sufferings; a people that loves and adores in Jesus Christ the first-born of all the oppressed, and in his cross the instrument of universal salvation. Give me, I say, a people formed in this mould and socialism will not merely be easily defeated, but impossible to be thought of...*
>
> Civiltà Cattolica [1]

> *'But when Napoleon began his advance, they (the Molokan heretic peasants) believed that he was that lion of the valley of Jehoshaphat, who, as their old hymns tell, is destined to overthrow the false Tsar and to restore the throne of the true White Tsar. And so the Molokans of Tambov province chose a deputation among themselves, which was to go to meet him and greet him, dressed in white raiment.'*
>
> Haxthausen, *Studien ueber ... Russland* [2]

I

What men think about the world is one thing; the terms in which they think about it, another. For most of history and over most of the world (China being perhaps the main exception) the terms in which all but a handful of educated and emancipated men thought about the world were those of traditional religion, so much so that there are countries in which the word 'Christian' is simply a synonym for 'peasant' or even 'man'. At some stage before 1848 this ceased to be so in parts of Europe, though not yet outside the area transformed by the two revolutions. Religion, from being something like the sky, from which no man can escape and which contains all that is above the earth, became something like a bank of clouds, a large but limited and changing feature of the human firmament. Of all the ideological changes this is by far the most profound, though its practical consequences were more ambiguous and undetermined than was then supposed. At all events, it is the most unprecedented.

What was unprecedented, of course, was the secularization of the masses. A gentlemanly religious indifference combined with the punctilious exercise of ritual duties (to set an example to the lower orders) had long been familiar among emancipated noblemen,[3] though ladies, like all their sex, remained far more pious. Polite and educated men might be technically believers in a supreme being, though one which had no function except existing and certainly did not interfere with human activities or require any form of worship except a gracious acknowledgement. But their views on traditional religion were contemptuous and often frankly hostile, and their views would have been no different had they been ready to declare themselves frank atheists. 'Sire,' the great mathematician Laplace is reported to have told Napoleon, when asked where God fitted into his celestial mechanics, 'I have no need of such an hypothesis.' Frank atheism was still comparatively rare, but among the enlightened scholars, writers and gentlemen who set the intellectual fashions of the later eighteenth century, frank Christianity was even rarer. If there was a flourishing religion among the late eighteenth-century élite, it was rationalist, illuminist and anti-clerical Freemasonry.

This widespread dechristianization of males in the polite and educated classes dated back to the late seventeenth or early eighteenth centuries, and its public effects had been startling and beneficial : the mere fact that trials for witchcraft, which had plagued western and Central Europe for several centuries, now followed trials for heresy and *autos-da-fé* into limbo, would be enough to justify it. However, in the earlier eighteenth century it hardly affected the lower or even the middle ranks. The peasantry remained totally beyond the range of any ideological language which did not speak with the tongues of the Virgin, the Saints, and Holy Writ, not to mention the more ancient gods and spirits which still hid beneath a slightly christianized façade. There were stirrings of irreligious thought among those craftsmen who would formerly have been drawn to heresy. The

cobblers, most persistent of working-class intellectuals, who had produced mystics like Jacob Boehme, seem to have begun to have their
doubts about any deity. At all events in Vienna they were the only
group of craftsmen to sympathize with the Jacobins, because it was
said that these did not believe in God. However, these were as yet tiny
ripples. The great mass of unskilled and miscellaneous poverty in the
cities remained (except perhaps for a few North European towns like
Paris and London) profoundly pious or superstitious.

But even among the middle ranks overt hostility to religion was
not popular, though the ideology of a rationalist progressive-minded,
anti-traditional enlightenment fitted excellently into the scheme of
things of a rising middle class. Its associations were with aristocracy
and immorality, which itself belonged to a noble society. And indeed the earliest really 'free thinkers', the *libertins* of the mid-seventeenth century, lived up to the popular connotation of their name :
Molière's *Don Juan* portrays not merely their combination of atheism and sexual freedom, but the respectable bourgeois horror of it.
There were good reasons for the paradox (particularly obvious in
the seventeenth century) that the intellectually most daring thinkers,
who thereby anticipated much of later middle class ideology, e.g.
Bacon and Hobbes, were as individuals associated with the old and
corrupt society. The armies of the rising middle class needed the
discipline and organization of a strong and single-minded morality
for their battles. Theoretically agnosticism or atheism is perfectly
compatible with this, and certainly Christianity unnecessary for it;
and the *philosophes* of the eighteenth century were never tired of
demonstrating that a 'natural' morality (of which they found illustrations among the noble savages) and the high personal standards of
the individual free-thinker were better than Christianity. But in
practice the tried advantages of the old type of religion and the
terrible risks of abandoning any supernatural sanction of morality
were immense; not only for the labouring poor, who were generally
held to be too ignorant and stupid to do without some sort of socially
useful superstition, but for the middle class itself.

The post-revolutionary generations in France are full of attempts
to create a bourgeois non-Christian morality equivalent to the Christian; by a Rousseauist 'cult of the supreme being' (Robespierre in
1794), by various pseudo-religious constructed on rationalist non-
Christian foundations, but still maintaining the apparatus of ritual

and cults (the Saint-Simonians, and Comte's 'religion of humanity'). Eventually the attempt to maintain the externals of old religious cults was abandoned, but not the attempt to establish a formal lay morality (based on various moral concepts such as 'solidarité') and above all on a lay counterpart to the priesthood, the schoolteachers. The French *instituteur*, poor, selfless, imbuing his pupils in each village with the Roman morality of Revolution and Republic, the official antagonist to the village curé, did not triumph until the Third Republic, which also solved the political problems of establishing bourgeois stability on the foundations of social revolution, at all events for seventy years. But he is already implicit in Condorcet's law of 1792 which established that 'the persons in charge of instruction in primary classes shall be called *instituteurs*', echoing Cicero and Sallust who spoke of 'founding the commonwealth' (*instituere civitatem*) and 'founding morality of commonwealths' (*instituere civitatum mores*).[4]

The bourgeoisie thus remained divided in its ideology between a minority of increasingly frank free-thinkers and a majority of the pious, Protestant, Jewish and Catholic. However, the new historic fact was that of the two the free-thinking sector was immeasurably more dynamic and effective. Though in purely quantitative terms religion remained immensely strong and, as we shall see, grew stronger, it was no longer (to use a biological analogy) dominant but recessive, and has remained so to this day within the world transformed by the dual revolution. There is little doubt that the great bulk of the citizens of the new USA were believers of one sort or another, mostly Protestant, but the Constitution of the Republic is, and in spite of all efforts to change it has remained, one of agnosticism. There is no doubt whatever that among the British middle classes of our period the Protestant pietists greatly and increasingly outnumbered the minority of agnostic radicals. But a Bentham moulded the actual institutions of their age far more than a Wilberforce.

The most obvious proof of this decisive victory of secular over religious ideology is also its most important result. With the American and French Revolutions major political and social transformations were secularized. The issues of the Dutch and English Revolutions of the sixteenth and seventeenth centuries had still been discussed and fought out in the traditional language of Christianity, orthodox, schismatic or heretical. In the ideologies of the American and French,

269

for the first time in European history, Christianity is irrelevant. The language, the symbolism, the costume of 1789 are purely non-Christian, if we leave aside a few popular-archaic efforts to create cults of saints and martyrs, analogous to the old ones, out of dead Sansculotte heroes. It was, in fact, Roman. At the same time this secularism of the revolution demonstrates the remarkable political hegemony of the liberal middle class, which imposed its particular ideological forms on a much vaster movement of the masses. If the intellectual leadership of the French Revolution had come only very slightly from the masses who actually made it, it is inconceivable that its ideology should not have shown more signs of traditionalism than it did.[5]

Bourgeois triumph thus imbued the French Revolution with the agnostic or secular-moral ideology of the eighteenth-century enlightenment, and since the idiom of that revolution became the general language of all subsequent social revolutionary movements, it transmitted this secularism to them also. With a few unimportant exceptions, notably among intellectuals like the Saint-Simonians and among a few archaic Christian-communist sectarians like the tailor Weitling (1808–1871), the ideology of the new working class and socialist movements of the nineteenth century was secularist from the start. Thomas Paine, whose ideas expressed the radical-democratic aspirations of small artisans and pauperized craftsmen, is as famous for having written the first book to demonstrate in popular language that the Bible is not the word of God (*The Age of Reason*, 1794), as for his *Rights of Man* (1791). The mechanics of the 1820s followed Robert Owen not only for his analysis of capitalism, but for his unbelief, and, long after the collapse of Owenism, their *Halls of Science* spread rationalist propaganda through the cities. There have been and are religious socialists, and a very large number of men who, while religious, are also socialists. But the predominant ideology of modern labour and socialist movements, insofar as they claim one, is based on eighteenth-century rationalism.

This is all the more surprising as we have seen the masses to have remained predominantly religious, and as the natural revolutionary idiom of masses brought up in a traditional Christian society is one of rebellion (social heresy, millennialism and the like), the Bible being a highly incendiary document. However, the prevalent secularism of the new labour and socialist movements was based on the equally novel and more fundamental fact of the prevalent religious indifference of the new proletariat. By modern standards the working-classes and urban masses which grew up in the period of the Industrial Revolution were no doubt rather strongly influenced by religion; by the standards of the first half of the nineteenth century there was no precedent for their remoteness from, ignorance of, and indifference to organized religion. Observers of all political tendencies agreed about this. The British Religious Census of 1851 demonstrated it to the horror of contemporaries. Much of this remoteness was due to the utter failure of the traditional established churches to cope with agglomerations – the great cities and the new industrial settlements – and with social classes – the proletariat – which were foreign to their routines and experience. By 1851 there were church places available for only 34 per cent of the inhabitants of Sheffield, only 31·2 per cent of those in Liverpool and Manchester, only 29 per cent of those in Birmingham. The problems of being a parish priest in an agricultural village were no guide to the cure of souls in an industrial town or urban slum.

The established churches therefore neglected these new communities and classes, thus leaving them (especially in Catholic and Lutheran countries) almost entirely to the secular faith of the new labour movements, which were eventually – towards the end of the nineteenth century – to capture them. (Where they had not by 1848 done so to any great extent, the incentive to recapture them from infidelity was not strong.) The Protestant sects were more successful, at all events in the countries such as Britain, in which such sectarianism was a well-established religio-political phenomenon. Nevertheless, there is much evidence that even the sects succeeded best where the social environment was nearest to that of the traditional small town or village community, as among the farm-labourers, miners, and fishermen. Moreover, among the industrial labouring classes the sects were never more than a minority. The working class as a group was undoubtedly less touched by organized religion than any previous body of the poor in world history.

The general trend of the period from 1789 to 1848 was therefore one of emphatic secularization. Science found itself in increasingly open conflict with the Scriptures, as it ventured into evolutionary fields (cf. Chapter 15). Historical scholarship, applied to the Bible in unprecedented doses – particularly from the 1830s by the professors of Tuebingen – dissolved the single text inspired, if not written, by the Lord into a collection of historical documents from various periods, with all the defects of human documentation. Lachmann's *Novum Testamentum* (1842–1852) denied that the Gospels were eyewitness accounts and doubted whether Jesus Christ had intended to found a new religion. David Strauss's controversial *Life of Jesus* (1835) eliminated the supernatural element from his subject's biography. By 1848 educated Europe was almost ripe for the shock of Charles Darwin. The trend was reinforced by the direct attack of numerous political régimes on the property and legal privileges of the established churches and their clergy or other ritual persons, and the increasing tendency for governments or other secular agencies to take over functions hitherto left largely to religious ones; especially – in Roman Catholic countries – education and social welfare. Between 1789 and 1848 monasteries were dissolved and their property sold from Naples to Nicaragua. Outside Europe, of course, conquering whites launched direct attacks upon the religion of their subjects or victims, either – like the British administrators in India who stamped out the burning of widows (*suttee*) and the ritual murder sect of the *thugs* in the 1830s – as convinced champions of enlightenment against superstition, or merely because they hardly knew what effect their measures would have on their victims.

II

In purely numerical terms it is evident that all religions, unless actually contracting, were likely to expand with the rise in population. Yet two types showed a particular aptitude for expansion in our period : *Islam* and *sectarian Protestantism*. This expansionism was all the more striking as it contrasted with the marked failure of other Christian religions – both Catholic and Protestant – to expand, in spite of a sharp increase in missionary activity outside Europe, increasingly backed by the military, political and economic force of European penetration. In fact, the revolutionary and Napoleonic decades saw the beginning of systematic Protestant missionary activity mostly by Anglo-Saxons. The Baptist Missionary Society (1792), the interdenominational London Missionary Society (1795), the evangelical Church Missionary Society (1799), the British and Foreign Bible Society (1804) were followed by the American Board of Commissioners for Foreign Missions (1810), by the American Baptists (1814), Wesleyans (1813–18), the American Bible Society (1816), the Church of Scotland (1824), the United Presbyterians (1835), the American Methodist Episcopalians (1819) and the rest. Continental Protestants, in spite of some pioneering by the Netherlands Missionary Society (1797) and the Basel Missionaries (1815), developed somewhat later : the Berlin and Rhenish societies in the 1820s, the Swedish, Leipzig and Bremen societies in the 1830s, the Norwegian in 1842. Roman Catholicism, whose missions were stagnant and neglected, revived even later. The reasons for this outpouring of bibles and trade over the heathen belong both to the religious, social and economic histories of Europe and America. Here we need merely note that by 1848 its results were still negligible, except in some Pacific Islands like Hawaii. A few footholds had been gained on the coast in Sierra Leone (whither anti-slavery agitation attracted attention in the 1790s) and in Liberia, formed as a state of liberated American slaves in the 1820s. Around the fringes of European settlement in South Africa foreign missionaries (but not the established local Church of England and Dutch Reformed Church) had begun to convert Africans in some quantities. But when David Livingstone, the famous missionary and explorer, sailed for Africa in 1840, the original inhabitants of that continent were still virtually untouched by Christianity in any shape.

As against this Islam was continuing that silent, piecemeal and irreversible expansion unbacked by organized missionary endeavour of forcible conversion, which is so characteristic of that religion. It expanded both eastwards, in Indonesia and North-western China, and westwards from the Sudan towards Senegal and, to a much smaller extent, from the shores of the Indian Ocean inland. When traditional societies change something so fundamental as their religion, it is clear that they must be facing major new problems. The Moslem traders, who virtually monopolized the commerce of inner Africa with the outside world and multiplied with it, helped to bring Islam to the notice of new peoples. The slave-trade, which broke down communal life, made it attractive, for Islam is a powerful means of reintegrating social structures.[6] At the same time the Mohammedan religion appealed to the semi-feudal and military societies of the Sudan, and its sense of independence, militancy and superiority made it a useful counterweight to slavery. Moslem Negroes made bad slaves : the Haussa (and other Sudanese) who had been imported into Bahia (Brazil) revolted nine times between 1807 and the great rising of 1835 until, in effect, they were mostly killed or deported back to Africa. The slavers learned to avoid imports from these areas, which had only recently been opened to the trade.[7]

While the element of resistance to the whites was clearly very small in African Islam (where there were as yet hardly any), it was by tradition crucial in South-east Asia. There Islam – once again pioneered by traders – had long advanced against local cults and the declining Hinduism of the spice islands, largely as a means of more effective resistance against the Portuguese and the Dutch, as 'a kind of pre-nationalism', though also as a popular counterweight to the Hinduized princes.[8] As these princes increasingly turned into narrowly circumscribed dependents or agents of the Dutch, Islam sunk its roots more deeply into the population. In turn, the Dutch learned that the Indonesian princes could, by allying with the religious teachers, unleash a general popular rising, as in the Java War of the Prince of Djogjakarta (1825–1830). They were consequently time and time again driven back to a policy of close alliance with the local rulers, or indirect rule. Meanwhile the growth of trade and shipping forged closer links between South-east Asian Muslim and Mecca, served to increase the number of pilgrims, to make Indonesian Islam more orthodox, and even to open it to the militant and revivalist influence of Arabian Wahhabism.

Within Islam the movements of reform and revival, which in this period gave the religion much of its penetrative power, can also be seen as reflecting the impact of European expansion and the crisis of the old Mohammedan societies (notably of the Turkish and Persian empires) and perhaps also of the growing crisis of the Chinese empire. The puritanical Wahhabites had arisen in Arabia in the mid-eighteenth century. By 1814 they had conquered Arabia and were ready to conquer Syria, until halted by the combined force of the westernizing Mohammed Ali of Egypt and Western arms; though their teachings spread eastwards into Persia, Afghanistan and India. Inspired by Wahhabism an Algerian holy man, Sidi Mohammed ben Ali el Senussi, developed a similar movement which from the 1840s spread from Tripoli into the Sahara desert. In Algeria Abd-el-Kader, in the Caucasus Shamyl, developed religio-political movements of resistance to the French and Russians respectively (see chapter 7) and anticipated a pan-Islamism which sought not merely a return to the original purity of the Prophet but also to absorb Western innovations. In Persia an even more obviously nationalist and revolutionary heterodoxy, the *bab* movement of Ali Mohammed, arose in the 1840s. It tended, among other things, to return to certain ancient practices of Persian Zoroastrianism and demanded the unveiling of women.

The ferment and expansion of Islam was such that in terms of purely religious history, we can perhaps best describe the period from 1789 to 1848 as that of a world Islamic revival. No equivalent mass movements developed in any other non-Christian religion, though by the end of the period we are on the verge of a great Chinese Taiping rebellion, which has many characteristics of such a one. Small religious reform movements of the evolués were founded in British India, notably Ram Mohan Roy's (1772–1833) *Brahmo Samaj*. In the United States the defeated Indian tribes began to develop religio-social prophetic movements of resistance to the whites, such as that which inspired the war of the largest recorded confederation of the Plains Indians under Tecumseh in the first decade of the century, and Handsome Lake's religion (1799), designed to preserve the Iroquois way of life against disruption by white American society. It is to the credit of Thomas Jefferson, a man of rare enlightenment, that he gave this prophet, who adopted some Christian and especially Quaker elements, his official blessing. However, the direct contact between an advanced capitalist civilization and animist peoples was still too rare to produce many of those prophetic and millenial movements which have become so typical of the twentieth century.

The expansionist movement of Protestant sectarianism differs from that of Islam in that it was almost entirely confined to the countries of developed capitalist civilization. Its extent cannot be measured, for some movements of this kind (for instance German pietism or English evangelicalism) remained within the framework of their respective established State churches. However, its size is not in doubt. In 1851 roughly half the Protestant worshippers in England and Wales attended religious services other than those of the Established Church. This extraordinary triumph of the sects was the result, in the main, of religious developments since 1790, or more precisely since the last years of the Napoleonic Wars. Thus in 1790 the Wesleyan Methodists had only 59,000 communicant members in the UK; in 1850 they and their various offshoots had something like ten times that number.[9] In the United States a very similar process of mass conversion multiplied the number of Baptists, Methodists and to a lesser extent Presbyterians at the relative expense of the formerly dominant churches; by 1850 almost three-quarters of all churches in the USA belonged to these three denominations.[10] The disruption of established churches, the secession and rise of sects, also marks the religious history of this period in Scotland (the 'Great Disruption' of 1843), the Netherlands, Norway and other countries.

The reasons for the geographical and social limits of Protestant sectarianism are evident. Roman Catholic countries provided no scope for and tradition of public sects. There the equivalent break with the established church or the dominant religion was more likely to take the form of mass dechristianization (especially among the men) than of schism.[11] (Conversely, the Protestant anticlericalism of the Anglo-Saxon countries was often the exact counterpart of the atheist anti-clericalism of continental ones.) Religious revivalism was likely to take the form of some new emotional cult, some miracle-working saint or pilgrimage within the accepted framework of the Roman Catholic religion. One or two such saints of our period have come to wider notice, e.g. the Curé d'Ars (1786–1859) in France. The Orthodox Christianity of Eastern Europe lent itself more readily to sectarianism, and in Russia the growing disruption of a backward society had since the later seventeenth century produced a crop of sects. Several, in particular the self-castrating Skoptsi, the Doukhobors of the Ukraine and the Molokans, were the products of the later eighteenth century and the Napoleonic period; 'Old Believers' dated from the seventeenth century. However, in general the classes to which such sectarianism made the greatest appeal – small craftsmen, traders, commercial farmers and other precursors of the bourgeoisie, or conscious peasant revolutionaries – were still not numerous enough to produce a sectarian movement of vast size.

In the Protestant countries the situation was different. Here the impact of the commercial and individualist society was strongest (at all events in Britain and the USA) while the sectarian tradition was already well-established. Its exclusiveness and insistence on the individual communication between man and God, as well as its moral austerity, made it attractive to, or a school for, rising entrepreneurs and small businessmen. Its gaunt, implacable, theology of hell and damnation and of an austere personal salvation made it attractive to men who lived harsh lives in a harsh environment : to frontiersmen and seamen, to small individual cultivators and miners, to exploited craftsmen. The sect could easily turn into a democratic, egalitarian assembly of the faithful without social or religious hierarchy, and thus appealed to the common man. Its hostility to elaborate ritual and learned doctrine encouraged amateur prophecy and preaching. The persistent tradition of millenarianism lent itself to a primitive expression of social rebellion. Finally, its association with emotionally overpowering personal 'conversion' opened the way for a mass religious 'revivalism' of hysterical intensity, in which men and women could find a welcome release from the stresses of a society which provided no equivalent outlets for mass emotion, and destroyed those which had existed in the past.

'Revivalism' did more than anything else to propagate the sects. Thus it was the intensely emotional, irrationalist, personal salvationism of John Wesley (1703–1791) and his Methodists which provided the impetus for the renaissance and expansion of Protestant dissent, at any rate in Britain. For this reason the new sects and trends were initially a-political or even (like the Wesleyans) strongly conservative, for they turned away from the evil outside world to personal salvation or to the life of the self-contained group, which often meant that they rejected the possibility of any collective alteration of its secular arrangements. Their 'political' energies generally went into moral and religious campaigns like those which multiplied foreign missions, anti-slavery and temperance agitations. The politically active and radical sectarians in the period of the American and French Revolutions belonged rather to the older, drier, and more tranquil dissenting and puritan communities which had survived from the seventeenth century, stagnant or even evolving towards an intellectualist deism under the influence of eighteenth-century rationalism : Presbyterians, Congregationalists, Unitarians, Quakers. The new Methodist type of sectarianism was anti-revolutionary, and the immunity of Britain to revolution in our period has even – mistakenly – been ascribed to their growing influence.

However, the social character of the new sects militated against their theological withdrawal from the world. They spread most readily among those who stood between the rich and powerful on one side, the masses of the traditional society on the other : i.e. among those who were about to rise into the middle class, those about to decline into a new proletariat, and the indiscriminate mass of small and independent men in between. The fundamental political orientation of all these inclined them towards a Jacobinical or Jeffersonian radicalism, or at least, a moderate middle-class liberalism. 'Nonconformism' in Britain, the prevalent Protestant churches in the USA, therefore tended to take their place as political forces on the left; though among the British Methodists the Toryism of their founder was overcome only in the course of the half-century of secessions and internal crises which ended in 1848.

Only among the very poor, or the very shaken, did the original rejection of the existing world continue. But there was often a primitive revolutionary rejection, taking the form of the millenarian prediction of the end of the world, which the tribulations of the post-Napoleonic period appeared (in line with the Apocalypse) to foreshadow. The Irvingites in Britain announced it for 1835 and 1838; William Miller, the founder of the Seventh Day Adventists in the USA, predicted it for 1843 and 1844, by which time 50,000 were said to follow him and 3,000 preachers to back him. In the areas where small stable individualist farming and petty trading were under the immediate impact of the growth of a dynamic capitalist economy, such as in upstate New York, this millenarian ferment was particularly powerful. Its most dramatic product was the sect of the Latter-Day Saints (the Mormons), founded by the prophet Joseph Smith who received his revelation near Palmyra, N.Y., in the 1820s, and led his people in an exodus towards some remote Zion which eventually brought them into the deserts of Utah.

These were also the groups among whom the collective hysteria of the mass revival meeting made the greatest appeal; whether because it relieved the harshness and drabness of their lives ('when no other entertainment offers, religious revivals will sometimes take its place' a lady observed of the girls in the Essex mills) [12] or whether its collective religious union created a temporary community of disparate individuals. In its modern form revivalism was the product of the American frontier. The 'Great Awakening' began around 1800 in the Appalachians with gigantic 'camp meetings' – the one at Kane Ridge, Kentucky (1801) united between ten and twenty thousand people under forty preachers – and a degree of sustained orgiastic hysteria difficult to conceive : men and women 'jerked', danced to exhaustion, fell into trances by the thousands, 'spoke with tongues' or barked like dogs. Remoteness, a harsh natural or social environment, or a combination of all these, encouraged such revivalism, which travelling preachers imported into Europe, thus producing a proletarian-democratic secession from the Wesleyans (the so-called Primitive Methodists) after 1808, who spread particularly among British North-country miners and small hill farmers, among North Sea fishermen, farm-labourers and the depressed domestic workers of the sweated industries in the Midlands. Such bouts of religious hysteria occurred periodically throughout our period – in South Wales they broke out in 1807–9, 1828–30, 1839–42, 1849 and 1859 [13] and account for the major increases in the numerical strength of the sects. They cannot be ascribed to any single precipitating cause. Some coincided with periods of acute tension and unrest (all but one of the periods of ultra-rapid Wesleyan expansion in our period did so), but sometimes also with rapid recovery after a depression, and occasionally they were precipitated by social calamities like the cholera epidemics, which produced analogous religious phenomena in other Christian countries.

III

In purely religious terms we must therefore see our period as one in which increasing secularization and (in Europe) religious indifference battled with revivals of religion in its most uncompromising, irrationalist, and emotionally compulsive forms. If Tom Paine stands at one extreme, William Miller the Adventist stands at the other. The frankly atheist mechanical materialism of the German philosopher Feuerbach (1804–1872) in the 1830s confronted the anti-intellectualist young men of the 'Oxford Movement' who defended the literal accuracy of the early medieval lives of the saints.

But this return to militant, literal, old-fashioned religion had three aspects. For the masses it was, in the main, a method of coping with the increasingly bleak and inhuman oppressive society of middle-class liberalism : in Marx's phrase (but he was not the only one to use such words) it was the 'heart of a heartless world, as it is the spirit of spiritless conditions . . . the *opium* of the people'.[14] More than this : it attempted to create social and sometimes educational and political institutions in an environment which provided none, and among politically undeveloped people it gave primitive expression to their discontents and aspirations. Its literalism, emotionalism and superstition protested both against the entire society in which rational calculation dominated and against the upper classes who deformed religion in their own image.

For the middle classes rising out of such masses, religion could be a powerful moral prop, a justification of their social existence against the united contempt and hatred of traditional society, and an engine of their expansion. It liberated them from the fetters of that society, if they were sectarians. It gave their profits a moral title greater than that of mere rational self-interest; it legitimized their harshness towards the oppressed; it united with trade to bring civilization to the heathen and sales to business.

For the monarchies and aristocracies, and indeed for all who rested on top of the social pyramid, it provided social stability. They had learned from the French Revolution that the Church was the strongest prop of the throne. Pious and illiterate peoples like the South Italians, the Spaniards, the Tyrolese and the Russians had leaped to arms to defend their church and ruler against foreigners, infidels and revolutionaries, blessed and in some instances led by their priests. Pious and illiterate peoples would live content in the poverty to which God had called them under the rulers which Providence had given them, simple, moral, orderly and immune from the subversive effects of reason. For conservative governments after 1815 – and what continental European governments were not? – the encouragement of religious sentiments and churches was as indispensable a part of policy as the organization of police-offices, and censorships, for the priest, the policemen and the censor were now the three main props of reaction against revolution.

For most established governments it was enough that Jacobinism threatened thrones and the churches preserved them. However, for a group of romantic intellectuals and ideologists the alliance between throne and altar had a more profound significance : it preserved an old, organic, living society against the corrosion of reason and liberalism, and the individual found it a more adequate expression of his tragic predicament than any provided by the rationalists. In France and England such justifications of the alliance between throne and altar had no great political importance. Neither did the romantic search for a tragic and personal religion. (The most important explorer of these profundities of the human heart, the Dane Søren Kierkegaard, 1813–1855, came from a small country and attracted very little contemporary attention : his fame is entirely posthumous.) However, in the German States and in Russia, the strongholds of monarchist reaction, romantic-reactionary intellectuals played some part in politics as civil servants, drafters of manifestos and programmes, and where monarchs were themselves inclined to mental imbalance (like Alexander I of Russia and Frederick William IV of Prussia) as private advisers. On the whole, however, the Friedrich Gentzes and Adam Muellers were minor figures, and their religious medievalism (which Metternich himself distrusted) was merely a slight traditionalist flourish to announce the policemen and the censors on whom their kings relied. The force of the Holy Alliance of Russia, Austria and Prussia which was to keep Europe in order after 1815 rested not on its titular crusading mysticism, but on the simple decision to put down any and every subversive movement by Russian, Prussian or Austrian arms. Moreover, genuinely conservative governments were inclined to distrust all intellectuals and ideologists, even reactionary ones, for, once the principle of thinking rather than obeying was accepted, the end was in sight. As Friedrich Gentz (Metternich's secretary) wrote in 1819 to Adam Mueller :

'I continue to defend the proposition : "In order that the press may not be abused, nothing whatever shall be printed in the next ... years. Period." If this principle were to be applied as a binding rule, a very few rare exceptions being authorized by a very clearly superior Tribunal, we should within a brief time find our way back to God and Truth.' [15]

And yet, if the anti-liberal ideologists were of small political importance, their flight from the horrors of liberalism into a truly godly and organic past was of considerable religious interest, for it produced a marked revival of Roman Catholicism among sensitive young men of the upper classes. For was not Protestantism itself the direct precursor of individualism, rationalism and liberalism? If a truly religious society alone would heal the sickness of the nineteenth century, was it not the only *truly* Christian society of the Catholic middle ages? [16] As usual, Gentz expressed the attraction of Catholicism with a clarity unsuited to the subject :

'Protestantism is the first, the true, the only source of all the vast evils under which we groan today. Had it merely confined itself to reasoning, we might have been able and obliged to tolerate it, for a tendency to argue is rooted in human nature. However, once governments agreed to accept Protestantism as a permitted form of religion, an expression of Christianity, a right of man; once they ... granted it a place in the State beside, or even on the ruins of, the only true church, the religious, moral and political order of the world was immediately dissolved. . . . The entire French Revolution, and the even worse revolution which is about to break over Germany, have sprung from this same source.' [17]

Groups of exalted young men thus flung themselves from the horrors of the intellect into the welcoming arms of Rome; embracing celibacy, the self-torture of asceticism, the writings of the Fathers, or merely the warm and aesthetically satisfying ritual of the Church with a passionate abandon. They came, as was to be expected, mostly from Protestant countries : the German Romantics were in general Prussians. The 'Oxford Movement' of the 1830s is the most familiar phenomenon of this kind to the Anglo-Saxon reader, though it is characteristically British inasmuch as only some of the young zealots who thus expressed the spirit of the most obscurantist and reactionary of universities, actually joined the Roman Church, notably the talented J. H. Newman (1801–1890). The rest found a compromise resting-place as 'ritualists' within the Anglican Church, which they claimed to be a true Catholic Church, and attempted, to the horror of 'low' and 'broad' churchmen, to garnish with vestments, incense and other popish abominations. The new converts were a puzzle to the traditionally Catholic noble and gentle families, who took their religion as a family badge, and to the mass of Irish immigrant labourers who increasingly formed the bulk of British Catholicism; nor was their noble zeal wholly appreciated by the careful and realistic ecclesiastical officials of the Vatican. But since they came from excellent families, and the conversion of the upper classes might well herald the conversion of the lower, they were welcomed as a heartening sign of the Church's power to conquer.

Yet even within organized religion – at least within the Roman Catholic, Protestant and Jewish kind – the sappers and miners of liberalism were at work. In the Roman Church their chief field of action was France, and their most important figure, Hugues-Felicité-Robert de Lamennais (1782–1854), who moved successively from romantic conservatism, to a revolutionary idealization of the people which brought him close to socialism. Lamennais' *Paroles d'un Croyant* (1834) created uproar among governments, who scarcely expected to be stabbed in the back with so reliable a weapon of the status quo defence as Catholicism, and he was soon condemned by Rome. Liberal Catholicism, however, survived in France, always a country receptive to trends in the Church slightly at variance with those in Rome. In Italy also the powerful revolutionary current of the 1830s and 1840s pulled some Catholic thinkers into its eddies, such as Rosmini and Gioberti (1801–52), the champion of the liberal Italy united by the Pope. However, the main body of the Church was militantly and increasingly anti-liberal.

Protestant minorities and sects naturally stood far closer to liberalism, at any rate in politics : to be a French Huguenot virtually meant to be at the very least a moderate liberal. (Guizot, Louis Philippe's Prime Minister, was one.) Protestant State churches like the Anglican and the Lutheran were politically more conservative, but their theologies were rather less resistant to the corrosion of biblical scholarship and rationalist enquiry. The Jews, of course, were exposed to the full force of the liberal current. After all, they owed their political and social emancipation entirely to it. Cultural assimilation was the goal of all emancipated Jews. The most extreme among the evolués abandoned their old religion for Christian conformity or agnosticism, like the father of Karl Marx or the poet Heinrich Heine (who discovered, however, that Jews do not cease to be Jews at least for the outside world when they stop going to the synagogue). The less extreme developed an attenuated liberal form of Judaism. Only in the small towns did the Torah- and Talmud-dominated life of the ghetto continue virtually unchanged.

NOTES

1 Civiltà Cattolica II, 122, quoted in L. Dal Pane, il socialismo e le questione sociale nella prima annata della Civiltà Cattolica, *Studi Onore di Gino Luzzato*, Milan, 1950, p. 144.
2 Haxthausen, *Studien ueber . . . Russland* (1847), I, p. 388.

3 cf. Antonio Machado's portrait of the Andalusian gentleman in *Poesias Completas* (Austral. ed.), pp. 152–4 :
'Gran pagano,
Se hizo hermano
De una santa cofradia' etc.

4 G. Duveau, *Les Instituteurs* (1957), pp. 3–4.

5 In fact only popular songs of the period do sometimes echo Catholic terminology, like the *Ça Ira*.

6 J. S. Trimingham, *Islam in West Africa* (Oxford 1959), p. 30.

7 A. Ramos, *Las Culturas negras en el mundo nuevo* (Mexico 1943), p. 277 ff.

8 W. F. Wertheim, *Indonesian Society in Transition* (1956), p. 204.

9 *Census of Great Britain 1851: Religious Worship in England and Wales* (London 1854).

10 Mulhall, *Dictionary of Statistics:* 'Religion'.

11 The sects and breakaways to Protestantism which occurred – not as yet very frequently – remained, and have since remained, numerically tiny.

12 Mary Merryweather, *Experience of Factory Life* (Third ed. London 1862), p. 18. The reference is to the 1840s.

13 T. Rees, *History of Protestant Nonconformity in Wales* (1861).

14 Marx-Engels, *Werke* (Berlin 1956), I, p. 378.

15 *Briefwechsel zwischen Fr. Gentz und Adam Müller*, Gentz to Müller, 7 October, 1819.

16 In Russia, where the truly Christian society of the Orthodox Church was still flourishing, the equivalent tendency was less one of a return to the unsullied godliness of the past, than one of a retreat into the limitless profundities of mysticism available in the Orthodoxy of the present.

17 Gentz to Müller, 19 April, 1819.

13

Ideology: Secular

(Mr Bentham) turns wooden utensils in a lathe for exercise, and fancies he can turn men in the same manner. He has no great fondness for poetry, and can hardly extract a moral out of Shakespeare. His house is warmed and lighted by steam. He is one of those who prefer the artificial to the natural in most things, and think the mind of man omnipotent. He has a great contempt for out-of-door prospects, for green fields and trees, and is for ever referring everything to Utility.

W. Hazlitt, *The Spirit of the Age* (1825)

The Communists disdain to conceal their views and aims. They openly declare that their ends can be attained only by the forcible overthrow of all existing conditions. Let the ruling classes tremble at a communist revolution. The proletarians have nothing to lose but their chains. They have a world to win. Working men of all countries, unite!

K. Marx and F. Engels, *Manifesto of the Communist Party* (1848)

I

Quantity must still make us give pride of place in the world of 1789–1848 to religious ideology; quality to secular. With a very few exceptions all the thinkers of importance in our period spoke the secular language, whatever their private religious beliefs. Much of what they thought (and what ordinary people took for granted without much self-conscious thought) will be discussed under the more specific headings of science and the arts; some has already been discussed. Here we shall concentrate on what was after all the major theme which arose out of the dual revolution, the nature of society and the way it was going or ought to go. On this key problem there were two major divisions of opinion : those who accepted the way the world was going and those who did not; in other words those who believed in progress and the others. For in a sense there was only one *Weltanschauung* of major significance, and a number of other views which, whatever their merits, were at bottom chiefly negative critiques of it : the triumphant, rationalist, humanist 'Enlightenment' of the eighteenth century. Its champions believed firmly (and correctly) that human history was an ascent, rather than a decline or an undulating movement about a level trend. They could observe that man's scientific knowledge and technical control over nature increased daily. They believed that human society and individual man could be perfected by the same application of reason, and were destined to be so perfected by history. On these points bourgeois liberals and revolutionary proletarian socialists were at one.

Up to 1789 the most powerful and advanced formulation of this ideology of progress had been classical bourgeois liberalism. Indeed, its fundamental system had been so firmly elaborated in the seventeenth and eighteenth centuries that its discussion hardly belongs to this volume. It was a narrow, lucid, and sharp-edged philosophy which found its purest exponents, as we might expect, in Britain and France.

It was rigorously rationalist and secular; that is to say convinced of the ability of men in principle to understand all and to solve all questions by the use of reason, and the tendency of irrational behaviour and institutions (among which traditionalism and all religion other than the rational) to obscure rather than to enlighten. Philosophically it tended towards materialism, or empiricism, as befitted an ideology which drew its force and methods from science, in this instance chiefly the mathematics and physics of the seventeenth-century scientific revolution. Its general assumptions about the world and man were marked by a pervasive individualism, which owed more to the introspection of middle-class individuals or the observation of their behaviour than to the *a priori* principles on which it claimed to be based, and which was expressed in a psychology (though the word was not yet in existence in 1789) that echoed seventeenth-century mechanics, the so-called 'associationist' school.

In brief, for classical liberalism the human world consisted of self-contained individual atoms with certain built-in passions and drives, each seeking above all to maximize his satisfactions and minimize his dissatisfactions, equal in this to all others,[1] and 'naturally' recognizing no limits or rights of interference with his urges. In other words, each man was 'naturally' possessed of life, liberty and the pursuit of happiness, as the American Declaration of Independence put it, though the most logical liberal thinkers preferred not to put this in the language of 'natural rights'. In the course of pursuing this self-interest, each individual in this anarchy of equal competitors, found it advantageous or unavoidable to enter into certain relations with other individuals, and this complex of useful arrangements – which were often expressed in the frankly commercial terminology of 'contract' – constituted society and social or political groups. Of course such arrangements and associations implied some diminution of man's naturally unlimited liberty to do what he liked, one of the tasks of politics being to reduce such interference to the practicable minimum. Except perhaps for such irreducible sexual groups as parents and their children, the 'man' of classical liberalism (whose literary symbol was Robinson Crusoe) was a social animal only insofar as he co-existed in large numbers. Social aims were therefore the arithmetical sum of individual aims. Happiness (a term which caused its definers almost as much trouble as its pursuers) was each individual's supreme object; the greatest happiness of the greatest number, was plainly the aim of society.

In fact, pure *utilitarianism*, which frankly reduced *all* human relations entirely to the pattern just sketched, was confined to very tactless philosophers like the great Thomas Hobbes in the seventeenth century of very confident champions of the middle class like the school of British thinkers and publicists associated with the names of Jeremy Bentham (1748–1832), James Mill (1773–1836) and above all the classical political economists. For two reasons. In the first place an ideology which so completely reduced all except the rational calculation of self-interest to 'nonsense on stilts' (to use Bentham's phrase), conflicted with some powerful instincts of the middle-class behaviour it aimed to advance.[2] Thus it could be shown that rational self-interest might well justify considerably greater interference in the individual's 'natural liberty' to do as he wished and to keep what he earned, than was at all agreeable. (Thomas Hobbes, whose works the British utilitarians piously collected and published, had actually shown that it precluded any *a priori* limits on state power, and the Benthamites themselves championed bureaucratic state management when they thought it secured the greatest happiness of the greatest number as readily as *laissez-faire*.) Consequently those seeking to safeguard private property, enterprise and individual freedom often preferred to give it the metaphysical sanction of a 'natural right' rather than the vulnerable one of 'utility'. Moreover, a philosophy which so completely eliminated morality and duty by reducing them to rational calculation, might well weaken that sense of the eternal fitness of things among the ignorant poor on which social stability rested.

Utilitarianism, for reasons such as these, therefore never monopolized middle class liberal ideology. It provided the sharpest of radical axes with which to chop down traditional institutions which could not answer the triumphant questions : is it rational? Is it useful? Does it contribute to the greatest happiness of the greatest number? But it was strong enough neither to inspire a revolution nor to safeguard against one. The philosophically feeble John Locke rather than the superb Thomas Hobbes remained the favourite thinker of vulgar liberalism; for he at least put private property beyond the range of interference and attack as the most basic of 'natural rights'. And the French Revolutionaries found it best to put their demand for free enterprise (*'tout citoyen est libre d'employer ses bras, son industrie et ses capitaux comme il juge bon et utile à lui-même. . . . Il peut fabriquer ce qui lui plaît et comme il lui plaît'*) [3] into the form of a general natural right to liberty (*'L'exercise des droits naturels de chaque homme n'a de bornes que celles qui assurent aux autres membres de la société la jouissance des mêmes droits'*).[4]

In its political thought classical liberalism thus swerved from the daring and rigour which made it so powerful a revolutionary force. In its economic thought, however, it was less inhibited; partly because middle-class confidence in the triumph of capitalism was much greater than confidence in the political supremacy of the bourgeoisie over absolutism or the ignorant mob, partly because the classical assumptions about the nature and natural state of man undoubtedly fitted the special situation of the market much better than the situation of humanity in general. Consequently classical political economy forms, with Thomas Hobbes, the most impressive intellectual monument to liberal ideology. Its great period is slightly earlier than that with which this volume deals. The publication of Adam Smith's (1723–90) *Wealth of Nations* in 1776 marks its beginning, that of David Ricardo's (1792–1823) *Principles of Political Economy* in 1817 its peak, and 1830 the beginning of its decline or transformation. However, its vulgarized version continued to gain adherents among businessmen throughout our period.

The social argument of Adam Smith's political economy was both elegant and comforting. It is true that humanity consisted essentially of sovereign individuals of a certain psychological constitution pursuing their self-interest in competition with one another. But it could be shown that these activities, when left to operate so far as possible unchecked, produced not only a 'natural' social order (as distinct from the artificial ones imposed by aristocratic vested interest, obscurantism, tradition or ignorant meddling), but the most rapid possible increase in the 'wealth of nations', i.e. the comfort and wellbeing, and therefore the happiness, of all men. The basis of this natural order was the social division of labour. It could be scientifically *proved* that the existence of a class of capitalists owning the means of production benefited all, including the class of labourers hiring themselves out to its members, just as it could be scientifically proved that the interests of both Britain and Jamaica were best served by the one producing manufactured goods and the other raw sugar. For the increase in the wealth of nations proceeded by the operations of property-owning private enterprise and the accumulation of capital, and it could be shown that any other method of securing it must slow it down or bring it to a stop. Moreover, the economically very unequal society which resulted inevitably from the operations of human nature was not incompatible with the natural equality of all men or with justice. For quite apart from securing to even the poorest a better life than he would otherwise have had, it was based on the most equal of all relationships, the exchange of equivalents in the market. As a modern scholar has put it : 'Nobody was dependent on the benevolence of others; for everything that one got from anybody, one gave an equivalent in exchange. Moreover, the free play of natural forces would be destructive of all positions that were not built upon contributions to the common good.'[5]

Progress was therefore as 'natural' as capitalism. Remove the artificial obstacles to it which the past had erected, and it must inevitably take place; and it was evident that the progress of production went hand in hand with that of the arts, the sciences and civilization in general. Let it not be supposed that the men who held such views were mere special pleaders for the vested interest of businessmen.

They were men who believed, with considerable historical justification at this period, that the way forward for humanity was through capitalism.

The power of this Panglossian view rested not merely on what was believed to be the unanswerable ability to prove its economic theorems by a deductive reasoning, but on the evident progress of eighteenth-century capitalism and civilization. Conversely, it began to falter not merely because Ricardo discovered contradictions within the system which Smith had overlooked, but because the actual economic and social results of capitalism proved to be less happy than had been forecast. Political economy in the first half of the nineteenth century became the 'dismal' rather than the rosy science. Naturally it might still be held that the misery of the poor who (as Malthus argued in the famous *Essay on Population*, 1798) were condemned to linger on the verge of starvation or who (as Ricardo argued) suffered from the introduction of machinery,[6] still constituted the greatest happiness of the greatest number, which merely happened to be much less than one might have hoped. But such facts, as well as the marked difficulties in capitalist expansion in the period from about 1810 to the 1840s, damped optimism and stimulated critical enquiry, especially into *distribution* as against the *production*, which had chiefly pre-occupied the generation of Smith.

David Ricardo's political economy, a masterpiece of deductive rigour, thus introduced considerable elements of discord into the natural harmony on which the earlier economists had put their money. It even stressed, rather more than Smith had done, certain factors which might be expected to bring the engine of economic progress to a stop by attenuating the supply of its essential fuel, such as a tendency for the rate of profit to decline. What is more, he provided the basic general labour theory of value which only needed to be given a twist to be turned into a potent argument against capitalism. Nevertheless, his technical mastery as a thinker, and his passionate support for the practical objects which most British businessmen advocated – free trade and hostility to landlords – helped to give classical political economy an even firmer place in liberal ideology than before. For practical purposes the shock-troops of British middle-class reform in the post-Napoleonic period were armed with a combination of Benthamite utilitarianism and Ricardian economics. In turn the massive achievements of Smith and Ricardo, backed by those of

British industry and trade, turned political economy into a largely British science, reducing the French economists (who had at the very least shared the lead in the eighteenth century) to the lesser role of predecessors or auxiliaries, and the non-classical economists to a scattering of snipers. Moreover, they made it an essential symbol of liberal advance. Brazil instituted a chair in the subject in 1808 – long before France – occupied by a popularizer of Adam Smith, J. B. Say (the leading French economist) and the utilitarian anarchist William Godwin. The Argentine had hardly become independent, when in 1823 the new university of Buenos Aires began to teach political economy on the basis of the already translated Ricardo and James Mill; but not before Cuba, which had its first chair as early as 1818. The fact that the actual economic behaviour of the Latin American rulers caused the hair of European financiers and economists to rise in horror, made no difference to their attachment to economic orthodoxy.

In politics, as we have seen, the liberal ideology was neither as coherent nor as consistent. Theoretically it remained divided between utilitarianism and adaptations of the age-old doctrines of natural law and natural right, with the latter prevailing. In its practical programme it remained torn between a belief in popular government, i.e. majority rule, which had logic on its side and also reflected the fact that what actually made revolutions and put the effective political pressure behind reform was not middle class argument but the mobilization of the masses,[7] and the more prevalent belief in government by a propertied élite – between 'radicalism' and 'whiggism' to use the British terms. For if government really were popular, and if the majority really ruled (i.e. if minority interests were sacrificed to it, as was logically inevitable), could the actual majority – 'the most numerous and poorest classes'[8] – be relied upon to safeguard freedom and to carry out the dictates of reason which coincided, as was obvious, with the programme of middle-class liberals?

Before the French Revolution the main cause for alarm in this respect was the ignorance and superstition of the labouring poor, who were only too often under the sway of priest and king. The Revolution itself introduced the additional hazard of a left-wing, anti-capitalist programme, such as was implicit (and some have argued explicit) in certain aspects of the Jacobin dictatorship. Moderate whigs abroad observed this danger early : Edmund Burke, whose economic ideology was one of pure Adam-Smithianism,[9] retreated in his politics into a frankly irrationalist belief in the virtues of tradition, continuity and slow organic growth, which have ever since provided the theoretical mainstay of conservatism. Practical liberals on the continent shied away from political democracy, preferring a constitutional monarchy with property suffrage, or at a pinch, any old-fashioned absolutism which guaranteed their interests. After 1793–4 only an extremely discontented, or else an extremely self-confident bourgeoisie, such as that of Britain, was prepared with James Mill to trust its own capacity to retain the support of the labouring poor permanently even in a democratic republic.

The social discontents, revolutionary movements and socialist ideologies of the post-Napoleonic period intensified this dilemma and the 1830 Revolution made it acute. Liberalism and democracy appeared to be adversaries rather than allies; the triple slogan of the French Revolution, liberty, equality, fraternity, to express a contradiction rather than a combination. Not unnaturally this appeared most obvious in the home of revolution, France. Alexis de Tocqueville (1805–59), who devoted a remarkably acute intellect to the analysis of the inherent tendencies of American democracy (1835) and later to those of the French Revolution, has survived best among the moderate liberal critics of democracy of this period; or rather he has proved particularly congenial to moderate liberals in the western world since 1945. Perhaps not unnaturally in view of his dictum: 'From the eighteenth century there flow, as from a common source, two rivers. One carries men to free institutions, the other to absolute power.'[10] In Britain too James Mill's sturdy confidence in a bourgeois-led democracy contrasts markedly with his son John Stuart Mill's (1806–73) anxiety to safeguard the rights of minorities against majorities, which dominates that generous but worried thinker's *On Liberty* (1859).

II

While the liberal ideology thus lost its original confident swoop – even the inevitability or desirability of progress began to be doubted by some liberals – a new ideology, socialism, reformulated the old eighteenth-century verities. Reason, science and progress were its firm foundation. What distinguished the socialists of our period from the champions of a perfect society of common ownership who periodically break into literature throughout recorded history, was the unqualified acceptance of the Industrial Revolution which created the very possibility of modern socialism. Count Claude de Saint-Simon (1760–1825), who is by tradition reckoned as the pioneer 'utopian socialist', though his thought actually occupies a rather more ambiguous position, was first and foremost the apostle of 'industrialism' and 'industrialists' (two words of Saint-Simonian coinage). His disciples became socialists, adventurous technologists, financiers and industrialists, or both in succession. Saint-Simonianism thus occupies a peculiar place in the history of both capitalist and anti-capitalist development. Robert Owen (1771–1858) in Britain was himself a highly successful pioneer of the cotton industry, and drew his confidence in the possibility of a better society not merely from his firm belief in human perfectibility through society, but also from the visible creation of a society of potential plenty by the Industrial Revolution. Frederick Engels, though reluctantly, was also in the cotton business. None of the new socialists wished to turn the clock of social evolution back, though many of their followers did. Even Charles Fourier (1772–1837), the least sanguine of the socialist founding fathers about industrialism, argued that the solution lay beyond rather than behind it.

Moreover, the very arguments of classical liberalism could and were readily turned against the capitalist society which they had helped to build. Happiness was indeed, as Saint-Just said, 'a new idea in Europe';[11] but nothing was easier than to observe that the greatest happiness of the greatest number, which was clearly not being achieved, was that of the labouring poor. Nor was it difficult, as William Godwin, Robert Owen, Thomas Hodgskin and other admirers of Bentham did, to separate the pursuit of happiness from the assumptions of a selfish individualism. 'The primary and necessary object of all existence is to be happy,' wrote Owen,[12] 'but happiness cannot be obtained individually; it is useless to expect isolated happiness; all must partake of it or the few will never enjoy it.'

More to the point, classical political economy in its Ricardian form could be turned against capitalism; a fact which led middle-class economists after 1830 to view Ricardo with alarm, or even to regard him, with the American Carey (1793–1879), as the source of inspiration for agitators and disrupters of society. If, as political economy argued, labour was the source of all value, then why did the bulk of its producers live on the edge of destitution? Because, as Ricardo showed – though he felt uncomfortable about drawing the conclusions of his theory – the capitalist appropriated in the form of profit the surplus which the worker produced over and above what he received back as wages. (The fact that the landlords also appropriated a part of this surplus did not fundamentally affect the matter.) In fact, the capitalist exploited the worker. It only remained to do without capitalists and thus to abolish exploitation. A group of Ricardian 'labour economists' soon arose in Britain to make the analysis and point the moral.

If capitalism had actually achieved what had been expected of it in the optimistic days of political economy, such criticisms would have lacked resonance. Contrary to what is often supposed, among the poor there are few 'revolutions of rising standards'. But in the formative period of socialism, i.e. between the publication of Robert Owen's *New View of Society* (1813–14) [13] and the *Communist Manifesto* (1848), depression, falling money-wages, heavy technological unemployment and doubts about the future expansive prospects of the economy were only too obtrusive.[14] Critics could therefore fix not merely on the injustice of the economy, but on the defects of its operation, its 'internal contradictions'. Eyes sharpened by antipathy thus detected the built-in cyclical fluctuations or 'crises' of capitalism (Sismondi, Wade, Engels) which its supporters overlooked, and indeed whose possibility a 'Law' associated with the name of J. B. Say (1767–1832) denied. They could hardly fail to notice that the increasingly uneven distribution of national incomes in this period ('the rich getting richer and the poor poorer') was not an accident, but the product of the operations of the system. In brief, they could show not merely that capitalism was unjust, but that it appeared to work badly and, insofar as it worked, to produce the opposite results to those predicted by its champions.

So far the new socialists merely made their case by pushing the arguments of classical Franco-British liberalism beyond the point where bourgeois liberals were prepared to go. Nor did the new society they advocated necessarily leave the traditional ground of the classical humanist and liberal ideal. A world in which all were happy, and every individual fully and freely realized his or her potentialities, in which freedom reigned and government that was coercion had disappeared, was the ultimate aim of both liberals and socialists. What distinguishes the various members of the ideological family descended from humanism and the Enlightenment, liberal, socialist, communist or anarchist, is not the gentle anarchy which is the utopia of all of them, but the methods of achieving it. At this point, however, socialism parted company with the classical liberal tradition.

In the first place it broke radically with the liberal assumption that society was a mere aggregate or combination of its individual atoms, and that its motive force was their self-interest and competition. In doing so the socialists returned to the oldest of all human ideological traditions, the belief that man is naturally a communal being. Men naturally live together and help one another. Society was not a necessary but regrettable diminution of man's unlimited natural right to do as he liked, but the setting of his life, happiness and individuality. The Smithian idea that the exchange of equivalents in the market somehow assured social justice, struck them as either incomprehensible or immoral. The bulk of the common people held this view even when they could not express it. Many critics of capitalism reacted against the obvious 'dehumanization' of bourgeois society (the technical term 'alienation', which Hegelians and the early Marx used, reflects the age-old concept of society as man's 'home' rather than as the mere locus of the unattached individual's activities) by blaming the entire course of civilization, rationalism, science and technology. The new socialists – unlike revolutionaries of the older craftsman type like the poet William Blake and Jean-Jacques Rousseau – were careful not to do so. But they shared not only the traditional ideal of society as man's home, but the age-old concept that before the institution of class society and property men had somehow lived in harmony; a concept which Rousseau expressed by idealizing primitive man, and less sophisticated radical pamphleteers by the myth of the once free and brotherly people conquered by alien rulers – the Saxons by the Normans, the Gauls by the Teutons. 'Genius,' said Fourier, 'must rediscover the paths of that primitive happiness and adapt it to the conditions of modern industry.' [15] Primitive communism reached out across the centuries or the oceans to provide a model for the communism of the future.

In the second place socialism adopted a form of argument which, if not outside the range of the classical liberal tradition, had not been greatly stressed within it; the evolutionary and historical. For the classical liberals, and indeed the earliest modern socialists, their proposals were natural and rational, as distinct from the artificial and irrational society which ignorance and tyranny had hitherto imposed on the world. Now that the progress of enlightenment had shown men what was rational, all that remained to be done was to sweep away the obstacles which prevented common sense from having its way. Indeed, the 'utopian' socialists (the Saint-Simonians, Owen, Fourier and the rest) tended to be so firmly convinced that the truth had only to be proclaimed to be instantly adopted by all men of education and sense, that initially they confined their efforts to realize socialism to a propaganda addressed in the first place to the influential classes – the workers, though they would undoubtedly benefit, were unfortunately an ignorant and backward group – and to the construction of, as it were, pilot plants of socialism – communist colonies and co-operative enterprises, mostly situated in the open spaces of America, where no traditions of historic backwardness stood in the way of men's advance. Owen's New Harmony was in Indiana, the USA contained some thirty-four imported or home-grown Fourieristic 'Phalanxes', and numerous colonies inspired by the Christian communist Cabet and others. The Saint-Simonians, less given to communal experiments, never ceased their search for an enlightened despot who might carry out their proposals, and for some time believed they had found him in the improbable figure of Mohammed Ali, the ruler of Egypt.

There was an element of historic evolution in this classical rationalist case for the good society; for an ideology of progress implies one of evolution, possibly of inevitable evolution through stages of historical development. But it was not until Karl Marx (1818–83) transferred the centre of gravity of the argument for socialism from its rationality or desirability to its historic inevitability that socialism acquired its most formidable intellectual weapon, against which polemical defences are still being erected. Marx derived this line of argument from a combination of the Franco-British and the German ideological traditions (English political economy, French socialism and German philosophy). For Marx human society had inevitably broken primitive communism into classes; inevitably evolved through a succession of class societies, each in spite of its injustices in its time 'progressive', each containing the 'internal contradictions' which at a certain point made it an obstacle to further progress and generating the forces for its supersession. Capitalism was the last of these, and

Marx, so far from merely attacking it, used all his world-shaking eloquence to trumpet forth its historic achievements. But capitalism could be shown by means of political economy to possess internal contradictions which inevitably made it at a certain point a bar to further progress and would plunge it into a crisis from which it could not emerge. Capitalism, moreover (as could also be shown by political economy), inevitably created its own grave-diggers, the proletariat whose numbers and discontent must grow while the concentration of economic power in fewer and fewer hands made it more vulnerable to overthrow. Proletarian revolution must therefore inevitably overthrow it. But it could also be shown that the social system which corresponded to the interests of the working class was socialism or communism. As capitalism had prevailed, not simply because it was more rational than feudalism, but because of the social force of the bourgeoisie, so socialism would prevail because of the inevitable victory of the workers. It was foolish to suppose that it was an eternal ideal, which men could have realized had they been intelligent enough in Louis XIV's day. It was the child of capitalism. It could not even have been formulated in an adequate manner before the transformation of society which created the conditions for it. But once the conditions were there, the victory was certain, for 'mankind always sets itself only such tasks as it can solve'.[16]

III

Compared to these relatively coherent ideologies of progress, those of resistance to progress hardly deserve the name of systems of thought. They were rather attitudes lacking a common intellectual method, and relying on the acuteness of their insight into the weaknesses of bourgeois society and the unshakeable conviction that there was more in life than liberalism allowed for. Consequently they require relatively little attention.

The chief burden of their critique was that liberalism destroyed the social order or community which man had hitherto regarded as essential to life, replacing it by the intolerable anarchy of the competition of all against all ('every man for himself and the devil take the hindmost') and the dehumanization of the market. On this point conservative and revolutionary anti-progressives, or the representative of rich and poor tended to agree even with the socialists, a convergence which was very marked among the Romantics (see chapter 14) and produced such odd compendia as 'Tory Democracy' or 'Feudal Socialism'. Conservatives tended to identify the ideal social order – or as near to the ideal as was practicable, for the social ambitions of the comfortable are always more modest than those of the poor – with whatever régime was threatened by the dual revolution, or with some specific state of the past, e.g. medieval feudalism. They also, naturally, stressed the element of 'order' in it, for it was this which safeguarded those on the upper steps of the social hierarchy against those on the lower. Revolutionaries, as we have seen, thought rather of some remoter golden time in the past when things had gone well with the people, for no present society is ever really satisfactory for the poor. Also, they stressed the mutual help and community feeling of such an age rather than its 'order'.

Nevertheless both agreed that in important respects the old régime had been or was better than the new. In it God made them high and lowly and ordered their estate, which pleased conservatives, but he also imposed duties (however light and badly carried out) on the high. Men were unequally human, but they were not commodities valued according to the market. Above all they lived together, in tight networks of social and personal relationships, guided by the clear map of custom, social institutions and obligation. Doubtless Metternich's secretary Gentz and the British radical demogogue and journalist William Cobbett (1762–1835) had a very different medieval ideal in mind, but both equally attacked the Reformation which had, they held, introduced the principles of bourgeois society. And even Frederick Engels, the firmest of the believers in progress, painted a notably idyllic picture of the old eighteenth-century society which the Industrial Revolution had disrupted.

Having no coherent theory of evolution, the anti-progressive thinkers found it hard to decide what had 'gone wrong'. Their favourite culprit was reason, or more specifically eighteenth-century rationalism, which sought foolishly and impiously to meddle with matters too complex for human understanding and organization : societies could not be planned like machines. 'It were better to forget, once for all,' wrote Burke, 'the *encyclopédie* and the whole body of economists, and to revert to those old rules and principles which have hitherto made princes great and nations happy.' [17] Instinct, tradition, religious faith, 'human nature', 'true' as opposed to 'false' reason, were marshalled, depending on the intellectual bent of the thinker, against systematic rationalism. But above all its conqueror was to be *history*.

For if conservative thinkers had no sense of historical progress, they had a very acute sense of the difference between societies formed and stabilized naturally and gradually by history as against those established suddenly by 'artifice'. If they could not explain how historical clothes were tailored, and indeed denied that they were, they could explain admirably how they were made comfortable by long wear. The most serious intellectual effort of the anti-progressive ideology went into historical analysis and the rehabilitation of the past, the investigation of continuity as against revolution. Its most important exponents were therefore not the freakish French emigrés like De Bonald (1753–1840) and Joseph De Maistre (1753–1821) who sought to rehabilitate a dead past, often by rationalist arguments verging on the lunatic, even if their object was to establish the virtues of irrationalism, but men like Edmund Burke in England and the German 'historical school' of jurists who legitimized a still existing old régime in terms of its historic continuities.

IV

It remains to consider a group of ideologies poised oddly between the progressive and the anti-progressive, or in social terms, between the industrial bourgeois and proletarian on one side, the aristocratic, mercantile classes and the feudal masses on the other. Their most important bearers were the radical 'little men' of Western Europe and the United States and the modest middle classes of Central and Southern Europe, comfortably but not wholly satisfactorily ensconced in the framework of an aristocratic and monarchical society. Both in some ways believed in progress. Neither was prepared to follow it to its logical liberal or socialist conclusions; the former because these would have doomed the small craftsmen, shopkeepers, farmers and businessmen to be transformed either into capitalists or labourers, the latter because they were too weak and after the experience of the Jacobin dictatorship too frightened, to challenge the power of their princes; whose officials in many cases they were. The views of both these groups therefore combine liberal (and in the first case implicitly socialist) components with anti-liberal, progressive with anti-progressive ones. Moreover, this essential complexity and contradictoriness allowed them to see more deeply into the nature of society than either liberal progressives or anti-progressives. It forced them into dialectics.

The most important thinker (or rather intuitive genius) of this first group of petty-bourgeois radicals was already dead in 1789 : Jean-Jacques Rousseau. Poised between pure individualism and the conviction that man is only himself in a community, between the ideal of the state based on reason and the suspicion of reason as against 'feeling', between the recognition that progress was inevitable and the certainty that it destroyed the harmony of 'natural' primitive man, he expressed his own personal dilemma as well as that of classes which could neither accept the liberal certainties of factory-owners nor the socialist ones of proletarians. The views of this disagreeable, neurotic, but, alas, great man need not concern us in detail, for there was no specific Rousseauist school of thought or, except for Robespierre and the Jacobins of the Year II, of politics. His intellectual influence was pervasive and strong, especially in Germany and among the Romantics, but it was not that of a system but of an attitude and a passion. His influence among plebeian and petty-bourgeois radicals was also immense, but perhaps only among the most woolly-minded, such as Mazzini and nationalists of his sort, was it predominant. In general it fused with much more orthodox adaptations of eighteenth-century rationalism, such as those of Thomas Jefferson (1743–1826) and Thomas Paine (1737–1809).

Recent academic fashions have tended to misunderstand him profoundly. They have ridiculed the tradition which bracketed him with Voltaire and the Encyclopaedists as a pioneer of the Enlightenment and the Revolution, because he was their critic. But those who were influenced by him then regarded him as part of the Enlightenment, and those who reprinted his words in small radical workshops in the early nineteenth century automatically did so in company with Voltaire, d'Holbach and the rest. Recent liberal critics have attacked him as the ancestor of 'totalitarianism' on the left. But in fact he exercised no influence at all on the main tradition of modern communism and Marxism.[18] His typical followers have been throughout our period and since, petty-bourgeois radicals of the Jacobin, Jeffersonian and Mazzini type : believers in democracy, nationalism and a state of small independents with equal distribution of property and some welfare activities. In our period he was believed to stand above all for *equality*; for freedom against tyranny and exploitation ('man is born free but everywhere he is in chains'), for democracy against oligarchy, for the simple 'natural man' unspoiled by the sophistications of the rich and educated, and for 'feeling' against cold calculation.

The second group, which can perhaps best be called that of German philosophy, was far more complex. Moreover, since its members had neither the power to overthrow their societies nor the economic resources to make an Industrial Revolution, they tended to concentrate on the construction of elaborate general systems of thought. There were few classical liberals in Germany. Wilhelm von Humboldt (1767–1835), the brother of the great scientist, is the most notable. Among German middle- and upper-class intellectuals a belief in the inevitability of progress and in the benefits of scientific and economic advance, combined with a belief in the virtues of an enlightened paternal or bureaucratic administration and a sense of responsibility among the upper orders was perhaps the most common attitude, well suited to a class containing so many civil servants and state-employed professors. The great Goethe, himself minister and privy councillor of a petty state, illustrates this attitude well.[19] Middle-class demands – often philosophically formulated as the inevitable working out of the tendencies of history – carried out by an enlightened state : these represented German moderate liberalism best. The fact that German states at their best had always taken a lively and efficient initiative in the organization of economic and educational progress, and that complete *laissez-faire* was not a particularly advantageous policy for German businessmen, did not diminish the appeal of this attitude.

However, though we can thus assimilate the practical outlook of the German middle class thinkers (allowing for the peculiarities of their historic position) to that of their opposite numbers in other countries, it is not certain that we can in this way explain the very marked coolness towards classical liberalism in its pure form which runs through much German thought. The liberal commonplaces – philosophical materialism or empiricism, Newton, Cartesian analysis and the rest – made most German thinkers acutely uncomfortable; mysticism, symbolism and vast generalizations about organic wholes visibly attracted them. Possibly a nationalist reaction against the French culture which predominated in the earlier eighteenth century helped to intensify this teutonism of German thought. More likely the persistence of the intellectual atmosphere of the last age in which Germany had been economically, intellectually, and to some extent politically, predominant accounts for it; for the decline of the period between the Reformation and the later eighteenth century had preserved the archaism of the German intellectual tradition just as it preserved unchanged the sixteenth-century look of small German towns. At all events the fundamental atmosphere of German thought – whether in philosophy, science or the arts – differed markedly from the main tradition of the eighteenth century in Western Europe.[20] At a time when the classical eighteenth-century view was approaching its limits, this gave German thought some advantage, and helps to explain its increasing intellectual influence in the nineteenth century.

Its most monumental expression was German classical philosophy, a body of thought created between 1760 and 1830 together with classical German literature, and in close connection with it. (It must not be forgotten that the poet Goethe was a scientist and 'natural philosopher' of distinction and the poet Schiller not only a professor of history [21] but a distinguished author of philosophical treatises.) Immanuel Kant (1724–1804) and George Wilhelm Friedrich Hegel (1770–1831) are its two great luminaries. After 1830 the process of disintegration which we have already seen in action at the same time within classical political economy (the intellectual flower of eighteenth-century rationalism) also occurred within German philosophy. Its products were the 'Young Hegelians' and eventually Marxism.

German classical philosophy was, it must always be remembered, a thoroughly bourgeois phenomenon. All its leading figures (Kant, Hegel, Fichte, Schelling) hailed the French Revolution and indeed remained loyal to it for a considerable time – Hegel championed Napoleon as late as the battle of Jena (1806). The Enlightenment was the framework of Kant's typically eighteenth-century thought, and the starting-point of Hegel's. The philosophy of both was profoundly impregnated with the idea of progress : Kant's first great achievement was to suggest a hypothesis of the origin and development of the solar system, while Hegel's entire philosophy is one of evolution (or, in social terms, historicity) and necessary progress. Thus while Hegel from the very beginning disliked the extreme left wing of the French Revolution and eventually became utterly conservative, he never for a moment doubted the historic necessity of that revolution as the foundation of bourgeois society. Moreover, unlike most subsequent academic philosophers, Kant, Fichte and notably Hegel studied some economics (the Physiocrats in Fichte's case, the British in Kant's and Hegel's); and there is reason to believe that Kant and the young Hegel would have regarded themselves as persuaded by Adam Smith.[22]

This bourgeois bent of German philosophy is in one respect more obvious in Kant, who remained all his life a man of the liberal left – among his last writings (1795) is a noble plea for universal peace through a world federation of republics which would renounce war – but in another more obscure than in Hegel. For in Kant's thought, confined in the bare and modest professor's lodgings in remote Prussian Koenigsberg, the social content which is so specific in British and French thought is reduced to an austere, if sublime, abstraction; particularly the moral abstraction of 'the will'.[23] Hegel's thought is, as all readers are painfully aware, abstract enough. Yet it is, at least initially, far clearer that his abstractions are attempts to come to terms with society – bourgeois society; and indeed in his analysis of *labour* as the fundamental factor in humanity ('man makes tools because he is a reasonable being, and this is the first expression of his Will', as he said in his lectures of 1805–6)[24] Hegel wielded, in an abstract manner, the same tools as the classical liberal economists, and incidentally provided one of the foundations for Marx.

Nevertheless, from the very beginning German philosophy differed from classic liberalism in important respects, more notably in Hegel than in Kant. In the first place it was deliberately idealist, rejecting the materialism or empiricism of the classical tradition. In the second place, while the basic unit of Kant's philosophy is the individual – even if in the form of the individual conscience – Hegel's starting-point is the collective (i.e. the community), which he admittedly sees disintegrating into individuals under the impact of historical development. And indeed Hegel's famous *dialectic*, the theory of progress (in whatever field) through the never-ending resolution of contradictions, may well have received its initial stimulus from this profound consciousness of the contradiction between individual and collective. Moreover, from the very beginning their position on the margins of the area of whole-hearted bourgeois-liberal advance, and perhaps their inability completely to participate in it, made German thinkers much more aware of its limits and contradictions. No doubt it was inevitable, but did it not bring huge losses as well as huge gains? Must it not in turn be superseded?

We therefore find classical, but especially Hegelian, philosophy runs oddly parallel with Rousseau's dilemma-ridden view of the world, though, unlike him, the philosophers made titanic efforts to include their contradictions in single, all-embracing, intellectually coherent systems. (Rousseau, incidentally, had an immense emotional influence on Immanuel Kant, who is said to have broken his invariable habit of taking a regular afternoon constitutional only twice, once for the fall of the Bastille and once – for several days – for the reading of *Emile*.) In practice the disappointed philosophical revolutionaries faced the problem of 'reconciliation' with reality, which in Hegel's case took the form, after years of hesitation – he remained in two minds about Prussia until after the fall of Napoleon, and, like Goethe, took no interest in the wars of liberation – of an idealization of the Prussian state. In theory the transitoriness of the historically doomed society was built into their philosophy. There was no absolute truth. The development of the historic process itself, which took place through the dialectic of contradiction and was apprehended by a dialectical method, or so at least the 'Young Hegelians' of the 1830s concluded, ready to follow the logic of German classical philosophy beyond the point at which their great teacher himself wished to halt (for he was anxious, somewhat illogically, to end history with the cognition of the Absolute Idea), as after 1830 they were ready to re-enter the road of revolution which their elders had either abandoned or (like Goethe) never chosen to walk. But the issue of revolution in 1830–48 was no longer the simple conquest of middle-class liberal power. And the intellectual revolutionary who emerged from the disintegration of classical German philosophy was not a Girondin or a Philosophic Radical, but Karl Marx.

Thus the period of the dual revolution saw both the triumph and the most elaborate formulation of the middle-class liberal and petty-bourgeois radical ideologies, and their disintegration under the impact of the states and societies they had themselves set out to create, or at least to welcome. 1830, which marks the revival of the major west-European revolutionary movement after the quiescence of the Waterloo period, also marks the beginning of their crisis. They were to survive it, though in a diminished form : no classical liberal economist of the later period had the stature of Smith or Ricardo (certainly not J. S. Mill, who became the representative British liberal economist-philosopher from the 1840s), no classical German philosopher was to have Kant's and Hegel's scope or power, and the Girondins and Jacobins of France in 1830, 1848 and after are pygmies compared to their ancestors of 1789–94. For that matter the Mazzinis of the mid-nineteenth century cannot compare with the Jean-Jacques Rousseaus of the eighteenth. But the great tradition – the mainstream of intellectual development since the Renaissance – did not die; it was transformed into its opposite. Marx was, in stature and approach, the heir of classical economists and philosophers. But the society whose prophet and architect he hoped to become was a very different one from theirs.

NOTES

1 The great Thomas Hobbes actually argued strongly in favour of the – for practical purposes – complete equality of all individuals in all respects except 'science'.
2 It should not be supposed that 'self-interest' necessarily meant an anti-social egoism. Humane and socially-minded utilitarians held that the satisfactions which the individual sought to maximize included, or might with proper education well include, 'benevolence' i.e. the urge to help one's fellow-men. The point was that this was not a moral duty, or an aspect of social existence, but something which made the individual happy. 'Interest,' argued d'Holbach in his *Système de la Nature* I, p. 268, 'is nothing but what each of us considers necessary for his happiness.'
3 *Archives Parlementaires* 1787–1860 t. VIII, p. 429. This was the first draft of paragraph 4 of the Declaration of Man and Citizen.
4 Declaration of the Rights of Man and Citizen 1798, paragraph 4.
5 E. Roll, *A History of Economic Thought* (1948 ed.), p. 155.
6 'The opinion entertained by the labouring class, that the employment of machinery is frequently detrimental to their interests, is not founded on prejudice and error, but is conformable to the correct principles of political economy.' *Principles*, p. 383.
7 Condorcet (1743–94), whose thought is virtually a compendium of enlightened bourgeois attitudes, was converted by the taking of the Bastille from a belief in limited suffrage to one in democracy, though with strong safeguards for the individual and for minorities.
8 *Oeuvres de Condorcet* (1804 ed.) XVIII p. 412; (*Ce que les citoyens ont le droit d'attendre de leur représentants.*) R. R. Palmer, *The Age of Democratic Revolution*, I, (1959), pp. 13–

20, argues – unconvincingly – that liberalism was more clearly 'democratic' than is here suggested.

9 cf. C. B. Macpherson, Edmund Burke (*Transactions of the Royal Society of Canada*, LIII, Sect. II, 1959, pp. 19–26).

10 Quoted in J. L. Talmon, *Political Messianism* (1960), p. 323.

11 Rapport sur le mode d'exécution du décrét du 8 ventôse, an II (*Oeuvres Complètes*, II, 1908, p. 248).

12 *The Book of the New Moral World*, pt. IV, p. 54.

13 R. Owen, *A New View of Society: or Essays on the Principle of the Formation of the Human Character.*

14 The word 'socialism' itself was a coinage of the 1820s.

15 Quoted in Talmon, op. cit., p. 127.

16 K. Marx, *Preface to the Critique of Political Economy.*

17 *Letter to the Chevalier de Rivarol*, June 1, 1791.

18 In almost forty years of correspondence with each other, Marx and Engels mentioned him just three times, casually, and rather negatively. However, in passing they appreciated his dialectical approach which anticipated Hegel's.

19 For his 'declaration of political faith,' see Eckermann, *Gespraeche mit Goethe*, 4.1.1824.

20 This does not apply to Austria, which had passed through a very different history. The main characteristic of Austrian thought was that there was none at all that deserves mention, though in the arts (especially music, architecture and the theatre) and in some applied sciences, the Austrian Empire was very distinguished.

21 His historical dramas – except the Wallenstein trilogy – contain so many poetic inaccuracies that one would not have thought so.

22 G. Lukacs, *Der junge Hegel*, p. 409 for Kant, *passim* – esp. II, 5 for Hegel.

23 Thus Lukacs showed that the very concrete Smithian paradox of the 'hidden hand', which produces socially beneficient results from the selfish antagonism of individuals, in Kant becomes the pure abstraction of an 'unsocial sociability'. *Der Junge Hegel*, p. 409.

24 Lukacs, op. cit., pp. 411–12.

The Arts

> *There is always a fashionable taste: a taste for driving the mail – a taste for acting Hamlet – a taste for philosophical lectures – a taste for the marvellous – a taste for the simple – a taste for the brilliant – a taste for the sombre – a taste for the tender – a taste for the grim – a taste for banditti – a taste for ghosts – a taste for the devil – a taste for French dancers and Italian singers, and German whiskers and tragedies – a taste for enjoying the country in November and wintering in London till the end of the dogdays – a taste for making shoes – a taste for picturesque tours – a taste for taste itself, or for essays on taste.*
>
> The Hon Mrs Pinmoney in T. L. Peacock,
> *Melincourt* (1816)

> *In proportion to the wealth of the country, how few in Great Britain are the buildings of any note . . .; how little is the absorption of capital in museums, pictures, gems, curiosities, palaces, theatres or other unreproductive objects! This which is the main foundation of the greatness of the country, is often stated by foreign travellers, and by some of our own periodical writers, as a proof of our inferiority.*
>
> S. Laing, *Notes of a Traveller on the Social and Political State of France, Prussia, Switzerland, Italy and other parts of Europe*, 1842 [1]

I

The first thing which strikes anyone who attempts to survey the development of the arts in this period of dual revolution is their extraordinary flourishing state. A half-century which includes Beethoven and Schubert, the mature and old Goethe, the young Dickens, Dostoievsky, Verdi and Wagner, the last of Mozart and all or most of Goya, Pushkin and Balzac, not to mention a regiment of men who would be giants in any other company, can stand comparison with any other period of similar length in the world's history. Much of this extraordinary record is due to the revival and expansion of the arts appealing to a literate public in practically all European countries which possessed them.[2]

Rather than weary the reader with a long catalogue of names it may be best to illustrate the width and depth of this cultural revival by taking occasional cross-sections through our period. Thus in 1798–1801 the citizen with an appetite for novelty in the arts could enjoy the *Lyrical Ballads* of Wordsworth and Coleridge in English, several works by Goethe, Schiller, Jean Paul and Novalis in German, while listening to Haydn's *Creation* and *Seasons* and Beethoven's First Symphony and first string quartets. In these years J-L David completed his *Portrait of Madame Recamier* and Goya his *Portrait of the Family of King Charles IV*. In 1824–6 he or she could have read several new novels by Walter Scott in English, Leopardi's poems and Manzoni's *Promessi Sposi* in Italian, Victor Hugo's and Alfred de Vigny's poems in French and, if suitably situated, the early parts of Pushkin's *Eugene Onegin* in Russian, and newly edited Norse sagas. Beethoven's *Choral Symphony*, Schubert's *Death and the Maiden*, Chopin's first work, Weber's *Oberon*, date from these years as do Delacroix's painting of *The Massacre at Chios* and Constable's *The Hay Wain.* Ten years later (1834–6) literature produced Gogol's *Inspector-General* and Pushkin's *Queen of Spades*, in France, Balzac's *Père Goriot* and works by Musset, Hugo, Théophile Gautier, Vigny, Lamartine and Alexander Dumas the Elder, in Germany works by Buechner, Grabbe and Heine, in Austria by Grillparzer and Nestroy, in Denmark by Hans Andersen, in Poland Mickiewicz's *Pan Tadeusz*, in Finland the fundamental edition of the national epic *Kalevala*, in Britain poetry by Browning and Wordsworth. Music provided operas by Bellini and Donizetti in Italy, by Chopin in Poland, by Glinka in Russia; Constable painted in England, Caspar David Friedrich in Germany. A year or two on either side of this triennium brings us within reach of Dickens's *Pickwick Papers*, of Carlyle's *French Revolution*, of Goethe's *Faust Part II*, of poems by Platen, Eichendorff and Moerike in Germany, of important contributions to Flemish and Hungarian literature as well as of further publications by the chief French, Polish and Russian writers; of Schumann's *Davidsbuendlertaenze* and Berlioz's *Requiem* in music.

Two things are evident from these casual samplings. The first is the extraordinarily wide spread of artistic achievement among the nations. This was new. In the first half of the nineteenth century Russian literature and music suddenly emerged as a world force, as, in a very much more modest way, did the literature of the USA with Fenimore Cooper (1787–1851), Edgar Allan Poe (1809–49) and Herman Melville (1819–91). So did Polish and Hungarian literature and music, and, at least in the form of the publication of folksong, fairytale and epic, the literature of the North and the Balkans. Moreover, in several of these newly-minted literate cultures, achievement was immediate and unsurpassed : Pushkin (1799–1837) for instance remains the classic Russian poet, Mickiewicz (1798–1855) the greatest Polish, Petoefi (1823–49) the Hungarian national poet.

The second evident fact is the exceptional development of certain arts and genres. Literature is a case in point, and within literature the novel. Probably no half-century contains a greater concentration of immortal novelists : Stendhal and Balzac in France, Jane Austen, Dickens, Thackeray and the Brontës in England, Gogol and the young Dostoievsky and Turgenev in Russia. (Tolstoi's first writing appeared in the 1850s.) Music is perhaps an even more striking case. The standard concert repertoire still rests largely on the composers active in this period – Mozart and Haydn, though these belong really to an earlier age, Beethoven and Schubert, Mendelssohn, Schumann, Chopin and Liszt. The 'classic' period of instrumental music was mainly one of German and Austrian achievement but one genre, opera, flourished more widely and perhaps more successfully than any other : with Rossini, Donizetti, Bellini and the young Verdi in Italy, with Weber and the young Wagner (not to mention the last two operas of Mozart) in Germany, Glinka in Russia and several lesser figures in France. The record of the visual arts, on the other hand, is less brilliant, with the partial exception of painting. Admittedly Spain produced in Francisco Goya y Lucientes (1746–1828) one of its intermittent great artists, and one of the handful of supreme painters of all time. It may be argued that British painting (with J. M. W. Turner, 1775–1851, and John Constable, 1776–1837) reached a peak of achievement and originality somewhat higher than in the eighteenth century, and was certainly more internationally influential than ever before or since; it may also be held that French painting (with J-L David, 1748–1825, J-L Géricault, 1791–1824, J-D Ingres, 1780–1867, F-E Delacroix 1790–1863, Honoré Daumier, 1808–79, and the young Gustave Courbet, 1819–77) was as eminent as it has ever been in its distinguished history. On the other hand Italian painting virtually came to the end of its centuries-old glory, German painting came nowhere near the unique triumphs of German literature or music, or its own sixteenth century. Sculpture in all countries was markedly less distinguished than in the eighteenth century and so, in spite of some notable achievements in Germany and Russia, was architecture. Indeed the greatest architectural achievements of the period were undoubtedly the work of engineers.

What determines the flowering or wilting of the arts at any period is still very obscure. However, there is no doubt that between 1789 and 1848 the answer must be sought first and foremost in the impact of the dual revolution. If a single misleading sentence is to sum up the relations of artist and society in this era, we might say that the French Revolution inspired him by its example, the Industrial Revolution by its horror, and the bourgeois society, which emerged from both, transformed his very existence and modes of creation.

That artists were in this period directly inspired by and involved in public affairs is not in doubt. Mozart wrote a propagandist opera for the highly political Freemasonry (*The Magic Flute* in 1790), Beethoven dedicated the *Eroica* to Napoleon as the heir of the French Revolution, Goethe was at least a working statesman and civil servant. Dickens wrote novels to attack social abuses, Dostoievsky was to be sentenced to death in 1849 for revolutionary activities. Wagner and Goya went into political exile, Pushkin was punished for being involved with the Decembrists, and Balzac's entire 'Human Comedy' is a monument of social awareness. Never has it been less true to describe creative artists as 'uncommitted'. Those who were, the gentle decorators of rococo palaces and boudoirs or the suppliers of collectors' pieces for visiting English milords, were precisely the ones whose art wilted away : how many of us remember that Fragonard survived the Revolution by seventeen years? Even the apparently least political of arts, music, had the strongest political associations. This was perhaps the only period in history when operas were written as, or taken to be, political manifestos and triggered off revolutions.[3]

The link between public affairs and the arts is particularly strong in the countries where national consciousness and movements of national liberation or unification were developing (cf. chapter 7). It is plainly no accident that the revival or birth of national literate cultures in Germany, Russia, Poland, Hungary, the Scandinavian countries and elsewhere should coincide with – and indeed should often be the first manifestation of – the assertion of the cultural supremacy of the vernacular language and of the native people, against a cosmopolitan aristocratic culture often employing a foreign longuage. Naturally enough, such nationalism found its most obvious cultural expression in literature and in music; both public arts, which could, moreover, draw on the powerful creative heritage of the common people – language and folksong. It is equally understandable that the arts traditionally dependent on commissions from the established ruling classes, courts and governments, architecture and sculpture and to a lesser extent painting, reflected these national revivals less.[4] Italian opera flourished as never before as a popular rather than a court art; Italian painting and architecture died. Of course it must not be forgotten that these new national cultures were confined to a minority of the literate and the middle or upper classes. Except perhaps for Italian opera and the reproducible forms of graphic art, and a few shorter poems or songs, none of the great artistic achievements of this period were within reach of the illiterate or the poor, and most inhabitants of Europe were almost certainly unaware of them, until mass national or political movements turned them into collective symbols. Literature, of course, would have the widest circulation, though mainly among the growing new middle classes, who provided a particularly grateful market (especially among their unemployed womenfolk) for novels and long narrative poetry. Successful authors have rarely enjoyed greater relative prosperity: Byron received £2,600 for the first three cantos of *Childe Harold*. The stage, though socially much more restricted, also reached a public of thousands. Instrumental music did less well, outside bourgeois countries like England and France and culture-starved ones like the Americas where large public concerts were well established. (Hence several continental composers and virtuosos had their eyes firmly on the lucrative, if otherwise undiscriminating English market.) Elsewhere court-employment, the subscription concert, maintained by a limited local patriciate or private and amateur performance, still held the field. Painting, of course, was destined for the individual purchaser and disappeared from sight after its original display at public exhibitions for sale or private dealers; though such public exhibitions were now well established. The museums and art galleries which were founded or opened to the public in this period (e.g. the Louvre and the British National Gallery, founded in 1826) displayed the art of the past rather than the present. The etching, print and lithograph, on the other hand, was ubiquitous, because it was cheap and began to penetrate the newspapers. Architecture, of course, continued to work mainly (except for a certain amount of speculative building of private dwellings) on individual or public commission.

II

But even the arts of a small minority in society can still echo the thunder of the earthquakes which shake all humanity. The literature and arts of our period did so, and the result was 'Romanticism'. As a style, a school, an era in the arts, nothing is harder to define or even to describe in terms of formal analysis; not even 'classicism' against which 'romanticism' claimed to raise the banner of revolt. The romantics themselves hardly help us, for though their own descriptions of what they were after were firm and decided, they were also often quite devoid of rational content. For Victor Hugo romanticism 'set out to do what nature does, to blend with nature's creations, while at the same time not mixing them all together : shadow and light, the grotesque and the sublime – in other words the body and the soul, the animal with the spiritual'.[5] For Charles Nodier 'this last resort of the human heart, tired of ordinary feelings, is what is called the *romantic* genre : strange poetry, quite appropriate to the moral condition of society, to the needs of surfeited generations who cry for sensation at any cost ...'[6] Novalis thought romanticism meant giving ' a higher meaning to what is customary, an infinite look to the finite'.[7] Hegel held that 'the essence of Romantic art lies in the artistic object's being free, concrete, and the spiritual idea in its very essence – all this revealed to the inner rather than the outer eye'.[8] Little illumination is to be derived from such statements, which is to be expected, for the romantics preferred dim and flickering or diffused lights to clear ones.

And yet, though it eludes the classifier, who finds its origins and conclusion dissolve as he tries to pin dates on them and its criteria turn into shapeless generalities as soon as he tries to define them, nobody seriously doubts the existence of romanticism or our capacity to recognize it. In the narrow sense it emerges as a self-conscious and militant trend in the arts, in Britain, France and Germany around 1800 (at the end of the decade of the French Revolution) and over a much wider area of Europe and North America after Waterloo. It was preceded before the Revolutions (again chiefly in France and Germany) by what has been called the 'pre-romanticism' of Jean-Jacques Rousseau, and the 'storm and stress' of the young German poets. Probably the revolutionary era of 1830-48 saw its greatest European vogue. In a wider sense it dominates several of the creative arts of Europe from the French Revolution onwards. In this sense the 'romantic' elements in a composer like Beethoven, a painter like Goya, a poet like Goethe, a novelist like Balzac, are crucial parts of their greatness, as they are not in, let us say, Haydn or Mozart, Fragonard or Reynolds, Mathias Claudius or Choderlos de Laclos (all of whom survived into our period); though none of these men could be described entirely as 'romantics' or would have described themselves as such.[9] In a yet wider sense the approach to art and artists characteristic of romanticism became the standard approach of nineteenth-century middle-class society, and still retains much of its influence.

However, though it is by no means clear what romanticism stood for, it is quite evident what it was against : the middle. Whatever its content, it was an extremist creed. Romantic artists or thinkers in the narrower sense are found on the extreme left, like the poet Shelley, on the extreme right, like Chateaubriand and Novalis, leaping from left to right like Wordsworth, Coleridge and numerous disappointed supporters of the French Revolution, leaping from royalism to the extreme left like Victor Hugo, but hardly ever among the moderates or whig-liberals in the rationalist centre, which indeed was the stronghold of 'classicism'. 'I have no respect for the Whigs,' said the old Tory Wordsworth, 'but I have a great deal of the Chartist in me'.[10] It would be too much to call it an anti-bourgeois creed, for the revolutionary and conquistador element in young classes still about to storm heaven fascinated the romantics also. Napoleon became one of their myth-heroes, like Satan, Shakespeare, the Wandering Jew and other trespassers beyond the ordinary limits of life. The demonic element in capitalist accumulation, the limitless and uninterrupted pursuit of *more*, beyond the calculation of rationality or purpose, need or the extremes of luxury, haunted them. Some of their most characteristic heroes, Faustus and Don Juan, share this unappeasable greed with the business buccaneers of Balzac's novels. And yet the romantic element remained subordinate, even in the phase of bourgeois revolution. Rousseau provided some of the accessories of the French Revolution, but he dominated it only in the one period in which it went beyond bourgeois liberalism, that of Robespierre. And even so, its basic costume was Roman, rationalist and neo-classic. David was its painter, Reason its Supreme Being.

Romanticism is therefore not simply classifiable as an anti-bourgeois movement. Indeed, in the pre-romanticism of the decades before the French Revolution, many of its characteristic slogans had been used for the glorification of the middle class, whose true and simple, not to say mawkish, feeling had been favourably contrasted with the stiff upper lip of a corrupt society, and whose spontaneous reliance on nature was destined, it was believed, to sweep aside the artifice of court and clericalism. However, once bourgeois society had in fact triumphed in the French and Industrial Revolutions, romanticism unquestionably became its instinctive enemy and can be justly described as such.

No doubt much of its passionate, confused, but profound, revulsion against bourgeois society was due to the vested interest of the two groups which provided its shock-troops : socially displaced young men and professional artists. There had never been a period for young artists, living or dying, like the romantic : the *Lyrical Ballads* (1798) were the work of men in their twenties, Byron became famous overnight at twenty-four, an age at which Shelley was famous and Keats was almost in his grave. Hugo's poetic career began when he was twenty, Musset's at twenty-three. Schubert wrote *Erlkoenig* at the age of eighteen and was dead at thirty-one, Delacroix painted the *Massacre at Chios* at twenty-five, Petoefi published his *Poems* at twenty-one. An unmade reputation or an unproduced masterpiece by thirty is a rarity among the romantics. Youth – especially intellectual or student youth – was their natural habitat; it was in this period that the Quartier Latin of Paris became, for the first time since the middle ages, not merely a place where the Sorbonne was, but a cultural (and political) concept. The contrast between a world theoretically wide open to talent and in practice, with cosmic injustice, monopolized by soulless bureaucrats and pot-bellied philistines, cried to the heavens. The shades of the prison-house – marriage, respectable career, absorption into philistinism – surrounded them, and birds of night in the shape of their elders predicted (only too often with accuracy) their inevitable sentence, as Registrator Heerbrand in E. T. A. Hoffmann's *Goldener Topf* predicts ('smiling cunningly and mysteriously') the appalling future of a Court Councillor for the poetic student Anselmus. Byron was clear-headed enough to foresee that only an early death was likely to save him from a 'respectable' old age, and A. W. Schlegel proved him right. There is, of course, nothing universal in this revolt of the young against their elders. It was itself a reflection of the society created by the double revolution. Yet the specific historic form of this alienation certainly coloured a great part of romanticism.

So, to an even greater extent, did the alienation of the artist who reacted to it by turning himself into 'the genius', one of the most characteristic inventions of the romantic era. Where the social function of the artist is clear, his relation to the public direct, the question of what he is to say and how to say it answered by tradition, morality, reason or some other accepted standard, an artist may be a genius, but rarely behaves like one. The few who anticipate the nineteenth-century pattern – a Michelangelo, Caravaggio or Salvator Rosa – stand out from the army of men with the standards of professional craftsmen and entertainers, the John Sebastian Bachs, Handels, Haydns and Mozarts, the Fragonards and Gainsboroughs of the pre-revolutionary age. Where something like the old social situation persisted after the double revolution, the artist continued as a non-genius, though very likely a vain one. Architects and engineers on specific orders continued to produce structures of obvious use which imposed clearly understood forms. It is significant that the great majority of the characteristic, and virtually all the most famous, buildings of the period from 1790 to 1848 are neo-classical like the Madeleine, the British Museum, St Isaac's cathedral in Leningrad, Nash's London, Schinkel's Berlin, or functional like the marvellous bridges, canals, railway constructions, factories and greenhouses of that age of technical beauty.

However, quite apart from their styles, the architects and engineers of that age behaved as professionals and not as geniuses. Again, in genuinely popular forms of art such as the opera in Italy or (on a socially higher level) the novel in England, composers and writers continued to work as entertainers who regarded the supremacy of the box-office as a natural condition of their art, rather than as a conspiracy against their muse. Rossini would no more have expected to produce an uncommercial opera than the young Dickens an unserializable novel or today the librettist of a modern musical a text which is performed as originally drafted. (This may also help to explain why Italian opera at this time was quite unromantic, in spite of its natural vulgarian fondness for blood, thunder and 'strong' situations.)

The real problem was that of the artist cut off from a recognizable function, patron or public and left to cast his soul as a commodity upon a blind market, to be bought or not; or to work within a system of patronage which would generally have been economically untenable even if the French Revolution had not established its human indignity. The artist therefore stood alone, shouting into the night, uncertain even of an echo. It was only natural that he should turn himself into the genius, who created only what was within him, regardless of the world and in defiance of a public whose only right was to accept him on his own terms or not at all. At best he expected to be understood, like Stendhal, by the chosen few or some undefined posterity; at worst he would produce unplayable dramas, like Grabbe – or even Goethe's *Faust* part II – or compositions for unrealistically gigantic orchestras like Berlioz; or else he would go mad like Hölderlin, Grabbe, de Nerval and several others. In fact, the misunderstood genius was sometimes amply rewarded by princes accustomed to the vagaries of mistresses or to the value of prestige expenditure, or by an enriched bourgeoisie anxious to maintain a tenuous contact with the higher things of life. Franz Liszt (1811–86) never starved in the proverbial romantic garret. Few have ever succeeded in realizing their megalomaniac fantasies as Richard Wagner was to do. However, between the 1789 and the 1848 Revolutions princes were only too often suspicious of the non-operatic arts [11] and the bourgeoisie engaged in accumulation rather than spending. Geniuses were therefore in general not only misunderstood but also poor. And most of them were revolutionary.

Youth and 'genius' misunderstood would have produced the romantic's revulsion against the philistine, the fashion of baiting and shocking the bourgeois, the liaison with *demi-monde* and *bohème* (both terms which acquired their present connotation in the romantic period) or the taste for madness or for things normally censored by respectable institutions and standard. But this was only a small part of romanticism. Mario Praz's encyclopedia of erotic extremism is no more 'The Romantic Agony' [12] than a discussion of skulls and ghosts in Elizabethan symbolism is a critique of Hamlet. Behind the sectional dissatisfaction of the romantics as young men (even occasionally as young women – this was the first period in which continental women artists appear in their own right in any quantity [13]) and as artists, there lay a more general dissatisfaction with the kind of society emerging out of the double revolution.

Precise social analysis was never the romantic forte, and indeed they distrusted the confident mechanical materialist reasoning of the eighteenth century (symbolized by Newton, the bugbear of both William Blake and Goethe) which they rightly saw as one of the chief tools with which bourgeois society had been built. Consequently we shall not expect them to provide a reasoned critique of bourgeois society, though something like such a critique wrapped in the mystical cloak of 'nature philosophy' and walking amid the swirling clouds of metaphysics did develop within a broadly 'romantic' framework, and contributed, among other achievements, to the philosophy of Hegel. (See above pp. 302–5.) Something like it also developed, in visionary flashes constantly close to eccentricity, or even madness, among early utopian socialists in France. The early Saint-Simonians (though not their leader) and especially Fourier can hardly be described as other than romantics. The most lasting results of these romantic critiques were the concept of human 'alienation', which was to play a crucial part in Marx, and the intimation of the perfect society of the future. However, the most effective and powerful critique of bourgeois society was to come not from those who rejected it (and with it the traditions of classic seventeenth-century science and rationalism) *in toto* and *a priori*, but from those who pushed the traditions of its classical thought to their anti-bourgeois conclusions. Robert Owen's socialism had not the slightest element

317

of romanticism in it; its components were entirely those of eighteenth-century rationalism and that most bourgeois of sciences, political economy. Saint-Simon himself is best regarded as a prolongation of the 'enlightenment'. It is significant that the young Marx, trained in the German (i.e. primarily romantic) tradition, became a Marxist only when combined with the French socialist critique and the wholly non-romantic theory of English political economy. And it was political economy which provided the core of his mature thought.

III

It is never wise to neglect the heart's reasons which reason knows nothing of. As thinkers within the terms of reference laid down by the economists and physicists, the poets were outclassed, but they saw not only more deeply but also sometimes more clearly. Few men saw the social earthquake caused by machine and factory earlier than William Blake in the 1790s, who had yet little except a few London steam-mills and brick-kilns to go by. With a few exceptions, our best treatments of the problem of urbanization come from the imaginative writers whose often apparently quite unrealistic observations have been shown to be a reliable indicator of the actual urban evolution of Paris.[14] Carlyle is a more confused but a more profound guide to England in 1840 than the diligent statistician and compiler J. R. McCulloch; and if J. S. Mill is a better one than other utilitarians, it is because a personal crisis made him alone among them aware of the value of the German and Romantic critiques of society: of Goethe and Coleridge. The romantic critique of the world, though ill-defined, was not therefore negligible.

The longing that haunted it was for the lost unity of man and nature. The bourgeois world was a profoundly and deliberately asocial one. 'It has pitilessly torn asunder the motley feudal ties that bound man to his "natural superiors", and has left no other nexus between man and man than naked self-interest, than callous "cash-payment". It has drowned the most heavenly ecstasies of religious fervour, of chivalrous enthusiasm, of philistine sentimentalism, in the icy water of egotistical calculation. It has resolved personal worth into exchange value, and in place of the numberless indefeasible freedoms, has set up that single, unconscionable freedom – Free Trade.' The voice is that of the Communist Manifesto, but it speaks

318

for all romanticism also. Such a world might make men wealthy and comfortable, though as a matter of fact it seemed evident that it also made others – a much greater number – hungry and miserable; but it left their souls naked and alone. It left them homeless and lost in the universe as 'alienated' beings. It left them cut off by a revolutionary chasm in world history from even the most obvious answer to alienation, the decision never to leave the old home. The poets of German romanticism thought they knew better than anyone that salvation lay only in the simple modest working life that went on in those idyllic pre-industrial little towns that dotted the dream-landscapes, which they described more irresistibly than they have ever been described by anyone. And yet their young men must leave to pursue the by definition endless quest for the 'blue flower' or merely to roam forever, homesick and singing Eichendorff lyrics or Schubert songs. The wanderer's song is their signature tune, nostalgia their companion. Novalis even defined philosophy in terms of it.[15]

Three sources assuaged this thirst for the lost harmony of man in the world : the middle ages, primitive man (or, what could amount to the same thing, exoticism and the 'folk'), and the French Revolution.

The first attracted chiefly the romanticism of reaction. The stable-ordered society of feudal age, the slow organic product of the ages, coloured with heraldry, surrounded by the shadowy mystery of fairy tale forests and canopied by the unquestioned Christian heavens, was the obvious lost paradise of the conservative opponents of bourgeois society, whose tastes for piety, loyalty and a minimum of literacy among the lower orders the French Revolution had only sharpened. With local modifications it was the ideal which Burke threw into the teeth of the rationalist Bastille-stormers in his *Reflections on the French Revolution* (1790). However, it found its classical expression in Germany, a country which in this period acquired something not far from a monopoly of the medieval dream, perhaps because the tidy *Gemuetlichkeit* which appeared to reign beneath those Rhine-castles and Black Forest eaves lent itself more readily to idealization than the filth and cruelty of more genuinely medieval countries.[16] At all events medievalism was a far stronger component of German romanticism than of any other, and radiated outwards from Germany, whether in the form of romantic opera or ballet (Weber's *Freischuetz* or *Giselle*), of Grimm's *Fairy Tales*, of historicist theories or of germanically inspired writers like Coleridge or Carlyle. However, in the more general form of a Gothic revival medievalism was the badge of the conservative and especially the religious anti-bourgeois everywhere. Chateaubriand exalted the Gothic in his *Génie du Christianisme* (1802) against the Revolution, the upholders of the Church of England favoured it against the rationalists and non-conformists whose buildings remained classical, the architect Pugin and the ultra-reactionary and catholicizing 'Oxford Movement' of the 1830s were gothicists to the core. Meanwhile from the misty remoteness of Scotland – long a country in which to set archaic dreams like the invented poems of Ossian – the conservative Walter Scott supplied Europe with yet another set of medieval images in his historical novels. The fact that the best of his novels dealt with fairly recent periods of history was widely overlooked.

Beside this preponderance of conservative medievalism, which the reactionary governments after 1815 sought to translate into ramshackle justifications of absolutism (cf. above pp. 280–1), left-wing medievalism is unimportant. In England it existed mainly as a current in the popular radical movement which tended to see the period before the Reformation as a golden age of the labourer and the Reformation as the first great step towards capitalism. In France it was very much more important, for there its emphasis was not on feudal hierarchy and catholic order, but on the eternal, suffering, turbulent, creative *people*: the French nation always reasserting its identity and mission. Jules Michelet, the poet as historian, was the greatest of such revolutionary-democratic medievalists; Victor Hugo's *Hunchback of Notre Dame*, the best-known product of the preoccupation.

Closely allied with medievalism, especially through its preoccupation with traditions of mystical religiosity, was the pursuit of even more ancient and profound mysteries and sources of irrational wisdom in the orient: the romantic, but also the conservative, realms of Kublai Khan or the Brahmins. Admittedly the discoverer of Sanskrit, Sir William Jones, was a straightforward Whiggish radical who hailed the American and French Revolutions as an enlightened gentleman should; but the bulk of the amateurs of the East and writers of pseudo-Persian poems, out of whose enthusiasm much of modern orientalism emerged, belonged to the anti-Jacobin tendency.

Characteristically Brahmin India was their spiritual goal, rather than the irreligious and rational Chinese empire, which had preoccupied the exotic imaginations of the eighteenth-century enlightenment.

IV

The dream of the lost harmony of primitive man has a much longer and more complex history. It has been overwhelmingly a revolutionary dream, whether in the form of the golden age of communism, of the equality 'when Adam delved and Eve span', the free Anglo-Saxon not yet enslaved by the Norman Conquest, or the noble savage showing up the deficiencies of a corrupt society. Consequently romantic primitivism lent itself more readily to left-wing rebellion, except where it served merely as an escape from bourgeois society (as in the exoticism of a Gautier or Mérimée who discovered the noble savage as a tourist sight in Spain in the 1830s) or where historic continuity made the primitive someone exemplifying conservatism. This was notably the case of 'the folk'. It was accepted among romantics of all shades that 'the folk', i.e. normally the pre-industrial peasant or craftsman, exemplified the uncorrupted virtues and that its language, song, story and custom was the true repository of the soul of the people. To return to that simplicity and virtue was the aim of the Wordsworth of *Lyrical Ballads*; to be accepted into the corpus of folksong and fairy-tale the ambition – achieved by several artists – of many a teutonic poet and composer. The vast movement for the collection of folksong, the publication of ancient epic, the lexicography of living language, was closely connected with romanticism; the very word *folklore* (1846) an invention of the period. Scott's *Minstrelsy of the Scottish Border* (1803), Arnim and Brentano's *Des Knaben Wunderhorn* (1806), Grimm's *Fairy-Tales* (1812), Moore's *Irish Melodies* (1807–34), Dobrovsky's *History of the Bohemian Language* (1818), Vuk Karajic's Serb Dictionary (1818) and Serbian Folksong (1823–33), Tegnér's *Frithjofssaga* in Sweden (1825), Lönnrot's *Kalevala* edition in Finland (1835), Grimm's *German Mythology* (1835), Asbjörnson and Moe's *Norwegian Folk Tales* (1842–71), are so many monuments to it.

'The folk' could be a revolutionary concept, especially among oppressed peoples about to discover or reassert their national identity, particularly those which lacked a native middle class or aristocracy.

There the first dictionary, grammar or collection of folksong was an event of major political importance, a first declaration of independence. On the other hand for those who were struck more by the folk's simple virtues of contentment, ignorance and piety, the deep wisdom of its trust in pope, king or tsar, the cult of the primitive at home lent itself to a conservative interpretation. It exemplified the unity of innocence, myth and age-old tradition, which the bourgeois society was every day destroying.[18] The capitalist and the rationalist were the enemies against whom king, squire and peasant must maintain their hallowed union.

The Primitive existed in every village; but he existed as an even more revolutionary concept in the assumed golden communistic age of the past, and as the free noble savage abroad; especially as the Red Indian. From Rousseau, who held it up as the ideal of free social man, to the socialists primitive society was a sort of model for utopia. Marx's triple divisions of history – primitive communism, class society, communism, on a higher level – echoes, though it also transforms, this tradition. The ideal of primitivism was not specially romantic. Indeed some of its most ardent champions were in the eighteenth-century illuminist tradition. The romantic quest took its explorers into the great deserts of Arabia and North Africa, among Delacroix's and Fromentin's warriors and odalisques, with Byron through the Mediterranean world, or with Lermontov to the Caucasus, where natural man in the shape of the Cossack fought natural man in the shape of the tribesman amid chasms and cataracts, rather than to the innocent social and erotic utopia of Tahiti. But it also took them to America, where primitive man was fighting and doomed, a situation which brought him closer to the mood of the romantics. The Indian poems of the Austro-Hungarian Lenau cry out against the red man's expulsion; if the Mohican had not been the last of his tribe, would he have become quite so powerful a symbol in European culture? Naturally the noble savage played an immeasurably more important part in American romanticism than in European – Melville's *Moby Dick* (1851) is his greatest monument – but in the *Leatherstocking* novels of Fenimore Cooper he captured the old world, as the conservative Chateaubriand's Natchez had never been able to do.

Middle ages, folk and noble savage were ideals anchored firmly to the past. Only revolution, the 'springtime of peoples', pointed exclusively to the future, and yet even the most utopian found it comforting to appeal to a precedent for the unprecedented. This was not easily possible until a second generation of romanticism had produced a crop of young men for whom the French Revolution and Napoleon were facts of history and not a painful chapter of autobiography. 1789 had been hailed by virtually every artist and intellectual of Europe, but though some were able to maintain their enthusiasm through war, terror, bourgeois corruption and empire, theirs was not an easy or communicable dream. Even in Britain, where the first generation of romanticism, that of Blake, Wordsworth, Coleridge, Southey, Campbell and Hazlitt, had been wholly Jacobin, the disillusioned and the neo-conservative prevailed by 1805. In France and Germany, indeed, the word 'romantic' had been virtually invented as an anti-revolutionary slogan by the conservative anti-bourgeois of the later 1790s (very often disillusioned former leftists), which accounts for the fact that a number of thinkers and artists in these countries who would by modern standards be reckoned fairly obvious romantics are traditionally excluded from this classification. However, by the later years of the Napoleonic wars new generations of young men began to grow up for whom only the great liberating flame of the Revolution was visible across the years, the ashes of its excesses and corruptions having dropped out of sight; and after Napoleon's exile even that unsympathetic character could become a semi-mythical phoenix and liberator. And as Europe advanced year by year more deeply into the low featureless plains of reaction, censorship and mediocrity and the pestilential swamps of poverty, unhappiness and oppression, the image of the liberating revolution became ever more luminous.

The second generation of British romantics – that of Byron (1788–1824), the unpolitical but fellow-travelling Keats (1795–1821) and above all Shelley (1792–1822) – was the first thus to combine romanticism and active revolutionism : the disappointments of the French Revolution, unforgotten by most of their elders, paled beside the visible horrors of the capitalist transformation in their own country. On the continent the junction between romantic art and revolution was anticipated in the 1820s, but only made fully in and after the French Revolution of 1830. This is also true of what may perhaps be called the romantic vision of revolution and the romantic style of being a revolutionary, whose most familiar expression is Delacroix's painting of *Liberty on the Barricades* (1831). Here saturnine young men in beards and top hats, shirt-sleeved workers, tribunes of the people in flowing locks under sombrero-like hats, surrounded by tricolours and phrygian bonnets, recreate the Revolution of 1793 – not the moderate one of 1789, but the glory of the year II – raising its barricades in every city of the continent.

Admittedly the romantic revolutionary was not entirely new. His immediate ancestor and predecessor was the member of the italianate and masonic revolutionary secret society – the Carbonaro or Phil-hellene, whose inspiration came directly from surviving old Jacobins or Babuvists like Buonarroti. This is the typical revolutionary struggle of the Restoration period, all dashing young men in guards or hussar uniforms leaving operas, soirées, assignments with duchesses or highly ritualized lodge-meetings to make a military coup or place them-selves at the head of a struggling nation; in fact, the Byronic pattern. However, not only was this revolutionary fashion much more directly inspired by eighteenth-century modes of thought, and perhaps socially more exclusive than the later one. It still lacked a crucial element of the romantic revolutionary vision of 1830–48; the barri-cades, the masses, the new and desperate proletariat; that element which Daumier's lithograph of the *Massacre in the Rue Trans-nonain* (1834), with its murdered nondescript worker, added to the romantic imagery.

The most striking consequence of this junction of romanticism with vision of a new and higher French Revolution was the over-whelming victory of political art between 1830 and 1848. There has rarely been a period when even the least 'ideological' artists were more universally partisan, often regarding service to politics as their primary duty. 'Romanticism,' cried Victor Hugo in the preface to *Hernani*, that manifesto of rebellion (1830), 'is liberalism in litera-ture.' [19] 'Writers,' wrote the poet Alfred de Musset (1810–57), whose natural talent – like that of the composer Chopin (1810–49) or the introspective Austro-Hungarian poet Lenau (1802–50) – was for the private rather than the public voice, 'had a predilection to speak in their prefaces about the future, about social progress, humanity and civilization.' [20] Several artists became political figures and that not only in countries in the throes of national liberation, where all artists tended to be prophets or national symbols : Chopin, Liszt and even the young Verdi among the musicians; Mickiewicz (who saw himself in a messianic role), Petöfi and Manzoni among the poets of Poland, Hungary and Italy respectively. The painter Daumier worked chiefly as a political cartoonist. The poet Uhland, the brothers Grimm, were liberal politicians, the volcanic boy-genius Georg Büchner (1810–37) an active revolutionary, Heinrich Heine (1797–1856), a close personal friend of Karl Marx, an ambiguous but powerful voice of the extreme left.[21] Literature and journalism fused, most notably in France and Germany and Italy. In another age a Lamennais or a Jules Michelet in France, a Carlyle or Ruskin in Britain, might have been poets or novelists with some views on public affairs; in this one they were publicists, prophets, philosophers or historians carried by a poetic afflatus. For that matter, the lava of poetic imagery accompanies the eruption of Marx's youthful intellect to an extent unusual among either philosophers or economists. Even the gentle Tennyson and his Cambridge friends threw their hearts behind the international brigade which went to support Liberals against Clericals in Spain.

The characteristic aesthetic theories developed and dominant during this period ratified this unity of art and social commitment. The Saint-Simonians of France on one hand, the brilliant revolutionary Russian intellectuals of the 1840s on the other, even evolved the views which later became standard in Marxist movements under such names as 'socialist realism',[22] a noble but not overpoweringly successful ideal deriving both from the austere virtue of Jacobinism, and that romantic faith in the power of the spirit which made Shelley call the poets 'the unacknowledged legislators of the world'. 'Art for art's sake', though already formulated, mostly by conservatives or dilettantes, could not as yet compete with art for humanity's sake, or for the nations' or the proletariat's sake. Not until the 1848 revolutions destroyed the romantic hopes of the great rebirth of man, did self-contained aestheticism come into its own. The evolution of such 'forty-eighters as Baudelaire and Flaubert illustrates this political as well as aesthetic change, and Flaubert's *Sentimental Education* remains its best literary record. Only in countries like Russia, in which the disillusion of 1848 had not occurred (if only because 1848 had not occurred), did the arts continue to remain socially committed or preoccupied as before.

Romanticism is the fashion in art as in life most characteristic of the period of dual revolution, but by no means the only one. Indeed, since it dominated neither the cultures of the aristocracy, nor those of the middle classes and even less of the labouring poor, its actual quantitative importance at the time was small. The arts which depended on the patronage or the mass support of the moneyed classes tolerated romanticism best where its ideological characteristics were least obvious, as in music. The arts which depended on the support of the poor were hardly of great interest to the romantic artist, though in fact the entertainment of the poor – penny dreadfuls and broadsheets, circuses, sideshows, travelling theatres and the like – were a source of much inspiration to the romantics, and in turn popular showmen reinforced their own stock of emotion-stirring properties – transformation scenes, fairies, last words of murderers, brigands, etc. – with suitable goods from the romantic warehouses.

The fundamental style of aristocratic life and art remained rooted in the eighteenth century, though considerably vulgarized by an infusion of sometimes ennobled nouveaux-riches; as notably in the Napoleonic *Empire* style, which was of quite remarkable ugliness and pretentiousness, and the British Regency style. A comparison of eighteenth century and post-Napoleonic uniforms – the form of art which most directly expressed the instincts of the officers and gentlemen responsible for their design – will make this clear. The triumphant supremacy of Britain made the English nobleman the pattern of international aristocratic culture, or rather unculture; for the interests of 'the dandy' – clean-shaven, impassive and refulgent – were supposed to be confined to horses, dogs, carriages, prize-fighters, gaming, gentlemanly dissipation and his own person. Such heroic extremism fired even the romantics, who fancied dandyism themselves; but probably it fired young ladies of lesser ranks even more, and set them dreaming (in Gautier's words) :

'Sir Edward was so splendidly the Englishman of her dreams. The Englishman freshly shaved, pink, shining, groomed and polished, facing the first rays of the morning sun in an already perfect white cravat, the Englishman of waterproof and mackintosh. Was he not the very crown of civilization? ... I shall have English silverware, she thought, and Wedgwood china. There will be carpets all over the house and powdered footmen and I shall take the air by the side of my husband driving our four-in-hand through Hyde Park. ... Tame spotted deer will play on the green lawn of my country house, and perhaps also a few blond and rosy children. Children look so well on the front seat of a Barouche, beside a pedigree King Charles spaniel ....' [23]

It was perhaps an inspiring vision, but not a romantic one any more than the picture of Royal or Imperial Majesties graciously attending opera or ball, surmounting expanses of jewelled, but strictly well-born, gallantry and beauty.

Middle- and lower-middle-class culture was no more romantic. Its keynote was soberness and modesty. Only among the great bankers and speculators, or the very first generation of industrial millionaires, who never or no longer needed to plough much of their profits back into the business, did the opulent pseudo-baroque of the later nineteenth century begin to show itself; and then only in the few countries in which the old monarchies or aristocrats no longer dominated 'society' entirely. The Rothschilds, monarchs in their own right, already showed off like princes.[24] The ordinary bourgeois did not. Puritanism, evangelical or Catholic pietism encouraged moderation, thrift, a comfortable spartanism and an unparalleled moral self-satisfaction in Britain, the USA, Germany and Huguenot France; the moral tradition of eighteenth-century illuminism and free-masonry did the same for the more emancipated or anti-religious. Except in the pursuit of profit and logic, middle-class life was a life of controlled emotion and deliberate restriction of scope. The very large section of the middle classes who, on the continent, were not in business at all but in government service, whether as officials, teachers, professors or in some cases pastors, lacked even the expanding frontier of capital accumulation; and so did the modest provincial bourgeois who knew that the small-town wealth which was the limit of his achievement, was not very impressive by the standards of the real wealth and power of his age. In fact, middle class life was 'un-romantic', and its pattern still largely governed by eighteenth century fashion.

This is perfectly evident in the middle-class home, which was after all the centre of middle-class culture. The styles of the post-Napoleonic bourgeois house or street derives straight from, and often directly continues, eighteenth-century classicism or rococo. Late-Georgian building continued in Britain until the 1840s, and elsewhere the architectural break (introduced mostly by an artistically disastrous rediscovery of the 'renaissance') came even later. The prevailing style of interior decoration and domestic life, best called *Biedermayer* after its most perfect expression, the German one, was a sort of domestic classicism warmed by intimacy of emotion and virginal dreaming (*Innerlichkeit, Gemuethlichkeit*), which owed something to romanticism – or rather to the pre-romanticism of the late eighteenth century – but reduced even this debt to the dimensions of the modest bourgeois playing quartets on a Sunday afternoon in his living room. Biedermayer produced one of the most beautifully habitable styles of furnishing ever devised, all plain white curtains against matt walls, bare floors, solid but mostly elegant chairs and bureaus, pianos, mineral cabinets and vases full of flowers, but it was essentially a late classical style. It is perhaps most nobly exemplified in Goethe's house in Weimar. It, or something like it, was the setting of life for the heroines of Jane Austen's (1775–1817) novels, for the evangelical rigours and enjoyments of the Clapham sect, for the high-minded Bostonian bourgeoisie or provincial French readers of the *Journal des Débats*.

Romanticism entered middle-class culture, perhaps mostly through the rise in day-dreaming among the female members of the bourgeois family. To show off the breadwinner's capacity to keep them in bored leisure was one of their main social functions; a cherished slavery their ideal fate. At all events bourgeois girls, like non-bourgeois ones, such as the odalisques and nymphs which anti-romantic painters like Ingres (1780–1867) brought out of the romantic into the bourgeois context, increasingly conformed to the same fragile, egg-faced, smooth-hair-and-ringlet type, the tender flower in shawl and bonnet so characteristic of the 1840s' fashion. It was a long way from that crouching lioness, Goya's Duchess of Alba, or the emancipated neo-Grecian girls in white muslin whom the French Revolution had scattered across the salons or the self-possessed Regency ladies and courtesans like Lady Lieven or Harriete Wilson, as unromantic as they were unbourgeois.

Bourgeois girls might play domesticated romantic music like Chopin's or Schumann's (1810–56). Biedermayer might encourage a kind of romantic lyricism, like that of Eichendorff (1788–1857) or Eduard Mörike (1804–75), in which cosmic passion was transmitted into nostalgia, or passive longing. The active entrepreneur might even, while on a business trip, enjoy a mountain pass as 'the most romantic sight I had ever beheld', relax at home by sketching 'The Castle of Udolpho' or even, like John Cragg of Liverpool, 'being a man of artistic taste' as well as an ironfounder, 'introduce cast-iron into Gothic architecture'.[25] But on the whole bourgeois culture was not romantic. The very exhilaration of technical progress precludes orthodox romanticism, at any rate in the centres of industrial advance. A man like James Nasmyth, the inventor of the steam-hammer (1808–90), was anything but a barbarian if only because he was the son of a Jacobin painter ('the father of landscape painting in Scotland'), brought up among artists and intellectuals, a lover of the picturesque and the ancient and with all the good Scotsman's thorough and wide education. Yet what more natural than that the painter's son should become a mechanic, or that on a youthful walking tour with his father the Devon Ironworks should interest him more than any other sight? For him, as for the polite eighteenth century citizens among whom he grew up, things were sublime but not irrational. Rouen contained simply a 'magnificent cathedral and the church of St Ouen, so exquisite in its beauty, together with the refined Gothic architectural remains scattered about that interesting and picturesque city'. The picturesque was splendid; yet he could not but note, on his enthusiastic holidays, that it was a product of neglect. Beauty was splendid; but surely, what was wrong with modern architecture was that 'the *purpose* of the building is . . . regarded as a secondary consideration'. 'I was reluctant to tear myself away from Pisa' he wrote; but 'what interested me most in the Cathedral was the two bronze lamps suspended at the end of the nave, which suggested to the mind of Galileo the invention of the pendulum.'[26] Such men were neither barbarians nor philistines; but their world was a great deal closer to Voltaire's or Josiah Wedgwood's than to John Ruskin's. The great toolmaker Henry Maudslay no doubt felt much more at home, when in Berlin, with his friends Humboldt, the king of liberal scientists, and the neo-classic architect Schinkel, than he would have done with the great but cloudy Hegel.

In any case, in the centres of advancing bourgeois society, the arts as a whole took second place to science. The educated British or

American manufacturer or engineer might appreciate them, especially in moments of family relaxation and holiday, but his real cultural efforts would be directed towards the diffusion and advancement of knowledge – his own, in such bodies as the British Association for the Advancement of Science, or the people's, through the Society for the Diffusion of Useful Knowledge and similar organizations. It is characteristic that the typical product of the eighteenth-century enlightenment, the *encyclopaedia*, flourished as never before; still retaining (as in the famous Meyer's Conversationslexicon of the Germans, a product of the 1830s) much of its militant political liberalism. Byron made a great deal of money out of his poems, but the publisher Constable in 1812 paid Dugald Stewart a thousand pounds for a preface on The Progress of Philosophy to introduce the supplement to the *Encyclopaedia Britannica*.[27] And even when the bourgeoisie was romantic its dreams were those of technology : the young men fired by Saint-Simon became the planners of Suez canals, of titanic railway networks linking all parts of the globe, of Faustian finance, beyond the natural range of interest of the calm and rationalist Rothschilds, who knew that plenty of money was to be made with a minimum of speculative soaring by conservative means.[28] Science and technology were the muses of the bourgeoisie, and they celebrated its triumph, the railway, in the great (and alas now destroyed) neo-classical portico of Euston station.

VI

Meanwhile, outside the radius of literacy, the culture of the common people continued. In the non-urban and non-industrial parts of the world it changed little. The songs and feasts of the 1840s, the costumes, designs and colours of people's decorative arts, the pattern of their customs, remained very much what they had been in 1789. Industry and the growing city began to destroy it. No man could live in a factory town as he had in the village, and the entire complex of culture necessarily fell to pieces with the collapse of the social framework which held it together and gave it shape. Where a song belongs to ploughing, it cannot be sung when men do not plough; if it is sung, it ceases to be a folksong and becomes something else. The nostalgia of the emigrant maintained the old customs and songs in the exile of the city, and perhaps even intensified their attraction, for they palliated the pain of uprooting. But outside cities and mills the dual revolution had transformed – or more accurately devastated – only patches of the old rural life, notably in parts of Ireland and Britain, to the point where the old ways of living became impossible.

Indeed even in industry social transformation had not gone far enough before the 1840s to destroy the older culture completely; all the more so as in Western Europe crafts and manufactures had had several centuries in which to develop an, as it were, semi-industrial pattern of culture. In the countryside miners and weavers expressed their hope and protest in traditional folksong, and the industrial revolution merely added to their number and sharpened their experience. The factory needed no worksongs, but various activities incidental to economic development did, and developed them in the old way: the capstan-chanty of the seamen on the great sailing ships belongs to this golden age of 'industrial' folksong in the first half of the nineteenth century, like the ballads of the Greenland whalers, the Ballad of the Coal-owner and the Pitman's Wife and the lament of the weaver.[29] In the pre-industrial towns, communities of craftsmen and domestic workers evolved a literate, intense culture in which Protestant sectarianism combined or competed with Jacobin radicalism as a stimulus to self-education, Bunyan and John Calvin with Tom Paine and Robert Owen. Libraries, chapels and institutes, gardens and cages in which the artisan 'fancier' bred his artificially exaggerated flowers, pigeons and dogs, filled these self-reliant and militant communities of skilled men; Norwich in England was famous not merely for its atheistical and republican spirit but is still famous for its canaries.[30] But the adaptation of older folksong to industrial life did not (except in the United States of America) survive the impact of the age of railways and iron, and the communities of the old skilled men, like the Dunfermline of the old linen-weavers, did not survive the advance of the factory and the machine. After 1840 they fell into ruin.

As yet nothing much replaced the older culture. In Britain, for instance, the new pattern of a wholly industrial life did not fully emerge until the 1870s and 1880s. The period from the crisis of the old traditional ways of life until then was therefore in many ways the bleakest part of what was for the labouring poor an exceedingly bleak age. Nor did the great cities develop a pattern of popular culture –

necessarily commercial rather than, as in the smaller communities, self-made – in our period.

It is true that the great city, especially the great capital city, already contained important institutions which supplied the cultural needs of the poor, or the 'little people', though often – characteristically enough – also of the aristocracy. These, however, were in the main developments of the eighteenth century, whose contribution to the evolution of the popular arts has been often overlooked. The popular suburban theatre in Vienna, the dialect theatre in the Italian cities, the popular (as distinct from court) opera, the commedia dell'arte and travelling mime-show, the boxing or race-meeting, or the democratized version of the Spanish bullfight [32] were products of the eighteenth century; the illustrated broadsheet and chapbook of an even earlier period. The genuinely new forms of urban entertainment in the big city were by-products of the tavern or drink-shop, which became an increasing source of secular comfort for the labouring poor in their social disorganization, and the last urban rampart of custom and traditional ceremonial, preserved and intensified by journeyman guilds, trade unions and ritualized 'friendly societies'. The 'music-hall' and dance-hall were to emerge from the tavern; but by 1848 it had not yet emerged far, even in Britain, though its emergence was already noted in the 1830s.[33] The other new forms of big-city urban entertainment grew out of the fair, always accompanied by its quota of itinerant entertainers. In the big city it became permanently fixed; and even in the 1840s the mixture of sideshows, theatres, hawkers, pickpockets and barrow-boys on certain boulevards provided the romantic intellectuals of Paris with inspiration and the populace with pleasure.

Popular taste also determined the shape and decoration of those relatively few individualized commodities which industry produced primarily for the market of the poor: the jugs which commemorate the triumph of the Reform Bill, the great iron bridge over the river Wear or those magnificent three-masters which sailed the Atlantic; the popular prints in which revolutionary sentiment, patriotism or famous crimes were immortalized, and such few articles of furnishing and clothing as the urban poor could afford. But on the whole the city, and especially the new industrial city, remained a gaunt place, whose few amenities – open spaces, holidays – were gradually diminished by the creeping blight of building, the fumes which poisoned all natural life, and the compulsion of unceasing labour, reinforced in suitable cases by the austere sabbatarian discipline imposed by the middle classes. Only the new gaslight and the displays of commerce in the main streets here and there anticipated the vivid colours of night in the modern town. But the creation of the modern big city and the modern urban ways of popular life had to await the second half of the nineteenth century. In the first destruction prevailed, or was at best held at bay.

NOTES

1 S. Laing, *Notes of a Traveller on the Social and Political State of France, Prussia, Switzerland, Italy and other parts of Europe, 1842* (1854 ed.), p. 275.

2 Those of non-European civilizations will not be considered here, except insofar as they were affected by the dual revolution, which was at this period hardly at all.

3 Apart from *The Magic Flute*, we may mention Verdi's early operas, which were applauded as expressions of Italian nationalism, Auber's *La Muette de Portici* which set off the Belgian revolution of 1830, Glinka's *A Life for the Tsar* and various 'national operas' such as the Hungarian *Hunyady László* (1844), which still keep their place in the local repertoire for their associations with early nationalism.

4 The absence of a sufficiently large literate and politically conscious population over most of Europe limited the exploitation of such newly invented cheap reproductive arts as lithography. But the remarkable achievements of great and revolutionary artists in this and similar mediums – e.g. Goya's *Disasters of War* and *Caprichos*, William Blake's visionary illustrations and Daumier's lithographs and newspaper cartoons, show how strong the attractions of these propagandist techniques were.

5 *Oeuvres Complètes*, XIV, p. 17.

6 H. E. Hugo, *The Portable Romantic Reader* (1957), p. 58.

7 Fragmente Vermischten Inhalts. (Novalis, *Schriften* (Jena 1923), III, pp. 45–6.)

8 From *The Philosophy of Fine Art* (London 1920), V.I., p. 106 f.

9 Since 'romanticism' was often the slogan and manifesto of restricted groups of artists, we risk giving it an unhistorically restricted sense if we confine it entirely to them; or entirely exclude those who disagreed with them.

10 E. C. Batho, *The Later Wordsworth* (1933), p. 227, see also pp. 46–7, 197–9.

11 The unspeakable Ferdinand of Spain, who maintained his patronage of the revolutionary Goya, in spite of both artistic and political provocation, was an exception.

12 Mario Praz, *The Romantic Agony* (Oxford 1933).

13 Mme de Staël, George Sand, the painters Mme Vigée Lebrun, Angelica Kauffman in France, Bettina von Arnim, Annette von Droste-Huelshoff in Germany. Women novelists had of course long been common in middle-class England, where this art form was recognized as providing a 'respectable' form of earning money for well-brought up girls. Fanny Burney, Mrs Radcliffe, Jane Austen, Mrs Gaskell, the Brontë sisters all fall wholly or partly into our period; as does the poet Elizabeth Barrett Browning.

14 L. Chevalier, *Classes Laborieuses et Classes Dangereuses à Paris dans la première moitié du XIX siecle.* (Paris 1958).

15 Ricarda Huch, *Die Romantik*, I, p. 70.

16 'O Hermann, O Dorothée! Gemuethlichkeit!' wrote Gautier, who adored Germany like all French romantics. 'Ne semble-t-il pas que l'on entend du loin le cor du postillon?' [17]

17 P. Jourda, *L'exotisme dans la littérature française depuis Chateaubriand* (1939), p. 79.

18 How we are to interpret the new popularity of folk-based ball-room dances in this period, such as the waltz, *mazurka* and *schottische*, is a matter of taste. It was certainly a romantic fashion.

19 V. Hugo, *Oeuvres Complètes*, XV, p. 2.

20 *Oeuvres Complètes*, IX (Paris 1879), p. 212.

21 It should be noted that this is one of the rare periods when poets not merely sympathized with the extreme left, but wrote poems which were both good and agitationally usable. The distinguished group of German socialist poets of the 1840s – Herwegh, Weerth, Freiligrath, and of course Heine – deserves mention, though Shelley's *Masque of Anarchy* (1820), a riposte to Peterloo, is perhaps the most powerful such poem.

22 cf. M. Thibert, *Le rôle social de l'art d'après les Saint-Simoniens* (Paris n.d.).

23 P. Jourda, op. cit., pp. 55–6.

24 M. Capefigue, *Histoire des Grandes Opérations Financières*, IV, pp. 252–3.

25 *James Nasmyth, Engineer, An Autobiography*, ed. Samuel Smiles (1897 edn.), p. 177.

26 Ibid. pp. 243, 246, 251.

27 E. Halévy, *History of the English People in the Nineteenth Century* (paperback ed.), I, p. 509.

28 D. S. Landes, Vieille Banque et Banque Nouvelle, *Revue d'Histoire Moderne et Contemporaine*, III, (1956), p. 205.

29 cf. the long-playing records '*Shuttle and Cage*' Industrial Folk

Ballads, (10T 13), *Row, Bullies, Row* (T7) and *The Blackball Line*, (T8) all on Topic, London.

30 'There yet stands many an old house', wrote Francis Horner in 1879 'deeply bedded in a town, that used to have its garden – oftentimes a florist's. Here for instance is the very window – curiously long and lightsome – at which a handloom weaver worked behind his loom, able to watch his flowers as closely as his work – his labour and his pleasure intermingled. . . . But the mill has supplanted his patient hand-machine, and brickwork swallowed up his garden.' [31]

31 Quoted in G. Taylor, Nineteenth Century Florists and their Flowers (*The Listener* 23.6.1949). The Paisley weavers were particularly enthusiastic and rigorous 'florists', recognizing only eight flowers worthy of competitive breeding. The Nottingham lace-makers grew roses, which were not yet – unlike the hollyhock – a working man's flower.

32 Its original version was knightly, the chief combatant being on horseback; the innovation of killing the bull on foot is traditionally ascribed to an eighteenth-century carpenter from Ronda.

33 *Select Committee on Drunkenness* (Parl. Papers VIII, 1834), Q 571. In 1852, 28 pubs and 21 beershops in Manchester (out of 481 pubs and 1,298 beershops for a population of 303,000 in the borough) provided musical entertainment. (John T. Baylee; *Statistics and Facts in reference to the Lord's Day* (London 1852), p. 20.)

15

Science

*Let us never forget that long before we did, the sciences
and philosophy fought against the tyrants. Their constant
efforts have made the revolution. As free and grateful
men, we ought to establish them among us and cherish
them for ever. For the sciences and philosophy will maintain the liberty which we have conquered.*

A member of the Convention [1]

*'Questions of science,' remarked Goethe, 'are very fre-
quently career questions. A single discovery may make a
man famous and lay the foundation of his fortunes as a
citizen. . . . Every newly observed phenomenon is a discovery, every discovery is property. Touch a man's property and his passions are immediately aroused.'*

Conversations with Eckermann, December 21, 1823

I

To draw a parellelism between the arts and the sciences is always
dangerous, for the relationships between either and the society in
which they flourish is quite different. Yet the sciences too in their
way reflected the dual revolution, partly because it made specific new
demands on them, partly because it opened new possibilities for
them and faced them with new problems, partly because its very
existence suggested new patterns of thought. I do not wish to imply
that the evolution of the sciences between 1789 and 1848 can be analysed exclusively in terms of the movements in the society round
them. Most human activities have their internal logic, which determines at least part of their movement. The planet Neptune was discovered in 1846, not because anything outside astronomy encouraged
its discovery, but because Bouvard's tables in 1821 demonstrated that
the orbit of the planet Uranus, discovered in 1781, showed unex-
pected deviations from the calculations; because by the later 1830s

these deviations had become larger and were tentatively ascribed to disturbances by some unknown celestial body, and because various astronomers set about to calculate the position of that body. Nevertheless even the most passionate believer in the unsullied purity of pure science is aware that scientific thought may at least be influenced by matters outside the specific field of a discipline, if only because scientists, even the most unworldly of mathematicians, live in a wider world. The progress of science is not a simple linear advance, each stage marking the solution of problems previously implicit or explicit in it, and in turn posing new problems. It also proceeds by the discovery of new problems, of new ways of looking at old ones, of new ways of tackling or solving old ones, of entirely new fields of enquiry, or new theoretical and practical tools of enquiry. And here there is ample scope for stimulation or the shaping of thought by outside factors. If in fact most sciences in our period had advanced in a simple linear way, as was the case with astronomy, which remained substantially within its Newtonian framework, this might not be very important. But, as we shall see, our period was one of radically new departures in some fields of thought (as in mathematics), of the awakening of hitherto dormant sciences (as in chemistry), of the virtual creation of new sciences (as in geology), and of the injection of revolutionary new ideas into others (as in the social and biological sciences).

As it happened of all the outside forces shaping scientific development the direct demands made on scientists by government or industry were among the least important. The French Revolution mobilized them, placing the geometer and engineer Lazare Carnot in charge of the Jacobin war-effort, the mathematician and physicist Monge (Minister of the Navy in 1792–3) and a team of mathematicians and chemists in charge of war production, as it had earlier charged the chemist and economist Lavoisier with the preparation of an estimate of the national income. It was perhaps the first occasion in modern or any other history when the trained scientist as such entered government, but this was of greater importance to government than to science. In Britain, major industries of our period were cotton textiles, coal, iron, railways and shipping. The skills which revolutionized these were those of empirical – too empirical – men. The hero of the British railway revolution was George Stephenson, a scientific illiterate, but a man who could smell what would make a machine go : a super-craftsman rather than a technologist. The attempts of scientists like Babbage to make themselves useful to the railways, or of scientific engineers like Brunel to establish them on rational rather than merely empirical foundations, came to nothing.

On the other hand science benefited tremendously from the striking encouragement of scientific and technical education and the somewhat less striking support for research, which arose during our period. Here the influence of the dual revolution is quite clear. The French Revolution transformed the scientific and technical education of its country, chiefly by setting up the *Ecole Polytechnique* (1795) – intended as a school for technicians of all sorts – and the first sketch of the *Ecole Normale Supérieure* (1794) which was firmly established as part of a general reform of secondary and higher education by Napoleon. It also revived the drooping royal academy (1795) and created, in the National Museum of Natural History (1794), the first genuine centre for research outside the physical sciences. The world supremacy of French science during most of our period was almost certainly due to these major foundations, notably to the *Polytechnique*, a turbulent centre of Jacobinism and Liberalism throughout the post-Napoleonic period, and an incomparable breeder of great mathematicians and theoretical physicists. The Polytechnique found imitators in Prague, Vienna and Stockholm, in St Petersburg and Copenhagen, all over Germany and Belgium, in Zürich and Massachusetts, but not in England. The shock of the French Revolution also jolted Prussia out of its educational lethargy, and the new University of Berlin (1806–10), founded as part of the Prussian revival, became the model for most German universities, which in turn were to create the pattern of academic institutions all over the world. Once again, no such reforms took place in Britain, where the political revolution neither won nor conquered. But the immense wealth of the country, which made private laboratories such as those of Henry Cavendish and James Joule possible, and the general pressure of intelligent middle-class persons for scientific and technical education, achieved comparable results. Count Rumford, a peripatetic illuminist adventurer, founded the Royal Institution in 1799. Its fame among laymen was chiefly based on its famous public lectures, but its real importance lay in the unique scope for experimental science it provided for Humphry Davy and Michael Faraday. It was in fact an early example of the research laboratory. Bodies for the encouragement of science, like the Birmingham Lunar Society and the Manchester Literary and Philosophical Society, mobilized the support of industrialists in the provinces : John Dalton, the founder of the atomic theory, came out of the latter. Then Benthamite Radicals in London founded (or rather took over and diverted) the London Mechanics Institution – the present Birkbeck College – as a school for technicians, London University as an alternative to the somnolence of Oxford and Cambridge, and the British Association for the Advancement of Science (1831) as an alternative to the aristocratic torpor of the degenerate Royal Society. These were not foundations intended to foster the pure pursuit of knowledge for its own sake, which is perhaps why specific research establishments were slow to make their appearance. Even in Germany the first university research laboratory for chemistry (Liebig's in Giessen) was not set up until 1825. (Its inspiration was French, needless to say.) There were institutions to provide technicians as in France and Britain, teachers, as in France and Germany, or to inculcate youth with a spirit of service to their country.

The revolutionary age therefore swelled the number of scientists and scholars and the output of science. What is more, it saw the geographical universe of science widen in two ways. In the first place the very process of trade and exploration opened new ranges of the world to scientific study, and stimulated thought about them. One of the greatest of the scientific minds of our period, Alexander von Humboldt (1769–1859), made his contributions primarily thus : as an indefatigable traveller, observer, and theorist in the fields of geography, ethnography and natural history, though his noble synthesis of all knowledge, the *Kosmos* (1845–59), cannot be confined within the limits of particular disciplines.

In the second place the universe of science widened to embrace countries and peoples which had hitherto made only the smallest contributions to it. The list of the great scientists of, say, 1750 contains few except Frenchmen, Britons, Germans, Italians and Swiss. But the shortest list of the major mathematicians of the first half of the nineteenth century contains Henrik Abel from Norway, Janos Bolyai from Hungary and Nikolai Lobachevsky from the even more remote city of Kazan. Here again science appears to reflect the rise of national cultures outside Western Europe, which is so striking a product of the revolutionary age. This national element in the expansion of the sciences was in turn reflected in the decline of the cosmopolitanism that had been so characteristic of the small scientific communiities of the seventeenth and eighteenth centuries. The age of the itinerant international celebrity who moved, like Euler, from Basel to St Petersburg, thence to Berlin, and back to the court of Catherine the Great, passed with the old régimes. Henceforth the scientist stayed within his linguistic area, except for shorter visits, communicating with his colleagues through the medium of the learned journals, which are so typical a product of this period : the *Proceedings of the Royal Society* (1831), the *Comptes Rendus de l'Académie des Sciences* (1837), the *Proceedings of the American Philosophical Society* (1838), or the new specialist journals such as Crelle's *Journal für Reine und Angewandte Mathematik* or the *Annales de Chimie et de Physique* (1797).

II

Before we can judge the nature of the impact of the dual revolution on the sciences, it is as well to survey briefly what happened to them. On the whole the classical *physical* sciences were not revolutionized. That is to say they remained substantially within the terms of reference established by Newton, either continuing lines of research already followed in the eighteenth century or extending earlier fragmentary discoveries and co-ordinating them into wider theoretical systems. The most important of the new fields thus opened up (and the one with the most immediate technological consequences) was electricity, or rather electro-magnetism. Five main dates – four of them in our period – mark its decisive progress : 1786, when Galvani discovered the electric current, 1799, when Volta constructed his battery, 1800, when electrolysis was discovered, 1820, when Oersted hit upon the connection between electricity and magnetism, and 1831, when Faraday established the relations between all these forces, and incidentally found himself pioneering an approach to physics (in terms of 'fields' rather than mechanical pushing and pulling) which anticipated the modern age : The most important of the new theoretical syntheses was the discovery of the laws of thermodynamics, i.e. of the relations between heat and energy.

The revolution which turned astronomy and physics into modern science had occurred in the seventeenth century; that which created

340

chemistry was in full swing when our period opens. Of all the sciences this was the most closely and immediately linked with industrial practice, especially with the bleaching and dyeing processes of the textile industry. Moreover, its creators were not only practical men, linked with other practical men (like Dalton in the *Manchester Literary and Philosophical Society* and Priestley in the *Lunar Society* of Birmingham), but sometimes political revolutionaries, though moderate ones. Two were victims of the French Revolution : Priestley, at the hands of the Tory mob, for sympathizing excessively with it, the great Lavoisier on the guillotine, for not sympathizing enough, or rather for being a big business man.

Chemistry, like physics, was pre-eminently a French science. Its virtual founder, Lavoisier (1743–94), published his fundamental *Traité Elémentaire de Chimie* in the year of revolution itself, and the inspiration for the chemical advances, and especially the organization of chemical research, in other countries – even in those which were to become major centres of chemical research later, like Germany – was primarily French. The major advances before 1789 consisted in bringing some elementary order into the tangle of empirical experiment by elucidating certain fundamental chemical processes such as burning, and some fundamental elements such as oxygen. They also brought precise quantitative measurement and a programme of further research into the subject. The crucial concept of an atomic theory (originated by Dalton 1803–10) made it possible to invent the chemical formula, and with it to open up the study of chemical structure. An abundance of new experimental results followed. In the nineteenth century chemistry was to be one of the most vigorous of all the sciences, and consequently one which attracted – as does every dynamic subject – a mass of able men. However, the atmosphere and the methods of chemistry remained largely those of the eighteenth century.

Chemistry had, however, one revolutionary implication – the discovery that life can be analysed in terms of the inorganic sciences. Lavoisier discovered that breathing is a form of combustion of oxygen. Woehler discovered (1828) that a compound hitherto encountered only in living things – urea – could be synthesized in the laboratory, thus opening up the vast new domain of *organic chemistry*. Yet, though that great obstacle to progress, the belief that living matter obeyed fundamentally different natural laws from the nonliving, was seriously crippled, neither the mechanical nor the chemical approach as yet enabled the biologist to advance very far. His most fundamental advance in this period, Schleiden and Schwann's discovery that all living things were composed of multiplicities of *cells* (1838–9), established a sort of equivalent of the atomic theory for biology; but a mature biophysics and biochemistry remained far in the future.

A revolution even more profound but, by the nature of the subject, less obvious than in chemistry took place in *mathematics*. Unlike physics, which remained within the seventeenth-century terms of reference, and chemistry, which fanned out on a broad front through the gap opened in the eighteenth, mathematics in our period entered an entirely new universe, far beyond the world of the Greeks, which still dominated arithmetic and plane geometry, and that of the seventeenth century, which dominated analysis. Few except mathematicians will appreciate the profundity of the innovation brought into science by the theory of the functions of complex variables (Gauss, Cauchy, Abel, Jacobi), of the theory of groups (Cauchy, Galois) or of vectors (Hamilton). But even the layman can grasp the bearing of the revolution by which Lobachevsky of Russia (1826–9), and Bolyai of Hungary (1831) overthrew that most permanent of intellectual certainties, Euclid's geometry. The entire majestic and unshakable structure of Euclidean logic rests on certain assumptions, one of which, the axiom that parallels never meet, is neither self-evident nor provable. It may today seem elementary to construct an equal logical geometry on some other assumption, for instance (Lobachevsky, Bolyai) that an infinity of parallels to any line L may pass through point P; or (Riemann) that no parallels to line L pass through point P; all the more so as we can construct real-life surfaces to which these rules apply. (Thus the earth, insofar as it is a globe, conforms to Riemannian and not Euclidean assumptions.) But to make these assumptions in the early nineteenth century was an act of intellectual daring comparable to putting the sun instead of the earth into the centre of the planetary system.

III

The mathematical revolution passed unperceived except by a few specialists in subjects notorious for their remoteness from everyday life. The revolution in the *social sciences*, on the other hand, could hardly fail to strike the layman, because it visibly affected him, generally, it was believed, for the worse. The amateur scientists and scholars in Thomas Love Peacock's novels are gently bathed in sympathy or a loving ridicule; not so the economists and propagandists of the Steam Intellect Society.

There were to be precise two revolutions, whose courses converge to produce Marxism as the most comprehensive synthesis of the social sciences. The first, which continued the brilliant pioneering of the seventeenth- and eighteenth-century rationalists, established the equivalent of physical laws for human populations. Its earliest triumph was the construction of a systematic deductive theory of *political economy*, which was already far advanced by 1789. The second which in substance belongs to our period and is closely linked with romanticism, was the discovery of historical evolution (cf. also above, pp. 288–9, 296–7).

The daring innovation of the classical rationalists had been to demonstrate that something like logically compulsory laws were applicable to human consciousness and free decision. The 'laws of political economy' were of this sort. The conviction that they were as far beyond liking and disliking as the laws of gravity (with which they were often compared) lent a ruthless certainty to the capitalists of the early nineteenth century, and tended to imbue their romantic opponents with an equally wild anti-rationalism. In principle the economists were of course right, though they grossly exaggerated the universality of the postulates on which they based their deductions, the capacity of 'other things' to remain 'equal'; and also, sometimes, their own intellectual abilities. If the population of a town doubles and the number of dwellings in it does not rise, then, other things being equal, rents *must* go up, whether anyone wants them to or not. Propositions of this kind made the force of the systems of deductive reasoning constructed by political economy, mostly in Britain, though also, to a diminishing degree, in the old eighteenth-century centres of the science, France, Italy, and Switzerland. As we have seen, the period from 1776 to 1830 saw it at its most triumphant. (See above pp. 288–9). It was supplemented by the first systematic presentation of a theory of demography purporting to establish a mechanical, and virtually inevitable, relationship between the mathematically describable rates of growth of population and of the means of subsistence. T. R. Malthus's *Essay on Population* (1798) was neither as original nor as compelling as its supporters claimed, in the enthusiasm of the discovery that somebody had proved that the poor must always remain poor, and why generosity and benevolence must make them even poorer. Its importance lies not in its intellectual merits, which were moderate, but in the claims it staked for a scientific treatment of so very individual and capricious a group of decisions as the sexual ones, considered as a social phenomenon.

The application of mathematical methods to society made another major advance in this period. Here the French-speaking scientists led the way, assisted no doubt by the superb mathematical atmosphere of French education. Thus Adolphe Quételet of Belgium, in his epoch-making *Sur l'Homme* (1835), showed that the statistical distribution of human characteristics obeyed known mathematical laws, from which he deduced, with a confidence since deemed excessive, the possibility of assimilating the social to the physical sciences. The possibility of generalizing statistically about human populations and basing firm predictions on such generalization had long been anticipated by the theorists of probability (Quételet's point of departure into the social sciences), and by practical men who had to rely on it, such as the insurance companies. But Quételet and the flourishing contemporary group of statisticians, anthropometrists and social investigators applied these methods to far wider fields and created what is still the major mathematical tool for the investigation of social phenomena.

These developments in the social sciences were revolutionary in the way chemistry was : by following through advances already theoretically made. But the social sciences also had an entirely new and original achievement to their credit, which in turn fertilized the biological sciences and even physical ones, such as geology. This was the discovery of history as a process of logical evolution, and not merely as a chronological succession of events. The links of this innovation with the dual revolution are so obvious that they hardly need argument. Thus what came to be called *sociology* (the word was invented by A. Comte around 1830) sprang directly out of the critique of capitalism. Comte himself, who is normally reckoned its founder, began his career as the private secretary to the pioneer utopian socialist, the Count of Saint-Simon,[2] and its most formidable contemporary theorist Karl Marx regarded his theory primarily as a tool for changing the world.

The creation of *history* as an academic subject is perhaps the least important aspect of this historization of the social sciences. It is true that an epidemic of history-writing overwhelmed Europe in the first half of the nineteenth century. Rarely have more men sat down to make sense of their world by writing many-volumed accounts of its past, incidentally often for the the the first time : Karamzin in Russia (1818–24), Geijer in Sweden (1832–6), Palacky in Bohemia (1836–67) are the founding fathers of their respective countries' historiography. In France the urge to understand the present through the past was particularly strong, and there the Revolution itself soon became the subject of intensive and partisan study by Thiers (1823, 1843), Mignet (1824), Buonarroti (1828), Lamartine (1847) and the great Jules Michelet (1847–53). It was an heroic period of historiography, but little of the work of Guizot, Augustin Thierry and Michelet in France, of the Dane Niebuhr and the Swiss Sismondi, of Hallam, Lingard and Carlyle in Britain, and of innumerable German professors, now survives except as historical document, as literature or occasionally as the record of genius.

The most lasting results of this historical awakening were in the field of documentation and historical technique. To collect the relics of the past, written or unwritten, became a universal passion. Perhaps in part it was an attempt to safeguard it against the steam-powered attacks of the present, though nationalism was probably its most important stimulus : in hitherto unawakened nations the historian, the lexicographer and the folksong collector were often the very founders of national consciousness. And so the French set up their *Ecole des Chartes* (1821), the English a *Public Record Office* (1838), the Germans began to publish the *Monumenta Germaniae Historiae* (1826), while the doctrine that history must be based on the scrupulous evaluation of primary records was laid down by the prolific Leopold von Ranke (1795–1886). Meanwhile, as we have seen (cf. chapter 14), the linguists and folklorists produced the fundamental dictionaries of their languages and collections of their peoples' oral traditions.

The injection of history into the social sciences had its most immediate effects in law, where Friedrich Karl von Savigny founded the historical school of jurisprudence (1815), in the study of theology, where the application of historical criteria – notably in D. F. Strauss's *Leben Jesu* (1835) – horrified the fundamentalists, but especially in a wholly new science, philology. This also developed primarily in Germany, which was by far the most vigorous centre of diffusion for the historical approach. It is not fortuitous that Karl Marx was a German. The ostensible stimulus for philology was the conquest of non-European societies by Europe. Sir William Jones's pioneer investigations into Sanskrit (1786) were the result of the British conquest of Bengal; Champollion's decipherment of the hieroglyphs (his main work on the subject was published in 1824), of Napoleon's expedition to Egypt; Rawlinson's elucidation of cuneiform writing (1835) reflected the ubiquity of the British colonial officers. But in fact philology was not confined to discovery, description and classification. In the hands chiefly of great German scholars such as Franz Bopp (1791–1867) and the brothers Grimm it became the second social science properly so described; that is to say the second which discovered general laws applicable to so apparently capricious a field as human communication. (The first was political economy). But unlike the laws of political economy those of philology were fundamentally historical, or rather evolutionary.[3]

Their foundation was the discovery that a wide range of languages, the Indo-European, were related to one another; supplemented by the obvious fact that every existing written European language had plainly been transformed in the course of the centuries and was, presumably, still undergoing transformation. The problem was not merely to prove and classify these relationships by means of scientific comparison, a task which was then being widely undertaken (for instance, in comparative anatomy, by Cuvier). It was also, and chiefly, to elucidate their historic evolution from what must have been a common ancestor. Philology was the first science which regarded evolution as its very core. It was of course fortunate because the Bible is relatively silent about the history of language, whereas, as the biologists and geologists knew to their cost, it is only too explicit about the creation and early history of the globe. Consequently the philologist was less likely to be drenched by the waters of Noah's flood or tripped by the obstacles of Genesis 1 than his unhappy confrère. If anything the Biblical statement 'And the whole earth was of one language, and one speech' was on his side. But philology was also fortunate, because of all the social sciences it dealt not directly with human beings, who always resent the suggestion that their actions are determined by anything except their free choice, but with words, which do not. Consequently it was left free to face what is still the fundamental problem of the historical sciences, how to derive the immense, and apparently often capricious variety of individuals in real life, from the operation of invariant general laws.

The pioneer philologists did not in fact advance very far in explaining linguistic change, though Bopp himself already propounded a theory of the origin of grammatical inflections. But they did establish for the Indo-European languages something like a table of genealogy. They made a number of inductive generalizations about the relative rates of change in different linguistic elements, and a few historical generalizations of very wide scope, such as 'Grimm's Law' (which showed that *all* Teutonic languages underwent certain consonantal shifts, and, several centuries later, a section of Teutonic dialects underwent another similar shift). However, throughout these pioneering explorations, they never doubted that the evolution of language was not merely a matter of establishing chronological sequence or recording variation, but ought to be explained by general linguistic laws, analogous to scientific ones.

IV

The biologists and geologists were less lucky. For them too history was the major issue, though the study of earth was (through mining) closely linked with chemistry and the study of life (through medicine) closely with physiology, and (through the crucial discovery that the chemical elements in living things were the same as those in inorganic nature) with chemistry. But for the geologist in any case the most obvious problems involved history – for instance, how to explain the distribution of land and water, the mountains, and above all the strongly marked strata.

If the historical problem of geology was how to explain the evolution of the earth, that of biology was the double one of how to explain the growth of the individual living thing from egg, seed or spore, and how to explain the evolution of species. Both were linked by the visible evidence of the fossils, of which a particular selection were to be found in each rock-stratum and not in others. An English drainage engineer, William Smith, discovered in the 1790s that the historic succession of strata could be most conveniently dated by their characteristic fossils, thus illuminating both sciences through the down-to-earth operations of the Industrial Revolution.

The problem had been so obvious that attempts to provide theories of evolution had already been made; notably, for the world of animals, by the stylish but sometimes slapdash zoologist Comte de Buffon (*Les Epoques de la Nature*, 1778). In the decade of the French Revolution these gained ground rapidly. The ruminative James Hutton of Edinburgh (*Theory of the Earth*, 1795) and the eccentric Erasmus Darwin, who shone in the Birmingham Lunar Society and wrote some of his scientific work in verse (*Zoonomia*, 1794), put forward fairly complete evolutionary theories of the earth and of plants and animal species. Laplace (1796) even brought out an evolutionary theory of the solar system, anticipated by the philosopher Immanuel Kant, and Pierre Cabanis, about the same time, envisaged the very mental faculties of man as the product of his evolutionary history. In 1809 Lamarck of France propounded the first systematic major modern theory of evolution, based on the inheritance of acquired characteristics.

None of these theories triumphed. Indeed they were soon met by the passionate resistance of those, like the Tory *Quarterly Review*, whose 'general attachment to the cause of Revelation is so decided'[4] What was to happen to Noah's Flood? What to the separate creation of the species, not to mention man? What, above all, to social stability? Not only simple priests and less simple politicians were troubled by such reflections. The great Cuvier, himself the founder of the systematic study of fossils (*Recherches sur les ossemens fossiles*, 1812), rejected evolution in the name of Providence. Better even to imagine a series of catastrophes in geological history, followed by a series of divine re-creations – it was hardly possible to deny *geological* as distinct from biological change – than to tamper with the fixity of Scripture and of Aristotle. The wretched Dr Lawrence, who answered Lamarck by proposing a Darwin-like theory of evolution by natural selection, was forced by the outcry of the conservatives actually to withdraw his *Natural History of Man* (1819) from circulation. He had been unwise enough not only to discuss the evolution of man but also to point out the implications of his ideas for contemporary society. His recantation preserved his job, assured his future career, and a permanent bad conscience, which he assuaged by flattering the courageous Radical printers who from time to time pirated his incendiary work.

Not until the 1830s – until politics had taken another turn to the left, we might observe – did mature evolutionary theories break through in geology, with the publication of Lyell's famous *Principles of Geology* (1830–33), which ended the resistance of the Neptunists, who argued, with the Bible, that all minerals had been precipitated from aqueous solutions which had once covered the earth (cf. Genesis 1, 7–9) and the catastrophists, who followed Cuvier's desperate line of argument.

In the same decade, Schmerling, researching in Belgium, and Boucher de Perthes, who fortunately preferred his hobby of archaeology to his post as director of customs at Abbeville, forecast an even more alarming development : the actual discovery of those fossils of pre-historic man whose possibility had been hotly denied.[5] But scientific conservatism was still able to reject this horrifying prospect on the grounds of inadequate proof, until the discovery of Neanderthal man in 1856.

It had now to be accepted (*a*) that the causes now in operation had in the course of time transformed the earth from its original state to the present, (*b*) that this had taken a vastly longer time than any calculable from the Scriptures and (*c*) that the succession of geological strata revealed a succession of evolving forms of animals, and therefore implied biological evolution. Significantly enough, those who accepted this most readily, and indeed showed the greatest interest in the problem of evolution were the self-confident Radical laymen of the British middle classes (always excepting the egregious Dr Andrew Ure, best known for his hymns of praise to the factory system). The scientists were slow to accept science. This is less surprising when we recall that geology was the only science in this period gentlemanly enough (perhaps because it was practised outdoors, preferably on expensive 'geological tours') to be seriously pursued in the Universities of Oxford and Cambridge.

Biological evolution, however, still lagged. Not until well after the defeat of the 1848 revolutions was this explosive subject once again tackled; and even then Charles Darwin handled it with considerable caution and ambiguity, not to say disingenuousness. Even the parallel exploration of evolution through embryology temporarily petered out. Here too early German speculative natural philosophers like

Johann Meckel of Halle (1781–1833) had suggested that during its growth the embryo of an organism recapitulated the evolution of its species. But this 'biogenetic law', though at first supported by men like Rathke, who discovered that the embryos of birds pass through a stage when they have gill-slits (1829), was rejected by the formidable Von Baer of Koenigsberg and St Petersburg – experimental physiology seems to have had a marked attraction for workers in the Slavonic and Baltic areas [6] – and this line of thought was not revived until the coming of Darwinism.

Meanwhile evolutionary theories had made striking progress in the study of society. Yet we must not exaggerate this progress. The period of the dual revolution belongs to the prehistory of all social sciences except political economy, linguistics and perhaps statistics. Even its most formidable achievement, Marx and Engels's coherent theory of social evolution, was at this time little more than a brilliant guess, put forward in a superb pamphlet-sketch – or used as the basis for historical narrative. The firm construction of scientific bases for the study of human society did not take place until the second half of the century.

This is so in the fields of social anthropology or ethnography, of pre-history, of sociology and of psychology. The fact that these fields of study were baptised in our period, or that claims to regard each as a self-contained science with it own special regularities were then first put forward – John Stuart Mill in 1843 was perhaps the first to claim this status firmly for psychology – is important. The fact that special Ethnological Societies were founded in France and England (1839, 1843) to study 'the races of man' is equally significant, as is the multiplication of social enquiries by statistical means and of statistical societies between 1830 and 1848. But the 'general instructions to travellers' of the French Ethnological Society which urged them 'to discover what memories a people has preserved of its origins, . . . what revolutions it has undergone in its language or behaviour (*moeurs*), in its arts, sciences and wealth, its power or government, by internal causes or foreign invasion' [7] is little more than a programme; though indeed a profoundly historical one. Indeed, what is important about the social sciences in our period is less their results (though a considerable amount of descriptive material was accumulated) than their firm materialist bias, expressed in a determination to explain human social differences in terms of the environment, and their equally firm commitment to evolution; for did not Cha-vannes in 1787, at the outset of the science, define ethnology as 'the history of the progress of peoples towards civilization'? [8]

One shady by-product of this early development of the social sciences must, however, be briefly mentioned : the theories of race. The existence of different races (or rather colours) of men had been much discussed in the eighteenth century, when the problem of a single or multiple creation of man also exercised the reflective mind. The line between the monogenists and the polygenists was not a simple one. The first group united believers in evolution and human equality with men relieved to find that on this point at least science did not conflict with Scripture : the pre-Darwinians Pritchard and Lawrence with Cuvier. The second, admittedly, included not only *bona fide* scientists, but also racialists from the American slave south. These discussions of race produced a lively outburst of anthropo-metry, mostly based on the collection, classification and measure-ment of skulls, a practice also encouraged by the strange contem-porary hobby of phrenology, which attempted to read character from the configuration of the skull. In Britain and France phreno-logical societies were founded (1823, 1832) though the subject soon dropped out of science again.

At the same time a mixture of nationalism, radicalism, history and field observation introduced the equally dangerous topic of per-manent national or racial characteristics in society. In the 1820s the brothers Thierry, pioneer French historians and revolutionaries, had launched themselves into the study of the Norman Conquest and of the Gauls, which is still reflected in the proverbial first sentence of French school readers ('*Nos ancêtres les Gaulois*') and on the blue packets of the *Gauloise* cigarette. As good radicals they held that the French people were descended from the Gauls, the aristocrats from the Teutons who conquered them, an argument later used for con-servative purposes by upper class racialists like the Count of Gobi-neau. The belief that specific racial stock survived – an idea taken up with understandable zeal by a Welsh naturalist W. Edwards for the Celts – fitted admirably into an age when men purported to dis-cover the romantic and mysterious individuality of their nations, to claim messianic missions for them if revolutionary, or to ascribe their wealth and power to 'innate superiority'. (They showed no tendency to ascribe poverty and oppression to innate inferiority.) But in mitigation it must be said that the worst abuses of racial theories occurred after the end of our period.

V

How are we to explain these scientific developments? How, in particular, are we to link them with the other historical changes of the dual revolution? That there are links of the most obvious kind is evident. The theoretical problems of the steam engine led the brilliant Sadi Carnot in 1824 to the most fundamental physical insight of the nineteenth century, the two laws of thermodynamics (*Reflexions sur la puissance motrice du feu* [9]), though this was not the only approach to the problem. The great advance of geology and palaeontology plainly owed much to the zeal with which industrial engineers and builders hacked at the earth, and the great importance of mining. Not for nothing did Britain become the geological country *par excellence*, setting up a national Geological Survey in 1836. The survey of mineral resources provided chemists with innumerable inorganic compounds to analyse, mining, ceramics, metallurgy, textiles, the new industries of gas-lighting and chemicals, and agriculture stimulated their labours. And the enthusiasm of the solid British bourgeois Radical and aristocratic Whig not merely for applied research but for daring advances in knowledge from which established science itself recoiled is sufficient proof that the scientific progress of our period cannot be separated from the stimulus of the Industrial Revolution.

Similarly the scientific implications of the French Revolution are obvious in the frank or concealed hostility to science with which political conservatives or moderates met what they regarded as the natural consequences of eighteenth century materialist and rationalist subversion. Napoleon's defeat brought a wave of obscurantism. 'Mathematics were the chains of human thought,' cried the slippery Lamartine, 'I breathe, and they are broken.' The struggle between a combative pro-scientific and anti-clerical left which has, in its rare moments of victory, built most of the institutions which allow French scientists to function, and an anti-scientific right, which has done its best to starve them,[10] has continued ever since. This does not imply that scientists in France or elsewhere were at this period particularly revolutionary. Some were, like the golden boy Evariste Galois, who dashed to the barricades in 1830, was persecuted as a rebel, and killed in a duel provoked by political bullies at the age of twenty-one in 1832. Generations of mathematicians have fed on the profound ideas he wrote down feverishly in what he knew to be his last night on earth. Some were frank reactionaries, like the Legitimist Cauchy, though for obvious reasons the tradition of the Ecole Poly-technique, which he adorned, was militantly anti-royalist. Probably most scientists would have reckoned themselves to be left of centre in the post-Napoleonic period and some, especially in new nations or hitherto unpolitical communities, were forced into positions of political leadership; notably historians, linguists and others with obvious connections with national movements. Palacky became the chief spokesman of the Czechs in 1848, the seven professors of Göttingen who signed a letter of protest in 1837 found themselves national figures,[11] and the Frankfurt Parliament in the German 1848 Revolution was notoriously an assembly of professors as well as other civil servants. On the other hand, compared with the artists and philosophers, the scientists – and especially the natural ones – showed only a very low degree of political consciousness, unless their subject actually required it. Outside the Catholic countries, for instance, they showed a capacity for combining science with a tranquil religious orthodoxy which surprises the student of the post-Darwinian era.

Such direct derivations explain some things about scientific development between 1789 and 1848, but not much. Clearly the indirect effects of contemporary events were more important. No one could fail to observe that the world was transformed more radically than ever before in this era. No thinking person could fail to be awed, shaken, and mentally stimulated by these convulsions and transformations. It is hardly surprising that patterns of thought derived from the rapid social changes, the profound revolutions, the systematic replacement of customary or traditional institutions by radical rationalist innovations, should become acceptable. Is it possible to connect this visible emergence of revolution with the readiness of the unworldly mathematicians to break through hitherto operative thought barriers? We cannot tell, though we know that the adoption of revolutionary new lines of thought is normally prevented not by their intrinsic difficulty, but by their conflict with tacit assumptions about what is or is not 'natural'. The very terms 'irrational' number (for numbers like $\sqrt{2}$) or 'imaginary' number (for numbers like $\sqrt{-1}$) indicate the nature of the difficulty. Once we decide that they are no more or less rational or real than any others, all is plain sailing. But it may take an age of profound transformation to nerve thinkers to make such decisions; and indeed imaginary or complex variables in mathematics, treated with puzzled caution in the eighteenth century, only came fully into their own after the Revolution.

Leaving aside mathematics, it was only to be expected that patterns drawn from the transformations of society would tempt scientists in fields to which such analogies appeared applicable; for instance to introduce dynamic evolutionary concepts into hitherto static ones. This could either happen directly, or through the intermediary of some other science. Thus the concept of the Industrial Revolution, which is fundamental to history and much of modern economics, was introduced in the 1820s frankly as an analogy to the French Revolution. Charles Darwin derived the mechanism of 'natural selection' by analogy with the model of capitalist competition, which he took from Malthus (the 'struggle for existence'). The vogue for catastrophic theories in geology, 1790–1830, may also owe something to the familiarity of this generation with violent convulsions of society.

Nevertheless, outside the most obviously social sciences, it is unwise to put too much weight on such external influences. The world of thought is to some extent autonomous : its movements are, as it were, on the same historical wave-length as those outside, but they are not mere echoes of them. Thus for instance, the catastrophist theories of geology also owed something to the Protestant, and especially the Calvinist, insistence on the arbitrary omnipotence of the Lord. Such theories were largely a monopoly of Protestant, as distinct from Catholic or agnostic workers. If developments in the field of the sciences parallel those elsewhere, it is not because each of them can be hooked on to a corresponding aspect of economic or political ones in any simple way.

Yet the links are hard to deny. The main currents of general thought in our period have their correspondence in the specialized field of science, and this is what enables us to establish a parallelism between sciences and arts or between both and politico-social attitudes. Thus 'classicism' and 'romanticism' existed in the sciences, and as we have seen each fitted in with a particular approach to human society. The equation of classicism (or in intellectual terms, the rationalist, mechanist Newtonian universe of the Enlightenment) with the milieu of bourgeois liberalism, and of romanticism (or in intellectual terms the so-called 'Natural Philosophy') with its opponents, is obviously an over-simplification, and breaks down altogether after 1830. Yet it represents a certain aspect of truth. Until the rise of theories like modern socialism had firmly anchored revolutionary thought in the rationalist past (cf. Chapter 13), such sciences as physics, chemistry and astronomy marched with Anglo-French bourgeois liberalism. For instance, the plebeian revolutionaries of the Year II were inspired by Rousseau rather than Voltaire, and suspected Lavoisier (whom they executed) and Laplace not merely because of their connections with the old régime, but for reasons similar to those which led the poet William Blake to excoriate Newton.[21] Conversely 'natural history' was congenial, for it represented the road to the spontaneity of true and unspoiled nature. The Jacobin dictatorship, which dissolved the French Academy, founded no less than twelve research chairs at the *Jardin des Plantes*. Similarly it was in Germany, where classical liberalism was weak (cf. chapter 13), that a rival scientific ideology to the classical was most popular. This was 'Natural Philosophy'.

It is easy to underestimate 'natural philosophy', because it conflicts so much with what we have rightly come to regard as science. It was speculative and intuitive. It sought for expressions of the world spirit, or life, of the mysterious organic union of all things with each other, and a good many other things which resisted precise quantitative measurement or Cartesian clarity. Indeed, it was flatly in revolt against mechanical materialism, against Newton, sometimes against reason itself. The great Goethe wasted a considerable amount of his Olympian time trying to disprove Newton's optics, for no better reason than that he did not feel happy about a theory which failed to explain the colours by the interaction of the principles of light and darkness. Such an aberration would cause nothing but pained surprise in the Ecole Polytechnique, where the persistent preference of the Germans for the tangled Kepler, with his load of mysticism, over the lucid perfection of the *Principia* was incomprehensible. What indeed was one to make of Lorenz Oken's

355

'The action or the life of God consists in eternally manifesting, eternally contemplating itself in unity and duality, externally dividing itself and still remaining one. . . . Polarity is the first force which appears in the world. . . . The law of causality is a law of polarity. Causality is an act of generation. The sex is rooted in the first movement of the world. . . . In everything, therefore, there are two processes, one individualizing, vitalizing, and one universalizing, destructive.' [13]

What indeed? Bertrand Russell's blank incomprehension of Hegel, who operated in such terms, is a good illustration of the eighteenth-century rationalist's answer to this rhetorical question. On the other hand the debt which Marx and Engels frankly acknowledged to natural philosophy [14] would warn us that it cannot be regarded as mere verbiage. The point about it is that it worked. It produced not merely scientific effort – Lorenz Oken founded the liberal German *Deutsche Naturforscherversammlung* and inspired the *British Association for the Advancement of Science* – but fruitful results. The cell theory in biology, a good deal of morphology, embryology, philology and much of the historical and evolutionary element in all the sciences, were primarily of 'romantic' inspiration. Admittedly even in its chosen field of biology 'romanticism' had eventually to be supplemented by the cool classicism of Claude Bernard (1813–78), the founder of modern physiology. On the other hand even in the physico-chemical sciences, which remained the stronghold of 'classicism', the speculations of the natural philosophers about such mysterious subjects as electricity and magnetism, brought advances. Hans Christian Oersted of Copenhagen, the disciple of the cloudy Schelling, sought and found the connection between the two when he demonstrated the magnetical effect of electric currents in 1820. Both approaches to science, in effect, mixed. They never quite merged, even in Marx who was more clearly aware than most of the combined intellectual origins of his thought. On the whole the 'romantic' approach served as a stimulus for new ideas and departures, and then once again dropped out of the sciences. But in our period it cannot be neglected.

If it cannot be neglected as a purely scientific stimulus, it can be even less neglected by the historian of ideas and opinions, for whom even absurd and false ideas are facts and historical forces. We cannot write off a movement which captured or influenced men of the highest intellectual calibre, such as Goethe, Hegel and the young Marx. We can merely seek to understand the deep dissatisfaction with the 'classical' eighteenth-century Anglo-French view of the world, whose titanic achievements in science and in society were undeniable, but whose narrowness and limitations were also increasingly evident in the period of the two revolutions. To be aware of these limits and to seek, often by intuition rather than analysis, the terms in which a more satisfactory picture of the world could be constructed, was not actually to construct it. Nor were the visions of an evolutionary, interconnected, dialectical universe which the natural philosophers expressed, proofs or even adequate formulations. But they reflected real problems – even real problems in the physical sciences – and they anticipated the transformations and extensions of the world of sciences which have produced our modern scientific universe. And in their way they reflected the impact of the dual revolution, which left no aspect of human life unchanged.

NOTES

1 Quoted in S. Solomon, *Commune*, August 1939, p. 964.
2 Though Saint-Simon's ideas are, as we have seen, not easily classifiable, it seems pedantic to abandon the established practice of calling him a utopian socialist.
3 Paradoxically, the attempt to apply the mathematical-physical method to linguistics considered as part of a more general 'communications theory' was not undertaken until the present century.
4 G. C. C. Gillispie, *Genesis and Geology* (1951), p. 116.
5 His *Antiquités celtiques et antediluviennes* was not published until 1846. In fact several human fossils had been discovered from time to time, but lay either unrecognized or simply forgotten in the corners of provincial museums.
6 Rathke taught at Dorpat (Tartu) in Estonia, Pander at Riga, the great Czech physiologist Purkinje opened the first physiological research laboratory in Breslau in 1830.
7 Quoted in Encyclopédie de la Pléiade, *Histoire de la Science* (1957), p. 1465.
8 *Essai sur l'éducation intellectuelle avec le projet d'une Science nouvelle* (Lausanne 1787).
9 His discovery of the first law was not, however, published until much later.

10 cf. Guerlac, Science and National Strength, in E. M. Earle ed. *Modern France* (1951).
11 They included the brothers Grimm.
12 This suspicion of Newtonian science did not extend to applied work, whose economic and military value was evident.
13 Quoted in S. Mason, *A History of the Sciences* (1953), p. 286.
14 Engels' *Anti-Duehring* and *Feuerbach* contain a qualified defence of it, as well as of Kepler as against Newton.

16

Conclusion: Towards 1848

> *Pauperism and proletariat are the suppurating ulcers which have sprung from the organism of the modern states. Can they be healed? The communist doctors propose the complete destruction and annihilation of the existing organism. . . . One thing is certain, if these men gain the power to act, there will be not a political but a social revolution, a war against all property, a complete anarchy. Would this in turn give way to new national states, and on what moral and social foundations? Who shall lift the veil of the future? And what part will be played by Russia? 'I sit on the shore and wait for the wind,' says an old Russian proverb.*
>
> Haxthausen, *Studien ueber . . . Russland* (1847) [1]

I

We began by surveying the state of the world in 1789. Let us conclude by glancing at it some fifty years later, at the end of the most revolutionary half-century in the history recorded up to that date.

It was an age of superlatives. The numerous new compendia of statistics in which this era of counting and calculation sought to record all aspects of the known world [2] could conclude with justice that virtually every measurable quantity was greater (or smaller) than ever before. The known, mapped and intercommunicating area of the world was larger than ever before, its communications unbelievably speedier. The population of the world was greater than ever before; in several cases greater beyond all expectation or previous probability. Cities of vast size multiplied faster than ever before. Industrial production reached astronomic figures: in the 1840s something like 640 million tons of coal were hacked from the interior of the earth. They were exceeded only by the even more

359

extraordinary figures for international commerce, which had multiplied fourfold since 1780 to reach something like 800 millions of pound sterling's worth, and very much more in the currency of less solid and stable units of currency.

Science had never been more triumphant; knowledge had never been more widespread. Over four thousand newspapers informed the citizens of the world and the number of books published annually in Britain, France, Germany and the USA alone ran well into five figures. Human invention was climbing more dazzling peaks every year. The Argand lamp (1728–4) had barely revolutionized artificial lighting – it was the first major advance since the oil-lamp and candle – when the gigantic laboratories known as gasworks, sending their products through endless subterranean pipes, began to illuminate the factories [3] and soon after the cities of Europe : London from 1807, Dublin from 1818, Paris from 1819, even remote Sydney in 1841. And already the electric arc-light was known. Professor Wheatstone of London was already planning to link England with France by means of a submarine electric telegraph. Forty-eight millions of passengers already used the railways of the United Kingdom in a single year (1845). Men and women could already be hurtled along three thousand (1846) – before 1850 along over six thousand – miles of line in Great Britain, along nine thousand in the USA. Regular steamship services already linked Europe and America, Europe and the Indies.

No doubt these triumphs had their dark side, though these were not so readily to be summarized in statistical tables. How was one to find quantitative expression for the fact, which few would today deny, that the Industrial Revolution created the ugliest world in which man has ever lived, as the grim and stinking, fog-bound back streets of Manchester already testified? Or, by uprooting men and women in unprecedented numbers and depriving them of the certainties of the ages, probably the unhappiest world? Nevertheless, we can forgive the champions of progress in the 1840s their confidence and their determination 'that commerce may go freely forth, leading civilization with one hand, and peace with the other, to render mankind happier, wiser, better'. 'Sir,' said Lord Palmerston, continuing this rosy statement in the blackest of years, 1842, 'this is the dispensation of Providence.' [4] Nobody could deny that there was poverty of the most shocking kind. Many held that it was even increasing and deepening. And yet, by the all-time criteria which measured the triumphs of industry and science, could even the gloomiest of rational observers maintain that in material terms it was worse than at any time in the past, or even than in unindustrialized countries in the present? He could not. It was sufficiently bitter accusation that the material prosperity of the labouring poor was often no better than in the dark past, and sometimes worse than in periods within living memory. The champions of progress attempted to fend it off with the argument that this was due not to the operations of the new bourgeois society, but on the contrary to the obstacles which the old feudalism, monarchy and aristocracy still placed in the way of perfect free enterprise. The new socialists, on the contrary, held that it was due to the very operations of that system. But both agreed that these were growing-pains. The ones held that they would be overcome within the framework of capitalism, the others that they were not likely to be, but both rightly believed that human life faced a prospect of material improvement to equal the advance in man's control over the forces of nature.

When we come to analyse the social and political structure of the world in the 1840s, however, we leave the world of superlatives for that of modest qualified statements. The bulk of the world's inhabitants continued to be peasants as before, though there were a few areas – notably Britain – where agriculture was already the occupation of a small minority, and the urban population already on the verge of exceeding the rural, as it did for the first time in the census of 1851. There were proportionately fewer slaves, for the international slave-trade had been officially abolished in 1815 and actual slavery in the British colonies in 1834, and in the liberated Spanish and French ones in and after the French Revolution. However, while the West Indies were now, with some non-British exceptions, an area of legally free agriculture, numerically slavery continued to expand in its two great remaining strongholds, Brazil and the Southern USA, stimulated by the very progress of industry and commerce which opposed all restraints of goods and persons, and official prohibition made the slave trade more lucrative. The approximate price of a field-hand in the American South was 300 dollars in 1795 but between 1,200 and 1,800 dollars in 1860;[5] the number of slaves in the USA rose from 700,000 in 1790 to 2,500,000 in 1840 and 3,200,000 in 1850. They still came from Africa, but were also increasingly bred for sale within the slave-owning area, e.g. in the border states of the USA for sale to the rapidly expanding cotton-belt.

Moreover, already systems of semi-slavery like the export of 'indentured labour' from India to the sugar-islands of the Indian Ocean and the West Indies were developing.

Serfdom or the legal bonding of peasants had been abolished over a large part of Europe, though this had made little difference to the actual situation of the rural poor in such areas of traditional latifundist cultivation as Sicily or Andalusia. However, serfdom persisted in its chief European strongholds, though after great initial expansion its numbers remained steady in Russia at between ten and eleven million males after 1811, that is to say it declined in relative terms.[6] Nevertheless, serf agriculture (unlike slave agriculture) was clearly on the decline, its economic disadvantages being increasingly evident, and – especially from the 1840s – the rebelliousness of the peasantry being increasingly marked. The greatest serf rising was probably that in Austrian Galicia in 1846, the prelude to general emancipation by the 1848 revolution. But even in Russia there were 148 outbreaks of peasant unrest in 1826–34, 216 in 1835–44, 348 in 1844–54, culminating in the 474 outbreaks of the last years preceding the emancipation of 1861.[8]

At the other end of the social pyramid, the position of the landed aristocrat also changed less than might have been thought, except in countries of direct peasant revolution like France. No doubt there were now countries – France and the USA for instance – where the richest men were no longer landed proprietors (except insofar as they also bought themselves estates as a badge of their entry into the highest class, like the Rothschilds). However, even in Britain in the 1840s the greatest concentrations of wealth were certainly still those of the peerage, and in the Southern USA the cotton-planters even created for themselves a provincial caricature of aristocratic society, inspired by Walter Scott, 'chivalry', 'romance' and other concepts which had little bearing on the Negro slaves on whom they battened and the red-necked puritan farmers eating their maize and fat pork. Of course this aristocratic firmness concealed a change : noble incomes increasingly depended on the industry, the stocks and shares, the real estate developments of the despised bourgeoisie.

The 'middle classes', of course, had increased rapidly, but their numbers even so were not overwhelmingly large. In 1801 there had been about 100,000 tax-payers earning above £150 a year in Britain; at the end of our period there may have been about 340,000;[9] say, with large families, a million and a half persons out of a total population of 21 millions (1851)).[10] Naturally the number of those who sought to follow middle-class standards and ways of life was very much larger. Not all these were very rich; a good guess [11] is that the number of those earning over £5,000 a year was about 4,000 – which includes the aristocracy; a figure not too incompatible with that of the presumable employers of the 7,579 domestic coachmen who adorned the British streets. We may assume that the proportion of the 'middle classes' in other countries was not notably higher than this, and indeed was generally rather lower.

The working class (including the new proletariat of factory, mine, railway, etc.) naturally grew at the fastest rate of all. Nevertheless, except in Britain it could at best be counted in hundreds of thousands rather than millions. Measured against the total population of the world, it was still a numerically negligible, and in any case – except once again for Britain and small nuclei elsewhere – an unorganized one. Yet, as we have seen, its political importance was already immense, and quite disproportionate to its size or achievements.

The political structure of the world was also very considerably transformed by the 1840s; and yet by no means as much as the sanguine (or pessimistic) observer might have anticipated in 1800. Monarchy still remained overwhelmingly the most common mode of governing states, except on the American continent; and even there one of the largest countries (Brazil) was an Empire, and another (Mexico) had at least experimented with imperial titles under General Iturbide (Augustin I) from 1822 to 1833. It is true that several European kingdoms, including France, could now be described as constitutional monarchies, but outside a band of such régimes along the eastern edge of the Atlantic, absolute monarchy prevailed everywhere. It is true that there were by the 1840s several new states, the product of revolution; Belgium, Serbia, Greece and a quiverful of Latin American ones. Yet, though Belgium was an industrial power of importance (admittedly to a large extent because it moved in the wake of its greater French neighbour [12]), the most important of the revolutionary states was the one which had already existed in 1789, the USA. It enjoyed two immense advantages : the absence of any strong neighbours or rival powers which could, or indeed wanted to, prevent its expansion across the huge continent to the Pacific – the French had actually sold it an area as large as the then USA in the 'Louisiana Purchase' of 1803 – and an extraordinarily rapid rate of economic expansion. The former advantage was also shared by Brazil, which, separating peacefully from Portugal, escaped the fragmentation which a generation of revolutionary war brought to most of Spanish America; but its wealth of resources remained virtually unexploited.

Still, there had been great changes. Moreover, since about 1830 their momentum was visibly increasing. The revolution of 1830 introduced moderate liberal middle-class constitutions – anti-democratic but equally plainly anti-aristocratic – in the chief states of Western Europe. There were no doubt compromises, imposed by the fear of a mass revolution which would go beyond moderate middle-class aspirations. They left the landed classes over-represented in government, as in Britain, and large sectors of the new – and especially the most dynamic industrial – middle classes unrepresented, as in France. Yet they were compromises which decisively tilted the political balance towards the middle classes. On all matters that counted the British industrialists got their way after 1832; the capacity to abolish the Corn Laws was well worth the abstention from the more extreme republican and anti-clerical proposals of the Utilitarians. There can be no doubt that in Western Europe middle-class Liberalism (though not democratic radicalism) was in the ascendant. Its chief opponents – Conservatives in Britain, blocs generally rallying round the Catholic Church elsewhere – were on the defensive and knew it.

However, even radical democracy had made major advances. After fifty years of hesitation and hostility, the pressure of the frontiersmen and farmers had finally imposed it on the USA under President Andrew Jackson (1829–37), at roughly the same time as the European revolution regained its momentum. At the very end of our period (1847) a civil war between radicals and Catholics in Switzerland brought it to that country. But few among moderate middle class liberals as yet thought that this system of government, advocated mainly by left-wing revolutionaries, adapted, it seemed, at best for the rude petty producers and traders of mountain or prairie, would one day become the characteristic political framework of capitalism, defended as such against the onslaught of the very people who were in the 1840s advocating it.

Only in international politics had there been an apparently whole-sale and virtually unqualified revolution. The world of the 1840s was completely dominated by the European powers, political and econo-mic, supplemented by the growing USA. The Opium War of 1839–42 had demonstrated that the only surviving non-European great power, the Chinese Empire, was helpless in the face of western military and economic aggression. Nothing, it seemed, could henceforth stand in the way of a few western gunboats or regiments bringing with them trade and bibles. And within this general western domination, Britain was supreme, thanks to her possession of more gunboats, trade and bibles than anyone else. So absolute was this British supremacy that it hardly needed political control to operate. There were no other colo-nial powers left, except by grace of the British, and consequently no rivals. The French empire was reduced to a few scattered islands and trading posts, though in the process of reviving itself across the Medi-terranean in Algeria. The Dutch, restored in Indonesia under the watchful eye of the new British entrepôt Singapore, no longer com-peted; the Spaniards retained Cuba, the Philippines and a few vague claims in Africa; the Portuguese colonies were rightly forgotten. British trade dominated the independent Argentine, Brazil and the Southern USA as much as the Spanish colony of Cuba or the British ones in India. British investments had their powerful stake in the Northern USA, and indeed wherever economic development took place. Never in the entire history of the world has a single power exercised a world hegemony like that of the British in the middle of the nineteenth cen-tury, for even the greatest empires or hegemonies of the past had been merely regional – the Chinese, the Mohammedan, the Roman. Never since then has any single power succeeded in re-establishing a com-parable hegemony, nor indeed is any one likely to in the foreseeable future; for no power has since been able to claim the exclusive status of 'workshop of the world'.

Nevertheless, the future decline of Britain was already visible. Intelligent observers even in the 1830s and 1840s, like de Tocqueville and Haxthausen, already predicted that the size and potential re-sources of the USA and Russia would eventually make them into the twin giants of the world; within Europe Germany (as Frederick Engels predicted in 1844) would also soon compete on equal terms. Only France had decisively dropped out of the competition for international hegemony, though this was not yet so evident as to reassure suspicious British and other statesmen.

In brief, the world of the 1840s was out of balance. The forces of economic, technical and social change released in the past half-century were unprecedented, and even to the most superficial observer, irresistible. Their institutional consequences, on the other hand, were as yet modest. It was, for instance, inevitable that sooner or later legal slavery and serfdom (except as relics in remote regions as yet untouched by the new economy) would have to go, as it was inevitable that Britain could not for ever remain the *only* industrialized country. It was inevitable that landed aristocracies and absolute monarchies must retreat in all countries in which a strong bourgeoisie was developing, whatever the political compromises or formulae found for retaining status, influence and even political power. Moreover, it was inevitable that the injection of political consciousness and permanent political activity among the masses, which was the great legacy of the French Revolution, must sooner or later mean that these masses were allowed to play a formal part in politics. And given the remarkable acceleration of social change since 1830, and the revival of the world revolutionary movement, it was clearly inevitable that changes – whatever their precise institutional nature – could not be long delayed.[13]

All this would have been enough to give the men of the 1840s the consciousness of impending change. But not enough to explain, what was widely felt throughout Europe, the consciousness of impending social revolution. It was, significantly enough, not confined to revolutionaries, who expressed it with the greatest elaboration, nor to the ruling classes, whose fear of the massed poor is never far below the surface in times of social change. The poor themselves felt it. The literate strata of the people expressed it. 'All well-informed people,' wrote the American consul from Amsterdam during the hunger of 1847, reporting the sentiments of the German emigrants passing through Holland, 'express the belief that the present crisis is so deeply interwoven in the events of the present period that "it" is but the commencement of that great Revolution, which they consider sooner or later is to dissolve the present constitution of things.'[14]

The reason was that the crisis in what remained of the old society appeared to coincide with a crisis of the new. Looking back on the 1840s it is easy to think that the socialists who predicted the imminent final crisis of capitalism were dreamers confusing their hopes with realistic prospects. For in fact what followed was not the breakdown of capitalism, but its most rapid and unchallenged period of expansion and triumph. Yet in the 1830s and 1840s it was far from evident that the new economy could or would overcome its difficulties which merely seemed to increase with its power to produce larger and larger quantities of goods by more and more revolutionary methods. Its very theorists were haunted by the prospect of the 'stationary state', that running down of the motive power which drove the economy forward, and which (unlike the theorists of the eighteenth century or those of the subsequent period) they believed to be imminent rather than merely in theoretical reserve. Its very champions were in two minds about its future. In France men who were to be the captains of high finance and heavy industry (the Saint-Simonians) were in the 1830s still undecided as to whether socialism or capitalism was the best way of achieving the triumph of the industrial society. In the USA men like Horace Greeley, who have become immortal as the prophets of individualist expansion ('Go west, young man' is his phrase), were in the 1840s adherents of utopian socialism, founding and expounding the merits of Fourierist 'Phalanxes', those *kibbutz*-like communes which fit so badly into what is now thought to be 'Americanism'. The very businessmen were desperate. It may in retrospect seem incomprehensible that Quaker businessmen like John Bright and successful cotton-manufacturers of Lancashire, in the midst of their most dynamic period of expansion, should have been prepared to plunge their country into chaos, hunger and riot by a general political lock-out, merely in order to abolish tariffs.[15] Yet in the terrible year of 1841–2 it might well seem to the thoughtful capitalist that industry faced not merely inconvenience and loss, but general strangulation, unless the obstacles to its further expansion were immediately removed.

For the mass of the common people the problem was even simpler. As we have seen their condition in the large cities and manufacturing districts of Western and Central Europe pushed them inevitably towards social revolution. Their hatred of the rich and the great of that bitter world in which they lived, and their dream of a new and better world, gave their desperation eyes and a purpose, even though only some of them, mainly in Britain and France, were conscious of that purpose. Their organization or facility for collective action gave them power. The great awakening of the French Revolution had taught them that common men need not suffer injustices meekly : 'the nations knew nothing before, and the people thought that kings were gods upon the earth and that they were bound to say that whatever they did was well done. Through this present change it is more difficult to rule the people.' [16]

This was the 'spectre of communism' which haunted Europe, the fear of 'the proletariat' which affected not merely factory-owners in Lancashire or Northern France but civil servants in rural Germany, priests in Rome and professors everywhere. And with justice. For the revolution which broke out in the first months of 1848 was not a social revolution merely in the sense that it involved and mobilized all social classes. It was in the literal sense the rising of the labouring poor in the cities – especially the capital cities – of Western and Central Europe. Theirs, and theirs almost alone, was the force which toppled the old régimes from Palermo to the borders of Russia. When the dust settled on their ruins, workers – in France actually socialist workers – were seen to be standing on them, demanding not merely bread and employment, but a new state and society.

While the labouring poor stirred, the increasing weakness and obsolescence of the old régimes of Europe multiplied crises within the world of the rich and influential. In themselves these were not of great moment. Had they occurred at a different time, or in systems which allowed the different sections of the ruling class to adjust their rivalries peaceably, they would no more have led to revolution than the perennial squabbles of court factions in eighteenth-century Russia led to the fall of Tsarism. In Britain and Belgium, for instance, there was plenty of conflict between agrarians and industrialists, and different sections of each. But it was clearly understood that the transformations of 1830–32 had decided the issue of power in favour of the industrialists, that nevertheless the political status quo could only be frozen at the risk of revolution, and that this must be avoided at all costs. Consequently the bitter struggle between free-trading British industrialists and the agrarian protectionists over the Corn Laws could be waged and won (1846) in the midst of the Chartist ferment without for a moment jeopardizing the unity of all ruling classes against the threat of universal suffrage. In Belgium the victory of the Liberals over the Catholics in the 1847 elections detached the industrialists from the ranks of potential revolutionaries, and a carefully judged electoral reform in 1848, which doubled the electorate,[17] removed the discontents of crucial sections of the lower middle class. There was no 1848 revolution, though in terms of actual suffering Belgium (or rather Flanders) was probably worse off than any other part of Western Europe except Ireland.

But in absolutist Europe the rigidity of the political régimes in 1815, which had been designed to fend off *all* change of a liberal or national kind, left even the most moderate of oppositionists no choice other than that of the status quo or revolution. They might not be ready to revolt themselves, but, unless there should be an irreversible social revolution, they would gain nothing unless someone did. The régimes of 1815 had to go sooner or later. They knew it themselves. The consciousness that 'history was against them' sapped their will to resist, as the fact that it was sapped their ability to do so. In 1848 the first faint puff of revolution – often of revolution abroad – blew them away. But unless there was at least such a puff, they would not go. And conversely the relatively minor frictions within such states – the troubles of rulers with the Prussian and Hungarian diets, the election of a 'liberal' Pope in 1846 (i.e. one anxious to bring the Papacy a few inches nearer to the nineteenth century), the resentment of a royal mistress in Bavaria, etc – turned into major political vibrations.

In theory the France of Louis Philippe should have shared the political flexibility of Britain, Belgium and the Dutch and Scandinavians. In practice it did not. For though it was clear that the ruling class of France – the bankers, financiers and one or two large industrialists – represented only a section of the middle-class interest, and moreover, one whose economic policy was disliked by the more dynamic industrialist elements as well as by various vested interests, the memory of the Revolution of 1789 stood in the way of reform. For the opposition consisted not merely of the discontented bourgeoisie, but of the politically decisive lower middle class, especially of Paris (which voted against the government in spite of the restricted suffrage in 1846). To widen the franchise might thus let in the potential Jacobins, the Radicals who, but for the official ban, would be Republicans. Louis Philippe's premier, the historian Guizot (1840–48), thus preferred to leave the broadening of the social base of the régime to economic development, which would automatically increase the number of citizens with the property qualification to enter politics. In fact it did so. The electorate rose from 166,000 in 1821 to 241,000 in 1846. But it did not do so sufficiently. Fear of the Jacobin republic kept the French political structure rigid, and the French political situation increasingly tense. Under British conditions a public political campaign by means of after-dinner speeches, such as the French opposition launched in 1847, would have been perfectly harmless. Under French conditions it was the prelude to revolution.

For, like the other crises in European ruling-class politics, it coincided with a social catastrophe: the great depression which swept across the continent from the middle 1840s. Harvests – and especially the potato crop – failed. Entire populations such as those of Ireland, and to a lesser extent Silesia and Flanders, starved.[18] Food-prices rose. Industrial depression multiplied unemployment, and the masses of the urban labouring poor were deprived of their modest income at the very moment when their cost of living rocketed. The situation varied from one country to another and within each, and – fortunately for the existing régimes – the most miserable populations, such as the Irish and Flemish, or some of the provincial factory workers were also politically among the most immature: the cotton operatives of the Nord department of France, for instance, took out their desperation on the equally desperate Belgian immigrants who flooded into Northern France, rather than on the government or even the employers. Moreover, in the most industrialized country, the sharpest edge of discontent had already been taken away by the great industrial and railway-building boom of the middle 1840s. 1846–8 were bad years, but not so bad as 1841–2, and what was more, they were merely a sharp dip in what was now visibly an ascending slope of economic prosperity. But, taking Western and Central Europe as a whole, the catastrophe of 1846–8 was universal and the mood of the masses, always pretty close to subsistence level, tense and impassioned.

A European economic cataclysm thus coincided with the visible corrosion of the old régimes. A peasant rising in Galicia in 1846; the election of a 'liberal' Pope in the same year; a civil war between radicals and Catholics in Switzerland in late 1847, won by the radicals; one of the perennial Sicilian autonomist insurrections in Palermo in early 1848: they were not merely straws in the wind, they were the first squalls of the gale. Everyone knew it. Rarely has revolution been more universally predicted, though not necessarily for the right countries or the right dates. An entire continent waited, ready by now to pass the news of revolution almost instantly from city to city by means of the electric telegraph. In 1831 Victor Hugo had written that he already heard 'the dull sound of revolution, still deep down in the earth, pushing out under every kingdom in Europe its subterranean galleries from the central shaft of the mine which is Paris'. In 1847 the sound was loud and close. In 1848 the explosion burst.

NOTES

1 Haxthausen, *Studien ueber . . . Russland* (1847), I, pp. 156-7.
2 About fifty major compendia of this type were published between 1800 and 1848, not counting the statistics of governments (censuses, official enquiries, etc.) or the numerous new specialist or economiic journals filled with statistical tables.
3 Boulton and Watt introduced it in 1798, the cotton-mills of Philips and Lee in Manchester permanently employed a thousand burners from 1805.
4 Hansard, 16 Feb. 1842, quoted in Robinson and Gallagher, *Africa and the Victorians* (1961), p. 2.
5 R. B. Morris, *Encyclopedia of American History* (1953), pp. 515, 516.
6 The extension of serfdom under Catherine II and Paul (1762–1801) increased it from about 3·8 million males to 10·4 millions in 1811.[7]
7 P. Lyashchenko, *History of the Russian National Economy*, pp. 273-4.
8 Lyashchenko, op. cit., p. 370.
9 J. Stamp, *British Incomes and Property* (1920), pp. 515, 431.
10 Such estimates are arbitrary, but assuming that everyone classifiable in the middle class kept at least one servant, the 674,000 female 'general domestic servants' in 1851 gives us something beyond the maximum of 'middle-class' households, the roughly 50,000 cooks (the numbers of housemaids and housekeepers were about the same) a minimum.
11 By the eminent statistician William Farr in the *Statistical Journal*, 1857, p. 102.
12 About a third of the Belgian coal and pig iron was exported, almost entirely to France.
13 This does not of course mean that all the precise changes then widely predicted as inevitable would necessarily come about; for instance, the universal triumph of free trade, of peace, of sovereign representative assemblies, or the disappearance of monarchs or the Roman Catholic Church.
14 M. L. Hansen, *The Atlantic Migration 1607–1860*, (Harvard 1945), p. 252.

15 N. McCord, *The Anti-Corn Law League 1838–46* (London 1958), chapter V.

16 T. Kolokotrones, quoted in L. S. Stavrianos, Antecedents to Balkan Revolutions, *Journal of Modern History*, XXIX, 1957, p. 344.

17 It was still no more than 80,000 out of 4,000,000.

18 In the flax-growing districts of Flanders the population dropped by 5 per cent between 1846 and 1848.

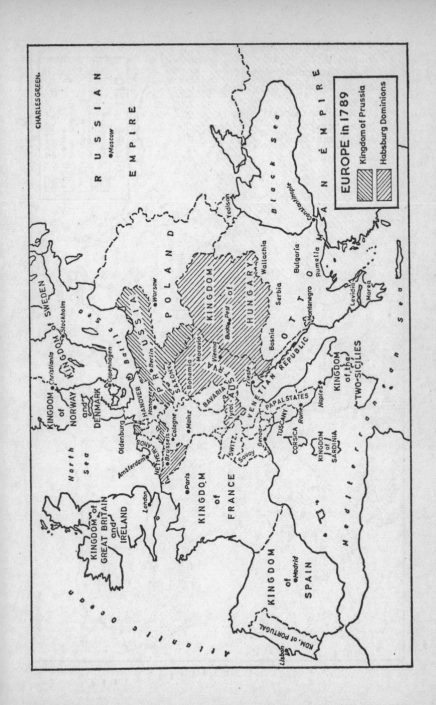

EUROPE in 1789

- Kingdom of Prussia
- Habsburg Dominions

CHARLES GREEN

RUSSIAN EMPIRE

Moscow

KINGDOM of SWEDEN

Stockholm

Christiania

KINGDOM of NORWAY and DENMARK

Copenhagen

North Sea

KINGDOM of GREAT BRITAIN and IRELAND

London

Atlantic Ocean

Oldenburg

Amsterdam

NETHERLANDS

Brussels

HANOVER

Hanover

Cologne

Mainz

Berlin

P R U S S I A

SAXONY

Bohemia

Moravia

Vienna

BAVARIA

AUST.

Tyrol

SWITZ.

Savoy

Genoa

KINGDOM of SARDINIA

CORSICA

KINGDOM of FRANCE

Paris

KINGDOM of SPAIN

Madrid

KDM. of PORTUGAL

Lisbon

Galicia

POLAND

Warsaw

KINGDOM of HUNGARY

Buda

Pest

Trieste

VENETIAN REPUBLIC

TUSCANY

PAPAL STATES

Rome

KINGDOM of the TWO SICILIES

Naples

Mediterranean Sea

Baltic Sea

Yedisan

Wallachia

Serbia

Bosnia

Montenegro

O T T O M A N   E M P I R E

Bulgaria

Rumelia

Constantinople

Black Sea

Levadia

Morea

Aegean Sea

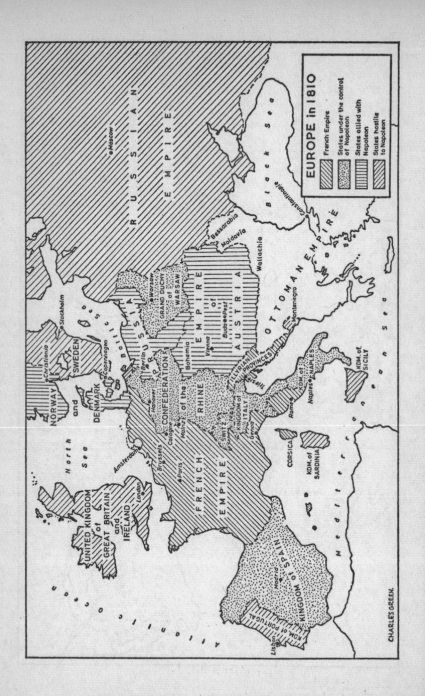

EUROPE in 1810

French Empire
States under the control of Napoleon
States allied with Napoleon
States hostile to Napoleon

RUSSIAN EMPIRE

Moscow

Baltic Sea

Stockholm

SWEDEN

NORWAY and DENMARK

Christiania

Copenhagen

North Sea

UNITED KINGDOM of GREAT BRITAIN and IRELAND

London

Amsterdam

Brussels

Paris

FRENCH EMPIRE

Atlantic Ocean

KINGDOM of SPAIN

Madrid

KDM. of PORTUGAL

Lisbon

Berlin

Hanover

CONFEDERATION of the RHINE

Cologne

Mainz

SWITZ.

KINGDOM of ITALY

Genoa

Rome

Naples

KDM. of NAPLES

CORSICA

KDM. of SARDINIA

Mediterranean Sea

KDM. of SICILY

Ionian Sea

Warsaw

GRAND DUCHY of WARSAW

Bohemia

Budapest

Vienna

AUSTRIA

EMPIRE

ILLYRIAN PROVINCES

Trieste

Montenegro

OTTOMAN EMPIRE

Moldavia

Bessarabia

Wallachia

Black Sea

Constantinople

CHARLES GREEN.

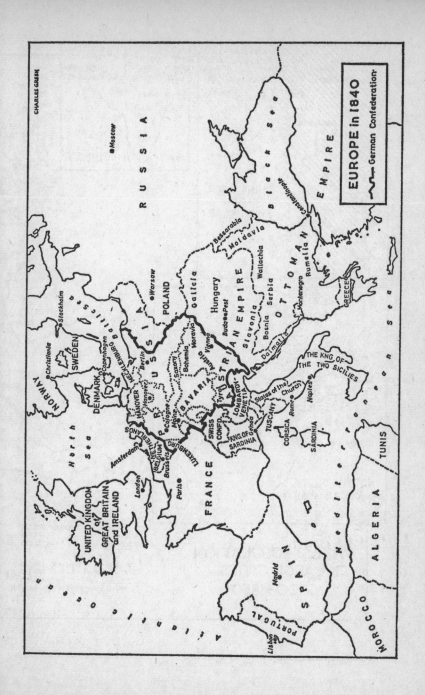

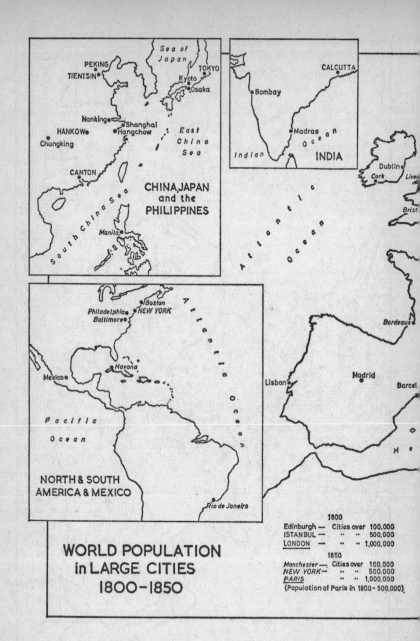

WORLD POPULATION
in LARGE CITIES
1800-1850

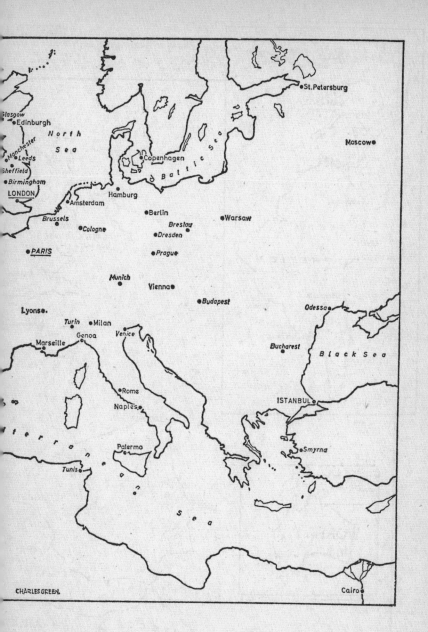

CHARLES GREEN.

WESTERN

Places and languages of performance of three

Corfu — Performances in French and Italian. London — Performances also or exclusively in vernacular.

...LTURE 1815—1848: OPERA

...ular operas: Rossini—'Almavia o sia l'inutile precauzione','Gazza Ladra': Auber:'La Muette de Portici'

...EL — Performances in
German.

ST.PETERSBURG — Performances in vernacular
and German.

NORWAY

SWEDEN

HELSINGFORS

ST.PETERSBURG

Christiania

Stockholm

North

RIGA

Sea

DENMARK

COPENHAGEN

Baltic Sea

RUSSIA

HAMBURG

P R U S S I A

AMSTERDAM
Rotterdam

BERLIN

Warsaw

Antwerp
Brussels

Braunschweig
DESSAU

POLAND

...ille

GERMANIC

RUDOLSTADT

...Paris

CONFEDERATION

PRAGUE

MANNHEIM

BRNO

Strasbourg

Munich

VIENNA

PRESSBURG

Odessa

BASEL

A U S T R I A N   E M P I R E

BUDAPEST

Klausenburg

Geneva

GRAZ

Hermannstadt

Lyons

Lugano

Kronstadt

Milan

Venice

Trieste

AGRAM

BUCHAREST

Black

Marseille

Florence

O T T O M A N

Sea

Bastia

I T A L Y

Rome

Constantinople

E

M

Naples

THE TWO SICILIES

P

Corfu

I

R

Cagliari

GREECE

E

Athens

Smyrna

terranean

Sea

...IA

TUNIS

Malta

CHARLES GREEN.

THE STATES OF EUROPE IN 1836

NAME	TOTAL POPULATION (THOUSANDS)	NUMBER OF CITIES (OVER 50,000)	LAND UNDER TILLAGE IN MORGEN (MILLION)	GRAIN PRODUCTION IN SCHEFFEL (MILLION)	BEEF CATTLE (MILLIONS)	IRON	COAL (MILLION CWT)
Russia, including Poland and Cracow	49,538	6	276	1125	19	2.1	—
Austria, including Hungary and Lombardy	35,000	8	93	225	10.4	1.2	2.3
France	33,000	9	74	254	7	4	20.0
Great Britain, including Ireland	24,273	17	67.5	330	10.5	13	200
German confederation (excluding Austria, Prussia)	14,205	4	37.5	115	6	1.1	2.2
Spain	14,032	8	30		3	0.2	0
Portugal	3,530	1	30		3	0.2	0
Prussia	13,093	5	43	145	4.5	2	4.6
Turkey, including Rumania	8,600	5					
Kingdom of Naples	7,622	2	20	116	2.8	0	0.1
Piedmont-Sardinia	4,450	2	20	116	2.8	0	0.1
Rest of Italy	5,000	4	20	116	2.8	0	0.1
Sweden and Norway	4,000	1	2	21	1.4	1.7	0.6
Belgium	3,827	4	7	5	2	0.4	55.4
Netherlands	2,750	3	7	5	2	0.4	55.4
Switzerland	2,000	0	2		0.8	0.1	0
Denmark	2,000	1	16		1.6	0	0
Greece	1,000	0					

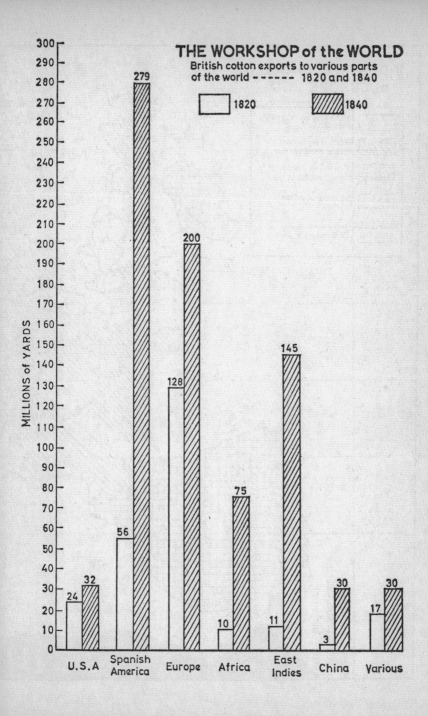

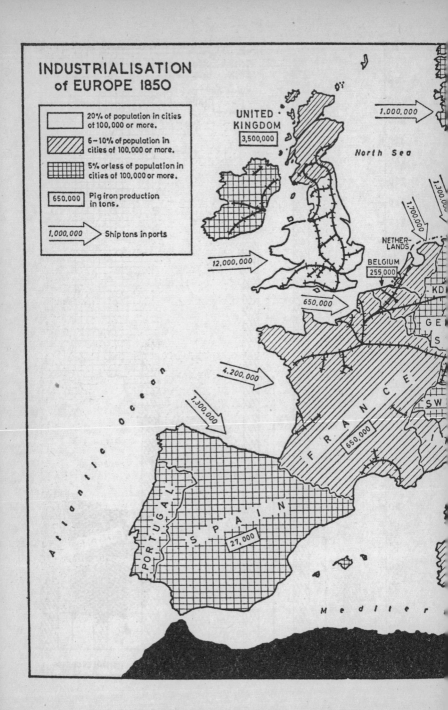

INDUSTRIALISATION of EUROPE 1850

	20% of population in cities of 100,000 or more.
	6-10% of population in cities of 100,000 or more.
	5% or less of population in cities of 100,000 or more.
650,000	Pig iron production in tons.
1,000,000 →	Ship tons in ports

UNITED KINGDOM
3,500,000

North Sea

1,000,000 →

1,300,000

1,700,000

NETHER-LANDS

BELGIUM
255,000

KD

12,000,000 →

GE

S

650,000

4,200,000 →

1,300,000

F R A N C E

650,000

SW

A t l a n t i c   O c e a n

P O R T U G A L

S P A I N

27,000

M e d i t e r

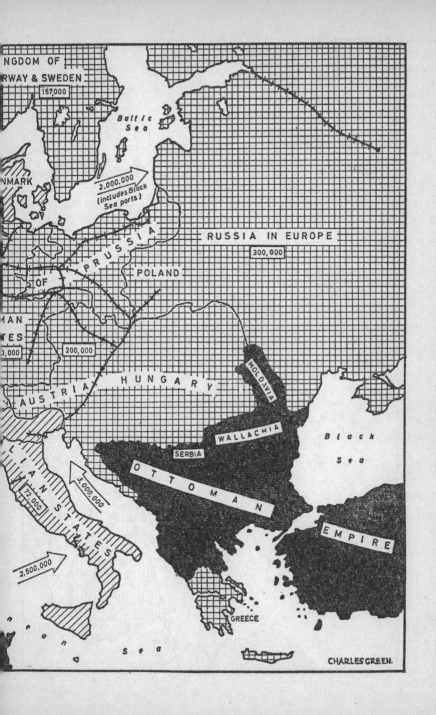

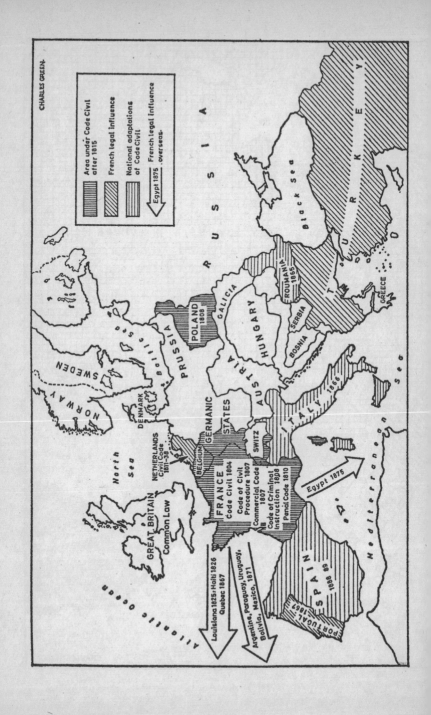

CHARLES GREEN.

Area under Code Civil after 1815

French legal influence

National adaptations of Code Civil

Egypt 1875 —→ French legal influence overseas.

RUSSIA

Black Sea

TURKEY

POLAND 1808

GALICIA

ROUMANIA 1865

SERBIA

BOSNIA

AUSTRIA HUNGARY

GREECE

PRUSSIA

Baltic Sea

SWEDEN

NORWAY

DENMARK

NETHERLANDS Civil Code 1811-38

BELGIUM

GERMANIC STATES

SWITZ

ITALY 1866

North Sea

GREAT BRITAIN Common Law

FRANCE
Code Civil 1804
Code of Civil Procedure 1807
Commercial Code 1807
Code of Criminal Instruction 1808
Penal Code 1810

Egypt 1875

Mediterranean Sea

SPAIN 1888-89

PORTUGAL 1867

Atlantic Ocean

Louisiana 1825; Haiti 1826 Quebec 1867

Argentine, Paraguay, Uruguay, Bolivia, Mexico, 1871

Bibliography

Both the subject and the literature are so vast that even a highly select bibliography would run into many pages. To refer to all subjects which might interest the reader is impossible. Guides to further reading on most subjects have been compiled by the American Historical Association (*A Guide to Historical Literature*, periodically revised) and for the use of students by some Oxford teachers; *A select list of works on Europe and Europe overseas 1715–1815*, edited by J. S. Bromley and A. Goodwin (Oxford 1956) and *A select list of books on European history 1815–1914*, edited by Alan Bullock and A. J. P. Taylor (1957). The former is better. Books marked * below also contain bibliographies which are recommended.

There are several series of general histories covering the period or part of it. The most important is *Peuples et Civilisations*, because it includes two volumes by George Lefebvre which are historical masterpieces : *La Révolution Française* (vol. 1, 1789–93 is available in English,1962) and *Napoléon* (1953). F. Ponteil *, L'eveil des nationalités 1815–48* (1960) replaces an earlier volume under the same title by G. Weill, which is still worth consulting. The equivalent American series *The Rise of Modern Europe* is more discursive and geographically limited. The available volumes are Crane Brinton's *A decade of revolution 1789–99* (1934), G. Bruun, *Europe and the French Imperium* (1938) and F. B. Artz, *Reaction and Revolution 1814–32* (1934). Bibliographically the most useful of the series is *Clio*, which is aimed at students and periodically brought up-to-date; note especially the sections summarizing current historical debate. The relevant volumes are : E. Préclin and V. L. Tapié, *Le xviiie siècle* (2 vols.); L. Villat, *La révolution et l'Empire* (2 vols.), J. Droz, L. Genet and J. Vidalenc, *L'époque contemporaine*, vol. I, 1815–71.

Though old, J. Kulischer, *Allgemeine Wirtschaftsgeschichte*, vol. II, *Neuzeit* (republished 1954) is still a good factual summary of economic history, but there are also numerous American college textbooks of approximately equal value, e.g. W. Bowden, M. Karpovitch and A . P. Usher, *Economic history of Europe since 1750* (1937). J. Schumpeter, *Business Cycles I* (1939) is broader than its title suggests. Of general interpretations, as distinct from histories, M. H. Dobb, *Studies in the development of capitalism* (1946) and K. Polanyi, *The great transformation* (published as *Origins of our Time* in England, 1945), as well as Werner Sombart's older *Der moderne Kapitalismus III: Das Wirtschaftsleben im Zeitalter des Hochkapitalismus* (1928) are recommended. For population, M. Reinhard, *Histoire de la population mondiale de 1700 à 1948* (1949), but especially the brief and quite excellent introductory C. Cipolla's *The economic history of world population* (1962). For technology, Singer, Holmyard, Hall and Williams' *A history of technology, IV: the Industrial Revolution 1750–1850* (1958) is myopic but useful for reference. W. H. Armytage, *A social history of engineering* (1961) is a better introduction and W. T. O'Dea, *The social history of lighting* (1958) is both entertaining and suggestive. See also the books on the history of science. For agriculture the obsolescent but convenient H. Sée, **Esquisse d'une histoire du régime agraire en Europe au 18e et 19e siècles* (1921) has not yet been replaced by anything as handy. There is as yet no good synthesis of the modern research work on farming. For money, Marc Bloch's very brief *Esquisse d'une histoire monétaire de l'Europe* (1954) is useful as is K. Mackenzie, *The banking systems of Great Britain, France, Germany and the USA* (1945). For want of a general synthesis R. E. Cameron, *France and the economic development of Europe 1800–1914* (1961), one of the most solid pieces of research to have appeared in recent years, can serve as an introduction to problems of credit and investment, together with the still unsurpassed L. H. Jenks, *The migration of British capital to 1875* (1927).

There is no good general treatment of the industrial revolution, in spite of much recent work on economic growth, not often of great interest to the historian. The best comparative conspectus is in the special number of *Studi Storici* II, 3–4 (Rome 1961) and the more specialised *First international conference of economic history, Stockholm 1960* (Paris-Hague 1961). P. Mantoux, *The industrial revolution of the 18th century* (1906), in spite of its age, remains basic for Britain. There is nothing as good for the period since 1800. W. O. Henderson, **Britain and industrial Europe 1750–1870* (1954) describes British influence and J. Purs, *The industrial revolution in the Czech lands (*Historica* II, Prague 1960) contains a convenient bibliography for seven countries; W. O. Henderson, *The industrial revolution on the continent: Germany, France, Russia 1800–1914* (1961) is aimed at the undergraduate. Among more general discussions Karl Marx, *Capital I* remains a marvellous, almost contemporary, treatment and S. Giedion, *Mechanisation takes command* (1948) is among other things a profusely illustrated and highly suggestive pioneer work on mass production.

A. Goodwin ed., *The European nobility in the 18th century* (1953) is a comparative study of aristocracies. There is nothing similar on the bourgeoisie. Luckily the best source of all, the works of the great novelists, notably Balzac, are easily accessible. For the working classes J. Kuczynski, *Geschichte der Lage der Arbeiter unter dem Kapitalismus* (Berlin, to be completed in 38 volumes) is encyclopedic. The best contemporary analysis remains F. Engels, *Conditions of the Working Class in England in 1844.* For the urban sub-proletariat, L. Chevalier, *Classes laborieuses et classes dangereuses à Paris dans le première moitié du 19e siècle* (1958) is a brilliant synthesis of economic and literary evidence. E. Sereni, *Il capitalismo nelle campagne* (1946), though confined to Italy and a later period, is the most useful introduction to the study of the peasantry. The same author's *Storia del paesaggio agrario italiano* (1961) analyses the changes in landscape made by man's productive activities, drawing most imaginatively on the arts. R. N. Salaman, *The history and social influence of the potato* (1949) is admirable on the historical importance of one type of foodstuff, but in spite of recent research the history of material life remains little known, though J. Drummond and A. Wilbraham, *The Englishman's food* (1939) is a pioneer work. J. Chalmin, *L'officier francais 1815–1871* (1957), Georges Duveau, *L'instituteur* (1957) and Asher Tropp, *The school teachers* (1957) are among the rare histories of professions. The novelists still provide by far the best guide to the social changes of capitalism; e.g. John Galt, *Annals of the Parish* for Scotland.

The most stimulating history of science is J. D. Bernal, *Science in history* (1954) and S. F. Mason, *A history of the sciences* (1953) is good on natural philosophy. For reference M. Daumas ed., *Histoire de la science* (Encyclopédie de la Pleiade 1957). J. D. Bernal, *Science and industry in the 19th century* (1953) analyses some examples of their interaction, R. Taton, The French Revolution and the progress of science (in S. Lilley ed., *Essays in the social history of science* Copenhagen 1953) may be the least inaccessible of several monographs. C. C. Gillispie, *Genesis and geology* (1951) is entertaining and illustrates the difficulties between science and religion. On education G. Duveau, *op cit.* and Brian Simon, *Studies in the history of education 1780–1870* (1960) will help to compensate for the absence of a good modern comparative study. On the press there is G. Weill, *Le journal* (1934).

There are numerous histories of economic thought, for the subject is much taught. E. Roll, *A history of economic thought* (various editions) is a good introduction. J. B. Bury, *The idea of progress* (1920) is still useful. E. Halévy, *The growth of philosophic radicalism* (1938) is an ancient but unshaken monument. L. Marcuse, *Reason and revolution: Hegel and the rise of social theory* (1941) is excellent and G. D. H. Cole, *A history of socialist thought I, 1789–1850*, a judicious survey. Frank Manuel, *The new world of Henri Saint-Simon* (1956) is the most recent study of that elusive but important figure. Auguste Cornu's *Karl Marx und Friedrich Engels, Leben u. Werk I, 1818–44* (Berlin 1954, in progress), appears definitive. Hans Kohn, *The idea of nationalism* (1944) is useful.

There is no general account of religion, but K. S. Latourette, *Christianity in a revolutionary age*, I–III (1959–61) surveys the entire world. W. Cantwell Smith, *Islam in modern history* (1957) and H. R. Niebuhr, *The social sources of denominationalism* (1929) may introduce the two expanding religions of the period, V. Lanternari, *Movimenti religiosi di libertà e di salvezza* (1960), what has been called the 'colonial heresies', S. Dubnow, *Weltgeschichte des juedischen Volkes*, VIII and IX (1929) deals with the Jews.

The best introductions to the history of the arts are probably N. L. B. Pevsner, *Outline of European architecture* (illustrated edition 1960), E. H. Gombrich, *The story of art* (1950) and P. H. Láng, *Music in western civilisation* (1942). There is unfortunately no equivalent for world literature, though Arnold Hauser, *The social history of art*, II (1951) covers this field also. F. Novotny, *Painting and sculpture in Europe 1780–1870* (1960) and H. R. Hitchcock, *Architecture in the 19th and 20th centuries* (1958), both in the Penguin History of Art, contain both illustrations and bibliographies. Among more specialised works mainly on the visual arts one might mention F. D.

Klingender, *Art and the industrial revolution* (1947) and *Goya and the democratic tradition* (1948), K. Clark, *The gothic revival* (1944), P. Francastel, *Le style Empire* (1944), and F. Antal's brilliant but capricious 'Reflections on Classicism and Romanticism' (*Burlington Magazine* 1935, 1936, 1940, 1941). For music, A. Einstein, *Music in the romantic era* (1947) and *Schubert* (1951) may be read; for literature, G. Lukacs' profound *Goethe und seine Zeit* (1955), *The historical novel* (1962) and the chapters on Balzac and Stendhal in *Studies in European realism* (1950); also the excellent J. Bronowski, *William Blake – a man without a mask* (1954 ed.). For a few general themes, consult R. Wellek, *A history of modern criticism 1750–1950*, I (1955), R. Gonnard, *Le légende du bon sauvage* (1946), H. T. Parker, *The cult of antiquity and the French revolutionaries* (1937), P. Trahard, *La sensibilité révolutionnaire 1791–4* (1936), P. Jourda, *L'exotisme dans la litterature française* (1938), and F. Picard *Le romantisme social* (1944.)

Only a few topics can be singled out from the history of events in this period. On revolutions and revolutionary movements the bibliography is gigantic for 1789, rather less so for 1815–48. G. Lefebvre's two works mentioned above and his *The coming of the French Revolution* (1949) are standard for the 1789 revolution; A. Soboul, *Précis d'histoire de la Révolution Française* (1962) is a lucid textbook and A. Goodwin, *The French Revolution* (1956) an English conspectus. The literature is too vast for summary. Bromley and Goodwin provide a good guide. To the works mentioned there A. Soboul, *Les sansculottes en l'an II* (1960), an encyclopedic work, G. Rudé, *The crowd in the French Revolution* (1959) and J. Godechot, *La contre-révolution* (1961) ought to be added. C. L. R. James, *The black Jacobins* (1938) describes the Haitian revolution. For the insurrectionaries of 1815–48, C. Francovich, *Idee sociali e organizzazione operaia nella prima metà dell' 800* (1959) is a good and brief study of a significant country, which can serve as introduction. E. Eisenstein, *Filippo Michele Buonarroti* (1959) leads us into the world of the secret societies. A. Mazour, *The first Russian revolution* (1937) deals with the Decembrists, R. F. Leslie, *Polish politics and the revolution of November 1830* (1956) is in effect a much broader book than its title suggests. On labour movements there is no general study, for E. Dolléans, *Histoire du mouvement ouvrier* I (1936) deals only with Britain and France. See also A. B. Spitzer, *The revolutionary theories of Auguste Blanqui* (1957), D. O. Evans, *Le socialisme romantique* (1948), and O. Festy, *Le mouvement ouvrier au début de la monarchie de Juillet* (1908).

On the origins of 1848, F. Fejtö ed., *The opening of an era, 1848* (1948) contains essays, mostly excellent, on numerous countries; J. Droz, *Les revolutions allemandes de 1848* (1957) is invaluable and E. Labrousse ed., *Aspects de la crise ... 1846–51* (1956) is a collection of detailed economic studies for France. A. Briggs ed., *Chartist studies* (1959) is the most up-to-date work on its subject. E. Labrousse, 'Comment naissent les révolutions?' (*Actes du centenaire de 1848*, Paris 1948) attempts a general answer to this question for our period.

On international affairs A. Sorel, *L'Europe et la Révolution Francaise* I (1895) still provides a good background and J. Godechot, *La Grande Nation*, 2 vols. (1956) describes the expansion of the revolution abroad. Vols. IV and V of the **Histoire des Relations Internationales* (by A. Fugier up to 1815 and P. Renouvin 1815–71, both 1954) are lucid and intelligent guides. On the process of war, B. H. Liddell Hart, *The ghost of Napoleon* (1933) remains a fine introduction to land strategy and E. Tarlé, *Napoleon's invasion of Russia in 1812* (1942) a convenient study of a particular campaign. G. Lefebvre, **Napoléon* contains by far the best concise sketch of the nature of the French armies, and M. Lewis, *A social history of the navy 1789–1815* (1960) is most instructive. E. F. Heckscher, *The Continental System* (1922) should be supplemented by F. Crouzet's massive *Le blocus continental et l'économie britannique* (1958) for the economic aspects. F. Redlich, *De praeda militari: looting and booty 1500–1815* (1955) casts interesting sidelights. J. N. L. Baker, **A history of geographical exploration and discovery* (1937) and the admirable Russian *Atlas geograficheskikh otkrytii i issledovanii* (1959) provide the background for the European world conquest; K. Panikkar, *Asia and Western dominance* (1954) an instructive account of it from an Asian point of view. G. Scelle, *Le traite negrière aux Indes de Castille*, 2 vols. (1906) and Gaston Martin, *Histoire de l'Esclavage dans les colonies françaises* (1948) remain basic for the slave-trade. E. O. v. Lippmann, *Geschichte des Zuckers* (1929) may be supplemented with N. Deerr, *The History of sugar*, 2 vols. (1949). Eric Williams, *Capitalism and slavery* (1944) is a general interpretation, though sometimes schematic. For the characteristic 'informal' colonisation of the world by trade and gunboat, M. Greenberg, *British trade and the opening* *of China* (1949) and H. S. Ferns, *Britain and Argentina in the 19th century* (1960) are case-studies. For the two large areas under direct European exploitation, W. F. Wertheim, *Indonesian society in transition* (Hague-Bandung 1959) is a brilliant introduction (see also J. S. Furnivall, *Colonial policy and practice*, 1956 which compares Indonesia and Burma), and out of a large but mainly disappointing literature on India the following may be selected : E. Thompson and G. T. Garratt, *Rise and fulfilment of British rule in India* (1934), Eric Stokes, *The English utilitarians and India* (1959) – a most illuminating work – and A. R. Desai, *The social background of Indian nationalism* (Bombay 1948). There is no adequate account of Egypt under Mehemet Ali, but H. Dodwell, *The Founder of Modern Egypt* (1931) may be consulted.

It is impossible to do more than point to one or two histories of some countries or regions. For Britain, E. Halévy, *History of the English people in the 19th century* remains fundamental, especially the great survey of England in 1815 in vol. 1; to be supplemented by A. Briggs, *The age of improvement 1780–1867* (1959). For France a classic of social history gives the eighteenth century background, P. Sagnac, *La formation de la société française moderne*, II (1946), and Gordon Wright, *France in modern times* (1962) a good introductory history since then. F. Ponteil, *La monarchie parlementaire 1815–48* (1949) and F. Artz, *France under the Bourbon restoration* (1931) are recommended. For Russia M. Florinsky, *Russia*, II (1953) covers the period since 1800 fully and M. N. Pokrovsky, *Brief history of Russia*, I (1933) and P. Lyashchenko, *History of the Russian national economy* (1947) include it. R. Pascal, *The growth of modern Germany* (1946) is brief and good, K. S. Pinson, *Modern Germany* (1954) is also introductory. T. S. Hamerow, *Restoration, revolution, reaction: economics and politics in Germany 1815–71* (1958), J. Droz, *op. cit.* and Gordon Craig, *The politics of the Prussian army* (1955) can be read with profit. On Italy G. Candeloro, *Storia dell' Italia moderna*, II, 1815–46 (1958) is by far the best, on Spain P. Vilar, *Histoire d'Espagne* (1949) is a superb brief guide and J. Vicens Vives ed., *Historia sociale de España y America Latina*, IV/2 (1959) is, among its other merits, beautifully illustrated. A. J. P. Taylor, *The Habsburg monarchy* (1949), is a good introduction. See also E. Wangermann, *From Joseph II to the Jacobin Trials* (1959). On the Balkans, L. S. Stavrianos, *The Balkans since 1453* (1953) and the excellent B. Lewis, *The emergence of modern Turkey* (1961), on the North, B. J. Hovde, *The Scandinavian countries 1720–1865*, 2 vols. (1943), will be found helpful. On Ireland, E. Strauss, *Irish nationalism and British democracy* (1951) and *The great famine, studies in recent Irish history* (1957). On the Low Countries, H. Pirenne, *Histoire de Belgique*, v–vi (1926, 1932), R. Demoulin, *La révolution de 1830* (1950) and H. R. C. Wright, *Free Trade and Protection in the Netherlands 1816–30* (1955).

A few final notes on general works of reference. W. Langer's *Encyclopedia of World History* (1948) or Ploetz' *Hauptdaten der Weltgeschichte* (1957) give the main dates, the admirable Alfred Mayer, *Annals of European civilisation 1501–1900* (1949) deals specially with culture, science and the like. M. Mulhall, *Dictionary of Statistics* (1892) remains the best compendium of figures. Among historical encyclopedias the new *Sovietskaya Istoricheskaya Entsiklopediya* in 12 volumes covers the world; the *Encyclopedie de la Pleiade* has special volumes on Universal History (3), the History of Literatures (2) Historical Research – very valuable – and the History of Science; but these are organised narratively and not under dictionary-headings. *Cassell's Encyclopedia of Literature* (2 vols.) is useful and E. Blom ed., Grove's *Dictionary of Music and Musicians* (9 vols.) (1954), though a little British, standard. The *Encyclopedia of World Art* (to be completed in 15 vols., I–V published) is outstanding. The *Encyclopedia of the Social Sciences* (1931), though getting old, remains very useful. The following atlases, not so far mentioned, may also be consulted with profit : *Atlas Istorii SSSR* (1950), J. D. Fage, *An Atlas of African history* (1958), H. W. Hazard and H. L. Cooke, *atlas of Islamic History* (1943), J. T. Adams ed., *Atlas of American History* (1957) and the general J. Engel *et. al Grosser Historischer Weltatlas* (1957) and the Rand McNally *Atlas of World History* (1957).

INDEX

Australia, 209, 219

Austria, 23, 24, 26, 35, 37, 38, 39, 94,
104, 109, 110, 111, 112, 114,
119, 120-1, 128, 129, 130-1, 132,
134, 135, 147, 155, 156, 157,
167, 169, 173, 176, 192, 209,
212, 215, 216, 235, 239, 281,
308, 309, 322

Austrian Empire, see Austria;
Bohemia; Croatia; Galicia;
Hungary; Illyria; Istria; Italy;
Milan; Moravia; Poland;
Salzburg; Tyrol; Venice

Austrian Netherlands, see Belgium

Avignon, 113

Babbage, Charles, scientist, 229,
338

Babeuf, Gracchus, communist;
Babouvists, 24, 77, 95, 142-3,
145, 153, 156, 324

Bach, J. S., composer, 315

Bacon, Francis, philosopher, 268

Baden, 110, 176

Baer, Von, 350

Bahia, see Brazil

Baines, Edward,
journalist-publisher, 228

Bakuninism, 195

Balkans, 23, 27, 31, 104, 112, 128,
133, 134, 144, 172, 174, 175,
207, 309

Baltic, 27, 32, 129, 187, 350

Balzac, H. de, writer, 43, 75, 225,
226, 227, 308, 309, 310, 313,
314

Banda Oriental, see Uruguay

Baptist Missionary Society, 272

Baptists, 228, 273, 276

Barings, financiers, 122

Barlow, Joel, 125n2

Baskerville, J., printer, 34

Basques, 194, 220

Bastille, storming of, 22, 43, 74, 82,
304, 305n7, 319

Batavian Republic, see Holland

Baudelaire, C. (1821-67), poet, 325

Baudrillart, Henri, academic, 242

Bavaria, 110, 194, 369

Beauvilliers, A., chef, 226

Bedouin, 172, 274

Beethoven, L. van, composer, 102-3,
307-8, 309, 310, 313

Bel-Ami (Maupassant), 226

Belgium, 31, 38, 43, 48, 60, 68, 74,
90, 96, 105, 106, 115, 118, 128,
129, 132, 140, 147, 148, 153,
158, 160, 167, 169, 191, 208,
209, 212, 213, 214, 216, 235,
260, 309, 338, 344, 349, 363,
368, 369, 370; see also Low
Countries

Belleville, 259

Bellini, V., composer, 308, 309

Benbow, William, pamphleteer, 255

Bengal, 40, 75, 197, 347

Bentham, Jeremy, reformer;
Benthamites, 15, 125n2, 144,
200, 234, 235, 243n13, 285, 287,
339

Béranger, P. J. de, poet (1780-1857),
154

Berg, Grand Duchy of, 106

Bergakademie (Prussian), 45

Berlin, 110, 210, 215, 226, 273, 315,
329, 338, 340

Berlioz, H., composer, 309, 316

Bernard, Claude, physiologist, 356

Berthollet, C.-L., chemist, 217

Bessarabia, 130

Bible, 346, 349; see also Chapter 12

Bible in Spain (Borrow), 162n7

Biedermayer, 215, 328

Birkbeck College, see London
Mechanics Institution

Birmingham, 34, 48, 154, 271, 339,
341, 348

Black George, King of Serbia, 173

Black Sea, 28, 174

Blake, William, poet, 103, 295, 317,
318, 323, 333n4, 355

Blanqui, Auguste, revolutionary,
153, 156, 158

Boehme, Jacob, mystic, 268

Also by E. J. Hobsbawm in Abacus

THE AGE OF CAPITAL 1848–1875

The first thorough major treatment of these critical years –
a penetrating analysis of capitalism throughout the world.

Professor Hobsbawm's intention is not to summarize facts, but
to draw facts together into an historical synthesis, to 'make sense of'
the period, and to trace the roots of the present world back to it.
He integrates economics with political and intellectual developments
in this objective yet original account of revolution and the failure of
revolution, of the cycles of boom and slump that characterize
capitalist economies, of the victims and victors of the bourgeois ethos.

'A major event in British historiography.... A work in the grand
manner.... It will undoubtedly be read and valued as highly as the
earlier *Age of Revolution* and that is high praise indeed.'
– *The Times Higher Educational Supplement*

HISTORY/ARCHAEOLOGY   0 349 11691 1   £3.50

Also available in Abacus

THE COLLAPSE OF DEMOCRACY

ROBERT MOSS

Could Britain's democratic system collapse? Will our liberal democracy evolve into a mass democracy and end up as no democracy at all?

In this timely and most disturbing book, Robert Moss analyses what is meant by democracy and how it relates to liberty. He makes a vital distinction between authoritarian and totalitarian government and shows that a democracy can drift into a state where it is forced to choose between them. He looks at the experiences of other societies, like Portugal, Chile and Czechoslovakia, and also Weimar Germany – where democracy broke down irretrievably – pointing out where we can learn from their mistakes. Most importantly, Robert Moss identifies the enemies to our free society and suggests ways in which they may be defeated.

'Brilliant' – *The Sunday Times*

WORLD AFFAIRS   0 349 12395 0   £1.50

A selection of bestsellers from SPHERE

FICTION
KEEPER OF THE CHILDREN

	William H. Hallahan	£1.00	☐
SPECIAL EFFECTS	Harriet Frank	£1.25	☐
BETHANY'S SIN	Robert R. McCammon	£1.40	☐
NOW, GOD BE THANKED	John Masters	£1.95	☐
SUMMER'S END	Danielle Steel	£1.50	☐

FILM AND TV TIE-INS
THE EMPIRE STRIKES BACK   Donald F. Glut £1.00 ☐
ONCE UPON A GALAXY:
A Journal of the Making of
The Empire Strikes Back   Alan Arnold £1.25 ☐
MIDNIGHT EXPRESS   Billy Hayes £1.00 ☐

NON-FICTION
THE BREAST BOOK   Anthony Harris £1.50 ☐
MANDY   Mandy Rice-Davies with Shirley Flack £1.25 ☐
NAZI GOLD   Ian K. Sayer & H. L. Seaman with
                                    Frederick Nolan £1.50 ☐
A NURSE'S WAR   Brenda McBryde £1.25 ☐
TIMEWARPS   John Gribbin £1.25 ☐
TRUE BRITT   Britt Ekland £1.50 ☐

All Sphere books are available at your local bookshop or
newsagent, or can be ordered direct from the publisher.
Just tick the titles you want and fill in the form below.

Name _____

Address _____

_____

Write to Sphere Books, Cash Sales Department, P.O. Box 11,
Falmouth, Cornwall TR10 9EN
Please enclose cheque or postal order to the value of the
cover price plus:
UK: 25p for the first book plus 12p per copy for each
additional book ordered to a maximum charge of £1.05.
OVERSEAS: 40p for the first book and 12p for each
additional book.
BFPO & EIRE: 25p for the first book plus 10p per copy for
the next 8 books, thereafter 5p per book.

*Sphere Books reserve the right to show new retail prices on
covers which may differ from those previously advertised in the
text or elsewhere, and to increase postal rates in accordance
with the PO.*